Anna
Best wis
Arana.

MADE OF GOLD

Angela Burdett Coutts, from a portrait by J. R. Swinton, c. 1865, in the Royal Marsden Hospital

MADE OF GOLD

*A Biography of
Angela Burdett Coutts*

by

DIANA ORTON

'You, like me, are supposed to be made of Gold.' – The Duke of Wellington in a letter to Angela Burdett Coutts

HAMISH HAMILTON

LONDON

First published in Great Britain 1980
by Hamish Hamilton Ltd
Garden House 57–59 Long Acre London WC2E 9JZ

Copyright © 1980 by Diana Orton

British Library Cataloguing in Publicaton Data

Orton, Diana
  Made of gold.
  1.   Burdett Coutts, Angela
  I. Title
  942.081'092'4   HV28.B7
  ISBN 0-241-89656-8

Printed and bound in Great Britain at
The Camelot Press, Southampton

CONTENTS

Foreword		ix
Prologue		1
1	Coutts and Burdett	9
2	Harriot and Hannah	28
3	The Richest Heiress in All England	47
4	The Irish Annoyance	62
5	Mr Dickens and Other Friends	77
6	The Bacon Affair	94
7	Oh Soldier, Soldier, will you marry me?	111
8	Urania Cottage	132
9	Guardian of the Poor	148
10	Domestic Matters	164
11	Wider Still and Wider	183
12	The Baroness	203
13	A Most Lamentable Act	223
14	The End of the Story	244
Epilogue		261
Select Bibliography		267
References		271
Coutts Family Tree		286–7
Index		288

ILLUSTRATIONS

Angela Burdett Coutts: portrait by J. R. Swinton, (*Mansell Collection*)	*frontispiece*
	page
Sir Francis Burdett: painted by Sir Thomas Lawrence (*Mary Evans Picture Library*)	15
Sophia Coutts; by Cosway (Courtesy of Lord Latymer)	15
Harriot Mellon as 'Volante': by Sir William Beechey (*Coutts & Co.*)	23
Thomas Coutts, after a portrait by Sir William Beechey (*Radio Times Hulton Picture Library*)	25
Hannah Meredith (*Courtesy of W. A. F. Burdett-Coutts*)	36
Angela Burdett: painted by J. J. Masquerier (*Courtesy of the Earl of Harrowby*)	41
Charles Dickens: by Samuel Laurence (*National Portrait Gallery*)	58
Angela's houses in Stratton Street and Piccadilly (*Sunday Times*)	82
Sir Francis Burdett: portrait by Sir Martin Archer Shee	92
Lord Dudley Coutts Stuart: by Thomas (*Mansell Collection*)	99
Angela laying the foundation-stone of St Stephen's Church, Rochester Row: from *The Illustrated London News* (*Mansell Collection*)	107
The Duke of Wellington: portrait by B. Haydon (*Courtesy of the 8th Duke of Wellington and The Courtauld Institute of Art*)	126
Dudley, 2nd Earl of Harrowby: by George Richmond (*Courtesy of the Earl of Harrowby*)	165
Angela in middle age: wood engraving by Skeolan (*Mary Evans Picture Library*)	177
Angela with Mrs Brown in 1864 (*Mansell Collection*)	181

John William Colenso: engraving by Biscombe Gardner (*Radio Times Hulton Picture Library*)	189
Sir James Brooke (*Radio Times Hulton Picture Library*)	199
Holly Lodge (*from the Potter Collection, courtesy of the Trustees of the British Museum*)	204
Columbia Market, from *The Illustrated London News* (*Tower Hamlets Libraries*)	208
The wedding of Baroness Burdett-Coutts and William Ashmead Bartlett	235
The Baroness: photograph taken in the late 1880s (*Reproduced by permission of the British Library*)	253

Every effort has been made to trace the copyright holders of the material used in this volume. Should there be any omissions in this respect we apologise and shall be pleased to make the appropriate acknowledgment in future editions.

FOREWORD

Angela Burdett Coutts, whose name was a household word in Victorian England, has been until very recently neglected by biographers. The reasons for the neglect are not hard to find. Despite a mass of original material, there is little about her personal life; many of her private papers have been destroyed. She left no diary, and if she had it would have taken years to decipher, for her handwritng was atrocious.

She is, nevertheless, a fascinating subject, as I found when I wrote an article about her several years ago, based mainly on the few (highly complimentary) published sources then available. When I agreed to write her biography I little realised what I was letting myself in for. Her life, after all, spanned the whole Victorian era with something to spare at either end; her charitable work, with its background of complex social issues, is a vast subject in itself; and many of the eminent men she knew – Dickens especially – had for so long been objects of scholarly scrutiny as to present a daunting prospect to the newcomer.

Most daunting of all, however, was the task of delineating the character of Angela herself. Not only did she often appear to be overshadowed by her famous friends, from whom there are several thousand letters in existence; but it was impossible at first to separate her from her good works. She was philanthropy personified, a candidate for canonisation if ever there was one. For once, it seemed, the panegyrics of earlier writers had been justified. But, as I got deeper into my research and then began writing, I found myself becoming more and more of a devil's advocate. The nagging question, 'What was she really like?' demanded to be answered.

When I began working I was aware that another biography of Angela had been in preparation for some years; it was published* just as I was completing my manuscript. The author's approach to the subject and the conclusions she comes to are different from my own, and the reader will obviously form his own opinion as to which interpretation is the more convincing. Questions of fact are, however, a

* Edna Healey, *Lady Unknown* (Sidgwick & Jackson, 1978).

different matter, and it has to be said that the earlier book contains many inaccuracies. Some of these – relating mainly to Dickens – have been pointed out elsewhere.* But there are others, concerning Angela herself and incidents in her life, which are likely to be less apparent to anyone unfamiliar with the subject.

It would, of course, be absurd for me to claim that my own book is free from factual errors, though I have naturally done my best to eliminate them. Nor, for that matter, do I believe that it is in any sense the last word on Angela Burdett Coutts, who will probably always be something of an enigma. But I have tried not to make assumptions for which I have had no evidence, and have checked and double-checked dates and figures and the exact wording of quotations. For any mistakes that remain I accept full responsibility.

There is some confusion over whether or not Angela's name should be hyphenated. Before she was created a baroness, Angela was generally known as 'Miss Coutts' and usually signed herself 'A. G. B. Coutts'. Afterwards, when she signed 'Burdett Coutts', she tended to run the two names together and it is not clear whether she intended a hyphen or not. When others wrote her name, it was sometimes with and sometimes without a hyphen. Sir Anthony Wagner, Clarenceux King of Arms, tells me that the Grant of Supporters of 1871 following the creation of the barony gives a hyphen. I have therefore adopted the practice, in the body of the text, of hyphenating the name *only* when it is preceded by the word 'Baroness' or 'Lady'. When using direct quotations, however, I have left the name as it was written or printed in the original, just as I have also retained the original spelling and punctuation (unless this has had to be altered to make the meaning clear).

I have to acknowledge the gracious permission of Her Majesty The Queen to use excerpts from material in the Royal Archives, and should like to thank Sir Robin Mackworth-Young and his staff for their kindness and helpfulness during the day I spent at Windsor.

Among all those who have helped me in my research, I am particularly grateful to Mrs Betty Coxon and to the Earl of Harrowby. Both have been kindness itself. Mrs Coxon, whom I first met when I was writing my original article, is a great-great-niece of Angela Burdett Coutts. For several years she entrusted me with valuable family papers and books, which were of the greatest possible use to me.

* Philip Collins, 'The Rich Full Life' (*Times Literary Supplement*, 13 January, 1978).

Foreword

Lord Harrowby not only allowed me the run of his family archives for days at a time, but has shown an unfailingly enthusiastic interest in my work from first to last. There are probably more of Angela's own letters at Sandon Hall than in any other single collection, as well as a large amount of other material relating to her. I am very grateful to Lord Harrowby for personally checking all the references of the letters I have used, and would like to thank him and the trustees of the Harrowby MSS Trust for permission to quote from them. I would also like to thank Lord Harrowby's daughter, Lady Frances Berendt, for ferrying me between London and Sandon on several occasions.

I am most grateful to the Duke of Wellington for allowing me access to the correspondence of the first Duke at Stratfield Saye, and to his archivist, Mrs Joan Wilson, for her help. For permission to quote from unpublished letters of Charles Dickens I should like to thank Mr Christopher Dickens. I also acknowledge the permission of Sir William Gladstone and Mr H. J. L. Osborne to quote from the Gladstone and Osborne papers in the British Library.

I should like to thank the staff of the British Library, London, and the Bodleian Library, Oxford, and to acknowledge the permission granted by both libraries to quote from material in their collections. I am grateful to the Pierpont Morgan Library, New York, for sending me microfilm of their Dickens correspondence and allowing me to quote from it, and to the Archbishop of Canterbury and the Trustees of Lambeth Palace Library for permission to quote from the Burdett-Coutts and Davidson Papers.

For assistance in various ways I should like to thank Miss M. V. Stokes, Archivist of Coutts & Co.; Miss Whimbrell Burdett-Coutts and Mr W. A. F. Burdett-Coutts; Mrs Barbier, Headmistress of the Burdett-Coutts School in Westminster; and the Reverend W. W. Davidson, Vicar of St Stephen's Church, Rochester Row. Sir Anthony Wagner kindly lent me copies of correspondence that had belonged to his cousin, Henry Wagner; and the Hon. John Twining lent me the typescript of his grandmother's unpublished memoir of Angela.

I also thank the following libraries and institutions for sending me material or allowing me to see it: the National Trust and its staff at Hughenden Manor (Disraeli Archives); University of London Library; the Fawcett Library; the Highgate Literary and Scientific Institute; the Torquay Natural History Society; Hertford Record Office; and public libraries in Camden, Tower Hamlets, the City of London, Westminster, East Sussex and Torquay. I should also like to thank Mr Howard M. Nixon, the Librarian at Westminster Abbey.

I have to thank the editors of the Pilgrim Edition of the Letters of Charles Dickens and Oxford University Press, on behalf of the Pilgrim Trust, for permission to quote from the Pilgrim Edition of the letters of Charles Dickens.

I am particularly grateful to K. J. Fielding, Saintsbury Professor of English Literature at the University of Edinburgh, who gave me valuable help and advice when I was beginning my research and who also read the typescript. His articles about Angela in the *Dickensian* and elsewhere have been most helpful and illuminating. I should also like to thank Timberlake Wertenbaker for her helpful comments and suggestions during the time I was revising my manuscript, Jane Everard, my editor, and Dorothy Seddon, my indexer.

To all those friends and members of my family who helped me in many ways during the time I was writing this book I should like to express my love and thanks.

D. O.

PROLOGUE

'I am very desirous to consult your grace upon a matter that has arisen,' wrote Basil Wilberforce, Archdeacon of Westminster, to Randall Davidson, Archbishop of Canterbury, on December 28, 1906:

> The aged Baroness Burdett Coutts is seriously ill. She *may* rally as she has many times before but it is not likely. No woman has ever more merited burial in the Abbey for her nobility of character and great services to the human race ... I am convinced that if a plebiscite of the English speaking peoples could be made this honour would be voted to her. She is the only woman upon whom a peerage has been conferred upon her *own* merits. As to her marriage, this was after all her own affair ...

Would the Archbishop write to the Dean of Westminster, suggesting that he should offer burial in the Abbey? 'The Dean will be sure to adopt your suggestion.'[1]

Archdeacon Wilberforce was a grandson of the great anti-slavery campaigner and son of Bishop Samuel Wilberforce, who had been a close friend of Baroness Burdett-Coutts. Like many of his generation, the Archdeacon's regard for the Baroness amounted almost to veneration. From the tone of his letter to the Archbishop it was clear that he had already raised the matter of the Baroness's burial with the Dean, Dr Joseph Armitage Robinson. A scholarly, eccentric man, still in his late forties but described as 'gaunt and prematurely bent', Dr Robinson could be difficult and capricious. *His* generation knew very little about the Baroness Burdett-Coutts — apart from her ridiculous marriage a quarter of a century ago. He was not at all sure that he wanted her remains in his Abbey.

The Archbishop's reply to Wilberforce was sympathetic but guarded. While realising the importance of all the Archdeacon had said about 'the good old Baroness', he could not really put pressure on the Dean:

You will I am sure realise the peculiar responsibility I should take were I to urge upon the Dean to do 'spontaneously' what he is really quite as well qualified to judge about as I am.

However, if the Dean were to ask his advice, he would 'say no deterrent word with reference to one who did such noble service to many good causes',[2] and from whom he personally had received much kindness. With that, for the time being, Wilberforce had to be satisfied.

*

Throughout the same day – Saturday, December 29 – telegrams and messages of enquiry were arriving in a constant stream at a large, brown-brick mansion on the corner of Stratton Street and Piccadilly. The building – it was two houses made into one – was a well-known landmark. Even those who had scarcely heard of its occupant were familiar with the white china cockatoo which hung 'on a level with the top of the passing omnibus'[3] on a circular perch in the big bay window looking on to Piccadilly. Like the Royal Standard at Buckingham Palace the bird's purpose was to indicate that its owner was in residence. In one passer-by it had caused 'a wild unreasoning hatred' as he peered short-sightedly at it day after day, trying to decide whether or not it was alive. In the end he decided it wasn't, because of its habit of sitting more and more backwards on its perch until it was in danger of falling off.*[4]

The house itself, situated as it was in the heart of London, had been both a centre of activity and a witness of events great and small during the time – nearly seventy years – the Baroness had lived there. From its balconies her guests had watched processions, pageants and parades held to mark momentous occasions, most of which had passed into almost-forgotten history. Here, on a sweltering July day in 1893 a party of working-class children from the Burdett-Coutts schools in Westminster had come with their head teachers to see the wedding procession of the Duke of York (later George V) and Princess May. Here, on a summer night nearly four decades earlier, a group of friends had gathered to watch the celebrations that followed the ending of the Crimean War. At least one onlooker on this occasion was amused by the 'childlike enjoyment of the fireworks' shown by Michael Faraday, the eminent scientist, who 'halloaed out, with wonderful vivacity, "There goes magnesium," "There's potassium, etc., etc." '[5]

* The cockatoo, now owned by Sir Anthony Wagner, still exhibits the same tendency and has to be straightened every now and then.

Prologue

There were more fireworks many years later as London went wild with Jubilee fever in 1887 and again in 1897. On these occasions, as on many others, the crowds in Piccadilly broke into enthusiastic cheers as they caught sight of the tall, stately figure of the Baroness Burdett-Coutts on the balcony or in one of the bay windows of 1 Stratton Street. More recently still, in February 1901, the crowds had been silent for the funeral procession of Queen Victoria. But even this was already fading from public memory. After all, the old Queen had been dead for nearly six years now. With her death, the present generation believed, the nineteenth century had finally come to an end.

But it hadn't, quite – not while the old lady of Stratton Street lived. She had been born Angela Georgina Burdett in this same house in 1814, five years before Victoria, whose coronation she had attended in 1838. Now, she lay in an upstairs room overlooking Green Park, her body gradually succumbing to acute bronchitis, her mind clear and untroubled. Sustained by an unshakeable, childlike faith, she was dying as she had lived: calmly, unhurriedly, with dignity and a minimum of fuss, but with a due regard for what was fitting.

At noon, the doctors pronounced her weaker. A telegram arrived – a message from Queen Alexandra; it was read to the Baroness and she indicated that she had understood. The older members of her household filed into the room to pay their last respects; she gave her hand to each in turn. Evening closed in on the short winter day, and her husband came to sit with her through the night.

*

She died peacefully at 10.30 the following morning, December 30. Like her grandfather, Thomas Coutts, and his second wife, Harriot Mellon – who between them had been responsible for the dramatic change in the fortunes of Angela Burdett at the age of 23 – she died on a Sunday. This, too, was as it should be. Beside her for the last twelve hours had been her husband, the former William Ashmead Bartlett, who had taken her name on their marriage. Now in his mid-fifties, he had been since 1885 Conservative Member of Parliament for Westminster, the constituency that her father, Sir Francis Burdett, had represented for thirty years. William Burdett-Coutts was to survive his wife for nearly fifteen years, dying in 1921 at the age of seventy.

In Westminster Abbey, the Dead March from *Saul* was played after morning service. Archdeacon Wilberforce inserted a brief eulogy into his sermon. The life of the Baroness Burdett-Coutts, he declared, stood next to that of Queen Victoria herself. In this he was echoing a remark of King Edward VII, who as Prince of Wales had once referred to the Baroness as 'After my mother, the most remarkable woman in the kingdom.'

'No arrangements have yet been made for the funeral,' the *Daily Telegraph* noted on Monday morning. In common with most other newspapers, the *Telegraph* devoted the best part of a page to its obituary of the Baroness, attempting to 'sum up very briefly the long record of her life'. That record, it declared,

> is one of the proudest and most satisfactory that the history of the nineteenth century can exhibit, for it is a record full of generous acts, of unstinted benevolence, and noble aspirations.

The Times called her 'a queen in her own circle'. It reminded its readers that most of her charitable work was done in the days when there was no Elementary Education Act; when no attempt had been made to solve the housing problem; when local government was 'extremely imperfect' and the sanitary laws 'more imperfect still'. It concluded:

> That in the face of so much general ignorance and disorganization one woman, furnished with nothing but wealth, a warm heart, and a clear head, should have accomplished so much is an astonishing fact; and, however the details of her achievements may be open to the criticisms of a later age, nothing can deprive the Baroness Burdett-Coutts of her claim to lasting public gratitude.

About her private life little was said. Most papers dwelt briefly on the numerous proposals of marriage that Angela Burdett Coutts had received on inheriting her grandfather's fortune in 1837. Some mentioned her friendships with the great men of her day; there were references to her hospitality at 1 Stratton Street and to the entertainments she gave at Holly Lodge, her 'semi-rural residence at Highgate'. When it came to her marriage, *The Times* was perhaps the most forthright. It recalled that, in 1881,

> to the surprise of the whole world, it was announced that her ladyship, who was then nearly 67 years of age and who was thought to be as much vowed to celibacy as the Virgin Queen herself, was about to be married. Her choice fell upon Mr William Lehman Ashmead-Bartlett, her private secretary . . ., who was born in 1851.

But it allowed itself no comment on how the marriage had turned out. It was left to the *Telegraph* to aver that all who have since had opportunities of observing her married life will concur in pronouncing that the step which many at the time deprecated turned out most favourably for her own happiness.

The next day, January 1, 1907, *The Times* published a correction: it had been asked to say that Mr Burdett-Coutts was never the Baroness's secretary: 'his position at the time of their marriage was that of an unpaid assistant in her philanthropic work'.

It was also announced that the burial would be in Westminster Abbey at noon on Saturday, January 5. The offer had been made to Mr Burdett-Coutts the previous afternoon by the Dean after consultation with his colleagues in the Chapter.

*

'Very many thanks,' wrote Archdeacon Wilberforce to the Archbishop of Canterbury on the following day:

> I am very glad it is settled. The Dean was very hard to persuade but the nation evidently expected it. The marriage seems to have been the obstacle in the Dean's mind yet *I* think she never showed her insight into character and her independence more than in her marriage ... Yesterday he and I knelt by the body and it was manifest that he was really deeply attached to her.[6]

On Thursday and Friday, January 3 and 4, while telegrams, messages and flowers continued to arrive from all over the world and all parts of the British Isles, the body of Angela Burdett Coutts lay in state in her house in Stratton Street. Surrounded by flowers, and with three large candles burning on either side, the coffin rested on a low, purple-draped platform in the great dining-room in whose bay window had hung the china cockatoo. Beside the coffin lay a bunch of herbs, with a card inscribed 'For my best and dearest. W. B-C'. About 14,000 people waited in the cold January air to file past the coffin on the first day, and a similar number on the second. 'The scene as the mourners passed silently through the room ... was an impressive one,' reported *The Times*. 'There were men and women of all ages and of all conditions in life, some of them in tears, and nearly all of them wearing some badge of mourning.'

On the day of the funeral an odd paragraph appeared in *The Times*:

> A report was circulated yesterday that the Baroness's remains have been cremated. Mr Burdett-Coutts asks us to state that nothing of the kind has taken place or will take place.

This curious denial was the only public intimation of a somewhat bizarre private drama that had been going on behind the scenes, the two protagonists being the Dean of Westminster, Dr Armitage Robinson, and the widower, William Burdett-Coutts. According to the journal of the Reverend R. B. Rackham, who acted as secretary to the Dean at the time, Dr Robinson had offered burial in the Abbey on condition that the Baroness's body was cremated. This condition (again according to Mr Rackham) was at first accepted by Mr Burdett-Coutts; but either there was a misunderstanding or he changed his mind. On the day of the funeral the Abbey authorities learned that the body had not been nor would be cremated. Telegrams were sent to the Dean, who had been ill and was convalescing in Devon. He left the decison to the Sub-Dean, who gave his consent for burial without cremation. Two canons stayed away from the funeral in protest at Mr Burdett-Coutts's conduct.*

The procession that set off from Stratton Street at 11 o'clock on Saturday, January 5, was a modest one: the hearse, drawn by four black horses, followed by a dozen or so private carriages. In one of these was Clara Burdett Patterson, a great-niece of the Baroness, who described the scene many years later: 'The whole of the route . . . , especially in the Green Park, was lined with people, and for once in my life I realised what it must be like to be Royalty.'[7] In Piccadilly, Grosvenor Place and Victoria Street flags flew at half-mast and blinds were drawn. What impressed the *Times* reporter most was 'the momentary lull in the busy traffic, and the silent reverence of the crowd'. Among the crowds waiting outside the Abbey was a group of costermongers, whose particular friend the Baroness had been. Inside, the vivid State robes of the Lord Mayor and other City dignitaries lent a splash of colour to the otherwise sombre scene.

To William Burdett-Coutts the service was 'infinitely noble and touching'. His wife had been laid to rest, he told the Archbishop of Canterbury, 'in a position she herself would have chosen, close to what is really the People's door'.[8] Actually, there is some evidence that she would have preferred to be buried in St Stephen's, Rochester Row, the church she had built fifty years before in memory of her father. In a specially-constructed vault under the High Altar lay the remains of her life-long companion and 'dearest Earthly friend', Hannah Brown, and it seems likely that it was the Baroness's wish to be laid in the same place.

Many, however, agreed with William Burdett-Coutts that the

---

* Apart from the Unknown Warrior, who was buried in 1920, the Baroness was the last person to be buried uncremated in Westminster Abbey.

position chosen for the grave was an appropriate one. The Baroness was buried in the nave, just inside the west (or people's) door, in the shadow of the statue of the seventh Earl of Shaftesbury. It was she who, some eighteen years before, had been invited to unveil this statue of her friend whose name, like hers, was synonymous with philanthropy.

*

'You, like me, are supposed to be made of Gold,'[9] the old Duke of Wellington had written to the young Miss Burdett Coutts more than half a century before; and many thought that the Baroness was still fabulously wealthy when she died. It was rumoured that she had framed, five-pound notes on the walls of her house. In fact, she left a relatively modest net personal estate of £63,325. A few days after the funeral her widower's solicitors issued a statement 'to set at rest the various rumours which have been circulated with regard to the will and property of the late Baroness'. It said that she had left everything to her husband, and that between 1881 and 1895 she had transferred to him 'nearly all the property which was at her disposal', including her houses in Stratton Street and Piccadilly and the Holly Lodge estate in Highgate. It also made clear that her wealth had derived mainly from the *income* from her half-share in the bank of Coutts & Co., and that she had had no power over the capital. At the time of her marriage this income had been greatly reduced, and on her death it ceased absolutely.[10]

So much for her wealth. But what about the woman herself? So little was known about her. Why, for instance, after years of single bliss, had she married a man forty years her junior? Had it really made her happy, as Archdeacon Wilberforce and many others were convinced it had? There were those who were equally convinced that it hadn't. It was said that her young husband brought his mistresses to her house; that he was cut at the clubs because of his remarks about his ageing wife; that he had once exclaimed aloud at a charity bazaar: 'By Jove, I must go and look after my grandmother.'[11]

What was she really like, this tall, reserved woman who might have married a duke or a prince but who preferred to devote herself to good works; who was the friend of every notable man of her day but whose affection had been reserved almost exclusively for the little lady who had been her governess? 'The story of her life and fortune reads like a series of romances from end to end,'[12] declared one newspaper in its obituary. Angela Burdett Coutts herself was aware, as she once wrote to a relative, that hers was a 'strange story'. For the beginning of the story we have to go back, not to her own birth in the year before Waterloo, nor even to those of her father and mother some forty years earlier; but to the middle of the eighteenth century, and the start of the career of one Thomas Coutts, a banker.

One

COUTTS AND BURDETT

In 1752, a young man of seventeen set out from his native Edinburgh to start a new life in London. Thomas Coutts, the youngest of four brothers, was an orphan, but not a poor one. His mother, Jean, daughter of Sir John Stuart of Allanbank, had died when he was just over a year old, having had six children in as many years (two died young). His father, John, who came from an old Scottish family variously known as Colt, Coult, Cowties or Coutts, had died in 1750. He had been one of the foremost merchants in Edinburgh, and had twice been elected Lord Provost. A wealthy man, hospitable and generous, he was reputedly the first Lord Provost to entertain official visitors at his own table instead of in a tavern at the city's expense.

John Coutts had begun in business as a corn merchant; but he also became a commission agent and negotiated bills of exchange. Soon after his four young sons – Patrick, John, James and Thomas – took over the business, they realised that a London office would be essential to further expansion. So Patrick and Thomas, the eldest and the youngest, moved south to open a branch in St Mary Axe, in the City. John and James, the two middle brothers, remained in Edinburgh.

In 1754 James Coutts, on a visit to his brothers in London, met and fell in love with a young woman called Mary Peagrim. She was the niece and heir of George Campell, sole partner in an old-established banking firm called Middleton, Campbell & Bruce. The following year, James and Mary were married. James, offered a partnership by Mary's uncle, left his father's firm and joined the bank, which was renamed Campbell & Coutts. When, five years later, George Campbell died, James invited his brother Thomas to join him in the bank. That year saw the break-up of the old family firm, for Patrick became insane and entered an asylum, and John, who had been running the Edinburgh business, died after a short illness. The branch at St Mary Axe came to an end, and after a time the Edinburgh firm passed into independent hands.

On February 1, 1762, Thomas Coutts began a twelve-year partnership with his brother James. Their bank, now called Coutts &

Coutts, had its offices at 59 Strand, and numbered among its customers King George III and many of the English and Scottish nobility. Thomas brought into the firm, besides an investment of £4,000, qualities that were to ensure his success as a banker during the next sixty years: sound business sense, a flair for diplomacy, and shrewd judgment of men and matters. They were qualities that people were to notice in his granddaughter, Angela Burdett Coutts. Both, too, had a gift for friendship, and both were generous in a clear-sighted, level-headed way.

Though the partnership between James and Thomas Coutts was successful in business terms, it was less so as far as their personal relations were concerned. To begin with, in 1763, Thomas defied convention and married a servant, Susannah Starkie, the nursemaid who looked after James's daughter, Fanny. Black-eyed Susannah, daughter of a Lancashire yeoman farmer, was almost certainly illiterate; but she was affectionate, good-looking and sensible, and Tom loved her. She was to prove a devoted wife and mother. 'Mrs Coutts ... took a great deal of pains with her Children, much more than Most Mothers,' Tom was to write years later, when the birth of his first grandchild had sparked off a discussion on Rousseau's ideas about rearing infants: 'I am inclined to prefer her Practice to Rousseau's Theory, who for ought I know never saw a new-born Infant in his life.'[1]

If James had qualms that his brother's marriage might damage the bank's relations with its royal and aristocratic customers, his fears were unfounded. Lord Dundonald, a cousin of the Coutts family, in later years described Susannah as 'a most respectable, modest, handsome young woman', whose 'good sense, amiable disposition, and exemplary conduct endeared her to all her husband's family, and commanded the respect of all who knew her'.[2] Certainly Susannah was accepted by such great society hostesses as Jane, Duchess of Gordon, and Georgiana, Duchess of Devonshire, both of whom were friends of her husband. In an age notorious for its spiteful and malicious gossip, very little seems to have been directed at Susannah Coutts.

Another source of conflict between the brothers was James's health. He suffered from a mental disorder which caused him to act erratically, adversely affecting his work. This threw a great burden on to Thomas, who found himself taking on more and more responsibility in bank affairs. When their partnership agreement came to an end in 1774, he insisted on a new arrangement. James agreed to retire, the terms were settled by two independent arbitrators, the Lords Bute and Rochford, and in August 1775, shortly before Tom's fortieth birthday, the bank became Thomas Coutts & Co. Two years later, James, on holiday in Italy, was taken seriously ill. He is said to have become so violent that it was decided to send him home 'in charge of keepers'. He died at Gibraltar in February 1778.

For the next forty years Thomas Coutts reigned supreme at the bank he was to make world-famous. As his business grew, he took on partners to share the work and the profits, always retaining a half-interest himself. The premises were considerably expanded and the staff increased: by the end of the century there were twenty-two clerks whose combined salaries came to £4,110.

But Thomas Coutts was more than an extremely successful banker. As his profits increased, so did his influence with the great men and women who were his customers. He became the confidant and adviser of princes, peers and Prime Ministers, the friend of men of every kind of distinction. He was above all proud of being banker to his king, George III; in 1787 he became a Gentleman of the King's Privy Chamber, with direct access to the sovereign. 'I was much in His Majesty's confidence which I never did anything to forfeit,'[3] he wrote later.

It says much for his diplomacy that he was also to gain and retain the confidence of the royal dukes, most of whom were at loggerheads with their father, the King. They found in Thomas Coutts a wise and sympathetic friend, though he was by no means always ready to grant their requests to borrow money. Fredrick, Duke of York, for instance, was refused a large loan in 1790, though two years later Coutts was prepared to lend £60,000 to the Prince of Wales (afterwards the Prince Regent) in return for suitable security.

In fact, as Coutts himself put it, his business was 'founded in the power of obliging my customers with loans of money'.[4] He saw the rôle of a banker as that of 'a trustee, accountable to his friends, for sums far beyond his private fortune'. His own fortune had grown to £900,000 by the time he died. Even so, in the memorandum book in which loans were recorded, there was often a note in his handwriting: 'Not to be pressed because it was lent out of compassion.'[5]

Thomas and Susannah Coutts had begun their married life in a house in St Martin's Lane, but in 1775 they moved to the spacious, comfortable apartments above the bank at 59 Strand. By this time they had had four sons, all of whom died in infancy, and three daughters. Coutts, who regarded his banking house as a sacred trust to be handed on to the next generation, hoped that his daughters 'would find me young men fit to take the oar from my hand'.[6]

Sophia, the future mother of Angela Burdett Coutts, was the youngest of the three Coutts daughters. She was born in 1775 into an exceptionally united family. Tom and Susannah, having lost all their sons, doted on the three girls – Susan, Fanny and Sophia – who, in turn, were devoted to their parents and to each other. From childhood they were known as the Three Graces, and were later painted as such, in Grecian dress, by Angelica Kauffmann.

The 'Graces' were expensively educated, first at a school in London known as the Ladies' Eton and then in France. At the age of twelve Sophia was sent to Paris with Susan, then sixteen; Fanny, who was delicate, stayed at home. After a year, discovering that the girls' French chaperon was not the soul of propriety he had thought her, Thomas Coutts removed his daughters from her care. The whole family went on a tour of France and Switzerland, after which all three girls were sent, on the recommendation of the Duchess of Devonshire, to one of France's most fashionable and exclusive educational establishments, the Couvent de Penthémont, where young ladies were prepared for a life of luxury and indulgence.

During the winter of 1788/89 Coutts and his wife stayed in Paris, entertaining lavishly and moving in the highest social circles. It has been suggested that during this protracted visit to France the banker was engaged in some discreet diplomacy on behalf of the King, whom he saw twice immediately on his return to England. Whether or not this is so, he was certainly making useful business contacts and introducing his daughters to the leaders of French Society. He could not have known that in a few short years the guillotine would claim many of these new friends and acquaintances; but of those who escaped the Terror and fled to England, many would turn to Coutts for help and advice.

Tom and Susannah returned home at the end of April. On July 14 the Bastille was stormed. Though assured by his friend Charles James Fox that his daughters were 'as safe in Paris as they would be in London',[7] Coutts had decided by October to bring them back to England. First, however, he took his family on another extensive tour, this time going as far as southern Italy. On their way home they were delayed in Augsberg by the illness of fifteen-year-old Sophia. She was attended by the personal physician of the Electrice of Bavaria, who, though ill herself, sent the doctor from Munich. The Scottish banker had become a person of no small importance.

By March 1791 the family were back in London, and in May, Sophia was presented at Court with her elder sisters. The Three Graces, wrote their proud father, were 'very flatteringly received at St James's' and were soon 'receiving visits from all the world and launching out into all companies'.[8] They were a striking trio. The Reverend William Bagshaw Stevens, who met them a few years later, described them as 'blooming brunettes . . . their long tresses flowing Nymphlike down their shoulders and bosoms'. Their manners, despite their French education, were 'perfectly simple, unspoiled by art'.[9]

Thomas Coutts watched anxiously as his daughters were courted by some of the most eligible young men in England. He was now nearing sixty and his health was not good. His partners at the bank were highly-valued colleagues, but his dearest wish was for a son-in-law to whom he could pass on his own responsibility as Head of the House. But, though each of his daughters was to make what the world regarded as a brilliant match, his hopes of finding a successor from among their husbands were not to be fulfilled. Sophia, the youngest, was the first to marry. And there could have been few men less cut out for the sober life of a banker than her impetuous young husband, Francis Burdett.

*

Francis Burdett was born in 1770. He was the grandson and eventual heir of Sir Robert Burdett of Foremarke Hall, Derbyshire. The Burdetts were an old family of Norman origin, their ancestors having been granted land by the Conqueror in return for services rendered. By the time the baronetcy was created by James I, much wealth and property had been acquired through prudent marriages – a process that continued up to the time of Sir Robert. His son married Eleanor Jones of Ramsbury Manor, Wiltshire, which in due course passed to Sir Robert's grandson, Francis.

Some intimate glimpses into the family life of the Burdetts in the last decade of the eighteenth century are provided by the journal of William Bagshaw Stevens, who was headmaster of Repton School and Domestic Chaplain to Sir Robert Burdett. The old baronet – he was seventy-seven in 1793 – was something of an autocrat. He kept his hands firmly on the family purse-strings and had grown mean with age. 'Dined at Foremarke . . . The Old Bart afraid to trust his Snuff Box on the Table. He cannot bear to lose a Pinch,'[10] wrote Stevens acidly in May 1793.

Young Francis Burdett, on the other hand, emerges very favourably from Stevens' journal, though his father is dismissed as almost an idiot:

Mr Burdett in higher Spirits than ever, an over-grown Baby, the manly sensible seriousness of his son contrasts curiously with the flippant nonsense, the loud causeless laugh, the hop-step-and-jump restless activity of the Father.[11]

But Francis was not always noted for his 'manly sensible seriousness'. He was something of a firebrand, and had inherited a good measure of his father's high spirits and restless energy. Expelled from the sixth form of Westminster School for taking part in a rebellion against the headmaster, he went up to Oxford in 1786 but left without taking a degree. At nineteen, he set off on a continental tour, arriving in Paris in April 1789, a few weeks before Tom and Susannah Coutts left the city. Whether Francis met his future wife and her family in the French capital is not known; but in any case he did not stay there long, finding it 'the most ill-contrived, ill built, dirty stinking Town that can possibly be imagined'.[12]

Francis returned to England in the summer of 1791. Excited, like many of his generation, by the French Revolution, he felt dissatisfied with the state of affairs in England but had not yet found a cause to embrace. He was no revolutionary. 'The French influence,' according to his biographer, 'was in him the thinnest veneer. His Radicalism, when it came, was . . . as racy of the English soil as was the Radicalism of Cobbett.'[13]

Francis Burdett and Sophia Coutts were married quietly on August 5, 1793. The bride was a gentle, romantic-looking girl of eighteen – 'very low of stature, very young and very girlish in appearance', wrote William Bagshaw Stevens, meeting her later. The bridegroom was tall, slim, elegant and rather vain, with very long legs and a prominent aquiline nose. The couple had had to overcome Sir Robert's opposition to the match, which was due mainly to fears of inherited insanity in the Coutts family. One is tempted to agree with Stevens' somewhat cynical view that what helped most to break down the old man's opposition was the dowry of £25,000 that Coutts provided, with the promise of more to come.

Even after the wedding had taken place, Sir Robert showed little inclination to be civil to Sophia's family. His discourteous attitude was only one of several factors that combined to make the first years of married life less happy than they might have been for Francis and Sophia. Less than three months after the wedding came news of an appalling and senseless tragedy: Francis Burdett's younger brother,

Sir Francis Burdett, an engraving from the portrait by Sir Thomas Lawrence

Sophia Coutts, from a miniature by Cosway

Sedley, had been drowned with Lord Montague of Cowdray in a mad attempt to shoot the falls of the Rhine at Schaffhausen in a small boat. Francis was heart-broken, and shut himself up alone in his room for four days.

At the end of the year the Coutts family were to pay their first visit to Foremarke with the newly-married pair. Sir Robert at first insultingly suggested that Sophia should come with her sisters but without her parents; later he gave way and invited the whole family, and the visit took place in January 1794. It was not a success. Sir Robert avoided his guests as much as possible, finding Coutts and his wife 'uncourtly'. * Stevens, though delighted with the daughters, thought Thomas Coutts 'a meagre withered man' and Susannah 'a strange outré Figure'. But, unlike the old baronet, he had sense enough to appreciate what lay beneath the surface: Coutts was 'mild and simple in manners, modest of speech but what he says to the point and sensible', while Susannah's 'Ugly Countenance and Vulgar Manner' were 'irradiated by a smiling Good-nature that seems to spring from the Heart'.[14]

The visit was cut short by the death of Francis's father on February 3. Francis was now heir to the baronetcy, which he inherited on the death of his grandfather three years later. On their return to London the couple lived in a large house in Piccadilly provided for them by Thomas Coutts, who later bought the house next door. Sophia, expecting her first child, was glad of her family's company and support, for Francis had become morose and preoccupied; he ignored her and spent all his time studying. In August he let their first anniversary go by unnoticed. Fanny Coutts told William Stevens that she was afraid Francis was making her sister miserable: Sophia had 'lost that gaity of Heart and sprightly Wit which once so graced her'.[15] And Stevens, who privately thought Sophia a 'spoiled child', was also confided in by Coutts, who had a string of complaints against his son-in-law:

> that he seemed to wish to walk in a little bye-path of his own; that he was constantly silent at table, so reserved at all times that no one could know even his wishes; ... that he returned no visits; that People now ceased to enquire after him; ... that he would be an unhappy man and make others so.[16]

* Coutts never paraded his great wealth. His tall, spare frame was habitually clad in a suit of sombre black. There is a story that once when he was staying in Brighton, a kindly stranger approached the shabbily-dressed old man and pressed a guinea into his hand. The 'lucky guinea' is preserved to this day at the bank.

Accused by Coutts of poring over his books, Francis wrote back wryly that it was odd

> that I whose bum underwent Martyrdom at School for eight years of my life, who notwithstanding its daily sufferings could never be forced to five minutes application, should now be thought to have too much.[17]

A few days later, perhaps feeling that he had been too flippant, he explained that he looked on the next two or three years 'as all that remains to me to acquire whatever can render me useful to my Fellow Men or estimable in the eyes of those who know me, and above all in my own'.[18]

It may have been during this period of intensive study that Burdett found the political inspiration he was seeking. He seems to belong to a type once described by Bertrand Russell in an essay on his grandfather, Lord John Russell – the type of 'the aristocratic reformer whose zeal is derived from the classics'. This type, now extinct, 'worshipped a goddess called Liberty' whose 'lineaments were rather vague'. Their creed was 'literary and poetic and romantic'. It had inspired the intellectual revolutionaries of France, and it inspired Byron to fight for Greece. 'It was quite untouched by the hard facts of economics which dominate all modern political thinking.'[19]

Certainly Burdett was a romantic. Ardent and imaginative, he was steeped in literature and poetry and would later become a close friend of Byron. His worship of the vaguely delineated goddess Liberty led him to champion what he saw as the ancient liberties of the English people and the ancient virtues of the English constitution – both of which, it must be said, he saw in a somewhat optimistic light.

More specifically, he was disgusted by the corrupt parliamentary system, whereby the majority of MPs were nominated by a handful of influential peers and elected by a small and unrepresentative minority of the people. For this reason Burdett was at first reluctant to become an MP. Ironically, it was as the Member for a rotten borough that he first entered Parliament in 1796. Boroughbridge was one of the Duke of Newcastle's seats. When the third Duke died in 1795, heavily in debt, Thomas Coutts in effect bought the seat for £4,000. In offering it to his son-in-law he hoped perhaps to wean the young man away from his books and make him a more congenial companion for Sophia. He little realised the force he was unleashing on an unsuspecting House of Commons.

Although the Duke of Newcastle was a Whig, Burdett never supported that party. During most of his political life he despised both the Whig and the Tory parties – and was in turn despised by them – though he joined the High Tories in the end. By the turn of the century he had inherited, besides the baronetcy, estates in Derbyshire, Wiltshire and Leicestershire and an income of perhaps £14,000 a year: he owed allegiance to no one. Fiercely independent, he was part extreme Radical, part aristocratic Tory. What he hated was the 'system', which was used by both parties for their own ends. 'All our evils can be traced to corruption,'[20] he declared in the House in 1797, and he fought for parliamentary reform long before it had become a burning political issue. Hazlitt called him 'the educator of his countrymen', and he is credited with having made free speech again possible in England.

Reform was not the only cause that Burdett espoused. As he wrote to Thomas Coutts in 1798, 'The best part of my character is a strong feeling of indignation at injustice & oppression & a lively sympathy with the sufferings of my fellows.'[21] Early in his career he pressed for an investigation into conditions in the notorious Coldbath Fields Prison, Clerkenwell, where the inmates languished in dark, damp, filthy cells, often in heavy irons. Debtors, vagrants, paupers, those awaiting trial, and even witnesses waiting to give evidence, were all herded together with convicted criminals. The entire staff from the governor downwards was corrupt. At one time Burdett was banned from visiting Coldbath Fields and other prisons; but his campaign eventually bore fruit. He also waged a life-long personal war against flogging in the army, and was ahead of his time in advocating Catholic emancipation. Twice imprisoned for acting on his principles, he would three times refuse a peerage on the grounds that he could do more good in the House of Commons.

In 1807 Sir Francis was elected as one of the members for Westminster, an 'open' constituency with a large electorate which he was to represent for nearly thirty years. He had become the most popular man in England, the idol of the mob – a remarkable feat for a wealthy, proud, fox-hunting member of the landed aristocracy at a time of political agitation and great social distress.

*

It is unlikely that Sophia shared her husband's political interests. Cocooned since infancy in the warmth and safety of a close family, she was as unsuited to the rough and tumble of public life as was Francis to cosy domesticity. Each felt disappointed in the other. Sophia wept and stormed, and complained to her father of Francis's neglect. Replying to a 'kind and sensible' letter from Coutts in January 1798, Francis candidly admitted that Sophia was to be 'pitied not blamed'. She was 'endowed with the purest & greatest virtues', but there was 'a certain something in our characters which does not assimilate'. Marriage, he had decided, was

> ill calculated to realise the fleeting dreams of happiness, much less those Ideas which youthful imagination creates: it is I think the worst bond & has with great truth been call'd the grave of love ... Indeed (you will think me wild) I am convinced all the present Ties of Society are calculated to obstruct human happiness.[22]

Seeking happiness outside marriage, Francis found it in the arms of the fascinating Lady Oxford. By August 1798 their affair was the talk of the town. Jane, wife of Edward Harley, Earl of Oxford, was later reputed to have had so many lovers that her children were referred to as 'the Harleian Miscellany'. Burdett was said to have been her first love and Byron (when half her age) the last. The question whether Sir Francis was a contributor to the 'Miscellany' was one that became the subject of a law case in 1811. Many years later, when Francis and Sophia were both dead, the question was raised again, much to the anguish of their youngest daughter Angela, who refused even to entertain the possibility that her father had been unfaithful to her mother.

Left more and more to her own devices, Sophia grew lonely and depressed. Between 1794 and 1800 she had three children – Sophia, Robert and Susannah – but caring for them was not enough: she pined for the difficult, moody man who could win over a crowd with his oratory but was often reserved and taciturn with his family and friends. She began to suffer from a variety of vague ailments, many of them no doubt psychological in origin, and eventually became a semi-invalid. Writing to her shortly after their tenth wedding anniversary in August 1803, Francis expressed exaggerated remorse for the 'dismal havock' his 'rugged barbarous folly' had caused. Beneath the self-dramatisation was a genuine concern and affection for his patient suffering wife, trying though he sometimes found her. Perhaps this letter led to a reconciliation, for in the following two years they had two more children, Joanna and Clara.

Thomas Coutts must sometimes have rued the day that he encouraged his son-in-law to enter politics, for Francis's Radical views and impetuous temper could be a source of acute embarrassment to the venerable banker. After the elections of 1802, for instance, a crowd of Burdett's supporters sang revolutionary songs outside Kew Palace, where George III was in residence. Furious, the King transferred his account from Coutts' to Drummonds'. It required all Thomas's diplomatic skill to get it back again.

Fortunately, Sophia's elder sisters had made less alarming choices when they came to marry, though neither son-in-law was interested in a banking career as Coutts had hoped. Both girls married widowers, who happened also to be the sons of former Prime Ministers. Susan, the eldest, became Lady Guilford, the wife of George Augustus, third Earl of Guilford and second Baron North. Fanny married the fifty-six-year-old John, Marquis of Bute, acquiring step-children older than herself. When Lord Guilford died in 1802 Susan and her two daughters moved into 1 Stratton Street, Piccadilly, where her parents now lived.

The adjoining house, 80 Piccadilly, was the home of the Burdetts and their growing family when they were in London. In April 1810 it was the scene of the most dramatic incident in Sir Francis's stormy career: his arrest on a warrant from the Speaker of the House of Commons after an exciting three-day 'siege'. It was a story that Angela, born four years later, never tired of hearing.

The Commons had imprisoned a well-known Radical called John Gale Jones for pasting up on the walls of Westminster an 'advertisement' protesting against secret debates in the House. Burdett denounced the action of his fellow-Members and called for Gale Jones's release. His motion was rejected. Twelve days later, a revised version of his speech in the form of an open letter to his constituents appeared in Cobbett's *Political Register*. The Commons, incensed, voted in the early hours of Friday, April 6 that the Honourable Member for Westminster should be committed to the Tower.

This was easier said than done. Sir Francis, maintaining that the warrant was illegal, refused to accompany the Serjeant-at-Arms who was sent to arrest him. If they wanted him, they would have to break into his house and take him by force. Thousands crowded into Piccadilly during that Friday and Saturday, pelting with mud anyone who did not profess support for Burdett. In the houses of his opponents windows were smashed, shutters, chandeliers and furniture destroyed. Revolt – perhaps even revolution – was in the air. So dangerous did the situation appear that the Guards were called out to disperse the crowds into side streets; an army of 50,000, it was said, was standing by.

The government, meanwhile, was at a loss to know what to do. On Sunday, while London waited tensely for the final outcome, the Prime Minister, Perceval, and the Speaker conferred with the Attorney-General on the legality of forcing an entry into Burdett's house. Eventually, just after breakfast on Monday morning, the Serjeant-at-Arms with some soldiers got in through a window. Sir Francis, arrested in his own drawing-room with his wife and son looking on, was escorted to a waiting coach and driven at top speed to the Tower by a route which avoided Westminster. In the ensuing riots, several people were killed and a number injured. Lady Burdett dashed off a note giving the news to her eldest daugher, sixteen-year-old Sophia, who was at Wimbledon with her younger sisters. On the back of the letter the young Sophia scribbled breathlessly: 'Papa forced from his house & taken by a military force to the Tower. *He* is *safe*, but *thinking* will drive me *mad. What a day.*'[23]

Sir Francis remained in the Tower for over two months, until Parliament was prorogued. He was comfortably housed and even entertained his friends to dinner. Letters of support and congratulation poured in from all over the country; petitions demanding his release were presented to the House of Commons. And *The Times* reported that a weaver in Dunfermline had had his son baptized by the name of Francis Burdett. He had wanted to call the child *Sir* Francis Burdett, but the Minister demurred.

To the disappointment of the huge crowds who waited outside the Tower on the day of his release to escort him to Piccadilly, Sir Francis left via the river and went quietly to his house in Wimbledon. As he explained later, he wished to avoid the possibility of further bloodshed. On July 31 he was given a celebratory public dinner by his Westminster constituents. His popularity was as great as ever, and remained so through the terrible years of distress and unemployment following the end of the Napoleonic Wars. On a summer night in 1816 a tipsy labourer told the diarist Henry Crabb Robinson that Sir Francis Burdett was 'the people's friend and only good man in the kingdom', adding sourly that he would never sing 'Britons never shall be slaves', for Britons were all slaves.[24]

*

Among those who visited Sir Francis in the Tower was Lady Oxford. Although they had long ceased to be lovers, their continued friendship was a constant thorn in Lady Burdett's side. It was not removed until

1813, when the Oxfords went to live abroad. The following year the Burdetts' last child, Angela, was born, after a childless gap of nearly ten years. It may well have been a turning-point in the marriage. Francis was by then forty-four; Sophia nearly forty. It was time to forget the past and build on the residue of mutual affection and respect that remained. Francis might still be impetuous, vain and proud, with a tendency to self-dramatisation. But while pursuing his tempestuous political career he had come to appreciate the blessings of family life. Sophia might still have in her something of the spoilt child; but she had remained a faithful wife and, it seems, a loving one. To Angela, they must have appeared a devoted couple.

Angela Georgina Burdett was born on April 21, 1814, into the elegant, extravagant world of the Regency. The Prince Regent, caricatured as gross and lascivious, was nevertheless a connoisseur of art and architecture who set a fashion for beautiful buildings as well as for self-indulgent living. It was the age of Scott and Jane Austen, of Lamb and Hazlitt, of Coleridge, Wordsworth and Byron. It was also an age of transition. The Regency was the watershed between the old world of stage coaches and ordered rural communities and the new world of railways and sprawling urban slums. The old social order was already beginning to crumble, with the newly-rich jostling for position and the new urban poor fighting for survival.

The great news at the time of Angela's birth was that Napoleon had finally been overthrown. On April 20, 1814, the defeated Emperor set off on his journey from Fontainebleau to Elba; in June, the Tsar of Russia and the King of Prussia, with assorted princes, generals and statesmen from all over Europe, assembled in London for three weeks of celebrations. But the celebrations turned out to be premature: the following March came news of Napoleon's triumphant return to France. Three months later, on June 18, 1815, the 'hundred days' ended at Waterloo, and England was at peace after more than twenty years of war.

In the Coutts and Burdett households, however, these great events had been overshadowed, as often happens, by domestic matters – by a crisis that threatened to shatter the peace of the whole family. In the spring of 1815, while Napoleon was mustering his forces in France, the nearest and dearest of Thomas Coutts found themselves for the first time in bitter conflict with the eighty-year-old head of the household.

Some years before, Susannah Coutts's health had begun to break down. Possibly she was becoming senile; but, whatever the illness was, it was most distressing in its effects and a heavy burden for old Coutts to bear on top of the cares of his business. For years his affection for Susannah was tried by her strange behaviour and shifting moods; all his reserves of patience and forbearance were needed to cope with her. Inevitably, he looked for sympathy outside his marriage; and he found it in a young actress called Harriot Mellon.

Daughter of an Irish seamstress and the self-styled Lieutenant Mellon of the Madras Infantry (who early disappeared from the scene), Harriot was born in about 1777 and made her first stage appearance at

Harriot Mellon in the rôle of 'Volante', by Sir William Beechey

the age of ten. A competent but not a great actress, she was good-looking and good-humoured, with an engaging personality and a warm heart. She played at Drury Lane and in the provinces, and is said to have first caught the banker's eye in Cheltenham in 1805, but they may have met earlier. By 1807 they were exchanging warmly affectionate letters, and Coutts was sending her large gifts of money.

Despite this compromising situation, Harriot always insisted that their friendship was innocent. The painter Joseph Farington, a close friend of Tom's, wrote in his diary:

The paragraphs in Newspapers insinuating that Mr Coutts has an Amour with Miss Mellon, the actress, are most unfounded, he being a most domestic man and attached to his old wife.[25]

In his letters to Harriot, Tom wrote affectionately of Susannah, giving details of her condition. With his family he made no secret of his friendship, naïvely hoping that Susannah would invite Harriot to the house, which she not unnaturally declined to do. Their daughters, however, were all on friendly, if somewhat patronising, terms with Harriot.

Between 1810 and 1814, as Susannah's condition deteriorated, Tom grew more and more attached to his 'sweet Harriot'. He installed her at Holly Lodge, Highgate, a modest house with beautiful gardens barely four miles from Piccadilly. Half a century later it would become world-famous as the summer home of Angela Burdett Coutts.

The Ladies Burdett, Bute and Guilford continued to be affable towards their father's friend, paying her visits at Holly Lodge. But they were completely unprepared for what was to follow. Early in January 1815 Susannah Coutts, who had scalded herself with boiling water, died after a painful last illness. She was buried on the 14th. And on the 18th, Thomas Coutts was secretly married to Harriot Mellon at Old St Pancras Church – or rather, he *thought* he had married her; in fact, there was only one witness and the ceremony was void. A second ceremony was held on April 12. By that time, the storm had broken.

After their first wedding, Tom and Harriot had returned to their respective homes – Tom straight to his bed, for he was very ill. What he had hoped to do was to present his daughters with a *fait accompli*, let them get used to the idea, and then bring the new Mrs Coutts to Piccadilly to preside over a happy united family. He had expected shock and initial dismay. What he had not bargained for was the prolonged and vehement opposition of his eldest and youngest daughters (Fanny was living abroad and could afford to be conciliatory), and of his son-in-law, Francis Burdett.

Susan and Sophia, torn between love of their father and distress at his conduct, made his life and their own a misery by extravagant displays of grief and outrage. Susan was more inclined to outrage, Sophia to grief. Tom wrote anguished letters to both. Susan, he told Sophia in July, had been 'hostile and violent' and had 'deeply wounded an innocent and good woman [who] is the greatest comfort and blessing of my age'. As for Sir Francis, Tom did not think it possible that anyone could 'spitefully or wantonly abuse or injure any person as he has done'.[26] He had behaved so cruelly to Harriot that Tom had to prevent them from being in the same room together.

It was obviously impossible for the family to live under one roof. Susan and her daughters had continued to occupy 1 Stratton Street, while Coutts and Harriot lived either at Holly Lodge or in a rented house near Covent Garden. By June 1817 the old man had had enough. He issued an ultimatum: 'I must have my house in Town to myself

Thomas Coutts, from an engraving after the portrait by Sir William Beechey

immediately.'[27] He got it. The Burdetts had already moved across Piccadilly to St James's Place; Lady Guilford and her daughters now vacated Stratton Street, in bitter mood. The quarrel simmered down, only to come to the boil again the following year, when Coutts went so far as to draft a 'declaration' breaking off all relations with Susan and Sophia.

London society took its cue from the Prince Regent and his brothers, who as early as June 1815 were dining with Tom and Harriot at their

'Highgate Cottage', as *The Times* called Holly Lodge. Of course there were the scoffers and the slanderers, as Tom had foreseen; scurrilous verses went the rounds of the London drawing-rooms. But a rhyme from a kinder pen delighted both Tom and Harriot:

> An apple we know was old Adam's disgrace,
> Who from Paradise quickly was driven,
> But yours my dear Tom is a happier case,
> For a Mellon transports you to Heaven.[28]

Though he had married in haste – in indecent haste – in the mistaken and ingenuous belief that he would forestall criticism and also, perhaps, because he was a very sick man and wanted to make Harriot his wife before he died, Thomas Coutts never for a moment regretted it. His cousin, Lord Chancellor Erskine, congratulated him on finding a wife

> so capable of dispensing pleasure to all around her, combining (which so rarely happens) the gaiest deportment with the most exemplary prudence and with so undivided an affection for yourself.[29]

Although relations with Susan Guilford were never quite the same as they had been before her mother's death, the more gentle and peace-loving Sophia was eventually restored to favour, despite her husband's boorish behaviour. The last years of Tom Coutts's life were spent peacefully with his 'most justly beloved Harriot . . . the preserver and the comforter and the delight of my life'.[30] There were visits from Sophia and her daughters, now all nearly grown-up except for little Angela. She was too young to have known anything about the storm surrounding her grandfather's second marriage, and was probably the only member of the family to have taken no part in the bitter quarrels.

No doubt old Tom had a particularly soft spot for the slightly solemn little girl, and knew how to get round her shyness. Theirs was the affinity of the very old and the very young. Harriot, too, with no children of her own, was drawn to her husband's youngest granddaughter, in whose affection there could be no hint of past animosity. So began the relationship that was to have such extraordinary and far-reaching consequences.

Thomas Coutts died on February 24, 1822, in his eighty-seventh year, and was buried at Wroxton beside his first wife, Susannah. In his will, made in 1818, after stating that he had given to each of his daughters £25,000 on her marriage and a further £20,000 since, he left the whole of his property, including his half-share in the bank, to his second wife, Harriot.

Two

HARRIOT AND HANNAH

Towards the end of her life, Angela Burdett Coutts told a young relative that she had had an 'ideal childhood'.[1] There is no reason to suppose that age had sweetened the memory. She was the youngest of a large family, with numerous relatives to make a fuss of her. She adored both her parents and, though her father was often away and her mother frequently ill, she probably saw more of them than did many upper-class children at a time when the nursery was often a self-contained and seldom visited part of the household.

One of Angela's earliest memories was of peacocks strutting in the grounds of Ramsbury Manor. This was the beautiful house in Wiltshire – built in the 1680s by Sir William Jones, Attorney-General under Charles II – that Sir Francis had inherited from his mother's family. More dignified and imposing, especially to a child, was Foremarke Hall, which had been re-built in Palladian style for Sir Robert Burdett in the 1760s. At these two great country houses, and at her father's London home in St James's Place, Angela spent much of her childhood.

Like most well-to-do families, the Burdetts never stayed long in one place. It was customary to divide one's time between town and country, with extended visits to friends and relations and to fashionable spa towns and seaside resorts like Bath and Brighton. To remain in the same place for more than a few months at a time was considered very tedious. Early in life Angela became accustomed to long, uncomfortable journeys with overnights stops at coaching inns which the railways would soon make redundant. She acquired a taste for travel which she never lost. In later years her friend the Duke of Wellington would tease her for her love of the new 'rail-road'.

Because of Lady Burdett's ill-health, the family often went to Bath for her to take the waters. Here they took a house in Royal Crescent, where their neighbours were the Brooke family. Young James Brooke, eleven years older than Angela, would one day be Rajah of Sarawak and one of her closest friends. 'I daresay the *ghost* of the girls and the Shetland pony . . . were familiar to me then,' wrote Brooke to Angela when they were both middle-aged; 'but ... were rather below my regard, as a *young gentleman.*'[2]

A more attentive observer of the Burdetts' life in Bath was the Irish poet Thomas Moore. He first met Sir Francis shortly after the publication of his most famous work, *Lalla Rookh*, which earned him a fame equal to that of Scott and Byron. He was then about thirty-eight. His Irish Melodies were sung in drawing-rooms up and down the country, and he himself was a performer of great charm, captivating the ladies with 'his singing and his conversational power, and his winning and deferential address'.[3]

The elder Miss Burdetts were all under Moore's spell, urging their mother to invite him to dinner when he visited their box at the theatre and singing for him themselves when he did come to call. Moore, for whom such adulation was as natural as the air he breathed, found them 'nice girls' and Joanna in particularly 'exceedingly pretty'.[4] There is no mention in his journal at this time of Angela, who had scarcely progressed from the nursery to the drawing-room; but it was she who was to be the friend of his old age.

It is probable that Angela was a rather solitary child. The youngest of her four sisters, Clara, was nine when she was born; Joanna, known as Tanzy, was a year older, Susan thirteen and Sophia nearly twenty. Sir Francis's brother, Jones Burdett, had married in 1811 and over the next twenty-five years produced a family of ten children; but Angela does not seem to have had a particular friend from among these cousins. She developed from an early age an affinity with people much older than herself. Quiet and attentive, intelligent and sweet-natured, she was a 'good' child, with none of the boisterous high spirits that can be so annoying to adults. She came to know many of her father's political associates – men like the brilliant, eccentric Lord Brougham, and John Cam Hobhouse, later Lord Broughton. Hobhouse, like Burdett a Radical MP, included little messages for 'Miss Angela' in his letters to her father. 'We have a little ball to-night,' he wrote in 1821, when Angela was six; 'I wish she was here, that I might have the honour of asking her to dance.'[5]

Angela never knew her only brother, Robert. From boyhood he had caused his parents much heartache, showing a complete disinclination to be educated. 'The command of money and of his own motions has utterly spoilt him,'[6] was the verdict of one schoolmaster when Robert was fifteen. In 1814, the year of Angela's birth, he went up to Oxford. Though he behaved wildly, running up debts and drinking heavily, his father still hoped that this only son would turn out to be 'a gentleman, a scholar and above all an honest man'.[7] A scholar, however, Robert was not cut out to be. He left Oxford after a year and went into the army – a profession Sir Francis detested – having obtained a commission through the influence of his grandfather Coutts with the Duke of York. From then on relations between father and son went from bad to worse, until eventually they were completely estranged.

According to family tradition, Angela met Robert only once at her father's house, when she neither knew who he was nor exchanged any words with him. This was in 1825, when Angela was eleven and Robert was said to have been temporarily ADC to the Duke of Wellington, though this is not confirmed. Robert, so the story goes, was sent to Sir Francis's house in St James's Place with some despatches and, on arrival, was asked by his father to join the family at lunch. Only afterwards did Angela discover that the stranger who had sat next to her was her brother. For a sensitive girl, such an incident would have been disturbing and upsetting. Even if the story is aprocryphal, the knowledge of the antipathy that existed between her father and brother must have been painful to her.

That Sir Francis was torn between love of his son and despair at his conduct is clearly shown in his letters to Robert. In March 1819 he wrote in language reminiscent of some of his earlier declarations to his wife:

> You are still dear to me, although I thought I had given you up, as having repeatedly evidenced a total want of affection, consideration, or regard for me; . . . I was endeavouring to forget that I ever had a son, and . . . could not help envying the good fortune of those who had none . . . The appearance of a desire for conciliation on your part undoes all my resolutions and makes me eager to receive you with open arms; . . . come when you will, you will always be as welcome to your too affectionate father as the precious drops from heaven to the parch't lips of the weary traveller o'er the sandy desert.[8]

Of Burdett's relations with his daughters little is known; but they are unlikely to have escaped the dramatic outbursts sparked off by his explosive temperament. As a 'too affectionate father' he may well have been possessive and over-protective towards his daughters: certainly, with the exception of Angela, they all stayed at home until an unusually late age. Sophia, the eldest, was thwarted in her desire to marry the man of her choice. She wrote bitterly to her cousin Frances that she had been 'cruelly deceived' in the matter of being allowed to decide for herself. We know nothing of the man in question; perhaps he was a scoundrel. But Sophia at the time was well over thirty – old enough, one would have thought, to make her own mistakes.

In the end it was Susan, the second daughter, who made an unfortunate choice: she married, in 1830, John Trevanion, an adventurer who squandered her fortune and later tried to extract money from Angela. Sophia married the Honourable Robert Otway-Cave, MP, a widower, in 1833. Joanna, the middle sister, did not marry at all, and Clara waited until she was forty-five.

Between Sir Francis and his youngest daughter there grew to be a particularly close bond. Angela, who knew nothing of her parents' past difficulties, was uncritically adoring of her famous papa, though she often had to worship him at a distance. Later, when gout slowed him down and he spent more time with his family, he turned to Angela for the intellectual companionship his wife had never been able to give him. They shared a love of Shakespeare, discussing quotations and the meanings of words. At times Angela also acted as his secretary, writing out his letters in a hand that her father charitably described as 'ready but not clear'.

The Burdetts lived very comfortably but not, it seems, in great luxury. Thomas Moore thought Sir Francis's style of living 'not at all equal to his means, either in expense or elegance. With such a fortune, he ought to make his private life a sort of counteraction to the plebeian tendency of his politics.'[9] A more plebeian observer, the Radical weaver Samuel Bamford, thought that Burdett's London home had a 'kind of dreary stateliness'. Bamford and his delegation from the Hampden Clubs felt a sense of disappointment in the man who was 'one of our idols'. In his 'cold, gloomy, barely furnished house' Sir Francis received them, dressed in

> a loose grey vest coat, which reached far towards his ancles [*sic*]. He had not a cravat on his neck; his feet were in slippers; & a pair of white cotton stockings hung in wrinkles on his long spare legs.[10]

Bamford also observed that the baronet, while talking 'candidly and freely' about Reform matters, appeared to be 'submitting to, rather than seeking conversation with men of our class'. The truth was that Burdett, though concerned throughout his political career for the rights and grievances of the people, was an aristocrat who had absolutely no desire to mix socially with the lower orders. He did, however, have many friends among those he called 'men of education'. At her father's house Angela first met a number of men from different professions who would become her lifelong friends. The artist Masquerier, the diarist Henry Crabb Robinson, the brilliant, sardonic banker-poet Samuel Rogers, famous for his literary breakfasts; lawyers, scientists, actors and musicians, as well as politicians – all were welcome at St James's Place and were sometimes asked to Foremarke or Ramsbury Manor.

It was at Ramsbury that Tom Moore first met Burdett, in 1818. Moore thought his host 'a most amiable man'; there was 'something peculiarly attaching in his manner; his gentleness, and almost bashfulness, forming such a contrast to the violence of his public career'.[11] Throughout her life Angela would also be noted for her gentle, almost self-effacing manner. But she, too, was capable of behaviour that was at variance with this seeming meekness.

*

No one could accuse Harriot Coutts of not living up to her means; nor was bashfulness one of her characteristics. Her position was not an easy one. Ridiculed – indeed, libelled – by the gutter press and sneered at behind her back, she could afford to ignore the insults while her husband still lived and the royal dukes dined at her table. But in her widowhood, deprived of the restraining influence of her beloved Tom as well as of his devotion and protection, she became more than ever a target for caricature and malicious gossip. Food and drink and a luxurious style of living were compensations she freely indulged in. Her ample figure was a gift to cartoonists, her maiden name with its juicy connotations was ripe for exploitation. In one cartoon the impecunious Duke of York kneels before her, his eyes on her money-bags, exclaiming: 'Oh delicious fruit. Could I but obtain a taste I should be myself again.'

But Harriot did have her friends and champions. One of them was Sir Walter Scott, a distant cousin of Thomas Coutts. He issued a warm invitation to her to stay with him at Abbotsford, though admitting to a friend that he would have to 'Reganise'* her a little if she thought of travelling with her usual retinue, which consisted of seven carriages and umpteen servants. In the end she brought only three coaches (each with four horses), which was still trying enough to Lady Scott. She had two doctors, in case one should fall ill, and two women to share the duties of keeping watch in her room at night, because she was afraid of ghosts.

* King Lear's daughters, Regan and Goneril, forced their father to reduce his retinue of 100 knights (*King Lear*, I, iv; II, iv).

But as Scott wrote in his diary, 'So much wealth can hardly be enjoyed without some ostentation.' He himself found her 'a kind, friendly woman, without either affectation or insolence in the display of her wealth, and most willing to do good if the means be shown to her'. She could also be very entertaining, talking 'without scruple of her stage life'.[12]

Would Harriot Coutts marry again? It was a question that not only occupied society gossips, but was of no small importance to her step-daughters and their families. Although under no obligation to do so, and despite their former treatment of her, Harriot paid regular and generous allowances to the Ladies Guilford, Bute and Burdett out of the income of about £60,000 a year that she received from her half-share in the bank. Many years later, Angela asserted that these payments had been a form of 'buying off' opposition to Thomas Coutts's will. The family, she said, had wanted to challenge the will in the courts, but had eventually been dissuaded from doing so by the bank partners. Whatever the truth of this, Harriot continued to pay the annuities without being compelled by law to do so.

In fact, Harriot's overriding concern was to carry out what she felt would have been Tom Coutts's wishes. Thus, she looked for her heir among her former husband's grandchildren. The most likely candidate was Lord Dudley Coutts Stuart, son of Fanny, Lady Bute. At the time of her father's re-marriage, Fanny – his favourite daughter – had been tactful and conciliatory: 'Pray always remember your Fanny very kindly to your dear wife, & also believe that I shall never cease to feel most kindly for her who makes the evening of your life comfortable.'[13] In 1817 she wrote to say how much it would please her if her son Dudley (then aged fourteen) were to enter the bank: 'My delight would be to have him the instrument of continuing your name and business when you and I shall have disappeared from this busy scene.'[14]

By the time Thomas disappeared, however, the matter had still not been settled. In the event Dudley did not go into the bank, and in 1824 he blotted his copybook irremediably as far as Harriot was concerned by marrying Christine Alexandrine Egypte, daughter of Lucien Bonaparte, Prince of Canino. The marriage was bigamous,* and it took several years for Christine's first marriage to be annulled; but this was not the reason for Harriot's disapproval. Young Dudley had allied

* Christine wrongly believed that her husband, a Swedish count, was dead. When she married Dudley, the count reappeared. The declaration of nullity was finally ratified in 1828.

himself to a niece of Napoleon, and in the patriotic Harriot's book this was unforgivable.

Fanny Bute, however, did not give up hope. Apart from the unsatisfactory Robert Burdett, Dudley was Thomas Coutts's only male grandchild; there was still a chance that Harriot would relent and leave him the half-share in the bank. And there was also the very large personal fortune that Thomas had bequeathed to Harriot: some at least of this would surely go to her step-granddaughters. So Fanny Bute, who now lived permanently abroad, sensibly urged her daughter, Lady Frances Sandon (afterwards Countess of Harrowby), to keep up with Mrs Coutts – a duty which Frances found tiresome and distasteful, to judge by her letters to her mother.

In June 1827, Frances Sandon passed on to her mother an important piece of news:

> I have just been doing an odious, but very necessary duty, which is, composing our respective letters of congratulations to Mrs Coutts on her approaching marriage with the Duke of St Albans . . . How it may affect our interests I am sure I cannot tell; . . . Our comfort, I should think would be increased by it, as probably she will care less for what we do, & have less wish to be with us than she has hitherto done.[15]

The Duke of St Albans was half Harriot's age. A quiet, shy young man, he had been pressing his suit for several years. Harriot had made Sir Walter Scott her confidant during a visit to Abbotsford in 1825, when she had been accompanied by the Duke and his sisters. Scott wrote in his journal:

> If the Duke marries her he ensures an immense fortune. If she marries him she has the first rank. If he marries a woman older than himself by twenty years She marries a man younger in wit by twenty degrees . . . The disparity of ages concerns no one but themselves – So they have my consent to marry if they can get each other's.[16]

Scott's daughter, Anne, commented more laconically in a letter to her former governess: 'I daresay the marriage will turn out very well, for, though he is a great fool, yet he is very good-natured.'[17]

The wedding was held in Stratton Street on June 16, 1827. George IV, to whom Harriot wrote informing him of the event, pronounced his blessing: 'Anything that can contribute to your happiness will always give me sincere Pleasure.'[18] Sir Walter Scott, too, wrote a congratulatory letter, which led Harriot to reflect in reply:

> What a strange, eventful life has mine been, from a poor little player child, with just food and clothes to cover me, dependent on a precarious profession, without talent or a friend in the world! . . . Is it not wonderful? is it true? Can I believe it – first the wife of the best, the most perfect being that ever breathed, his love and unbounded confidence in me, his immense fortune . . . all at my command . . . and now the wife of a Duke. You must write my life; the History of Tom Thumb, Jack the Giant Killer, and Goody Two Shoes, will sink compared with my true history written by the author of *Waverley*.[19]

*

Angela Burdett was thirteen at the time of Harriot's marriage. Neither she nor her mother attended the wedding, for they had left England the previous summer for a prolonged stay in Europe. They were away for about three years, travelling extensively in France, Germany, Switzerland and Italy. Angela's sisters were with them for part of the time, and Sir Francis joined them when he could. The tour was undertaken partly for the sake of Lady Burdett's health: she was still plagued by rheumatism, headaches and general nervous debility, and it was hoped that treatment at some of the numerous continental resorts and spas might help. But Sophia, remembering her own residence in Paris and travels in Europe with her family, was also anxious to give her intelligent youngest daughter a similar opportunity.

Angela learned to speak several languages fluently, absorbed information on the culture and customs of the countries she lived in, and mixed with people of a wide cross-section of opinion, if not of class. It was an education at once liberalising and liberating, laying the foundations for the independent life she was to take up a decade later. She left England a shy and awkward schoolgirl. When she returned, though still only fifteen, she was an accomplished young woman, quietly self-confident and already possessing something of the social poise and composure for which she would be noted throughout her life.

Though her travels and studies abroad had helped to bring about this transformation, there was another factor that contributed to Angela's new self-assurance. Some time before leaving England – exactly when is not clear – Lady Burdett had engaged a governess for Angela, Miss Hannah Meredith. Miss Meredith had apparently been recommended to Lady Burdett in glowing terms by a friend in Lancashire. Her origins are obscure. It has been suggested that her father, James William Meredith, was a clergyman; but this is not confirmed. Even her date of birth is unknown. When she died in 1878 she was a very old woman, but perhaps no more than eighty; so she was probably in her twenties when she first came to the Burdetts.

There was nothing particularly distinctive about Hannah Meredith's appearance. Small in stature – particularly in comparison to Angela, who was always tall for her age – she was known to her friends in later

Hannah Meredith

years as 'Tiny'. Her portrait shows a plumpish young woman with brown hair and brown eyes and a slightly quizzical, enigmatic smile. The face is that of a woman at once sensitive and determined, a shrewd, intelligent woman who knows her own mind and likes to get her own way, and who is not without a sense of humour.

Hannah Meredith was to be more important than any other single person in the life of Angela Burdett. Her extraordinary influence remains to some extent a mystery. But it is probable that what drew them together initially was the simple fact that each had a need which the other was able to fulfil. Angela, with few companions of her own age, was shy and reserved; and a reserved child often needs the undivided attention of one person to draw her out and help her to discover her own identity. Angela's mother was gentle and loving, but ill-health kept her preoccupied with herself to a greater or lesser degree. Her adored father, more demonstrative in his affections perhaps, was often busy with politics, with hunting, or with managing his estates. Besides, he was almost public property; she had to share him with the vast majority of the populace; for he was still, as Hazlitt wrote in 1825, 'a prodigious favourite of the English people'.[20] As for her sisters, fond as they were of the baby of the family, they were a group of young ladies, with interests of their own.

If Angela found in Miss Meredith the special friend that she needed, in the same way did Hannah warm to the child whose trust and affection were freely given once a certain reserve had been overcome. In a house full of young women whose social equal she could never be, Hannah's situation was not an easy one. In Angela, she found not only a mind willing and eager to be trained and formed according to her own precepts and principles but, beneath a slightly wary exterior, a heart that was capable of strong attachment.

It was from Miss Meredith that Angela imbibed her religious faith – an unquestioning, childlike faith that would remain virtually unchanged throughout her long life. She was to become a devoted member of the Church of England, never wavering in her support of the established Protestant faith. But the particular creed that appealed to her was that of the Evangelicals, with their earnestness, their piety, their total commitment to the service of God and man. As an intensely private person Angela was drawn to Evangelicalism because it was concerned essentially with the saving of the individual soul. As a person with an already strongly-developed sense of duty, she approved of the emphasis the Evangelicals placed on social responsibility.

The great religious movement that came to be known as the Evangelical Revival had begun in the second half of the eighteenth century with John Wesley. Hannah Meredith's parents may well have been among those who flocked to hear this remarkable priest and preacher, who could hold a crowd of several thousand miners enthralled at an open-air meeting at five o'clock on a winter morning. Wesley's conviction was total; his power almost hypnotic. For over fifty years he travelled the length and breadth of the country, addressing congregations of up to 20,000 people. At his meetings those who underwent 'conversion' often fainted, wept, shouted out or even went into convulsions. Though he and his followers were frequently ridiculed and abused, the impact of the movement on an easy-going, self-indulgent society was profound. The Evangelicals, wrote the historian Lecky,

> gradually changed the whole spirit of the English Church. They infused into it a new fire and a passion of devotion, kindled a spirit of fervent philanthropy, raised the standard of clerical duty, and completely altered the whole tone and tendency of the ministers.[21]

By the time Wesley died in 1791 Evangelicalism had spread to the middle and upper classes. Writers like Hannah More produced books and tracts which became best-sellers. It is easy to imagine Angela reading *Thoughts on the Importance of the Manners of the Great to General Society*, first published in 1788, which urged the rich and privileged to use their power wisely. The French Revolution gave to this message a new political urgency. What had happened in France was a terrible example to the English upper classes, as William Wilberforce – later to be famous for his anti-slavery campaign – pointed out in his popular *Practical View of Christianity*,* which has been called the Bible of Evangelicalism. Writing of 'the blessed effects of Christianity on the temporal well-being of political communities', Wilberforce described how Christianity could 'root out our natural selfishness' and 'rectify the particular faults' of each class:

> Affluence she teaches to be liberal and beneficent; authority to bear its faculties with meekness . . . Those in the humbler walks of life . . . she instructs, in their turn, to be diligent, humble, patient; reminding them that their more lowly path has been allotted to them by the hand of God; that it is their part faithfully to discharge its duties, and contentedly to bear its inconveniences.[22]

As G. M. Young has remarked, the Evangelicals gave Victorian England 'a creed which was at once the basis of its morality and the justification of its wealth and power'.[23] Certainly it was the Evangelicals, of whom the most famous was Lord Shaftesbury, who led

---

* Full title: *A Practical View of the Prevailing Religious Systems of Professed Christians in the Higher and Middle Classes in this Country contrasted with Real Christianity* (1797).

the fight to improve the lot of 'those in the humbler walks of life'. As Victoria's reign progressed, charitable work in some form or other came to be regarded as the duty of every good Christian. Nevertheless, few questioned Wilberforce's assumption that men's stations were 'allotted to them by the hand of God'. If Angela's religion inspired her to spend a large part of her fortune for the benefit of others, it also allowed her to enjoy to the full the benefits she herself received from her wealth, and to relish, in her quiet way, the power and prestige that went with her position as a great heiress and a great public figure.

The Evangelicals left another legacy to nineteenth-century England: their language. The Victorians were steeped in what one might call 'sermonese'; its influence on speech and writing was even more pervasive, perhaps, than that of journalese in our own day. Angela, at twenty, wrote of the death of her sister Susan's little girl: 'As to the poor babe, whatever sorrow one may feel on one's own account, it would almost be unkind to regret its early release from a world of sorrow.'[24] Many years later, in paying tribute to Hannah Meredith – by then her inseparable companion – she expressed herself in terms not unworthy of Wesley himself. To her 'dear friend', she wrote, she was indebted

> not only for whatever information I may possess, but . . . for the first direction of my mind to the observation of the multitude of objects of usefulness and beauty with which a merciful Father has surrounded us. From her I first learnt that happiness and comfort are the exclusive possession of no condition in life, but are attainable by most people; proceeding out of common things and simple pleasures, and seldom indeed, if ever, to be wholly missed by those who walk carefully and reverently in the footsteps of our Great Example, and who cherish a humble sympathy with all the work He has intrusted to the hearts and hands of His children.[25]

*

Whether Harriot, Duchess of St Albans, would have agreed with these sentiments it is difficult to say. Her extravagant entertainments were hardly 'simple pleasures', but she fondly believed they made others happy. As Sir Francis Burdett wrote to his wife in Germany, the Duchess was very good-natured and had the best of intentions; but she went on 'at such a rate' with her parties and fêtes that he was afraid it would annoy Lady Burdett.

It certainly annoyed Angela's cousin, Frances Sandon. 'I cannot express how disagreeable we felt it,' wrote Frances to her mother after attending a grand *fête champêtre* at Holly Lodge in June 1829 to celebrate the St Albans' second wedding anniversary. Nevertheless, she had to admit that it was 'a very pretty sight', with 'all sorts of amusements' – displays of archery, haymakers *en costume*, Spanish dancing, and singers from various countries. There were 'heaps of people never seen elsewhere, dressed in all the colours of the rainbow'; Frances was particularly struck by the 'Moorish-looking' Spanish women with their 'immense sparkling eyes & white teeth'. Invited by the Duchess to sit at the top table among the royal guests, Frances felt obliged to talk to her hostess but 'only gave myself as much trouble as civility required'.[26]

If Frances Sandon was not prepared to be more than civil to the Duchess, her young cousin Angela was. In the autumn of 1829 Angela returned to England. From then on she saw much of the Duke and Duchess of St Albans and soon became a favourite with Harriot. Exactly how this rather unlikely friendship began is not known. There is a tradition in the Harrowby family that it was Miss Meredith who pushed Angela forward; but we have no evidence of this. In any case Harriot, who was no fool, would hardly have allowed herself to be influenced against her own judgment and inclination. That she had taken a particular fancy to Angela and found in her a congenial companion seems certain. She was also looking for an heir – a responsibility she took seriously – and she was perfectly capable of assessing Angela's suitability without the intervention of an ambitious governess.

All the same, one cannot help thinking that in the ordinary course of events Harriot was someone of whom Hannah would not have wholeheartedly approved. As for Angela herself – serious, thoughtful, reserved, ladylike, with that composed look which made her seem older and wiser than her years – one wonders what she made of the extrovert and extravagant Harriot, ageing now but still full of gusto, warm-hearted, generous, slightly eccentric and not a little vulgar.

There is every reason to suppose that Angela returned Harriot's affection. As a small child she had warmed to this kind, amusing lady who loved to spoil her with party dresses and other presents. Now that she was older she could see beyond the glamour and understand something of the woman. Angela was as good a listener as Harriot was an entertaining talker. During their long drives together to the Lakes,

Angela Burdett as a young girl, from the painting by J. J. Masquerier

the West Country and Scotland, there was ample opportunity to hear Harriot's life history several times over, and to gain an insight into what it was like to be a 'poor little player child, with just food and clothes to cover me'. And often in the carriage would appear another figure, brought to life by Harriot's vivid recollections: Tom Coutts, 'the best, the most perfect being that ever breathed'.

'To me, the Duchess comes back stately, benignant, in black velvet and diamonds,' recalled the writer George Augustus Sala towards the end of the century. Harriot would have done well to stick to black; the white satin she loved to wear was not the best choice for her ample figure. Sala remembered as 'a little urchin' going to a Twelfth Night entertainment at the Duchess's house in Brighton. The huge Twelfth Cake was 'ornamented with a vast number of musical instruments in miniature'. When it was cut, 'the slice which fell to Miss Angela Burdett contained a magnificent diamond ring'.[27]

If Harriot counterbalanced the pietistic Evangelical influence of Hannah Meredith, she was not without her own brand of social responsibility. But, though anxious to use at least some of her wealth to relieve poverty and suffering, she went about it in a rather haphazard way. She set up a soup kitchen outside the gates of Holly Lodge, gave money and coal to the aged poor, distributed food, clothes and other necessities on Christmas Day, and did her best to help in individual cases of hardship that came to her notice. Activities of this kind struck a sympatheitc chord in the mind of Angela Burdett, which had been so well prepared by Miss Meredith. But they also made her realise that stop-gap charity, while often necessary, was not enough.

Sir Francis, now in his sixties and often laid low by gout, missed his youngest daughter when she was away on her jaunts with the Duchess, but he seems to have raised no objection to her going. His relations with Harriot had become more cordial, particularly since she continued to make a generous allowance to Lady Burdett and took a great interest in all his daughters. In July 1829 Sir Francis wrote Harriot an effusive letter of thanks for her 'kind, considerate, & judicious' conduct, adding: 'I write this as a record which may be produced in evidence against me, in case I should ever so far forget myself as to fall into that odious but common vice of ingratitude.'[28]

Alas for such extravagant declarations! Two years later, almost to the day, Harriot received from the same pen an extraordinary outburst – violent, vindictive, and insultingly hostile. Economic necessity had compelled her to reduce the allowances she had been paying to Thomas

Coutts's three daughters. 'So then, Duchess,' began Sir Francis, 'you really grudge Mr Coutts's Daughters the crumbs that fall from their Father's Table?' He went on to threaten legal action on the grounds that Thomas Coutts had not been of sound mind when he made his will; and, as a final insult, announced that he had transferred 'all my affairs from the Strand to the House of Messrs Drummond'.[29]

Harriot's reply was a model of magnanimity and restraint. She hoped that he would now 'as you have done before acknowledge your error and unkindness'. But, if he wished to investigate the legality of Mr Couts's will, nothing would give her greater joy,

> when I trust every circumstance of my connection before and after my marriage with Mr Coutts, and my conduct to him and his Family, will appear as clear and honourable in the eyes of man as I know and feel it does in the knowledge of God.[30]

Rash and impetuous as ever, Burdett had written in haste, and she allowed him to repent at leisure. In due course he acknowledged that he had been in the wrong and apologised. How much Angela, then seventeen, knew of the affair we do not know. But, loth as she was to believe any ill of her father, she may have reflected that it was this streak of impetuous anger in him that had helped to estrange him from her brother Robert.

*

In 1832, a year after this incident, occurred the event towards which Sir Francis Burdett had been working all his political life: the passing of the Reform Bill. Elections for the first reformed Parliament were held in December, and Burdett and his friend Hobhouse were again returned for Westminster. The following year, the new Parliament abolished slavery and passed the first Factory Act; in 1834 came the controversial Poor Law Amendment Act, of which more will be said later.

When Lord Melbourne, on becoming Prime Minister, offered Burdett a peerage it was declined, as two previous offers had been. 'They seem determined to make me a Peer. How odd people are,'[31] wrote Sir Francis to his wife. Some people thought that he was the odd one, suddenly displaying alarming Tory tendencies now that Reform had been won. The fact was that he had never adhered to either party, but with the great political aim of his life achieved, his innate Toryism began to assert itself. Some of his colleagues in the House recognised this; the people resented it. Nevertheless, they re-elected him in January 1835, though during the next two years his gout was so bad that he seldom attended the House.

The Duchess of St Albans, kind as ever, lent him Holly Lodge while she carried Angela off to the Continent. 'I was truly sorry not to be able like a good and dutiful Papa to join you and the Duchess at Dover,' he wrote on March 11, 1836, 'but the doctor would not hear of it. Give my love to the Duchess and tell her nothing can be more comfortable than Holly Lodge nor anybody more so than I am.' [32]

On June 20, 1837, King William IV died. His young niece, eighteen years old and trained from childhood for her great destiny, entered on a reign which would last for nearly sixty-four years. The Victorian Age had begun. On the King's death Parliament was dissolved, and a general election took place in August. Sir Francis, giving health as the reason, declined to stand again for Westminster. He was, after all, sixty-seven, though he had written to his daughter Joanna only a few months earlier that he didn't know when he had felt so well, and 'almost as foolish as ever I was in my life'. [33] His next action seemed to some to confirm his foolishness: he agreed to stand as *Conservative* MP for North Wiltshire, a district in which he was well-known as the squire of Ramsbury. The church bells rang for him and people pledged him their votes. The old baronet was in his element. 'This is a new epoch in my life,'[34] he wrote jubilantly to his sister-in-law Susan, Lady Guilford.

It was, indeed, the beginning of a new epoch for many people. But the strange, eventful life of Harriot Mellon was drawing to a close. Taken ill at Stratton Street, she had a longing to be at Holly Lodge. In days gone by it had been a feature of her entertainments to be drawn in a phaeton up and down the hilly grounds, preceded by a band of musicians and followed by her guests in procession. Now, for the last time, she was driven slowly round the beautiful grounds, resplendent in their summer glory. Increasingly her thoughts returned to her dear Tom. Knowing that she had not long to live, she asked to be taken back to Stratton Street to die on the bed where Tom had expired. It was her wish to leave the earth, as he had done, on a Sunday, the day of the Resurrection, 'in the humble hope of gaining admission where there are many mansions'.[35] Her wish was fulfilled, and she died on Sunday, August 6, 1837.

Sir Francis, in the thick of the election battle at Devizes, replied to Angela's note telling him of Harriot's death:

My dear Angy, You may well say as to the Duchess, that her life, the latter part of her life at least, was truly a fitful fever. Tell your dear

Mama I can no more quit this place now than the Duke of Wellington could have quitted Flanders just before the battle of Waterloo. . . . I shall keep this open till the close of the Poll.[36]

At 6 p.m. he added the voting figures: he had come top of the poll. On the same day (August 7) he wrote to his sister-in-law, Susan Guilford: 'What [the Duchess] has done Heaven alone knows – she always talk'd of herself as being left as trustee for you all. We shall ere long see . . .'[37]

*

The last will and testament of the Most Noble Harriot, Duchess of St Albans,[38] was read in Stratton Street on August 10, 1837. Besides the Duke and his solicitor, there were present the two senior partners of Coutts & Co., Edward Marjoribanks and Sir Edmund Antrobus, and representatives from the families of two of Thomas Coutts's daughters, Susan Guilford and Fanny Bute (Fanny had died in 1832). Lord Dudley Coutts Stuart was there, and his brother-in-law Viscount Sandon, husband of Lady Frances Sandon. In a letter to his father written on the same day, Lord Sandon described the scene and outlined the will's provisions. A slip in the first sentence – 'The Will was opened this morning at 2 p.m.' – betrays his agitation. The letter also makes clear that, ironically, there was no representative of Thomas Coutts's third daughter, Sophia, present. Sir Francis Burdett, wrote Sandon, 'was not . . . able as yet to quit the scene of his triumph'.[39]

It was an immensely long will. Harriot had left her husband an annuity of £10,000, plus Holly Lodge and 80 Piccadilly during his lifetime. There were small annuities to some of her own family, friends and servants, £5,000 each to two of Edward Marjoribanks' children (the godchildren of herself and Tom), but nothing whatever for Lady Guilford or her descendants, or for Fanny Bute's family. Lady Burdett, however, was left £20,000, 'for her sole and separate use and benefit, exclusively of any husband'. The bulk of Harriot's estate, including all her jewellery, property, money, stocks and securities, and her half-share in the banking house, she left on trust for Lady Burdett's youngest daughter, Angela.

There were certain conditions attaching to the bequest. Angela must take the additional surname of Coutts within six months; and should she 'intermarry with any person being by birth an alien', she would forfeit all benefit under the will 'as if she were dead'. On her death the trust was to pass to her son, if she had one, failing which it would go successively to her two sisters, Joanna and Clara, and to their sons.

Each person inheriting was to take the name of Coutts and was debarred from marrying a foreigner.

After the solicitor had finished reading the will, there was silence from the seven men in the room. It was broken by the Duke, who nervously expressed his gratitude to his late wife for what she had left him (in a codicil, as it happened), adding:

'I hope none of the family grudge it me, and that we shall all live in harmony.'

It was Lord Dudley who replied:

'I see no reason to the contrary.'

There was nothing more to be said. They all bowed and left the room.

Three

THE RICHEST HEIRESS IN ALL ENGLAND

According to the newspapers, the amount of Angela Burdett's inheritance was £1,800,000 in gold and an income of £80,000 a year. In fact, they were exaggerating: Harriot's personal estate was valued at under £600,000, not all of which went to Angela, and the income from the bank was nearer £50,000 than £80,000, at least in the early years. Even so, at a time when a London clerk could keep himself and his family on a salary of £100 a year, and a skilled workman made do with much less, £50,000 was a staggering sum. There had always been great heiresses in terms of landed property, but it had never been known for any young woman to possess, in hard cash at the bank, the kind of wealth that Sir Francis Burdett's youngest daughter now possessed. She had become, overnight, 'the richest heiress in all England'.[1]

There is a family tradition that Sir Francis, incensed by the terms of the Duchess of St Albans' will, turned Angela out of his house in St James's Place at an hour's notice. With Miss Meredith she walked across to the Stratton Street mansion she had inherited and – so the story goes – they had to sleep in blankets for several nights because there were no servants to prepare the bedrooms and no sheets aired.

While such an act might not have been beyond a man of Sir Francis's temper, the story is not supported by the facts. To begin with, as we have seen, Angela's father was not at home when the will was read. He remained in Wiltshire for several days after the election, then, having attended Harriot's funeral, spent several weeks in London before returning to Devizes in mid-September. He was certainly in a bad humour when he wrote to Angela on September 17, but only because his servant had forgotten to pack his 'little red writing box which contains everything I want and can't do without'.[2] Would she please send it on to him? The letter was addressed to Angela at 25 St James's Place, so by that time she had not yet left the family home.

Sir Francis begins this letter 'My dear ABC'. Angela had lost no time in complying with the Duchess's will, and on September 14 had assumed the name of Coutts by royal licence. The change of name was symbolic of her changed status. At twenty-three she was independent, her own mistress, with a huge fortune at her command. Hers was a unique position for a young woman at that time.

'I suppose you are quite inundated not only with torrents of congratulatory letters, but with sonnets in every variety of metre, from despairing and disinterested admirers,' wrote her father's old friend and fellow-MP, Sir George Sinclair. His letter – endorsed on the outside 'N.B.: This is not a proposal' – was sincere, earnest and prophetic, and must have made a deep impression on Angela:

> You . . . may easily believe, that I *cordially rejoice* in your accession to a princely fortune, which, however, I should consider as no blessing, if you were not enabled to employ it, as I trust you will be, in promoting the Glory of God, and furthering the interests of your fellow-creatures. This is my heart's desire and prayer for you – and knowing your kind, amiable and generous disposition I am quite happy to think, that you have now the means of giving full scope to it. May you be happy, and a source of happiness to thousands . . .[3]

Not everyone was so ready to rejoice. Angela's cousin, Frances Sandon, thought her 'poor Grandfather's fortune' had been 'a *curse* rather than a blessing hitherto to those concerned in it. I know little or nothing of my young cousin Angela,' she told a friend. 'May it not be to her what it has been to others!'[4]

Whether the inheritance would prove eventually to be a blessing or a curse to Angela, in those early days it brought her more disquiet than happiness. Its immediate effect was to make her a target for publicity, which she hated. For a short time she escaped by accompanying her mother on a visit to Foremarke. By the time she returned to London, she was beginning to take stock and to plan her new life. Whatever the future might hold, she knew she could count on one unfailing source of support – Hannah Meredith, the ex-governess who was now her constant companion. With Hannah, she prepared to take her first big step, which was to install herself at 1 Stratton Street.

By Christmas 1837 the move had been made. It caused a further raising of eyebrows: for a young unmarried woman to set herself up in an independent establishment was most unusual. If Angela did incur her father's wrath, it was more likely to have been over this than because of the inheritance *per se*. But Angela, the quiet, sweet-tempered and dutiful daughter, was not to be deterred once her mind was made up.

Outwardly calm and dignified but no doubt quaking within, she took leave of the family home and, with the faithful Hannah, crossed the threshold of the great house on the corner of Piccadilly which would be her home for nearly seventy years.

Whatever the manner of her going, she had started as she meant to continue. She was independent and intended to lead her own life, however strange it might seem to her relations. Frances Sandon, staying at the Harrowby family seat of Sandon Hall, Staffordshire, was kept up-to-date with all the London news by her husband Dudley Ryder, Viscount Sandon. 'I called today on Aunt Burdett,' he wrote early in December, 'and found her sitting in the dark with two persons.' One of these turned out to be 'the heiress':

> I must say she was very unassuming & rather agreeable in the turn of her conversation. I see that already she is treated as a distinct, as well as distinguished personage, & dines out I think, by herself, at any rate without either of her elder sisters. What a strange position, & how much it must disturb, if it ever existed, the natural relation of the sisters.[5]

Others, too, were to find that Miss Coutts, despite her apparent disregard for some of the conventions of society, was in her demeanour at least the very model of a conventional young lady. The more acute observer realised that behind the modest, unassuming manner was a woman to be reckoned with, though she was still very young and still feeling her way in a new situation. Benjamin Disraeli, meeting her the following year during 'a brilliant evening at the Salisburys', found her 'a very quiet and unpretending person; not unlike her father, nevertheless'.[6] Which could have meant many things, but indicated that there was more to Miss Angela than met the eye.

*

It was taken for granted that Miss Coutts would not long remain alone in her mansion with only her companion for company. She would, of course, marry; it only remained to be seen who would be the lucky man. There was no shortage of suitors. As one leader of Society – Richard Monkton Milnes, afterwards Lord Houghton – said, almost all the young men of good family proposed to her: 'Those who did their duty by their family *always* did.'

In fact, Angela had no intention of marrying any of these young hopefuls. It was Richard Monkton Milnes who described the procedure generally adopted at Stratton Street when a proposal was imminent. Miss Meredith, who received visitors with Angela, became expert at judging the moment, and retired into an adjoining room, leaving the door slightly ajar. A few minutes later a discreet cough would tell her that it was all over, and back she would go to help steer the conversation towards more general topics. Monkton Milnes, who later fell in love with Florence Nightingale (she refused him in 1849 after a seven-year courtship), never went through the experience himself. 'Miss Coutts likes me,' he once remarked, 'because I never proposed to her.'[7]

Who Miss Coutts would marry was a question that occupied everyone, from Queen Victoria downwards. Rumour linked Angela's name with many of the eligible bachelors of the day. On March 5, 1838, the Queen discussed with Lord Melbourne, her Prime Minister, mentor, and chief source of gossip, the 'supposed marriage' of Lord Fitzalan, heir to the Duke of Norfolk, with Miss Coutts. Ten days later, Her Majesty noted in her journal that the marriage was 'off'. It was almost certainly never on. Leaving aside personal feelings, it is highly unlikely that Angela, with her strong Evangelical tendencies, would have considered allying herself with the foremost Catholic family in the country, even though Lord Fitzalan, who became the 14th Duke in 1856, did not formally enter the Roman Catholic Church until 1839.

It appeared that a match-making grandmother, the Duchess Countess of Sutherland, had been responsible for the reports in this instance, as the Queen discovered some months afterwards. The Duke of Norfolk's agent, she recorded in her journal,

> told Lady Holland how shocked they were at the Duchess Countess trying to make a match between the young man and Miss Coutts, and the violently open and apparent manner in which the Duchess Countess set about it; for, that though they (the Duke of Norfolk etc) were a little embarrassed in their circumstances, still they had quite enough.[8]

'Miss Burdett (or Miss Coutts),' added the 19-year-old Queen, momentarily confused, 'behaved very well about it.' Indeed, Miss Burdett Coutts – or Miss Coutts, as she was almost invariably called – was discovering that her position called for discretion and restraint, qualities which, fortunately, were in keeping with her reserved temperament. She was to give away thousands during her lifetime; but she was a woman who gave away little about herself.

There was another matter over which Angela 'behaved very well', according to Lord Melbourne, who was again the Queen's informant.

Early in 1838 Victoria was shocked to find that her mother, the Duchess of Kent, was in debt to the tune of £70,000. She herself, at the beginning of her reign, had had to borrow money from Coutts & Co., as had her father before her. The Duke of Kent had died in 1820, heavily in debt. Now, the young Queen was paying off her father's debts out of her Privy Purse, only to find that her mother's finances were in an appalling state. Miss Coutts was approached for a loan, and, reported the Queen in her journal:

> Lord Melbourne said she was clever, for . . . when they came to her (as she is the principal person in the House), she made no difficulty about it; they told her she must not speak of it; 'she said she never told her father these things as he was engaged in Politics, but that she would not mention this even to her mother'.[9]

It may have been partly in recognition of services rendered that Angela received Her Majesty's command to attend the Coronation. This took place on June 28, 1838, and was perhaps the only occasion, as the writer Harriet Martineau remarked, 'on which a lady could be alone in public, without impropriety or inconvenience'. Sir Francis Burdett, as a Member of Parliament, would also have attended, but is unlikely to have sat with Angela. Miss Martineau wrote that she 'knew of several daughters of peeresses who were going singly to different parts of the Abbey, their tickets being for different places in the building'.

London went wild with Coronation fever. Hyde Park was a sea of tents, gay with flags and bunting; the streets were crammed with people. Those living near the Park or on the processional route slept little the night before, and were wakened at four by the booming of the twenty-one-gun salute. Well before six, ladies dressed in their finery were making their way to the Abbey to secure a good seat. Harriet Martineau, who had a ticket for the transept gallery, settled herself into a back seat, which gave her 'a pillar to lean against, and a nice corner for my shawl and bag of sandwiches'.

Harriet wore her mother's pearls; Angela the Duchess of St Albans' diamonds. We do not have Angela's impressions of the day to compare with Miss Martineau's detailed account. But even that Radical middle-class blue-stocking, critical alike of the ageing peeresses with their dyed hair and exposed wrinkled flesh and of the 'blasphemous' religious ceremony with its 'mixing up of the Queen and the God', had to admit that 'it was a wonderful day'.[10]

If Harriet Martineau was already a celebrity at thirty-five owing to her literary achievements, Angela Burdett Coutts, at twenty-four, was an object of far greater interest because of her fortune. For Angela, as for the Queen herself, the Coronation was a day of exposure – exposure to the curious stares and comments of those around her in the crowded Abbey. Her face was not yet well known – these were the days before illustrated papers – but people who had met her or knew her by sight were able to point her out to their neighbours. She was singled out for mention by the anonymous author (E. H. Barham) of the *Ingoldsby Legends*, in 'Mr Barney Maguire's Account of the Coronation':

> 'Twould have made you crazy to see Esterhazy*
> All joo'ls from his jasey to his di'mond boots,
> With Alderman Harmer, and that swate charmer,
> The famale heiress, Miss Anja-ly Coutts.

Whether Angela was really a 'charmer' is open to question. By the standards of the day she was not conventionally beautiful, though her expression was 'sweet and engaging', according to Hobhouse. Tall and slim, with a long face and a broad brow, she had inherited her father's nose and her mother's slightly pouting mouth, though in old age her lips would be thin. Her eyes were dark blue, with well-shaped brows; her dark brown hair was always dressed simply, drawn down from a centre parting and either plaited in 'earphones' or swept straight and smooth into a bun at the back. Not for her the elaborate ringlets, or plaits looped beneath the ears like snakes, that were worn by young women of fashion. Her father, who thought such plaits 'tasteless and unnatural', approved.

Strictly brought up by Miss Meredith, Angela had been discouraged from vanity. But she loved to wear beautiful clothes and jewellery, and took as much trouble over her toilette as any lady of fashion. By the beginning of Queen Victoria's reign the simple Empire line had given way to the tight-waisted, full-skirted style which was to culminate in the exaggerated crinolines of the middle of the century. Evening and Court gowns, in silks and satins sometimes richly embroidered with silver thread and pearls and trimmed with exquisite lace, were cut low to

---

* 'Prince Esterhazy . . . was covered with diamonds and pearls; and as he dangled his hat, it cast a dancing radiance all round. While he was thus glittering and gleaming, people were saying . . . that he had to redeem those jewels from pawn, as usual, for the occasion.' (Harriet Martineau: *Autobiography*.)

reveal their wearers' statuesque shoulders. Angela was perhaps a little on the thin side to be statuesque; but she had a natural grace and dignity of carriage that would be remarked upon until the end of her life.

It was her misfortune, however, to suffer from a skin condition – probably eczema – which gave her face a red, blotchy appearance, possibly affecting other parts of her body too. 'If her complexion were good she would have a pleasing face',[11] Hobhouse noted in his diary; and there are references in family correspondence to 'dear Angy's face'. No doubt all kinds of treatments, remedies and special diets were tried, as they still are today for eczema. In August 1838 Lady Burdett passed on the recommendation of one doctor, who had declared that

> nothing was accounted so bad for any irruption in the face or otherwise in France, as the use of *coffee*, leave it off love a little while to see and take cocoa, or try to use milk, which he says is by far the best if it agrees tis so *bland* to the system – you take a good deal of coffee you know but you should take NONE![12]

Perhaps Angela's great-niece, Clara Burdett Patterson, was right in suggesting that Angela was 'never very attractive to young men, except as regards her fortune'.[13] Certainly Angela herself was intelligent enough to be aware of the chief source of her sudden eligibility. If the knowledge sometimes pained her, she was also sensible enough not to take it too much to heart. On each suitor who presented himself at Stratton Street she practised that sang-froid for which she would become so famous; as each retired discomfited she and Hannah no doubt shared (in Mrs Patterson's words) 'many a good laugh'.

After all, Angela – like Jane Austen's Emma – had 'none of the usual inducements of women to marry'. She already enjoyed wealth, status, security; she was mistress of her own house and, like Emma, she had 'a friend and companion such as few possessed, intelligent, well-informed, useful . . .; one to whom she could speak every thought as it arose, and who had such an affection for her as could never find fault'.[14] Why should she risk her happiness with a man who might be nothing but a fortune-hunter? So she continued to turn away all who queued at her door for her hand, not caring much whether they found her attractive and not herself being much attracted to any of them.

*

Unwanted suitors might cause some amusement, but there were other consequences of being an heiress that were less easy to laugh off. By every post came begging letters from people in every conceivable (and inconceivable) kind of distress. This was disturbing enough; but worse still were the appeals for help from members of Angela's own family. Harriot's will had, not surprisingly, caused bad feeling among the rest of Thomas Coutts's grandchildren: it was, wrote Frances Sandon, 'not only so unjust but in so bad a spirit . . . No other individual of the family is even *mentioned*.'[15]

Frances felt particularly keenly about the exclusion of her brother, Lord Dudley Coutts Stuart, the erstwhile heir presumptive, and appeared to have some support from their father's family, the Stuarts. 'I do think it strange,' Lord James Stuart had written to Frances in December 1837, 'that up to this moment the possessor of the vast fortune of Mr Coutts has done nothing for your brother.'[16] Poor Dudley had been unlucky in his marriage to Christine Bonaparte; she had proved to be a heavy financial liability and eventually he was compelled to deny responsibility for her debts. Moreover, Dudley was deeply involved in the cause of Polish independence and the welfare of Polish refugees, the victims of Tsarist oppression. For over twenty years, until his death in 1854, he was the indefatigable champion of the Poles, and there is no doubt that had the Coutts inheritance passed to him, some of it would have gone to this cause that was so dear to him.

More hurtful to Angela than the murmurings among her cousins was the attitude of her own sisters. It was understandable that they should have resented being excluded from Harriot's will, but their resentment caused Angela much heartache. She was prepared to be generous to them, but she drew the line at helping Susan's scoundrel of a husband, John Trevanion, get himself out of debt. 'Poor Susan,' wrote her father to Angela, 'is only made a catspaw of to work upon your feelings.' Sir Francis urged her not to give way to this 'improper and unfair application', even though Susan was complaining bitterly of her younger sister's 'unkindness'.[17]

It was partly to escape from these worries that, about a month after the Coronation, Angela left London with Hannah to take a holiday in the North. The spa waters of Harrogate, they hoped, would soothe her inflamed skin and calm her jangling nerves. From London, Lady Burdett wrote Angela a comforting motherly letter:

> Your papa *may* have said something to Dudley but it must not affect you . . . A casual conversation without *any participation of yours*, never can signify, besides, *your* position is *really* different to the late

Duchess's – *all* your cousins might do the same with Dudley if admitted! And I might according to *that* come forward as most rightful heir of *all* Papa's property being *his child* the rest only grand ones . . . As to Susan, she is settled as far as you are concerned, and you must not WORRY love pray do not. Get health and FAT, and *then* we will see – No *hurry* for anything. God bless you.[18]

It was all very well to be told not to worry. But a new and sinister cause for concern had in the meantime appeared on the scene. At the beginning of August, her father had forwarded Angela some letters, with the comment, 'I don't know what your correspondent means nor who he is'. Her correspondent was a certain Richard Dunn, and his two letters were couched in such strange terms that she thought they must have been written by a madman, and threw them away. Exactly what they said we do not know, but they were love letters – of a kind.

A few days later, a new guest arrived at the Queen's Hotel, Harrogate, where Angela and Miss Meredith were staying, and occupied a room almost opposite Angela's bedroom. He was a man in his late thirties, of medium height, dark, well dressed, intelligent-looking, with a confident and gentlemanly manner. Shortly after his arrival Angela, returning to her room, found to her dismay that a visiting card had been left there. The name on the card was Richard Dunn: the dark stranger and her eccentric would-be lover were one and the same person.

Annoyed and uneasy, Angela left the Queen's Hotel the next day and, with Miss Meredith and their servants, settled into some apartments on the other side of the town. It was a fruitless move. For the rest of their stay they were haunted by Dunn. Never a day passed without their seeing him. He wrote Angela a constant stream of letters, kept calling at the house, and dogged her footsteps when she was out walking, trying to engage her in conversation. She began to be afraid he might become violent.

Not wishing to worry her parents, Angela appealed to Edward Marjoribanks, the senior partner of Coutts & Co., who promptly came to Harrogate and advised her to apply to the local magistrates for protection. At the same time a police officer, Ballard, was despatched from London to guard her. Armed with the magistrates' warrant, Ballard arrested Dunn as he was on his way to the house where Angela was staying. At first Dunn denied that he was going anywhere near her, then he shouted:

'If she's done this, she's worse than the damnedest whore that ever walked the streets!' He went on abusing her as he was taken before the magistrates, declaring that she deserved to be 'tarred, feathered and burnt'.[19]

On September 29, Dunn was ordered by the magistrates to keep the peace and stay away from Miss Coutts, on his own recognisance of £500 and two others of £250 each. When he failed to pay, he was sent to prison until the opening day of the new sessions, October 16. By that time Angela had left Harrogate. She was advised to take no further action, and Dunn was released.

'I cannot express how rejoiced I feel at the conviction of this fool (or madman – or both),'[20] wrote Edward Marjoribanks to Sir Francis on October 1. The old baronet, understandably, was mortified that Angela had not sent for him: 'I could have put an end to your annoyance sooner than anybody, but you mentioned it so slightly that I had no idea of its being so tormenting and distressing.'[21] Neither he nor Marjoribanks could have foreseen that Angela would be tormented and distressed by Richard Dunn for a period of nearly eighteen years, during which time he and his victim would come face-to-face in a court of law on several occasions, and he would spend a number of years in jail for his pains.

*

It would be a mistake, however, to imagine that Angela's new life was all anxiety and distress. She enjoyed a very full social life, and though never aspiring to become a leader of Society, she herself entertained on a grand scale. Her house in Stratton Street was ideal for the purpose, with its magnificent ballroom and spacious reception rooms, lavishly fitted out and filled with priceless furniture, pictures and *objets d'art*. A dinner party was often followed by a much larger late evening party, which might take the form of a ball or a concert. It was not unusual for several hundred of the *haut ton* to attend Miss Coutts's functions, and invitations were eagerly sought after. Often, people would write to Sir Francis, who passed on the names to Angela with his comments:

> Sir E^d Kerrison's son a very young and agreeable man and a good dancer having neither sister father nor mother as an encumbrance is very anxious to make no inconsiderable figure at your ball . . .[22]

Good dancers, it seems, were sometimes in short supply. A guest who attended one of Angela's balls wrote that, though she 'found a large, crowded and brilliant party, saw all the fine people and spoke to many', there was very little dancing, and 'not dancing men enough for the numbers of pretty girls, many of whom never danced at all. Elderly gentlemen were certainly too numerous.' It was, nevertheless, 'a satisfaction to be seen there'.[23]

Angela may well have felt more at ease with 'elderly gentlemen' – many of them her father's friends – than with the young 'dancing men' who clamoured for invitations to her parties. Her circle of friends and acquaintances was in fact already very wide, ranging from the distinguished men she had met at her father's house to actors, singers and others connected with the theatre whom she had come to know through Harriot St Albans. There were, too, the partners in the bank: Edward Marjoribanks, a tall, good-looking man in his mid-fifties with a slight stoop and the preoccupied air of one who carries grave responsibilities, and his colleagues Sir Edmund Antrobus and William Coulthurst. Angela's relations with these sober gentlemen would at times be somewhat strained; but they became her trusted friends and advisers and in turn developed a healthy respect for the young heiress.

She had much to learn. Like Queen Victoria, she was determined 'to be good'. Much as she loved entertaining, theatre-going and the delights of good conversation, these alone were not enough to satisfy her. She had been entrusted with a great fortune which it was her duty to use, in Sir George Sinclair's words, 'in promoting the glory of God, and furthering the interests of her fellow-creatures'. But how could this best be done?

One obvious channel through which her bounty could flow was the Church of England. The Bishop of London, Charles James Blomfield, soon to become a close friend, was campaigning vigorously for funds to build churches in the metropolis to save the souls of the poor – something of which both Angela and Miss Meredith wholeheartedly approved. But what of the bodily needs of the poor? Angela knew that there were many who lacked the basic necessities of life – adequate shelter, food and clothing. Her step-grandmother had tried in her haphazard way to relieve the misery of some of these unfortunates. Now she herself was inundated with appeals. From the start, her private charity was extensive. Her father, too, passed on requests for assistance from friends of deserving individuals. But, as he wrote, there was no end to applications of this kind, and she 'ought to do greater and more useful things, and not dribble away great resources in this sort of way.'[24]

Angela agreed. But she was by nature cautious; her knowledge was incomplete, her experience limited. Above all, she shrank from publicity. These factors combined to prevent her from rushing into ambitious schemes of her own at this stage. With Hannah Meredith as her chief adviser, she was content to give through the Church and the many charitable agencies and societies that were springing up, as well as helping anonymously those who appealed direct to her. It would be some years before she would be ready to follow a more independent line. A number of influences were already at work, and several unexpected events would play their part in shaping the future course of her philanthropy. In the meantime, the gaps in her knowledge were being filled in by someone with first-hand experience of how the poor really lived.

We do not know exactly when Angela first met Charles Dickens, but it was probably in 1838 or early the following year. We do know that it

Charles Dickens in 1838, at about the time Angela first met him, by Samuel Laurence

was at a dinner given by Edward Marjoribanks, and it was on a Friday
– or so Dickens insisted many years later, because 'I have never in my
life ... begun anything of interest to me, or done anything of
importance to me, but it was on a Friday'.[25] That included the most
important beginning of all – his entry into the world on Friday,
February 7, 1812.

Bursting with vitality, restless, impetuous, his manner earnest and
sincere, his expression open and eager, his whole being charged as if
with an electric current – this was Charles Dickens. 'What a face is his
to meet in a drawing-room!' wrote Leigh Hunt. 'It has the life and soul
in it of fifty human beings.'[26] It was a face framed at that time with
luxuriant chestnut-brown hair, and without the beard and moustache of
later years. He had, wrote John Forster, his friend and biographer, 'a
capital forehead, a firm nose with full wide nostrils, eyes wonderfully
beaming with intellect and running over with cheerfulness, and a rather
prominent mouth strongly marked with sensibility'.[27]

The first *Sketches by Boz* had been published in February 1836,
followed by a second series in December. In March of the same year
had appeared the first instalment of *The Pickwick Papers*, the book
which was to make its author a household name. In the middle of
Pickwick, Dickens started work on *Oliver Twist*, which was also
published monthly, beginning in January 1837. By that November the
young author, now married to Catherine Hogarth and with a baby son,
Charley, felt sufficiently confident to open a bank account at Coutts &
Co. It was quite likely soon after this that Edward Marjoribanks invited
Miss Coutts to meet the bank's new and famous customer.

The first of the many hundreds of letters from Dickens to Angela that
have come down to us is a note dated July 1, 1839, in which he
'exceedingly regrets' that he is unable to accept her invitation for the
9th. Angela lost no time in renewing it, however, and Dickens duly
dined with her on July 25. By the end of the year he was writing to his
solicitor, albeit a little prematurely, that he was 'on terms of intimacy
with Miss Coutts'.

His confidence was well justified. Angela was captivated by this
brilliant young man in whom, perhaps, she fancied she saw something
of her father in his youth. During 1840 she invited Dickens to a number
of parties, causing him on one occasion to write in mock distress to
Edward Marjoribanks to enquire whether, since 'Miss Coutts's card . . .
has solemn mention of a Royal Duke and Duchess', gentlemen were
expected to wear court-dress:

I have already appeared in that very extraordinary costume and am prepared for the worst; but I have no confidence in my legs, and should be glad to hear that the etiquette went in favor of trowsers [*sic*].[28]

Whichever way the etiquette went, Dickens evidently went with it and didn't disgrace himself, for within a fortnight he was asked again. By the turn of the year their friendship was well established. Angela lent him her box at Covent Garden, and in the new year invited him to several informal 'library dinners'.

It did not take Dickens long to discover that the great heiress with the calm, quiet manner had an intense desire to use her fortune for the benefit of others. He himself felt a passionate concern for the poor. In 1836, under the pseudonym of Timothy Sparks, he had written a strongly-worded booklet called *Sunday Under Three Heads*, attacking those who, through the Sunday Observance Bill, wanted to deprive the working classes of their 'innocent Sunday recreations'. It was dedicated, in scorn and anger, to Bishop Blomfield, who had been 'among the first . . . to expatiate on the vicious addiction of the lower classes of Society to Sunday excursions'.

If Angela and Miss Meredith had read this publication, or knew of it, they would surely not have approved. But they were unlikely to have connected Timothy Sparks with the delightful young author whom they welcomed so warmly at Stratton Street. Nor could they have known, because it was not something he talked about, that his indignation at social conditions was born partly of his own experiences in childhood – of visiting his father in the Marshalsea debtors' prison, of daily trips to the pawnbroker, and, above all, of six months' despairing drudgery, at the age of twelve, in a rat-infested blacking warehouse.

In his frequent wanderings through the London slums Dickens had learned much about the appalling conditions in which the very poor existed. Some of this knowledge had gone into *Oliver Twist*, which profoundly shocked many people by revealing a world they would have liked to ignore but whose existence could no longer be denied. Sir Francis Burdett, who mentioned *Oliver* in one of his speeches, told Angela that he found the book

> very interesting, very painful, very disgusting, and as the old woman at Edinburgh, on hearing a preacher on the sufferings of Jesus Christ, said, Oh dear, I hope it isn't true. Whether anything like it exists or

not I mean to make enquiry for it is quite dreadful, and to society in this country, most disgraceful.[29]

Charles Dickens opened Angela's eyes and widened her sympathies. He was to be her partner and adviser in philanthropy for the best part of twenty years.

*

On February, 10, 1840, Queen Victoria married her Prince Charming in the Chapel Royal, St James's. The gay, wilful little Queen (she was under five feet) and the tall, serious, quietly determined heiress had been catapulted to fame and fortune in the same year. Each had begun her new life with a former governess turned devoted companion – Angela with Hannah Meredith, Victoria with her dearest Baroness Lehzen. Now, the Queen had a handsome young husband, her 'DEAREST DEAREST DEAR Albert', with whom she was blissfully in love. Angela, twenty-six next birthday, was still unmarried. She had many friends and a full and interesting life. But in the background hovered the nightmare figure of Richard Dunn. Since he was to loom so large in her life over so long a period, we must now take a closer look at this Irish 'suitor' and his extraordinary eighteen-year 'courtship'.

Four

THE IRISH ANNOYANCE

Richard Dunn was an Irish barrister; an unsuccessful barrister – or perhaps just an unlucky one, for his knowledge of the law was acute. His avowed aim was to marry Angela. But, like so many of her suitors, what he was really after was her money. So, at least, it seemed to Angela, and with good reason. His tactics were those of a blackmailer, an insidious and subtle blackmailer whose legal training enabled him to take advantage of loopholes in the law and to use its intricacies for his own ends.[1]

Not that his methods were in the least subtle. On the contrary, his harassment took the crudest forms. Released from York Castle, where he had been imprisoned, in October 1838, he hotfooted back to London and took a room in the Gloucester Hotel, Piccadilly, just up the road from Angela's house and separated from it only by the courtyard of Devonshire House. From his window he could look across to the front door of 1 Stratton Street and watch all Angela's comings and goings. Whenever she went out, either on foot or in the carriage, he would appear and try to talk to her. He followed her everywhere. He wrote notes and letters, in terms both loving and abusive, and was for ever calling at the house. He seemed intent on making her life a misery.

When she recognised his handwriting on the envelope, Angela usually passed Dunn's letters unopened to her solicitor, Mr Parkinson. It was becoming clear that they would have to resort to the law again if she was to have any peace. 'Mr Parkinson may safely be relied upon for taking good care concerning the Irish annoyance,' wrote Sir Francis optimistically, adding: 'I shall carefully keep it from your Mama – and from everybody.'[2]

This was easier said than done. Everybody was interested in Miss Coutts's affairs, and it was part of Dunn's plan to stir up as much publicity as possible in the hope of embarrassing his victim.

At last, on December 21, an application was made on Angela's behalf to Bow Street Police Court. Dunn was arrested on a warrant from the Chief Magistrate, ordered to keep the peace and, unable to find the necessary sureties, was again sent to prison. But not for long. He applied to the Court of Queen's Bench, was released on a technicality, and at once resumed his former activities.

He did not go back to the Gloucester Hotel, but he was constantly in the Piccadilly area. He would walk up and down outside 1 Stratton Street, waiting for Angela to come out, and repeatedly tried to gain admittance both to her house and to her father's in St James's Place. Angela never went out unless accompanied by a manservant; she had to give up walking in Kensington Gardens because servants in livery were not admitted there. For long periods Ballard or another Bow Street police officer took up residence at Stratton Street. She could not even go to church without being followed, and went instead to a private chapel in Albemarle Street. But even there, on one occasion, Dunn turned up, created a disturbance and had to be thrown out. It was a war of nerves, and it continued all through 1839 and into the New Year.

In April 1840, just before her twenty-sixth birthday, Angela, accompanied as always by Miss Meredith, went to stay with her parents at the Park Hotel in Norwood, then a resort in rural Surrey. They arrived on a Saturday. Next day, when they were at church, someone – probably Angela's footman – recognised Dunn among the congregation. Afterwards, he was seen on the road between the church and the hotel, watching his prey. During the next few days he kept popping up, almost out of the ground, wherever Angela happened to be walking – in the hotel's private gardens, on the road, in the nearby fields. He waved his handkerchief, blew kisses, and made other gestures. Once, he squeezed through a gap in the hedge and confronted Angela and Hannah as they walked in the hotel grounds. They rushed indoors. He was far too clever to do anything that might constitute an assault, but he was bent on causing as much annoyance and distress as he could.

He succeeded only too well. By the end of the week Angela had had enough. She and Hannah decided to cut short their visit, returning to London on April 25. About a fortnight later, Angela received a letter from Dunn insisting that she should meet him. If she refused to do so, he wrote, she would 'repent a course the consequences of which will sooner or later fall on yourself and your family'. She gave the letter to her solicitor.

The Season that year was particularly brilliant. Balls, levees and drawing-rooms were held to celebrate the Queen's marriage and her twenty-first birthday. At many of these events could be seen the tall, graceful figure of Miss Coutts, exquisitely dressed and glittering with fine jewels, including the famous tiara, inherited from Harriot St Albans, that had once belonged to Marie Antoinette. The unwelcome attentions of her Irish 'suitor' had again brought her into the limelight. Would she now, people wondered, overcome her reluctance to marry? A husband, after all, would be the best form of protection against this menace. But if Angela was tempted, she did not give in.

On June 10 an attempt on Queen Victoria's life shocked the nation. The Queen and Prince Albert were driving up Constitution Hill in an open carriage when shots rang out. They were fired, wrote the Queen afterwards in her journal, by 'a little man on the footpath with his arms folded over his breast, a pistol in each hand'.[3] Edward Oxford, aged eighteen, was at first charged with high treason, but was later judged to be insane and sent to a criminal lunatic asylum.

There was little similarity between Angela's tormentor and the Queen's pathetic young assailant – but might not Dunn be capable of a similar act? What about the threat in his letter of May 8? Couldn't his bizarre behaviour – not to mention the extraordinary language of his never-ending correspondence – be indicative of an unhinged mind? The fears of the ladies at Stratton Street increased.

A week after the attack on Queen Victoria, Angela and Miss Meredith went for a drive to Regent's Park, where they hoped to be able to walk unmolested. They had seen Dunn walking down Bond Street as they drove up the other way; so they assumed they were safe. But hardly had they stepped out of the carriage and started their walk when the ubiquitous Dunn triumphantly appeared, right in their path. Terrified, Angela called the footman, who rushed forward and planted himself between Dunn and the two women. Fortunately, they were very near the home of some friends, the Boyd Alexanders, with whom Angela had dined the night before. Sophia Alexander was the half-sister of Sir Francis Burdett's old friend, John Cam Hobhouse. Angela and Hannah made for the Alexanders' house and took refuge there. Unabashed, Dunn followed, knocked at the door and, when he was not admitted, hung about outside.

Seeing the state the two ladies were in, Boyd Alexander went out to remonstrate with Dunn, but, as a police constable happened to be passing, it seemed a better idea to have the man arrested on the spot. Dunn was taken off to Marylebone Police Court to appear once more before a magistrate. The result was the same as before: he was bound over to keep the peace, this time on his own personal recognisance of £200, and was ordered to appear at Middlesex Sessions later that month.

On his way to the court, Dunn, playing the injured suitor, had protested that he would 'never have gone near the lady if she hadn't given him encouragement'. He repeated this at the hearing, shouting excitedly that he had forty or fifty letters from Miss Coutts, which he could produce if necessary. He added, 'Tomorrow morning there will be a flaming report of all this in the newspapers.'

He was right. There was, and it was just what he wanted. It did him no harm for the world to read his assertion that Angela, far from rejecting his advances as she claimed, had in fact been replying to his letters. No matter that Angela's solicitor went to court the next day to deny the allegation about the letters. Not everyone who had seen the reports in Friday's newspapers would read the denial in Saturday's.

There must, however, have been many who agreed with *The Times*, which asked: 'Should there not be some inquiry as to the state of mind of Mr Dunn? He seems to be labouring under some insane delusion.' But, during all the years that Dunn pestered Angela, no such enquiry was ever ordered by the courts.

On June 29, 1840, Angela, with her father and her aunt, Lady Langham, attended the hearing of her case against Dunn at Middlesex Quarter Sessions. Her 'Articles of the Peace' set out the story of her two-year persecution, ending by asking the court to call upon Dunn to 'keep the peace towards her'. Sworn statements from William Ballard, the police officer who had at various times protected her, and from her footman, supported her plea that she was 'in constant danger from the said defendant'. Dunn himself was not in court to hear the Chairman make his order: once again, he was to find £500 himself and two sureties of £250 each, to be forfeited if he failed to 'keep the peace and be of good behaviour to Miss Angela Georgina Burdett Coutts for two years'. Once again, Angela's hopes rose: perhaps at last she would be free to resume a normal life.

And it seemed as if it might indeed be so. The time allowed for the payments by Dunn and his sureties expired; the money was not paid; Dunn was arrested and once more sent to jail. A few weeks later, he attempted to show that there had been an irregularity in the depositions of Ballard and the footman; but his plea was rejected and he was returned to prison. For the time being, at least, he was safely behind bars.

*

Now at last, after many months, Angels could leave her house without fear of being watched or followed. She and Hannah could again take their daily walk in Kensington Gardens, and attend services at a public church – the fashionable St George's, Hanover Square, as it happened, whose congregation of fine people had been lampooned by the irreverent Timothy Sparks in *Sunday Under Three Heads*.

But Dunn had not given up. He had been twice imprisoned before and had twice obtained his release. Now, again drawing on his knowledge of the law and of the way in which it could be used to his advantage, he was planning his next move. It came in November 1840, less than five months after his committal. He issued two writs in the High Court, claiming that the 'Articles of the Peace' exhibited by Angela at the Middlesex Quarter Sessions provided insufficient grounds for his detention. The case was heard in the Court of Queen's Bench by the Lord Chief Justice, Lord Denman, sitting with three other judges; the Crown was represented by the Attorney-General, whose rôle was to speak in support of the Articles of the Peace; two counsel appeared for Angela. Dunn may have been a briefless barrister, but he was pitting his wits against some of the best legal brains in the country.

The case of *R. v. Dunn* attracted enormous interest. Reporters and members of the public crowded into the small court room on Wednesday, November 4, eager to see the man who had gained such notoriety as the self-styled suitor of Miss Burdett Coutts. Dunn, conducting his own case, spoke at great length, taking up the whole day. He made a number of legal points, but his main contention was that the Articles of the Peace were 'insufficient to deprive him of his liberty'. He admitted that he had 'intruded upon the lady and annoyed her', but denied that he had threatened her. Nothing criminal could be proved against him.

The next day, Thursday, it was the Attorney-General's turn. The decision of the justices at the Middlesex Court of Quarter Sessions, he said, should be upheld. Threats could be made other than by words, and depended upon the condition or position of the parties. In this case, Dunn was a perfect stranger to Miss Burdett Coutts, who had grounds to fear bodily harm. Their Lordships, he suggested, would have acted in the same way if applied to.

Their Lordships, however, were not so sure. When the case for the Crown was concluded, Counsel for Miss Coutts having added their contribution, the judges conferred briefly together. Then Lord Denman announced that they thought the case was of such importance that they would take until the following Monday to consider their decision. For Angela, it meant three days of agonising suspense. As her legal advisers felt bound to tell her, the situation did not look hopeful.

On Monday morning, the Lord Chief Justice delivered his judgment. He dwelt at length on the legal issues that had been raised, tracing the powers of justices of the peace to a statute of Edward III. The nub of the matter was: did the lower courts have jurisdiction in this case? A person who asked the justices, or the Court of Quarter Sessions, for protection, must make a statement on oath that 'he went in fear and danger of personal violence by reason of threats'. In ordering Dunn to enter into recognisances merely on the statement of a third party, Boyd Alexander, the Marylebone magistrate had exceeded his power.

As for the Articles of the Peace that had been exhibited at Middlesex Quarter Sessions, they made no mention of specific threats. 'Whatever the Court may think of the defendant's conduct,' said Lord Denman, 'an essential part of it is a letter written by him, which has not been set forth in full, but only a short extract given. The Court would have required to see that letter.' This was the letter that Angela had received in May, containing vague threats about the 'consequences' that would fall on herself and her family if she refused to meet Dunn.

In short, their Lordships upheld Dunn's contention that there was nothing in the Articles of the Peace that could justify his being imprisoned. 'Perhaps the law of England might be justly reproached for its inadequacy to repress such conduct as that of the prisoner,' Lord Denman admitted. But, in all the circumstances, the Court was bound to decide that the prisoner must be discharged. Even an application by the Attorney-General that Dunn should be required to give security to be of good behaviour was refused; the Court considered, said Lord Denman, that the whole matter was disposed of up to the present time. It was a bitter blow for Angela.

Were her legal advisers at fault in not wording the Articles of the Peace in the proper terms? It would be easy to blame them at this distance. The point raised by Dunn was, as the Lord Chief Justice himself admitted, 'of great nicety'. Nothing quite like it had come up before; in fact the case of *R. v. Dunn* established a precedent. As for the letter that had not been quoted in full, it may be that the reason Angela's lawyers decided against using the whole of it was that its contents were too vile for publication. Their client had suffered enough unwelcome publicity without dragging her name down still further by the publication of scurrilous letters. This, again, is something that Dunn would have been only too aware of: if he was writing her obscene letters – and it seems very likely – he could be pretty certain that they would never see the light of an open court.

Clever and cunning Richard Dunn certainly was. But his next step proved to be too clever for his own good. In February 1841 he sued Boyd Alexander for damages for wrongful arrest and imprisonment. In giving Dunn into police custody the previous June, Alexander had acted under a recent statute which authorised the arrest of anyone ringing or knocking at a house without lawful excuse, and with intent to alarm or disturb the inhabitants. Dunn claimed that the statute did not apply, and that he had been justified in knocking at Alexander's door.

Once more, Dunn conducted his own case, representing himself as the aggrieved suitor. It was Miss Coutts's father and friends, he told the packed court, who had 'thwarted her wishes' and forced her to reject his advances. She herself had given him cause for hope. He then called Angela as a witness. He had subpoenaed her to give evidence on his behalf – an extraordinary step to take, on the face of it, since she was bound to deny his allegations. But he knew that nothing could be more distasteful to her than having to appear in court and submit to his questioning. And it gave him the opportunity to sow the seed of doubt in the minds of those listening and of the public at large. Why, for instance, had she not returned his very first letter, in which he announced his intention of following her to Harrogate? Wasn't he entitled to regard this as tacit acceptance of what he had proposed?

Alexander's counsel was quickly able to establish, in his cross-examination of Angela, that for the past two and a half years Dunn's conduct to her had been 'one continued source of annoyance'. The jury, directed by the judge, returned a verdict for the defendant, Alexander. But they added that if Alexander was *not* protected by the statute – once again, Dunn had raised a 'nice' legal point – then they assessed the damages he should pay Dunn at one farthing.

This was not the end of the matter, however. Dunn was ordered to pay the costs of the case and, when he failed to do so, was arrested and committed to jail for the fourth time. He remained in the Fleet Prison for nearly four years, continuing to write letters to Angela, at one moment declaring his love, at another demanding compensation for what he had suffered at her hands, at still others requesting her to pay his debts. Then, at the beginning of 1845, it occurred to him that he could obtain his release by declaring himself a bankrupt. This he proceeded to do, and he was released that April. And then he had another idea.

*

On January 13, 1846, Edward Marjoribanks, senior partner of Coutts & Co., received a letter from Richard Dunn. The letter informed Marjoribanks that Dunn had in his possession an authority from Miss Coutts 'to draw upon your bank for compensation for the injuries, etc, she has inflicted on me'. He intended to act upon the authority, and would call at the bank to see Marjoribanks.

On the same day, Angela also received a letter from Dunn. He would be going to the bank, he said, 'to test your sincerity and liberality'. But before doing so, he wished 'to solicit the honour of an interview with you, that we might possibly come to some understanding, to remove the bitterness of the past and the future'. The letter ended:

> If you ever wish to have the protection of a man's arm, send for the man who writes this, and if any man's arm can protect you, mine is at your command.

On January 15, Dunn presented himself at Coutts & Co., producing, as his 'authority' from Miss Coutts, a set of doggerel verses which he said he had received from her. He was told they were not in her handwriting. Undeterred, he wrote again to Angela, saying that he would be taking steps to prove her handwriting, and that this would 'enlighten the eyes of the community'. The object of the letter appeared to be to give Angela the chance of buying him off before he went any further. Receiving no reply, however, he went back to the bank and presented a draft for £100,000, again producing the verses as his authority. Once more, he was shown the door.

In mid-March, Dunn wrote to Angela's solicitor stating his intention to proceed under the bankruptcy law to enforce payment of the £100,000. And, on March 31, he swore an affidavit in the Court of Bankruptcy that 'A. B. Coutts is justly and truly indebted to this deponent, Richard Dunn, in the sum of £100,000 . . . , which sum she promised in writing should be duly paid'.

Having instituted the case, Dunn did not pursue it ('from motives of delicacy', as he later explained). But Angela's legal advisers were not prepared to let the matter rest. Dunn's affidavit was clearly an absurdity. But it was more than that. In swearing it in a court of law, he had committed a criminal offence. He should not be allowed to get away with it. Accordingly, he was indicted on a charge of wilful and corrupt perjury.

The case was heard at the Guildhall on February 27, 1847, before Lord Denman, the Lord Chief Justice, whose judgment in November 1840 had resulted in Dunn's being released from jail. Once again the court was densely packed for this latest in a series of entertainments which rivalled anything on offer at the London theatres. The public were agog to see if Miss Coutts's tormentor would be hoist with his own petard.

Dunn arrived promptly at 9.30. His appearance, according to *The Times*, was decidedly Hibernian' but 'not unprepossessing'. He was, this report continued,

> a man between 40 and 50 years of age, his hair rather gray, about the middle height, well-dressed, with a gentlemanly bearing and an intelligent expression. His manner throughout the proceedings was confident and unabashed, and . . . he never appeared to lose the self-possession which a firm reliance on the merits of one's cause is generally supposed to inspire.

Angela, who arrived with her eldest sister, Sophia Otway-Cave (now a widow), and her cousin by marriage, Lord Sandon, sat beside Lord Denman on the bench. Throughout the hearing, wrote *The Times* reporter,

> she preserved a dignified composure of manner, which gained for her general sympathy, and all felt how deeply her feelings must have been wounded by the details of this extraordinary and yet ridiculous trial.

Not the least extraordinary and ridiculous feature of the trial was the set of rhymes which Dunn alleged Angela had sent him in prison and which he claimed constituted her 'authority' to pay him the £100,000. The verses, all eleven of them, were read out by Sir Frederick Thesiger, counsel for the prosecution, causing vast amusement in the crowded court room. They began:

> Oh, Mr D - - -
> You've spoilt all our fun
> By your very imprudent advances;
> Why didn't you meet
> Me, except in the street –
> Why not meet me at routs or at dances?

The history of Dunn's pursuit of Angela was then related, in similar vein, the last three stanzas indicating that she had had a change of heart and wished to make it up to him:

> But at last I'm relenting,
> My jewel, repenting
> Of all that you've suffered for me;
> Nay, I'm even grown tender,
> Disposed to turn lender
> Of cash, your sweet person to free.
>
> Send to Coutt's your bill –
> There are lots in the till –
> I'll give the clerk orders to do it.
> Then get your discharge,
> Your dear body enlarge,
> And in Stratton-street do let me view it.
>
> And, by the by, love,
> My affections to prove,
> For your long cruel incarceration
> Fill a good round sum in
> (As I've plenty of tin),
> To make you a fair compensation.

It was signed 'A.B.C.'

Was Dunn responsible for this bizarre composition? Either he wrote it himself, claimed the proscution, or someone did it for him. It is just possible that it was the work of a practical joker; if so, it gave Dunn a golden opportunity, in the words of Sir Frederick Thesiger, 'to act upon Miss Burdett Coutts's fears of a ludicrous exposure, and to exort money thereby'.

This was the second occasion on which Angela had to go through the ordeal of submitting to Dunn's questioning. She gave her evidence sitting beside the judge, referring to Dunn always as 'this person' and not addressing her replies directly to him. During her cross-examination by Dunn she remained calm. Only when Dunn produced some letters and asked her to identify the handwriting did she show any emotion. One of the letters was from her father, who had been dead for several years. Unable to conceal her agitation, Angela pulled her veil down over her face to hide her tears. A thrill of outrage ran through the court, and Dunn was sternly rebuked by the judge.

After the evidence for the prosecution had been concluded, Dunn delivered a long speech in his own defence. There were shouts of laughter when he declared that it was Mr Marjoribanks who stood between him and 'this most unhappy lady – for unhappy she is in every way'. He claimed that Angela had written him letters, including a poem which began, 'Art thou not dear unto my heart?' He insisted that he had good grounds for believing the 'authority' to be in Angela's handwriting, and called witnesses to prove it. Unfortunately for him, they contradicted each other.

Summing up, Lord Denman gave a clear direction to the jury: in his opinion, the prosecution's case had been proved beyond doubt. The jury immediately returned a verdict of Guilty, and the court held its breath as the Lord Chief Justice, in tones solemn and severe, pronounced sentence: 'Richard Dunn, you have been convicted upon the clearest evidence of a most base and malignant act, founded on the most corrupt motives . . .' No man in his senses could imagine that Miss Coutts wrote the verses: 'I cannot entertain the smallest doubt that that paper was fabricated by yourself.'

Here Dunn caused a great sensation by shouting out: 'As I stand before Almighty God, my Maker, I never did nor do I know whom it came from. May I never enter into the Kingdom of God if I know who wrote it.'

His Lordship, after expressing shock at such 'horrid imprecations', continued unperturbed. This matter had been long before the public, and had 'gained a disgusting sort of familiarity'. He had considered whether to pass sentence of transportation, but had decided against it partly because of 'the feeling of the public mind with regard to that punishment'. He had therefore decided on a sentence of eighteen months' imprisonment, after which Dunn would be required to enter into securities. The sentence would be extended for so long as the securities remained unpaid.

*

Dunn served his eighteen months' sentence and then, unable to find the necessary sureties, was kept in custody for a further two years, eventually being released in August 1851. That November he brought another action for the £100,000, repeating the same claims and allegations that he had made previously. The trial was appointed to be heard the following February, but at the last moment Dunn withdrew, alleging that his witnesses had been suborned by Angela's advisers. Angela then sued him for the costs she had incurred in preparing her defence – over £150. In April 1853 Dunn was again arrested and imprisoned, this time under a writ of *capias*. Charles Dickens, whose indignation on Angela's behalf was matched by his contempt for the law, wrote to her to explain the lawyers' latest move:

> I am heartily rejoiced to read the enclosed – the more so as I *do* understand it!!!!!!! If he had had any goods, they would have been taken in execution under another absurd machine called a Fi Fa; but having nothing but himself, *he* is taken in execution under our friend ca sa . . . I shall sustain myself through the Academy Dinner . . . by the comfortable hope that his fellow Dunn will never get out again.[4]

But get out he did. A few months later, Dunn successfully petitioned the Insolvent Debtors' Court for his release. Giving judgment, Chief Commissioner Law admitted that Dunn had repeated his perjury by swearing to the schedule now before the Court. He had 'suffered imprisonment as the lawful result of his own conduct'. It was 'deplorable that such a fate should be so studiously sought by one whose intelligence and energies are such as might have gained for him the highest honours of his profession'. Nevertheless, the Commissioner ordered that Dunn should be discharged in ten months' time.

Dickens was enraged at the decision of the 'asinine commissioner'. It would be unwise, he thought, to prosecute Dunn again for perjury, because it would 'run the hazard of making a Martyr of him . . . , coupled with all the annoyance and uncertainty of our monstrous Law'.[5] He proposed to vent his wrath against Dunn and the monstrous Law with an article in his journal *Household Words*, which he hoped would 'cast a little more reproach and disgrace about the gentleman than the Judges do'. The article, 'Things That Cannot Be Done', appeared in October 1853. It mentioned no names, but there could be no mistaking the matter it referred to. With biting sarcasm, it outlined 'an impossible case, to illustrate at once my admiration of the Law, and its tender care for women'.

It was three years before the law finally disposed of Richard Dunn – and the tender care it then displayed was not on Angela's behalf. Dunn, at last giving her up as a bad job, had transferred his affections elsewhere. The new object of his attentions was a young friend of Angela's, Princess Mary Adelaide of Cambridge, first cousin to the Queen. Dunn's letters to the Princess had a familiar ring: he had acted in accordance with her wishes – she had encouraged him and taught him to entertain 'a warm and ardent affection' for her. The whole Empire knew that money couldn't buy his heart: 'I loved with truth and sincerity. I acted with candour and honesty . . .'

It was the beginning of the end for Dunn. He was brought before the Bow Street Magistrate, who ordered that an enquiry should be made into his state of mind by two specialists. At the adjourned hearing on July 10, 1856, the doctors reported their findings. Both testified that they believed Dunn to be insane and suffering from delusions. He was alleged to have said that a number of noble ladies were in love with him, including the Queen. Dunn put up a last desperate fight, cross-examining the doctors in a hectoring way about the definition of insanity and making long excited speeches. But his fate was sealed. The Magistrate declared him to be of unsound mind and ordered him to be placed under restraint. He lived on in an asylum for many years.

'I could not help saying when I read the case,' wrote Dickens to Angela,

> that it is remarkable how brisk people are to perceive his madness, the moment he begins to trouble the blood royal. As to his being mad, I believe he is as mad as any other obstinate and persistent scoundrel – and no more.[6]

Angela, we are told, agreed with Dickens that Dunn was an unscrupulous blackmailer: in later life, wrote her great-niece, Clara Patterson, she spoke of him with indignation as having been not insane but 'extremely cunning and malicious'. Queen Victoria felt the same about the various 'madmen' who made attempts on her life. 'In her heart,' wrote her biographer, 'she never believed that they were too mad to know what they were doing.'[7]

Her sufferings at Dunn's hands – particularly in the early years – underlined for Angela the vulnerability of her position. As a great heiress she was an unwilling focus of attention and a target for public censure. People would be willing to believe anything about her, given half a chance. Dunn knew this. Sane or insane, he was clever enough to go straight for this sensitive spot again and again.

Paradoxically, however, Dunn's persecution probably had something to do with Angela's emergence as a fully-fledged philanthropist. Described by Chief Commissioner Law in 1853 as 'a lady whose exemplary life commands the esteem and respect of all classes – who is always actively employed in doing good without ostentation', Miss Coutts had by then become famous not just because of her money, but because of what she did with it; her reputation was virtually unassailable. No longer content to give anonymously to worthy causes, she had stepped into the limelight and was initiating public projects in her own name. In this development the machinations of Richard Dunn played their part.

*

As a postscript to the extraordinary story of Richard Dunn, it seems appropriate to mention here the 'fantastic domestic legend' about Angela that Sir Compton Mackenzie recalled in his autobiography – that she was 'afflicted by lice self-generated'. As a small boy in the 1880s Sir Compton

> heard this repeated over and over again, but I was too young at the time to be ready with the right response and remind the tellers of this ludicrous tale that any woman with as much money as Lady Burdett-Coutts was liable to be afflicted by parasites.[8]

To this day the ludicrous tale is still repeated, especially by old Highgate residents; indeed, it is frequently the first thing people call to mind in connection with Angela Burdett Coutts. It seems likely that it had something to do with her skin complaint: one of the symptoms of eczema is a dry, irritated, itching skin, which comes away in small flakes when scratched. Did some one make a joke about Miss Coutts and her parasites, thinking of Dunn and the way he stuck to her for so many years? Or is it possible that Dunn himself, incarcerated in his asylum and nursing a grudge against Miss Coutts, could have started the rumour deliberately? There is no evidence, and the lice legend will doubtless remain one of the mysteries of Angela's life. But it is perhaps not too fanciful to suggest that Dunn, who did his best to bring her name into disrepute, was in some way connected with this unpleasant and persistent story.*

---

* The slang word *cootie* (or *cooty*), meaning a louse, or lousy, does not appear to have anything to do with Angela's name. According to the *OED Supplement*, it dates from the First World War and is derived from the Malay *kutu*, a parasitic biting insect.

Five

MR DICKENS AND OTHER FRIENDS

It was no wonder that, pursued by hordes of unwanted suitors and menaced by the unsavoury Dunn, Angela should have felt safest when surrounded by the 'elderly gentlemen' she had known since childhood. Any feelings she might have been expected to have for men nearer her own age went underground; her love was reserved exclusively for her parents and for Hannah Meredith, the mainstay of her life. With Hannah as her trusted adviser and partner, she settled down to devoting herself to good works while conducting her social life in a style befitting her new station.

But, if she renounced the joys (and anguish) of sexual love, she discovered instead the more tranquil delights of true friendship — friendship with many of the most eminent men of the day, as well as with the less exalted. Initially, to be sure, it was curiosity that drew men to her. Her wealth and her unique position acted like a magnet. What was she like, this fabulously rich young woman living all alone (for her companion scarcely counted) in her great house? At any rate, she was worth getting to know. Money meant influence, and there must have been many who hoped for some personal advancement through old Coutts's granddaughter, or at the very least support for a favourite cause.

When they met her, however, they were disarmed by her simple dignity, charmed by her very lack of charm — by her unaffected manner and the quiet, unobtrusive way she had of putting her guests at their ease. Her friend John Hobhouse was expressing the general sentiment when he wrote that Miss Coutts 'supports her station with great propriety and good feeling in every respect, and it is lucky that her vast wealth has fallen into such hands'.[1]

Angela was not a star in her own circle, like the witty and beautiful Marguerite, Countess of Blessington, who (wrote Dickens when she was in her fifties) 'wears brilliantly, and has the gloss upon her, yet'.[2] Angela had no gloss. She was a woman of independent mind, intelligent and well-educated, but with no desire to shine in a man's world: the perfect friend for a Victorian male. Her innate qualities of restraint and circumspection set the bounds of her relationships. She did not probe too deeply into her friends' affairs and feelings.

She must have had, indeed, from the beginning, what was later described as 'the gift of erecting impassable yet imperceptible barriers against familiarity'.[3] But the men (and they were mainly men) who were invited to Stratton Street were not seeking a relationship of familiarity; or if they were, they were not invited again. In Miss Coutts they found a woman who was genuinely interested in them and in what they had achieved or hoped to achieve, who was always ready to help and encourage them in whatever ways she could. Few realised that beneath the calm exterior was a woman of steady, slow-burning passions which, once kindled, were not easily extinguished. She was an ally to be relied upon; and an enemy to be reckoned with.

By and large, it was not the thinkers of the day who became Angela's friends. She was more attracted to the doers. Her serious nature sought out and approved a sense of purpose in others. She befriended and encouraged explorers, scientists, soldiers, politicians, artists – and, of course, anyone who was engaged in furthering the spread of the gospel, at home or overseas.

In Charles Dickens she found a doer *par excellence*. In a few short years this son of an improvident, would-be genteel Civil Service clerk had rocketed to success through his own stupendous talent and incredible energy. Though he and Miss Coutts were poles apart in background, upbringing, temperament and life-style, they shared an earnestness of purpose with which went a seriousness less obvious in Dickens than in Angela. Less obvious, too, was Dickens's deep reserve about his innermost feelings – something else he had in common with Miss Coutts. For all his apparent spontaneity and open-heartedness, Dickens shied away from complete intimacy with anyone, even with his wife, Kate, whom he probably never told about the humiliation of working in the blacking warehouse (though John Forster, his closest friend, knew of it). He had lost his heart to his first love, Maria Beadnell, who had spurned him; and, though he loved Kate, he could never make himself so vulnerable to another human being again.

For Dickens, as for Angela, there was no element of sexual attraction in their friendship. Miss Coutts, Dickens was to write enthusiastically to Forster, was 'a most excellent creature' for whom he had 'a most perfect affection and respect'.[4] As for Angela – even if she hadn't put her feelings into cold storage, Mr Dickens was married and that defined the limits of their relationship. Indeed their friendship, which was to become so close over the years, would not have been possible at all had Dickens not been married.

Dickens's reputation as a novelist was consolidated by *The Old Curiosity Shop*, which appeared in weekly instalments from April 1840. In January 1841 he included Angela among the handful of special friends to whom he sent advance copies of the number in which Little Nell finally perishes, 'beseeching you to with-hold this mighty revelation from all the world – except Miss Meredith, who is free to share it to the utmost'.[5] Angela replied that she would 'successfully preserve the secret' and was 'so *very* glad not to be kept in suspense a week'.[6]

Dickens's breezy notes must have been a welcome diversion from the shoals of begging letters that poured into Stratton Street. As Angela and Hannah sat surrounded by piles of paper, trying to sort out the genuine appeals from the frauds and the forgeries, they dissolved into laughter at a gloriously nonsensical account of Mr Dickens's recently-deceased pet raven, which had 'left a considerable property (chiefly in cheese and halfpence) buried in different parts of the garden'.[7]

Busy as he was, with *Barnaby Rudge* following immediately on *The Old Curiosity Shop*, Dickens was already beginning to become involved in Angela's charitable work. He had always enjoyed long solitary walks through London's slum districts, absorbing sights, sounds and smells that others would experience only through his books. Now, investigating cases for Miss Coutts, his excursions into these murky regions took on an added purpose. His first mention of this new rôle comes in a letter of April 1841. He has at length, he writes, 'been enabled to discover the benevolent Porkman'[8] – a pork butcher who had refused to prosecute a woman who had stolen meat from him to feed her starving children. Presumably, having discovered the porkman, Dickens was able to locate the family and pass on Miss Coutts's assistance.

In the summer of 1841 Angela temporarily lost touch with Dickens. He had gone to Edinburgh in June, where a public dinner was given in his honour and he received the Freedom of the City. After a fortnight's tour of Scotland he and Kate returned to London for a short while before setting off for the family holiday in Kent. Notes and cards from Angela had meanwhile been following him all over the country. He wrote to her on August 16:

> A kind of daymare comes upon me sometimes, under the influence of which I have dismal visions of your supposing me careless of your kind Invitations – regardless of your notes – insensible to your friendship – and a species of moral monster with the usual number of legs and arms, a head, and so forth, but no heart at all.⁹

In his reply, Angela was tempted (perhaps unconsciously) to imitate his style – always a risky undertaking but particularly so with a writer of Dickens's calibre. As one of the few letters of any length from her to Dickens that have survived, it is of some interest. It begins, despite its informal tone, with the formal 'My dear Sir':

> Notes and Cards were not the only means employed to find you, these failing, a body of Cavalry, headed by Mr Marjoribanks and myself last Thursday week, made an attempt on your House, but with no other result, than the ascertaining that the House belonged to an Individual of your name, who was *just* gone out of Town, (the invariable answer to all enquiries) ... Visionary reports of your having made excellent speeches in Scotland reached us, but like a Ghost, no one had themselves seen the Papers in which they were reported, at last on one occasion we traced a Newspaper into somebody's possession but on asking for it, were told it was just sent into the country that day, at last we gave ourselves up to the most gloomy reflections as to your probable or improbable fate, & as to the likelihood of your ever having existed & other useful speculations. . . .¹⁰

And so on.

It would, of course, be unfair to compare Angela's epistolary style with that of her famous correspondent. But, though her letter is lively enough, its rambling, erratically-punctuated sentences leave the reader gasping for breath. For a woman of her education, Angela often wrote surprisingly badly, judging by the comparatively few letters that have come down to us out of what must have been a vast output. The influence of 'sermonese' that we have already noted is partly to blame. Her prose is often tortuous and long-winded, overburdened with clauses and sadly lacking in full stops. There is scarcely an elegant, witty or memorable phrase – which is odd, since she was to become renowned as a first-rate public speaker and was a good conversationalist.

Charles Osborne, who was Angela's secretary at a much later stage in her life (from 1887 to 1898) said that she wrote with great difficulty –

altering, transposing paragraphs, turning round sentences, substituting words and re-writing often. Certainly one cannot imagine her dashing off the kind of easy, relaxed, newsy letters that Victorian ladies so delighted in writing to one another. Nor, if she kept a journal, could it have been as racy, pithy and, above all, as revealing of herself as Queen Victoria's. What strikes one about Angela's letters is that they reveal so little: lacking Victoria's openness and candour, she seemed to take refuge in a thick undergrowth of verbiage in which the tender plant of her sensibility could be safely hidden. To such an intensely private person, composition – which exposes the writer to himself as well as to his readers – must indeed have been a painful process.

*

When Dickens gave a party for his friends, it was likely to develop into a wildly gay affair, with frenetic country dancing and displays of conjuring by the ever-inventive author himself. The gatherings at Stratton Street were more staid. But they were enlivened by good conversation and by the talents of some of the greatest actors and musicians of the day. Charles Mayne Young, a contemporary of Harriot Mellon who was famed as a tragedian but also possessed comic gifts, amused the company with anecdotes of his early days on the stage. His wife, the Italian actress Julia Griamani, had died shortly after the birth of their son Julian in 1806. Julian entered the Church, and in due course joined the band of devoted clerics who clustered round Miss Coutts. Churchmen, like elderly gentlemen, were 'safe'. The Reverend Julian Young was a man of singular charm, 'ardent and impulsive from his Italian mother'[11] and with an attractive streak of ingenuousness. One evening, he 'happened, casually, to mention to Miss Coutts' that he had never seen Charles Dickens. The very next day, both were invited to luncheon. 'I am delighted to have eaten, drunk, and chatted with "Boz",' wrote Young in his journal.[12]

Angela and Dickens had a number of friends in common, among them the great Shakespearian actor William Charles Macready. They both knew Samuel Rogers, now approaching eighty and as acid-tongued as ever. Rogers had, however, a soft spot for Catherine Dickens, so often eclipsed by her husband's dazzling brilliance, and an even softer one for Angela, who, though not easily eclipsed, had the great virtue of not wishing to dazzle anyone. Rogers' house in St James's Place was stuffed with artistic and literary treasures. When he died in 1855, aged ninety-two, Angela bought many of his pictures, including several by Reynolds, two Gainsboroughs, and Raphael's *Agony in the Garden*, which held pride of place in her collection.

Not everyone was delighted to meet 'Boz' at Angela's house. Old Tom Moore, the former spoilt darling of the drawing-rooms who had captivated the young Miss Burdetts in Regency Bath, was jealous of the young man's success. He was becoming crotchety and missed the public adulation that had for so long been his life-blood. Julian Young described how, when he was once staying at Stratton Street, Moore

> called and lunched, and Miss Coutts asked him to stay and dine. Charles Dickens was there that day; and Moore, who had been buoyant and delightful before he came, became taciturn and sulky after. When he had gone, Moore . . . spoke to me with much chagrin of the fickleness of public opinion and the instability of literary reputation. He said, 'I dare say Dickens is pointed out as "Boz" wherever he goes. So was I once pointed out as "Tom Little".'[13]

For Angela herself, Moore retained a great affection. One summer evening he called to see her as she was preparing to set out for a royal ball, dressed 'in all her splendours'. Next morning he called again, 'and

Angela's houses on the corner of Stratton Street and Piccadilly, from the drawing by Hanslip Fletcher

found her preparing to send it all back to the Bank'. She led him upstairs so that he could see the treasures by daylight, including Marie Antoinette's tiara. 'On my asking her what, altogether, might be the value of her dress last night, she answered, in her quiet way, "I think about a hundred thousand pounds."'[14]

A few weeks later, Moore dined with Angela at Stratton Street. Samual Rogers was there, and another old friend, John Cam Hobhouse. Also present was Charles Babbage, the mathematician and inventor of the world's first mechanical computer. One of the greatest brains of the nineteenth century, Babbage was once described as 'quite odious to look at'.[15] He was in many ways an unhappy and disappointed man. Having spent thousands of his own and other people's money on his two 'calculating engines', he was forced to abandon them in 1842 through lack of further funds. Successive governments had refused to back him. The only person who seems to have believed wholeheartedly in his computer was Byron's daughter Augusta, Countess of Lovelace. She worked with him for ten years and, herself an exceptionally gifted mathematician, was able to grasp the theory behind the machines. Parts of them may be seen today in the Science Museum.

One of Babbage's less-known accomplishments was the telling of children's stories. In January 1855 Angela asked him if he would write some 'pretty fanciful sketches' for children, since she found 'most of the instructive books are deficient in imagination and works of imagination alone are seldom wholly unobjectionable'.[16] The great mathematician evidently complied with with her request, for a few years later she wrote to tell him how delighted she was with 'How I became a governess' and other stories; she would be sending them to some young friends and would also see if she could get them included in the booklist of the Society for Promoting Christian Knowledge.

By far the most distinguished of Angela's scientific friends, however, was Michael Faraday, whose three volumes of *Experimental Researches in Electricity* were published between 1839 and 1855. As a girl she had attended his lectures at the Royal Institution. He was a brilliant speaker, especially when addressing a young audience. Angela often spoke of his simplicity and 'nobility of purpose', which, together with his humble origins, gave him a special appeal for her; she always admired self-made men. It was Faraday who suggested that she should become a member of the Royal Institution, which had been founded in 1799 for the purpose of popularising scientific knowledge and 'facilitating the general introduction of useful mechanical inventions and improvements'. From the first the Institution had been open to women, and Faraday hoped to encourage more ladies to join. Angela was admitted as a member in 1847.

She was fascinated by science. It was an exciting and disturbing new world, holding out the promise of unlimited progress for mankind. The threat that it posed to traditional religious thought apparently did not worry her. A decade or so later the cult of the scientific method reached its peak and faith in science clashed head-on with faith in God. In the 1840s the young Miss Coutts appeared to be serenely unaware of the storms ahead. Whether Miss Meredith shared her former pupil's enthusiasm for the new knowledge we cannot say. She may well have felt less sanguine about it. But if she had qualms, she must have comforted herself with the thought that Angela's religious faith was of a kind to withstand any assault that might be made on it; and time was to prove her right.

In fact, many men of science were also men of God. The great Faraday himself joined a small Christian sect, the Sandemanians, at the age of thirty, and from then on until his death in 1867 his faith never wavered. All the same, it must have been a comfort to Hannah to know that her dear Angela had so many friends in the Church. There was old Bishop Phillpotts of Exeter, dogmatic, doctrinaire and reactionary – Dickens once told Angela that Phillpotts had done 'as much harm to real Christian brotherhood and good will . . . since he has been a Bishop as any mere mortal man could well do in his lifetime'.[17] More liberal (though still not to Dickens's taste) was the energetic reforming Bishop Blomfield of London. Then there was John Sinclair,* Vicar of Kensington and Archdeacon of Middlesex, who was closely involved in the Church's educational work for the poor; besides the charming Julian Young and many others.

Hannah must have been happy, too, to know that Angela's generous support for missionary societies was being put to good use. Later, Miss Coutts would become the close friend and financial backer of the most famous missionary-explorer of them all, David Livingstone. In the early years it was Livingstone's father-in-law and fellow-Scot, Robert Moffat, who enjoyed her help and friendship.

Moffat, born in 1795, was a man after Angela's own heart. The pioneer of South African missionary work, he had gone to the Cape in 1816 and, after twenty-three years of unceasing labours, returned to England in June 1839 for his first home leave. He was of striking, even

* Brother of Sir George Sinclair; see page 48.

formidable, appearance, with his shaggy beard, piercing eyes, and 'grave, apostolic, blackish yellow Africa-burnt face' – as the novelist Maria Edgeworth described it. Moffat had, she wrote, 'an unconquerably laborious mind with a calm cool outside, fire burning within and every ray of light and heat directed to one point'. Did he, one wonders, demonstrate for Angela, as he did for Miss Edgeworth, the 'clucking' language of the Hottentots which was 'indescribable and inimitable'? 'Tis done Madam,' he told her, 'by pressing my tongue quick withinside of my cheek and withdrawing it sudden.'[18]

Moffat returned to South Africa in 1843, having met David Livingstone in London and recruited the young man for his own mission. Livingstone sailed for Africa in December 1840, and in 1844 married Moffat's eldest daughter, Mary. He would not meet Miss Coutts until after his triumphant return to England in December 1856.

*

One thing that Miss Coutt's friends – old and new – soon learned was that her companion was not to be ignored. Miss Meredith, far from not counting, was to be treated as an equal. Indeed, it was Hannah Meredith's unfailing love and support that counted most through these first few difficult years. The story goes that, at the time of Angela's inheritance in 1837, Miss Meredith was engaged to be married to Dr William Brown, of the medical firm of Tupper, Chilvers & Brown, but Angela begged her to postpone the marriage because she could not bear the thought of losing Hannah at this critical time. If this is true, it shows remarkable devotion on Hannah's part and an even more remarkable forbearance on Dr Brown's. In the end they did not marry until December 1844.

Charles Dickens's letters throw some light on to Hannah's character. The woman whose husband called her his 'little mouse' does not emerge as very mouse-like, though she could doubtless be as unobtrusive as that animal when necessary. Significantly, when sending the *Old Curiosity Shop* instalments to Angela, Dickens had taken care not to exclude Miss Meredith from 'this mighty revelation'. He knew the power she wielded in the household. Nearly all his early letters contain regards or compliments to her. Later, when he discovered she had a sense of humour, he paid her the compliment of teasing her. Thus, he ends his letter of August 16, 1841:

> If Miss Meredith should remember a fair young man with whom she had a community of feeling in reference to the impossibility of getting

up in the morning during the Great Frost of eighteen hundred and forty one, – I beg to say that I am the person, and that I send my compliments.[19]

To which Angela, delighted, ended her own letter (part of which has already been quoted):

Miss Meredith desires her best Compts., her forebodings *were* of the *most melancholy* kind, as she thought most likely you were smothered or expired suddenly trying to get up, if at least you had suffered as much as she has done during the severe summer 1841 from the same 'community of feeling' as during the winter.[20]

The joke was resurrected that November, when Dickens was planning his trip to America: 'I am told that getting up in the morning *there* in the winter time, is beyond Miss Meredith's conception.'[21] He was away for the first half of 1842. On his return, he gave Angela a rocking-chair and presented Hannah with an eagle's feather whose 'rightful owner fell over the great fall at Niagra'.[22]

In the spring of the following year, when Hannah became ill with a mysterious 'rheumatic' malady, Dickens was all affectionate concern. He was himself, he wrote, 'kept within doors by the doctor for a kind of rheumatism in the face, which penetrates into the depths of my ears, and makes me feel at times as if a beehive had been upset in the intricacies of my brain'.[23] But he hoped to be well enough to call the next day. Throughout that summer and autumn, as the illness persisted, he continued to make kind enquiries; his children became convinced that 'That Lady' lived upstairs in bed. Her long illness, so worrying to Angela, produced an unexpected bonus for Dickens in the shape of the inspiration for one of his most memorable comic characters, Sairey Gamp in *Martin Chuzzlewit*.

The original of Mrs Gamp was a 'nurse' employed for a short time to look after Hannah Meredith. Dickens was regaled with an account of this lady's oddities, and he was so taken with her that he introduced Sairey Gamp into the book in chapter 19. Among the attributes that she shared with her original were her habit of rubbing her nose along the top of the tall fender while sitting by the fire; her sniffs; her fondness for tea and for stronger drink when she felt 'so dispoged', and her 'yellow nightcap of prodigious size'. 'I don't wish Mrs Brown would be ill again,' wrote Dickens to Angela some years later, 'but I wish she would do something, which would lead to her suggesting another character to me, as serviceable as Mrs Gamp.'[24] When *Martin Chuzzlewit* appeared in book form in 1844, it was dedicated to Miss Coutts 'with the true and earnest regard of the author'.

Hannah herself was thought by John Forster to have been the lady friend, 'very familiar to [Dickens] indeed', who inspired Rosa Dartle's* 'peculiarity of never saying anything outright, but hinting it merely, and making more of it that way'.[25] This can surely have been only partly true, for Hannah emerges from Dickens's letters as a very outspoken lady. She is 'our dear obstinacy' and 'the General Objector', and later has a new nickname – 'O' – which could have stood for either. 'I think you are in your way as obstinate as – Mrs Brown – I can't say more,'[26] Dickens once told Angela. When Hannah was recovering from another of her illnesses he hoped she would soon be 'in a good contradictory humour again!'[27] And on another occasion he wrote that he was 'collecting some materials for a pitched battle with her'.[28]

But there came a time when the pitched battle ended in tears. There was an argument about the French: Hannah said they were immoral. At least, retorted Dickens, they were not as hypocritical as the English, who pretended that social evils and vices didn't exist. 'Don't say that!' she cried. 'Don't say that! It gives me such pain to hear you say anything I can't agree with!' But he must say it, Dickens insisted, 'when, according to our national vanity and prejudice, you disparage an unquestionably great nation'.[29] Mrs Brown burst into a storm of weeping, but he remained unmoved; he, too, could be obstinate.

Such incidents, however, appeared to be rare. If there were undercurrents of tension between them, they do not come to the surface in Dickens's letters. He seems to have had a genuine affection for Hannah, and an appreciation of the lively mind that had helped to form Miss Coutts's. If it occasionally occurred to him that Angela's emotional dependence on her companion was not altogether a good thing – that it tended at times to cloud her judgment or narrow her vision – he knew that any remonstrance from him would have been worse than useless. Indeed, it would probably have brought their relationship to an abrupt end, which was the last thing he wanted.

*

By the end of 1843 Dickens was firmly established as Miss Coutts's unofficial almoner – a position he was to fill with zest and competence for the next twelve years. 'Trust me,' he had written that July, 'that I will

* Rosa Dartle: Mrs Steerforth's companion in *David Copperfield*.

be a faithful steward of your bounty; and that there is no charge in the wide World I would accept with so much pride and happiness as any such from you.'[30] She had just sent him a generous donation for the seven orphaned children of an actor called Edward Elton, 'a struggling man through his whole existence' who had perished in a disaster at sea. Many were the struggling men and their families who would be helped (usually anonymously) by Miss Coutts after a visit from Charles Dickens the social worker. The reports that flowed into Stratton Street, however, whether consisting of a concise paragraph or several closely-written pages, were unmistakably from the pen of Dickens the novelist. Not that he made anything up; but when his sympathies were engaged by some 'affecting and distressful' case, there could be no more eloquent pleader of it. Nor, when he suspected humbug, could there have been a more telling detractor. 'I did not like,' he warned Angela, one applicant's

> mention of his "revered and lamented father", and his "beloved mother" in his letter to you. A man who is quite in earnest, can afford to leave his estimation of his parents, I think, to the understanding of his reader.[31]

Private charity was all very well. But Dickens longed to direct Angela's larger efforts away from the Church and towards schemes that would directly benefit the very poorest members of society, the vast majority of whom couldn't even write their own names, let alone concoct a begging-letter. Poverty in England there had always been; and the rich had, to a greater or lesser extent, always regarded it as their duty to relieve the sufferings of the poor. The tradition of philanthropy went back hundreds of years. But the degree of human misery and degradation that now existed in the slums of London and other large cities was something new. By the 1830s the full horror of the situation was just beginning to be realised; it was confirmed in the 1840s by a spate of government reports – the 'Blue Books' – from whose grim statistics the writers of the day took their themes. The Blue Books inspired Elizabeth Barrett's *The Cry of the Children* and Disraeli's *Sybil, or The Two Nations*.

Overcrowding, filth, disease, starvation, ignorance – with all these existing side-by-side in the new urban slums, the problem for the reformers, and the philanthropists, was to know where to start. Radical proposals for State intervention were turned down: the country was not ready for them. But in one area, education, some progress was made.

Mr Dickens and Other Friends

Although a number of bills for creating a rate-aided system of national education had been rejected by Parliament, in 1833 it had voted the first government money – £20,000 – for popular education. Six years later, in 1839, the grant was increased and an Education Committee of the Privy Council – the forerunner of the Ministry of Education – was set up to administer it.

Education for the masses was not a subject that particularly interested Sir Francis Burdett, though in 1825 he had been persuaded by his friend Henry Brougham to take two shares in the new University College, London. For Angela, however, the subject was to become one of her life-long concerns. Lord Brougham, the brilliant but highly eccentric former Lord Chancellor, was her friend, too; perhaps he infected her with his own abiding passion for the cause of popular education. And the Secretary of the new Education Committee, Dr James Kay (later Sir James Kay-Shuttleworth), became a friend for life.

Born in 1804, Kay (who became Kay-Shuttleworth when he married the heiress Janet Shuttleworth in 1842), qualified in Edinburgh and practised for some years in a poor district of Manchester, where he drew attention to the need for proper housing and sanitation. His interest in education stemmed from his work as an Assistant Poor Law Commissioner, when he reported on the dismal fate of children confined to the workhouse. As Secretary to the Education Committee he faced a formidable task.

Up till then, the government grant had been divided between two rival organisations founded early in the century which had shared responsibility for educating the poor – and with some success. These were the National Society for the Education of the Poor in the Principles of the Established Church – which, as its name implies, was run by the Church of England, and whose Secretary was Angela's friend John Sinclair; and the British and Foreign School Society, which was predominantly Nonconformist. Sectarian animosity, that 'most intense of Victorian emotions',[32] had early entered the field of education. With the increased grant of 1839 Dr Kay had hoped to set up the first teacher training college with a model school; but because of irreconcilable differences between Churchmen and Dissenters the scheme had to be abandoned. Instead, Kay and a friend, E. Carleton Tufnell, established a college in Battersea with their own funds. The two societies promptly founded their own colleges.

Sectarian animosity was the greatest stumbling-block to progress in educational reform. It led to the rejection of proposals, incorporated in the Factory Bill of 1843, for the part-time education of factory children. The new factory schools, it was suggested, should be substantially under Church control, but with security for freedom of conscience. This did not satisfy the Dissenters, whose howls of protest wrecked the Bill. In such an atmosphere James Kay had to work; and, gradually, through conciliation and compromise, he succeeded. A School Inspectorate was set up, new schools built, and the profession of teaching established. Matthew Arnold, who himself spent some years as a school inspector, called Kay-Shuttleworth the founder of the English system of popular education.

Like many of Angela's friends, Kay-Shuttleworth was a man with a mission. He was earnest, sincere, serious and conscientious – in fact, he worked so hard that his health broke down temporarily in 1849, the year he was created a baronet. Dickens lamented over his lack of imagination: there was, he once complained to Angela, too much 'Boredom and Red Tape, and what I may call Kayshuttleworry'[33] associated with the word education. And Maria Edgeworth, visiting Battersea Training College in 1841, was a little tried by 'the high flying over-zeal of young Dr Kay'.[34]

That the ill-educated poor needed the services of the zealous Dr Kay there could be no doubt. But not even he could reach the very dregs of humanity – the young gutter-snipes, half-starved and destined for a life of crime, who foraged for a living in the grim back streets. There was little hope of getting *them* inside a school – and, once they were inside, of teaching them anything. And yet, amazingly, it was being done.

Some time in the summer of 1843 Angela received an appeal from a Mr Samuel Starey, treasurer of the Field Lane Ragged School, off Saffron Hill, Clerkenwell. Perhaps he had been emboldened to write after seeing Miss Coutts's name as a subscriber (of £200) to the National Society, which had recently taken a four-column advertisement in *The Times* to promote its object of providing education 'in the principles of the Established Church'. In eloquent contrast was Starey's own modest appeal, published in *The Times* some months earlier, for funds and 'left off garments'. The Ragged School movement had been in existence for some years, but it may have been Starey who first coined the rather touching – and apposite – name. Angela asked Dickens to investigate, and on September 16, in a long letter, he made his report.

Even he was shocked by what he found. The 'school' was held 'in three most wretched rooms on the first floor of a rotten house'. There was 'no such thing as dress among the seventy pupils; certainly not the elements of a whole suit of clothes, among them all. I have very seldom seen, in all the strange and dreadful things I have seen in London and elsewhere, anything so shocking as the dire neglect of soul and body exhibited in these children.'

The school was run by a group of laymen drawn from both the established Church and the Nonconformists. Here, at least, was an advance. 'The Masters,' wrote Dickens, 'are extremely quiet, honest, good men. You may suppose they are, to be there at all. It is enough to break one's heart to get at the place: to say nothing of getting at the children's minds afterwards.' The children, nevertheless, 'knew about the Saviour, and the Day of Judgment . . . [and] understood that the Deity was everywhere'. This in itself was a major triumph, for

> To impress them, even with the idea of a God, when their own condition is so desolate, becomes a monstrous task . . . And here it is that the viciousness of insisting on creeds and forms in educating such miserable beings, is most apparent . . . To get them, whose whole lives from the moment of their birth, are one continued punishment, to believe even in the Judgment of the Dead and a future state of punishment for their sins, requires a System in itself.[35]

Strong words to use to such a staunch Churchwoman as Miss Coutts! Possibly Dickens was being deliberately outspoken to see how she would react; perhaps it was Hannah Meredith's conventional Church piety that he felt he had to combat. His whole report, as he told his friend Forster, was 'a sledge-hammer account'; and, having seen Angela's name down for £200 'in the clergy education subscription list', he had taken pains 'to show her that religious mysteries and difficult creeds wouldn't do for such pupils'.[36]

In fact, his appeal to Angela was irresistible. He ended on a personal note: not only was this a cause he passionately believed was worthy of her support; but only *she* would be large-hearted enough to help in so 'squalid and terrible' a case:

> There is a kind of delicacy which is not at all shocked by the existence of such things, but is excessively shocked to know of them . . . The reasons I have, for doubting its being generally assisted, all assure me that it will have an interest for you.

He was not mistaken. Just over a week later, he was writing to Forster that Miss Coutts had asked him what the rent of some large airy premises would be, and what the expense of erecting a regular bathing or purifying place; touching which points I am in correspondence with the authorities. I have no doubt she will do whatever I ask her in the matter.[37]

Dickens had struck a chord in Angela. Strong-willed, independent, but in many ways ultra-conventional, she could be rigid in her religious views, as he was to discover. As a philanthropist, however, she could also be unexpectedly broad-minded. She would later work happily with

This portrait by Sir Martin Archer Shee of Sir Francis Burdett hung over the chimney-piece of Angela's small private drawing-room at 1 Stratton Street

people of many different denominations for causes she believed in, though if her religious prejudices were aroused she could be implacable.

Angela's support of the Ragged School movement continued for many years. It was the first public work that she and Dickens did together. He must have hoped that it would lead to greater things – as indeed it did; but not immediately. For one thing, within a month or two of his 'sledge-hammer' letter both Sir Francis and Lady Burdett were taken seriously ill. The new year of 1844 was to be an unhappy one for Angela. To the shock of bereavement was added almost immediately another shock of a different kind – a revelation that would cause her more pain, probably, than any other single incident in her life. But, distressing as it was, it may well have played a decisive part in the emergence of Miss Coutts as a great public benefactor. Aware of her father's stricture on 'dribbling away great resources' she was still searching for some large undertaking which would make fitting use of the fortune that had been entrusted to her. Not until after his death did she feel ready to embark on such a project. And when she did, she was determined that it should be not only worthy of her fortune, but a fitting memorial to the father who, in her eyes, could do no wrong.

Six

THE BACON AFFAIR

Lady Burdett died on January 12, 1844, after many years as an invalid. 'I have very often thought of Miss Coutts in her long and arduous attendance upon her poor mother', wrote Dickens to Miss Meredith,

> and but that I know how such hearts as hers are sustained in such duties, should have feared for her health. For her peace of mind in this and every trial, and for her gentle fortitude always, no one who knows her truly, can be anxious in the least. If she has not the materials of comfort and consolation within herself, there are no such things in any creature's nature.[1]

Angela needed all the fortitude she could muster, for her father, too, was gravely ill. So serious was his condition that it was thought best to postpone his wife's funeral. For years his gout had been getting steadily worse; early in 1842 he had complained that his foot was so 'monstrously swell'd' that he could 'scarcely put it to the ground'. He had tried a number of unorthodox remedies, finally settling in October 1843 for hydropathy, or the 'cold-water cure'. This probably hastened his demise, for it was said that he took to riding out on horseback enveloped in wet towels. His daughters eventually dismissed the hydropathist who had been treating him, but it was too late. Very soon afterwards the old baronet became delirious. He died on January 23. Large crowds followed the funeral procession to Ramsbury parish church, where he and Sophia were buried together in the family vault on the last day of January. They had been married for just over fifty years.

'The death of no man, out of my own family, could have affected me so much,'[2] wrote Hobhouse in his diary, adding that the obituary notices in *The Times* and the *Chronicle* did his friend scant justice. Many people still did not understand Burdett's apparent *volte-face* from Radicalism to Toryism: 'The English public,' wrote Disraeli many years later, '. . . joined in the taunts of his inconsistency, when, late in life, the Boromongers having been got rid of, Burdett turned out to be

The Bacon Affair

what he started as, a high aristocratic English politician.' Sir Francis, added Disraeli, was 'the greatest gentleman I ever knew'.[3]

The new baronet was Robert, Angela's only brother, now in his forty-eighth year. Despite repeated attempts at reconciliation by both his parents, Robert seems to have remained estranged from them to the end. 'Let me entreat of you to come and see your mother,' Sir Francis had written in May 1831, adding rather touchingly that he would like to show Robert what he had done at Foremarke: 'you will find I have not been a bad steward at least.' And in April 1836 Lady Burdett had written that she could not let Robert's fortieth birthday pass 'without sending you my blessing'.[4]

Between Robert and his sisters the lack of communication appears to have been total. For Angela, meeting this unknown elder brother virtually for the first time at their parents' funeral must have been a strange and upsetting experience. But worse was to come.

In February 1844, scarcely a month after his father's death, Sir Robert Burdett received several letters from a General Bacon, asking to see him about certain matters connected with his late father's estate. In reply, Robert declined to discuss any transactions between Bacon and his father and referred the General to Sir Francis's executors. A few weeks later, Robert received a pathetic appeal from the General's wife, Lady Charlotte Bacon, written 'without the advice or knowledge of anyone'. It was in Robert's power, she wrote, to save her and her seven children from 'disgrace and utter destitution . . . We have endeavoured to struggle on, but in vain, & *starvation* is before me . . . I plead for my children . . . May God open your heart.'[5]

Who were the desperate Bacons, and what was their claim upon Sir Robert? Anthony Bacon, who had served in the Peninsular War and fought at Waterloo, had been one of the most outstanding cavalry officers in the British Army. He had been expected to succeed to the command of the 17th Lancers, in which he was senior major, but in 1826 the command had been bought by another officer for £20,000 above the usual price. Bacon, who could not have hoped to find such a sum, resigned and became a mercenary in the services of the King of Portugal. Now, back in England and near to bankruptcy, he was unable to support himself and his large family.

General Bacon had married Lady Charlotte Harley in 1823. Their devotion was legendary; she even rode with him on his campaigns. Lady Charlotte was the daughter of the celebrated Lady Oxford, whom we have met before. She had inherited her mother's beauty; when she was a young girl, Byron – who was in love with Lady Oxford – had dedicated the first canto of *Childe Harold* to her.

When Lady Charlotte Harley was born, in 1801, her mother was still the constant companion of Sir Francis Burdett. In 1811 had appeared in an unknown newspaper a choice piece of gossip in the form of a so-called 'Advertisement Extraordinary':

> Lately was published an additional volume of the 'Harleian Miscellany' carefully edited by Sir F.B. Baronet, and imprinted nearly eleven years ago at the Oxford Press. This beautiful work was arranged by the Editor during a trip to France in 1801, & the proof sheets were delivered in Paris. On his return to England, both this work & his baggage were bonded, which has occasioned the extraordinary delay in the publication.[6]

The appearance of this 'advertisement' coincided with the bringing of a law suit by Sir Francis Burdett against Lady Oxford's brother, William Scott. Burdett claimed that Scott had given him his bond for £5,000. Scott, in his defence, declared that Burdett had paid him the money on trust for the maintenance of a child born to 'a lady, whose name it is unnecessary to mention'. (It was thought at the time that the child was Lady Oxford's son, Lord Harley, born in 1800).

Sir Francis's counsel vigorously denied the whole of Scott's story. But when the Judge ordered that Scott should produce evidence in support of his defence, Burdett dropped his action. To many, this was proof of his guilt. However, in a long letter to his wife, Sir Francis insisted that Scott had been trying to blackmail him. Scott, he told Sophia, had informed him that the Oxfords were about to separate on his (Burdett's) account, and that Lady Oxford would be left destitute. Sir Francis had therefore deposited £5,000 with Scott for the lady's maintenance. But he soon discovered from Lady Oxford herself that the separation story was completely false, and demanded his money back from Scott, who had by that time misappropriated it. Scott then gave Burdett his bond; when it fell due, he could not pay, and Burdett sued him for the £5,000.

If all this was true, why did Sir Francis withdraw from the case? The reason, it has been suggested, was that he was not prepared to put Lady Oxford in the witness box – a necessary step if he was to prove that her brother was a blackmailer. William Scott was, in fact, a strange sort of brother, having brought an action for libel against his sister a few years earlier. But whatever the truth behind the case of 1811, it was neither proved nor disproved that Lady Charlotte Harley was the daughter of Sir Francis Burdett. And when the whole subject was re-opened in the spring of 1844, neither Jane, Lady Oxford (who had died in 1824) nor Sir Francis was there to give evidence either way.

The essence of Lady Charlotte's appeal to Sir Robert Burdett was this: for several years before his death, Sir Francis had been paying her an annuity; she had been led to understand that a settlement of perhaps £20,000 would be provided for her under his will; he had made no such provision, and the loss of the annuity left her and her family in desperate straits.

Sir Robert's reply was unequivocal: he would entertain no claims other than strictly legal ones, nor could any transactions between his father and any other person possibly concern him,

> because, from my first entry into life, Sir Francis Burdett & myself, never executed any transaction together, nor had I ever any acquaintance with any such transaction, as we were totally alienated from, and strangers to each other.[7]

There remained only one hope for Lady Charlotte: one other member of the Burdett family who certainly had the means to help her and might be persuaded for her father's sake to do so.

*

The Bacons did not go direct to Angela. Instead, they sought to influence her through several of her father's old friends and through her cousin, Dudley Coutts Stuart. He was to be the one to approach her.

Among the intermediaries was the handsome and charming Count D'Orsay, who, though professedly 'much attached' to Sir Francis, was hardly the kind of man to have any appeal for Angela. Separated from his wife, he had been a reckless spender and a compulsive gambler, and lived with the widowed Lady Blessington (his wife's stepmother) in relations which were probably innocent but which caused scandalous gossip. He was also a talented artist: Dickens, a close friend, had twice sat to him. Angela's acquaintance with this 'Prince of Dandies', whose extravagant mode of dress had influenced Dickens and Disraeli, was no doubt slight. But each was well-known to the other by repute. 'Sir F. Burdett,' wrote D'Orsay now to Lord Dudley,

> has so often spoken to me of the goodness of heart and estimable qualities of Miss Burdett Coutts, that it has occurred to me that if you

my Dear Dudley as a relative would disclose to her the disturbing position into which the death of her father has plunged an amiable and unfortunate family, she would not withhold the assistance of which they so much stand in need, more especially when the granting of it will prevent censure from falling on the memory of her parent.[8]

Another pleader of the Bacons' cause was Lord Brougham. Described by the diarist Greville in 1837 as 'a noble wreck', he was still an impressive if no longer a powerful figure in public life. He was a flawed genius whose erratic behaviour had culminated in his putting about, in October 1839, reports of his own death in a carriage accident. Years before, in 1820, he had become a popular hero after successfully defending Queen Caroline at her extraordinary 'trial' for adultery in the House of Lords. Now, he took up with gusto the cause of another wronged woman. 'I know your active benevolence will not let my affair rest,' Lady Charlotte wrote to him. She was about to be turned out of her house and would be left homeless, 'with no shelter for my children'. And she added (though not mentioning Angela by name):

> Surely no one with such ample, such superfluous wealth would permit so great a blot to rest upon a Father's name, if by fulfilling a sacred obligation, she can remove it.[9]

For Brougham, the removal of the 'blot' from Burdett's name was the most important consideration. He sent Lady Charlotte's letter on to Lord Dudley with a scribbled note and a postscript directed at Angela:

> I assure you if she does not do what is right for her fathers memory, I would not for ten times her large fortune be the possessor of her conscience.[10]

The situation, as everybody saw it, was simple: Lady Charlotte Bacon was the daughter (and the 'living image', according to D'Orsay) of Sir Francis Burdett, who had paid her an allowance for some years but who by an oversight – they all agreed it could not have been deliberate – had omitted to provide for her in his will. His son and heir having washed his hands of the whole affair, it was up to Angela to step in and save the Bacons – and her father's reputation.

To Angela, the matter was not quite so cut and dried. On May 14, Dudley called to see her at Stratton Street. She was shattered by what he told her. That her beloved father could have been unfaithful to her mother; that he might even have had an illegitimate child; that *she* was expected to confirm the fact by helping to maintain this child, now a grown woman with a husband to support her – it was all too much. She could not, she would not, do it. After Dudley had left she sat down, quivering with distress but bristling with determination, to write to him:

Angela's cousin, Lord Dudley Coutts Stuart, engraved by H. Linton after a drawing by Thomas

The subject upon which you spoke to me this day was so very painful that I am afraid I did not explain my feelings clearly enough . . . I have no course but one, I *cannot* be expected to make enquiries in such a case, to admit it upon mere assertion I will not – I have never heard a word till now upon the subject, perhaps as you said, it was not one likely to be brought before me, all I know is, that Lady Charlotte Bacon, was *Lady Charlotte Harley*, . . . & that for a *very very* few years previous to his death, my dear Father afforded her & her family some pecuniary assistance . . . For me to come forward to the world to acknowledge more than this would be I think a most ungrateful return for the affection of the kindest parent ever given.

She acknowledged that Dudley had approached her with the best of motives, but he could only have done so

> with great violence to your own feelings when you consider what mine must have been to find myself placed in such a position.[11]

Dudley's own position was not an enviable one. Pressed on all sides to plead for Lady Charlotte, he seems himself to have believed wholeheartedly in the justness of her claim. But his cousin Angela could be utterly unyielding once her mind was made up. She had been very unwell, she told him, and was 'still far from strong' — but there was no doubting the strength of her resolve.

For a couple of months, Dudley let the matter rest. Angela, meanwhile, had left for the continent. She may have had 'the materials of comfort and consolation within herself', but the trials of the past few months had strained those inner resources to the limit. She needed to get away from England, to spend the summer at spas and resorts regaining her health and strength. But she could not escape entirely from the affairs of the unfortunate Lady Charlotte Bacon. Early in August she received a letter from Dudley which had been forwarded to her in Germany.

In four closely-written pages, Dudley earnestly urges her to reconsider her decision. His own opinion remains unshaken — has indeed been strengthened by 'consultation with others to whose judgment I look up' — and he writes 'in obedience to what I feel to be my duty'. He can understand her 'reluctance to believe the allegations made' and her 'repugnance to make enquiries', but

> I cannot help thinking that if you examine into the matter more closely you will find that that very feeling of respect for your parent's memory should rather lead you to do that from which at first you shrunk . . . Suppose, for a moment, the story to be true. What will then be the state of the case? This – a person having your Father's blood in her veins will be left, with a large family to struggle with all the evils of penury while you are in the possession of comparatively boundless wealth. Surely you never could wish this to happen simply because it is painful to you to believe it.

Once more he lays before her 'the facts which ought to guide your judgment, and which are known to all the world': that her father

> lived in great intimacy with the mother of Lady Charlotte – that this person always spoke of her as his child – that he was at no great

pains to deny it himself – that as she grew up her likeness to him became extraordinary, and the theme of general remark, – that none of his contemporaries, or companions of his own standing had, or have any doubt of the fact, – that, indeed, in the Courts of law proceedings took place which strongly corroborate the prevailing belief, – that, after making her many handsome presents of money at different periods, he at length, agreed to pay her an annuity of £300 a year.

Dudley himself was 'brought up from a boy to regard Sir Francis with attachment and admiration', and will never cease to do so. It is for the sake of his memory, as much as for the plight of Lady Charlotte and her family, that he is urging Angela not to persist in her refusal:

If the fact of his paying her an annuity be (as you maintain) no proof of the relationship, how can your continuing the annuity be considered as establishing it? . . . the general opinion as to Lady Charlotte's birth will remain unaffected either by your granting, or withholding from her assistance . . . It is my firm conviction that Sir Francis did not deliberately leave her unprovided for . . . If, however, she is known to be in want his memory will be loaded with grievous, though, as I am persuaded, unmerited censure . . . In urging you then, thus earnestly, to continue to this unfortunate lady the assistance granted by Sir Francis I am less influenced by considerations of what is humane and charitable and generous than by a concern for his memory.[12]

It would be hard to fault Dudley's letter. He had taken great pains (and some 1,700 words) to express to Angela his concern for her feelings, his affection for her father, and his conviction of the rightness of his view 'in relation to this painful affair'. His arguments were unanswerable; and Angela did not attempt to answer them. She ignored his letter completely. She returned to England in the autumn and resumed her charitable work, for the time being without Dickens, who was spending a year in Italy.

*

In December occurred an event that Angela had been half-dreading for years. The marriage of Hannah Meredith and William Brown could no longer be put off. As it turned out, Angela was not losing a companion but gaining a resident physician and adviser, for Dr Brown gave up his medical partnership and moved with Hannah into apartments in the spacious Piccadilly mansion. Thenceforth, though he kept up some private practice, he seems to have been quite happy to be one of the household, taking an active part in Angela's schemes and becoming one of her valued friends and counsellors.

The Christmas season that year inevitably brought unhappy memories of the last illnesses of Sir Francis and Lady Burdett. Angela cheered herself up by sending out to Italy a huge Twelfth Cake, magnificently decorated, for Charley Dickens's eighth birthday on January 6. 'It was *exhibited*,' wrote Dickens, 'to the principal Inhabitants [of Genoa] as a wonder and a marvel.'[13] Having no nephews or nieces of her own, Angela had become a sort of unofficial aunt to the Dickens children, who regularly sent her, through their father, their 'best love', entrusting him on one occasion with 'messages full of partially unintelligible enthusiasm'.[14] Charley, the eldest, was a particular favourite. 'He is still full of his last visit to you', Dickens had written when Charley was six, 'and brightened up like burnished copper . . . when I asked him if he had any message to send.'[15]

The first anniversary of her parents' deaths came and went. Angela was too busy to brood. She had resolutely put Dudley's letter and the whole unpleasant Bacon affair out of her mind. There were calls enough on her charity, in any case. Dickens wrote appealing on behalf of the widow and six children of John Overs, a poor carpenter-turned-writer whose literary career Dickens had encouraged and who had recently succumbed to tuberculosis. Here was a destitute family whom Angela could have no hesitation in helping. 'Mrs Overs tells me,' wrote Dickens to Forster in March,

> that Miss Coutts has sent her, at different times, sixteen pounds, has sent a doctor to her children, and has got one of the girls into an Orphan School. When I wrote her a word in the poor woman's behalf, she wrote me back . . . that it was a kindness to herself to have done so, 'for what is the use of my means but to try and do some good with them?'[16]

But nothing could persuade Angela to use her means to help Lady Charlotte Bacon and her family. A letter from Lord Brougham to Dudley Coutts Stuart that February re-opened the whole subject. Brougham had heard from Lady Charlotte that her husband was to be declared a bankrupt and that she had 'literally not one shilling in the world'. Brougham wrote to Dudley:

Surely Miss C for whom I really have the greatest affection & of whom I have a very high opinion also – should step in to save her father's memory. You cannot conceive what a searching scrutiny a Bkt undergoes . . . There is no one private particular that is not publicly disclosed. I believe there are people – attached to Burdett's memory, who would themselves pay some considerable sums of money than let all this scandal happen. But they never will come forward when it is rather a duty of B's own family.[17]

Armed with this letter, Dudley made one last attempt to breach the impregnable fortress of his cousin Angela's determination. Had she, he asked somewhat reproachfully, received his last letter, written seven months ago and delivered by him personally to Sir Edmund Antrobus in the Strand to be forwarded to her in Germany? He had hoped that she would see reason; at the very least, he had expected her to acknowledge his letter. Now, in sending her Lord Brougham's note, he was actuated as before 'by no motives except concern for the memory of your Father and (if I may say so without offence) for your own good repute'.[18]

Angela's reply was couched in such terms as to make further communication on the subject useless. She had not acknowledged his previous letter, she wrote, because

I scarcely thought you would expect an answer, unless I had indeed altered my opinions, which are quite unchanged. I return you Lord Broughams letter & I still conceive it to be quite unfit for me, to adopt this version of a story, contradicted by the fact, of the position the Lady holds as an Earls daughter, her birth and marriage being recorded as such, in the Peerage . . . I must add, that though I may feel that something of what *was done* to me, may have been overlooked, I fully believe that you and all who have brought this under my notice have fulfilled what you considered a duty.[19]

She never forgot what *was done* to her, though she bore no grudge against Dudley or Lord Brougham. It was monstrous, in her opinion, that the matter should ever have been raised with her; and indeed the first claim, as everyone acknowledged, was on her brother Robert, if on any of the Burdetts. In Angela's view it was not a matter that affected her family at all: she steadfastly refused to face the fact that her father had been an adulterer. Ironically, she saw herself, like Dudley and the rest, as protecting Sir Francis's reputation; in reality she was (as Dudley realised) intent on preserving intact her own image of the 'dear Father' whose 'unsuspecting generous nature' had been taken advantage of, as she explained it to Dudley. She is said to have bought up every copy she could lay her hands on of an anonymous pamphlet published in 1811 called 'Adultery and Patriotism', which was an attack on Sir Francis. And she refused permission for his biography to be written while she was alive.

As for the Bacons, the General, despite gloomy predictions to a friend that he would not last long, lasted for another twenty years, dying in 1864. Lady Charlotte lived on until 1880. In 1853, on the death of her brother, she and her sister inherited the Oxford estate, thereby in a sense vindicating Angela's contention that she was an acknowledged member of the Oxford family – though another relative, according to D'Orsay, had earlier disinherited Lady Charlotte on the grounds that she was Burdett's daughter.

How the Bacons managed financially in the intervening years we do not know; perhaps the friends to whom Lord Brougham alluded stepped into the breach to save the General from bankruptcy. We can be fairly certain, however, that no aid was forthcoming from one quarter, from which it had been so urgently, but vainly, solicited.

*

With her letter to Dudley of March 3, 1845, Angela may well have thought that she was closing the subject. But painful experiences cannot be eliminated from the mind by an act of will. Angela's determination not to allow a life of her father to be written is one indication of the far-reaching effects of the Bacon affair. That it also affected the general course of her own life from then onwards seems likely. 1845 marked a turning-point in her career as a philanthropist. It was in this year that she embarked on two large-scale projects – the first of those public works which would make her name synonymous with philanthropy throughout her own country and in many other parts of the world. At last she felt able to do 'greater and more useful things' with her money.

Bishop Blomfield of London, whom Angela admired and Dickens disliked, had set up two funds, the first for church building in London, the second to establish new bishoprics in the Godless colonies. It was to this second cause that Angela was at first drawn. She had been approached by the Reverend Edward Coleridge, Fellow of Eton College, who had sent her his brief history of the church in Australia. From it, we learn that the first group of just over a thousand souls (three-quarters of them convicts) had settled in that vast territory in

1788. Among them was one clergyman, who was joined six years later by a second. By the early 1800s the population had increased to over 6,000. And by 1836, when the first Bishop of Australia was appointed, it had grown to well over 60,000, with the proportion of convicts to 'others' now reversed.

It may have been Coleridge who first kindled Angela's interest in the colonies. At any rate, by 1845 she had decided to provide the money for the endowment of a bishopric in Adelaide, South Australia, and for another in Cape Town. The amount involved was £35,000 – by far the largest single sum she had given away so far. In an effusive letter of thanks, Coleridge referred to 'your truly noble disposition of that treasure, which the Almighty has not placed in your hands in vain'.[20]

It was all very well to minister to the spiritual needs of fellow-countrymen in far-away places. But, as Angela well knew, there were those on her own doorstep who were desperately in need of the kind of aid her 'treasure' could provide. For some years, indeed, she had been considering what she could do for London's poor that would bring lasting benefit rather than temporary alleviation. She was aware of the reports of commissions and committees on such matters as education, public health and housing, and of the woeful inadequacy of all three. She had consulted Blomfield and other concerned churchmen, as well as friends such as Dickens and Kay-Shuttleworth, and well-informed members of her own family circle like Dudley Ryder, Viscount Sandon (afterwards Lord Harrowby), who was MP for Liverpool. She knew the Prime Minister, Sir Robert Peel, whose 'frigid efficiency covered an almost passionate concern for the welfare of the people',[21] and Lord Ashley (later Shaftesbury), who felt no need to conceal his passionate concern.

She had resolved to give £35,000 to the church overseas. Should she simply donate a similar amount to the church at home? The church was, after all, one of the main channels through which aid to the poor flowed, either directly via the parishes or indirectly through the ever-increasing number of relief organisations that were being formed, many of them with church patronage. To have given large sums to such worthy bodies as the Metropolitan Visiting and Relief Association and the Society for Improving the Condition of the Labouring Classes (to name but two) would have been to assist in much good work; and by giving under her habitual designation of 'a lady', Angela would have preserved her much-prized anonymity.

The alternative was to step out of the shadow of that anonymity into the full glare of public benefaction by inaugurating a project in her own name; and this is what she eventually decided to do. She would build a church, with vicarage and schools – the nucleus of an entire parochial organisation – in the heart of one of the worst slum districts of London.

The development was, to some extent, a natural one. Angela's confidence had increased over the years and she had an understandable desire to exercise some control over what happened to her money. Even so, for a woman of her reserved temperament it was a remarkable step to take. The impetus, one cannot help thinking, came from outside events: specifically, from the Bacon affair and from her experiences with Richard Dunn. If her name was to be dragged before the public by a blackmailer or a madman, the public might as well know how Miss Coutts was spending her money. Similarly, if there was a suspicion that she had acted ungenerously to a family in distress, let it be seen that she was aiding other families whose distress was infinitely greater. And, most important of all, to prove to the world the unimpeachable character of her father, she would build her church as a memorial to him and create her 'model parish' in his old constituency of Westminister.

Westminster in those days was not a place of imposing mansion blocks and smart office buildings. It consisted for the most part of mean streets, narrow alleys and filthy courtyards, of wretched, run-down tenements in which the dregs of humanity were ever more tightly packed – a situation all the more shocking when it is remembered that much of the land was owned by the Dean and Chapter of Westminster Abbey. Worst of all was the area to the west and south of the Abbey, known as the Devil's Acre, where every variety of criminal was to be found and the law-abiding dared not venture. It was on the fringes of the Devil's Acre, in Rochester Row, that Angela's new church and schools of St Stephen's were to be built.

A rising young architect, Benjamin Ferrey, who had superintended the restoration of parts of Wells Cathedral, was engaged to design a church in fourteenth-century Gothic style, the other buildings to be in keeping. The cost of the whole project was originally estimated at £30,000, but this soon proved to be unrealistic and the final figure was more in the region of £100,000. Compensation for the tenants on the site, for example, was at first agreed at £4,700, but came to more than double that in the end.

Angela was interested in every detail. She carried on a voluminous correspondence with the architect, Ferrey, and with Bishop Blomfield, who was also personally involved in the minutiae. It is pleasant to think of the Bishop of London and the great heiress corresponding at some length, as they did, on the problems of one Mr Richards, a rope-maker, who was paid £100 to compensate him for the loss of his rope-walk but later claimed he was destitute because he had been unable to find another strip of land long enough for spinning his ropes.* He eventually received a further £50; but it is not known if he ever resumed his rope-making.

A contemporary drawing showing Angela laying the foundation-stone of St Stephen's Church, Rochester Row, in 1847

Not until the summer of 1847 was the foundation stone of St Stephen's laid. The ceremony, held on July 20, was attended by nearly a thousand distinguished guests, who sat on tiers of wooden seats specially erected for the occasion. In the centre was a raised platform on which stood Angela with the bishop and other dignitaries. It was an affecting scene. Miss Catherine Sinclair, a writer of children's books and sister of the Sinclair brothers, heard several of the ladies present say they would have liked 'to retire out of sight that they might relieve their

* Rope-walks were 600 or 1,200 feet long. The spinners, who walked backwards and forwards first drawing out the fibres and then reeling in the yarn, covered about eighteen miles a day.

hearts with tears'.[22] After Angela had spread the mortar with a silver trowel presented to her by the local inhabitants, the stone was lowered into place. Its Latin inscription recorded that the church was being built as a memorial to Sir Francis Burdett by his youngest daughter.*

Among the old friends of Sir Francis who were invited to the ceremony was Lord Brougham. He had evidently been forgiven for his outspoken interference in the Bacon affair. Now nearly seventy, he spent a part of each year in retirement at Cannes, where he had built a château; but he still attended the House of Lords, making long speeches on law reform. In case he could not get away from the House on the 20th, he told Angela,

> I send you a substitute namely half a Tyne salmon – just arrived. It is parboiled at Newcastle but you must give strict & positive order to your kitchen people to *dress it exactly as if it were not boiled at all* – else it will be underdone.[23]

In the end he did attend both the ceremony and the dinner that Angela gave the same evening, much to the gratification of Catherine Sinclair, who was delighted to meet him: 'He is so amusing and looked so animated,' she wrote to Angela. 'I thought him *quite handsome.*'[24]

Three weeks earlier, on June 29, there had been another important public occasion for Angela: the consecration of 'her' two bishops – Robert Gray of Cape Town and Augustus Short of Adelaide – at Westminster Abbey. 'Thousands will bless your name beyond those who now value and praise you,'[25] wrote Mary Howley, wife of the Archbishop of Canterbury. Miss Coutts, for ten years an unwilling focus of public attention, was at last beginning to come out of her shell.

*

Human nature being what it is, there were probably thousands who were more interested in Angela's personal life than in her church-building schemes. The big question was: would Miss Coutts ever marry, and if so, whom? She was now in her early thirties: quite an old maid. Her name had recently been linked with that of Louis Napoleon, who had fled to England the previous summer after escaping from the French fortress where he had been imprisoned since 1840. Angela had got to know the Prince during his previous exile in London. In November 1846 she gave a dinner party in his honour, taking a

---

* The present vicar, The Rev. W. W. Davidson, says that he has never been able to find the foundation stone.

banqueting suite in the Bedford Hotel for the purpose, since presumably not even the large dining-room at Stratton Street could accommodate the numbers. One of those invited was Julian Young, who found himself unexpectedly elevated when the party went into dinner:

> Miss Coutts sat, as she always does when she has a very large dinner party, in the centre of one side of the table, with the Prince at her right hand. As the most insignificant person present, I entered the room last, and *sans dame*. As I could not go below the salt, I made for the lowest place near to it; but found every place but the chair next to Miss Coutts on the left already occupied. She beckoned me up, told me to fill the vacant seat, and presented me to the Prince.[26]

Inevitably, after this dinner, it was rumoured that Louis Napoleon had become engaged to Miss Coutts – a match that would have made Harriot St Albans turn in her grave. Whether or not the Prince did propose we do not know. In 1852, after he had at last achieved his ambition and been proclaimed Emperor of the French, he made overtures for the hand of Queen Victoria's niece, Princess Adelaide of Hohenlohe, but without success. He married instead the beautiful Eugenie de Montijo, who was tall and elegant; the Emperor himself was short and dapper, with long waxed moustaches. Angela remained on the friendliest terms with Napoleon, who died in Chislehurst in 1873; the Empress, too, became a close friend.

Among others who were rumoured to be contenders for Angela's hand was Samuel Wilberforce, third son of the anti-slavery campaigner, who had been enthroned in December 1845 as Bishop of Oxford. Born in 1805, Wilberforce had risen rapidly in the clerical hierarchy since his ordination. He was, wrote Greville in 1845, 'a very quick, lively, and agreeable man, who is in favor at Court'. Quite likely he was already a widower when Angela first met him: his wife died in 1841, leaving him an estate in Sussex which raised him by several notches on the social scale. He and Angela became friends for life; but there appears to have been no romance.

Angela herself had not completely given up the idea of marriage. She had always preferred the company of older men, and by the end of 1846 she had found someone on whom she could lavish her considerable store of affection. In that same summer of 1847 when her two church projects were launched, tongues were wagging about this latest friendship of Miss Coutts's. On September 24 the arch-gossip Princess Lieven wrote from Paris to her friend Lady Palmerston:

Tell me if it is true that the Duke of Wellington is marrying Miss Coutts. I can hardly believe it, yet such extraordinary things happen in this world that I should never say that anything was impossible.[27]

Wellington had been a widower for fifteen years and had never shown any inclination to re-marry. But his new friend Miss Angela was a very determined woman, particularly when her passions were aroused. Remembering the marriage of her grandfather Coutts and Harriot Mellon, she might well have agreed with Princess Lieven that anything was possible. And what woman, after all, would even consider a bishop, or give more than a backward glance at a refugee French prince, when there was a chance that she might share the last years of that greatest of Englishmen, the Duke of Wellington?

Seven

OH SOLDIER, SOLDIER, WILL YOU MARRY ME?

'I hope that you will write to me, whenever you wish to communicate with a friend!'[1] wrote Field Marshal the Duke of Wellington, aged seventy-seven, to the 32-year-old Miss Angela Burdett Coutts in August 1846. Thirty years after the Battle of Waterloo, its hero was still the greatest figure in England. Despite an unhappy three years (1828–30) as Prime Minister and an uncompromising hostility to Reform, Wellington was the elder statesman who was universally respected and admired by men of all classes and shades of political opinion. Mistaken though he had been in some of his policies, his courage and integrity were never in question. The young Queen had come to rely on his kindness, common sense, and unswerving loyalty. Above all, he was loved for what Lord Holland had once called 'the ineffable charm of unassuming simplicity'.[2]

On the fall of Sir Robert Peel's government in June 1846 after the repeal of the Corn Laws, the Duke ceased to be the leader of the Conservative peers. But he was still active in public life. He was Commander-in-Chief of the Army, Lord Warden of the Cinque Ports, Constable of the Tower of London and Chancellor of Oxford University. Everyone asked his advice; it seemed as if nothing really important could happen without his being in some way involved. His incredible energy was matched by the clarity and incisiveness of his mind. He liked to claim that even the costermonger's donkey was allowed some rest, while the Duke of Wellington got none. But it was his sense of duty and his willingness to serve that drove him on, as much as external pressures.

Sir Francis Burdett had had a great admiration for Wellington, his erstwhile political opponent. While their friendship was never close, they dined at each other's houses and spoke the same language. The old Duke had for some years taken a grandfatherly interest in Angela, inviting her to balls and concerts at Apsley House, his London home at Hyde Park Corner which was known as 'No 1 London', and sending her tickets for the House of Lords. 'Nothing will give me greater pleasure,' he had assured her in July 1840, 'than to wait upon you whenever you invite me.'[3] But in practice he had often been obliged, through pressure of parliamentary business, to decline her invitations to dinners and parties. Now, he would have more time to devote to this serious young woman whose charitable activities he heartily applauded.

The Duke, as everybody knew, had always enjoyed feminine company; and he had never lacked it. Susceptible to beauty, he appreciated intelligence too: a clever woman, he once told Lady Salisbury, had the virtue of 'anticipating one's meaning'.[4] Such a one was Harriet Arbuthnot, whose death in 1834 had been a great loss. Almost certainly they were not lovers; Harriet's husband, Charles Arbuthnot, was as devoted to the Duke as Harriet was. In his anguish after his wife's death Arbuthnot poured his heart out to the Duke: 'I am writing all my thoughts to you, for we were *three*, & you will understand . . .'[5]

Harriet had had a passion for politics and had been the Duke's confidante on political matters for many years. This consuming interest in public affairs was something that Angela never shared with the Duke; nor was their friendship sparked off by an exchange of news and gossip about mutual friends and acquaintances, for they tended to move in different social circles, though meeting at Court functions and in each other's houses. So what was it that brought them together?

For many women, to know the Duke of Wellington was to love him: that ineffable charm still worked its magic even as he approached his eighties. With his 'beautiful silver head',[6] his simple manner, his unfailing kindness behind the sometimes 'iron' mask, the Duke in old age represented an ideal of manhood. But most women had their own menfolk with first claim on their affections. Not so Angela. She had never – as far as we know – lost her heart to a man. Her father, the man she had loved most, was dead. There was a yawning void in her life which her charitable work, however absorbing, her friends, however devoted, could not fill. With the marriage of Hannah Meredith, the void became wider. Into this great gap stepped the Great Duke.

As for Wellington, he had initially, no doubt, been as curious as anyone to make the acquaintance of the richest heiress in England, who happened to be his neighbour in Piccadilly. As he got to know her he discovered in her a fellow-feeling: she, like him, was anxious to be of service. He applauded her strong sense of duty, though at times he must have sighed over her excessive earnestness. Probably what drew him to her more than anything in the early days was her request for help and guidance. This was something he had never been able to resist. She consulted him about the dreadful Dunn, about a dispute she was having with the bank partners, about her charities. He responded with his customary courtesy and assiduity, showing a flattering interest in her affairs and a concern for her well-being. In the summer of 1846 their friendship began to blossom.

September of that year found them both in Kent, the Duke at Walmer Castle and Angela just along the coast at Ramsgate. He called on her, and a few days later wrote to invite her and Mrs Brown to dine and stay the night. They accepted for the 9th. As Lord Warden of the Cinque Ports (an honorary post carrying great prestige*), Wellington lived for part of each year at Walmer Castle, and was much attached to it. Harriet Arbuthnot had once described it as 'the most charming marine château';[7] but Lady Lyttelton, who stayed there with the royal family in November 1842, called it 'a big round tower, with odd additions stuck on'. It wasn't necessary, she added, to go outside for air: 'doors and windows all chatter and sing at once, and hardly keep out the . . . wind and rain.'[8]

No doubt the weather was less wild and stormy in early September, when Angela's first visit to Walmer took place; but in any case she could hardly have had a more attentive and solicitous host. There was nothing the Duke loved more than fussing over his women guests, especially if they had a slightly delicate air. To receive such attention from 'the foremost man of all the world',[9] as Sir Francis had once called the Duke, was enough to turn any woman's head. Angela, seemingly indifferent to all suitors but with as great a need to love and be loved as any other human being, was no exception. With the Duke she felt 'safe'; she had found someone who was utterly dependable as well as eminently lovable.

That autumn saw the beginning of the almost daily (and sometimes twice-daily) correspondence between them. As was his usual custom, the Duke destroyed all Angela's letters; only one note from her has survived. But she carefully preserved his letters, and in due course they were returned to his family. There are nearly 850 of them at Stratfield Saye, the country house near Reading that was presented to Wellington by a grateful nation in 1817. Written on pale-grey writing-paper in a sloping hand that becomes ever more difficult to read as the writer

---

* More recent Lords Warden have included Sir Winston Churchill and Sir Robert Menzies.

advances in years, the letters are a tantalisingly one-sided record of a most unusual friendship.

By October 1846 'My dear Miss Coutts' has become 'My dear Miss Angela', and the formal ending 'ever yours most faithfully, Wellington', gives way to greater warmth and the more intimate signature 'Wn.'. Always pleased to hear from her, the Duke is 'delighted with the prospect of seeing' her, or 'much concerned' not to see her. 'You may', he writes, 'rely upon being informed of all my movements, so that you may communicate to me your wishes at any moment.'[10] One of Angela's wishes was that the Duke should be a trustee of a settlement that she was making on Mrs Brown. After what looks like some initial hesitation he was 'delighted' to act in this capacity – surely a unique distinction for an ex-governess and an indication of the Duke's desire to please his new young friend.

*

In her battle with the partners of Coutts & Co. the Duke was Angela's staunch supporter, though the wisdom of his advice was questionable. Her position vis-à-vis the bank was an anomalous one. It was widely believed that she was 'head of the House'. For example, as we have seen, when a loan was needed to pay off the Duchess of Kent's debts it was Miss Coutts whom the Queen's Ministers approached. In fact, she was not even a partner, as the Duchess of St Albans had been. Under the Duchess's will her half-share was held on trust during her lifetime, the trustees being the senior partners. The will provided that any power or control she might exercise in the running of the business must depend upon the partners' consent. What seems to have happened was that a 'gentleman's agreement' was arrived at whereby Angela's opinions and wishes were taken into consideration but final decisions rested with the partners.

The situation was a tricky one. Edward Majoribanks and his colleagues, while wishing to conduct their affairs without too much interference from Thomas Coutts's granddaughter, nevertheless recognised the advantage to the bank of her being generally regarded as head of the firm that bore her name. As for Angela, whatever the Duchess's will might say she saw herself as having taken over the sacred trust to which her grandfather had devoted his life. She always referred to 'my House', and felt a personal responsibility for the bank. Inevitably, she sometimes came into conflict with the partners, and in the summer of 1846 her relations with Edward Majoribanks were going through a sticky patch.

'I am much concerned to learn that Mr Marjoribanks continues so unreasonable,'[11] wrote the Duke of Wellington on August 31. In October he agreed to go and see Marjoribanks if Angela wished it; by November they had decided that she should send a stiffly-worded letter before bringing up the big Wellingtonian guns. The Duke wrote a draft for her; it asked Marjoribanks to

> ... recollect that there are points connected with the management of my House, upon which I cannot alter my opinions founded as they are upon the Invariable Practice of my Grandfather, and of the Duchess of St Albans.[12]

The points at issue were, first, the appointment of a new partner and, secondly, 'an arrangement for a general rise in the Publick Salaries of the Clerks of the House', which had not taken place for some years. In the end Angela sent her own letter, approved by the Duke, who assured her it was much better than the one he had drafted. There followed a meeting at the Strand between Angela and the partners. The results were disappointing, but the Duke counselled patience: 'all will come right!' He was fully sensible, he assured her, of her excellent understanding, justice, rectitude and moderation. She was right to go through the stationery accounts, 'notwithstanding that you were bored by the same!' It would show the partners

> that you can and will go through any thing however dry and little interesting; & which it may be your duty to attend to as the Head of the House! Any thing of this kind will do good inasmuch as it will increase your Influence and Power; and establish more firmly in the Minds of those about you, a confidence in your steadiness and power of giving your attention to business.[13]

Influence and power, as Angela must have realised, were the almost inevitable concomitants of great wealth; but she would have denied being interested in them for their own sake, or for selfish ends. Like her money, her influence and power were to be used to benefit others, whether the poor of Westminster or the clerks of Coutts & Co. At the same time, she was becoming accustomed to having her own way and was more self-confident and assured; the determined young woman now doing battle in the Strand had come a long way from the shy and inexperienced girl of nine years before. And yet, despite the constant support of the faithful Hannah, she often felt the loneliness of her position. How delightful, now, to know that she had the Great Duke on her side, applauding her decisions and encouraging her endeavours. She basked in the warmth of his approbation and was more than ever drawn to him.

As Angela's devotion increased so the Duke's attachment deepened. When she sent him a purse she had made he told her it would 'strengthen the regard we feel for each other'. He urged her to come and visit him at Stratfield Saye – but first, she must send him a pair of her shoes, 'that I may have some galoshes made for you'.[14] On New Year's Eve she wrote to tell him how happy the past year had been for her. Touched by her letter and its complimentary references to himself, he replied that he was sorry he had not written to her in similar vein, as he had intended: 'How much better you treated me than I deserve!' In the same letter he encouraged her to take up skating: 'Don't repine! My Dear! that you are a Woman! There is nothing to prevent your skaiting . . . Women skait habitually in the Countries in which the Ice is certain annually, and in England I have seen Ladies skait beautifully.'[15] It is interesting that Angela, while prepared to tackle business matters at the bank, was doubtful about taking part in such an 'unfeminine' pursuit as 'skaiting'!

The year was to be one of great activity for Angela, and she wrote fully to the Duke of all her plans. He was 'delighted' with her letter, and with her approach to philanthropy:

> It appears to me that in administering Charities as well as in most other matters, your Mind and mine very naturally travel on the same Road. You as well as I like and endeavour to do good effectually. I cannot bear to be called upon and to be used [as a] Stop Gap to provide the Means for going on in the same vicious course, and there to leave the matter. You appear to have the same feeling, and you are quite right!

His only reservation concerned her plan to establish a refuge for 'fallen' women – something she and Dickens had first discussed the previous spring. The Duke was pessimistic about the chances of 'saving in this World that particular Class of Unfortunates', though he himself was later moved to send money to prostitutes wishing to start a new life in the colonies.

He ends this letter with a postscript urging her to come and visit him at Stratfield Saye:

I shall be here quite alone on Saturday. If you and Mrs Brown could come down and dine here on that day, and stay Sunday I could show you my House and Place! There will be nobody here excepting myself from Friday till Monday. If you will come . . . I will send my carriage over to Reading to meet you.[16]

The invitation was repeated two days later, when the weather had become slightly milder; in any case, as the Duke frequently boasted, Stratfield Saye was a very warm house. But Angela was recovering from a cold and did not want to risk catching another one; she may also have been concerned for Mrs Brown's health. The Duke was becoming impatient: 'I feel the want of your society,' he writes on January 9. 'I shall certainly be in town on Wednesday . . . I will take care to keep you informed of my movements!'[17]

When he did return to Apsley House in mid-January they saw each other almost daily. Never had Angela been so busy. There was the supervision of her St Stephen's, Westminster, scheme, under way at last after long delays; there were final arrangements to be made in connection with her colonial bishoprics; there were the plans for the proposed 'home for homeless women'; not to mention the never-ending stream of begging-letters to be waded through, without the help of Dickens who was abroad. But this was not all. The trial of Richard Dunn for perjury was due to take place shortly, and there were conferences with her lawyers about the case. While outwardly maintaining her usual composure, Angela was inwardly steeling herself for the ordeal of attending court and giving evidence.

Through all this the Duke sustained her, encouraging, counselling, but never obtruding his own views. 'You have a clear correct judgment, which with an excellent heart will always keep you right,'[18] he told her. His confidence in her was exactly what she needed. It boosted her morale as no amount of advice, however sound, could have done. When she told him at the beginning of February that she would be devoting a day to young Charley Dickens, who was arriving from France to start his career at King's College School (for which she was paying), he replied:

Although I am sorry that I shall not see you this day, I hope you will believe that I am delighted that you have determined to attend to your little Boy! This course is entirely consistent with all that you do! Ever yours with sincere regard and affection.[19]

The Duke may have been a father-figure, but he was neither over-protective nor dictatorial. He was happy for her to be herself. There could be no greater proof of his regard for her.

Two days later, he was writing of the 'admirable good sense and goodness of heart' which had prompted her letter of the previous night. And he continued, rather mysteriously:

> You are quite right! There can be no secrets between us on any subjects! We will talk of this as of other subjects or not, as we may like! and neither of us can have any reluctance or restraint in touching upon it. The subject is now exactly as it ought to be between us! and as every other is one on which either can think aloud![20]

Was 'the subject' in question their feelings for each other, and the possibility of marriage? It seems highly likely. To Angela, the temptation to 'think aloud' proved irresistible. The Duke might believe that the subject was exactly as it ought to be between them; she felt differently. He had invited her to speak without 'reluctance or restraint', and on the following day, February 7, speak she did. She asked the Duke of Wellington to make her his wife.

Sincerely attached to her though he was, it is difficult to believe that the Duke had ever seriously considered marrying her. He was getting on for eighty and, despite his vigorous constitution and undiminished interest in life, he was often tired and felt the need for rest and solitude. With Angela at his side there would be little chance of either. Besides, he may well have felt the impropriety of such a match. Twelve years earlier he had written to another young woman who had wanted to marry him: 'What would be said if I ... were to take in marriage a lady young enough to be my Granddaughter?'[21]

So, tackfully, he declined Miss Angela's proposal. It would not make her happy, he told her; she would be throwing herself away. Remembering her grandfather and Harriot Mellon, Angela couldn't agree: she *knew* she would be happy, as Harriot had been. When the Duke left her that evening, she must have allowed herself to hope that he might change his mind. But her hopes were dashed the next morning with the arrival of a letter in the familiar grey envelope. It was one of the most affectionate and endearing that the Duke ever wrote to her – but it was a refusal nonetheless:

> My dearest Angela! I have passed every moment of the Evening and Night since I quitted you in reflecting upon our conversation of

yesterday! Every word of which I have considered repeatedly! My first duty towards you is that of Friend, Guardian, Protector! You are Young, my Dearest! You have before you the prospect of at least twenty years of enjoyment of Happiness in Life. I entreat you again . . . not to throw yourself away upon a Man old enough to be your Grandfather! who however Strong, Hearty and Healthy at present! must and will certainly in time feel the consequences and infirmities of Age! . . . I cannot too often and too urgently entreat you to consider this well! I urge it as your Friend, Guardian, Protector. But I must add as I have frequently that my own happiness depends upon it. My last days would be embittered by the reflection that your Life was uncomfortable and hopeless. God bless you my Dearest! Believe me Ever Yours Wn.[22]

The Duke, it may be noted in passing, kept a copy of this letter.

*

For several days it was as if the great Stratton Street mansion was in mourning. Wellington, passing it on his way to the House of Lords on February 11, saw 'the windows all closed and the blinds down even of your apartments. It looked melancholy.'[23] No doubt Angela was feeling melancholy; not that she admitted as much to the Duke. She was ill with earache, she told him. By the 16th he was relieved to know that she was better. Having got over the initial disappointment of his rejection, she must have taken comfort in the realisation that she still held a unique place in his affections. Their friendship was as close as ever; and it was even possible that she might still persuade him to change his mind and marry her.

At the same time, what an immense satisfaction it would have been to have faced her old adversary, Richard Dunn, in court at the end of that month as the future Duchess of Wellington! The very name would have put fear into the soul of that hateful man as well as silencing the gossips. As it was, she came through the ordeal very well; the Duke was delighted at the quiet way in which she wrote to him of it. But the emotional strain, coupled with the enormous burden of her charitable work, affected her health. It was altogether a trying time. Dr Brown was seriously ill and unable to give her his usual solid support; and Dickens, though back in London, was heavily involved in family matters and in keeping up with his monthly instalments of *Dombey and Son*.

The Duke was all affectionate concern, sending flowers and enquiring tenderly after her health. Early in April, when she was better, he urged her to come to Stratfield Saye, but she went off instead on a visit to Oxfordshire with another of her elderly admirers, Samuel Rogers (then in his eighty-fourth year). Later in the month the Duke renewed his invitation: would she not come and dine at Stratfield Saye alone? No; she would bring Mrs Brown with her. 'My dearest! Act as your excellent judgment suggests respecting the manner in which you will come to me!' he replied, resignedly. 'At all events I shall be delighted to see Mrs Brown. But it amused me that you might come alone . . . But you are always right!' Somewhat incongruously, he ends this letter (in answer to her enquiry, it would appear) with a reference to his underwear:

> I do wear Muslin next my Skin. It imbibes the moisture which in a state of Health ought always to be on the skin, and is not cold as Linen or Cambrick would be. I wear the finest Bengal Muslin if I can find any.[24]

In May there were long, newsy letters, and, when the Duke returned to London in June, short affectionate notes. She was unwell again, and he entreats her 'not to think of moving even from your bed till you will be permitted to do so by your medical attendant . . . God bless you my dearest.' A week later he advised her not to 'carry into execution your plan of coming here this evening through the gardens . . . The India rubber galoshes will keep your feet dry but the skirts of your cloathes will be wet about your feet and ankles and I earnestly intreat you not to make the experiment.'[25]

Inevitably, the Duke's attentions to Miss Coutts did not go unnoticed. This 'strange intimacy' was 'astonishing the world' and was one the the 'lamentable appearances of decay in his vigorous mind',[26] wrote Greville in July. It should be remembered, however, that Charles Greville was not an entirely unbiased witness as far as the Duke's relations with women were concerned: his own mother had had an affair with Wellington some twenty-five or thirty years before, and the bitterness felt then by the young Charles still simmered below the surface. In fact the Duke's later reputation as a roué owed much to the publication in the seventies and eighties of Greville's famous *Memoirs*, which one contemporary reader likened to 'Judas writing the lives of the Apostles'.[27] (Greville had been Clerk of the Privy Council.)

Late August found the Duke at Walmer again and Angela with the Browns at nearby Sandgate. The Duke wrote every day, often sending a leaf or a flower, the marks of which can be seen today on his writing-paper. His letters ranged over a wide variety of subjects. He reflected on the present state of the country, on the 'anxiety and uneasiness' he felt when he contemplated the danger ahead and realised that he might 'no longer have the Power of Mind or Body to contend with it'. He advised Angela on what to read. Nicholas Wiseman's *Lectures on Science and Revealed Religion* would 'amuse' her: 'Dr Wiseman is a Bishop of the R.C. Church . . . He is by [no] means bigoted. His particular creed never appears.' The Duke himself was a sincere believer in Christianity as a guiding principle for mankind. Dr Wiseman's book, he thought, would be better for Angela than one he had previously recommended, Lamartine's *Histoire des Girondins*, with its grisly details of the 'Horrors of the French Revolution'.[28]

'Keep me informed exactly of your movements my Dearest! and let me know all that you feel and think!'[29] he urged as Angela prepared to leave for an autumn holiday in France. She needed no persuading to write. Long letters in her execrable handwriting arrived almost by every post – from Abbeville, Amiens, Paris, Tours and other Loire Valley towns. The Duke acknowledged them with delight, relishing the detailed accounts of herself, her 'health, feelings, thoughts and amusements!' Throughout October, whether in Walmer, London or Windsor (where he was the Queen's guest for two days), he was with Miss Angela in spirit. 'You were ever in my mind . . . I am become like you! I have you with me constantly!' he wrote. His feelings seemed to reach a peak during her absence: 'My Dearest! for so I must call you. Your constant recollection of and kindness to me, charm me; and I cannot express what I feel for you . . .'[30]

Yet one wonders exactly what it was he was trying to express. These could hardly be called love letters. Perhaps the key to his feelings lies in the excerpt just quoted: deeply attached to her as the old Duke undoubtedly was, it was Angela's own devotion to him that provided the mainspring of their relationship. One cannot help thinking of Tom Coutts and Harriot Mellon. Did Harriot ever show Angela Tom's 'declaration' to his 'dearest, most justly beloved Harriott'? Old Coutts had had no compunction about marrying a woman young enough to be his granddaughter.* 'My happiness with you is perfect', he had written. The inescapable fact seems to be that Angela could never be for the Duke what Harriot had been for Tom: 'the preserver and the comforter and the delight' of his life.[31]

* There were forty-two years between Tom and Harriot; forty-five between the Duke and Angela.

Nevertheless, a letter from the Duke of November 9 that year hints at a greater degree of intimacy: 'I have been here entirely alone now nearly a week. My companion constantly with me, day and night! with whom I think aloud, whom I coax and caress, who is happy and delighted, and smiles on me in return! So that I cannot complain of my solitude.'[32] That Angela should have allowed herself to become his lover seems unthinkable – though not impossible, given the strength of her feelings for him. More likely, however, the old man was indulging in a little harmless fantasy as he dozed by his fireside, awaiting the return of his 'companion'. Solitude, for him, was no hardship but a luxury: relieved of the burden of entertaining unwanted guests, he had time to reflect and to dream a little.

Ten days earlier, writing of the importance of a healthy skin and a good circulation, he had been quite carried away in describing how he kept his feet warm at night:

> ... I rub them against each other... as I have intreated you to do! I think of you when I am in the act of doing so, and whether you have adopted that practice and it succeeds in making you as comfortable as it does me and that immediately... It would warm you throughout and would relieve you of the tenderness of skin of which you complain! Then you might think again of your companion who has given you this advice! Do this my Dearest and tell me how you feel. Let me know and feel that you have enjoyed it.[33]

In this foot-warming exercise, it has been suggested, the Duke had 'devised an innocent and endearing substitute for sexual intercourse'![34]

Certainly it seemed that Angela's absence had made his heart grow fonder. But hardly had she returned home, full of health and spirits, before she was reproaching him for his lack of attention. At Christmas she was in London, the Duke at Stratfield Saye. He had not complained recently, she wrote, of their being apart. He at once acknowledged his omission. But, he added:

> when you mentioned the fact which is very undeniable! the thought immediately occurred it would be ridiculous to complain when I know and feel, God Bless you! that I have only to say the Word! and that I shall have you at my side at all times! Is that reflection very presumptuous? No. It is the truth! You delight in it as I do![35]

Whether Angela shared the Duke's delight is questionable. It was, after all, very unlikely that he ever would 'say the Word' and make her his

Duchess. But she still had the assurance of his continued affection and regard. And with that, as they entered the new year of 1848, she had to be content.

*

'It appears probable that we alone of the Nations of the earth may . . . be saved from Wreck and Destruction!'[36] declared the Duke of Wellington to a friend in March 1848, as revolution swept through Europe like a forest fire. In France, old King Louis-Philippe had been forced to abdicate. He and his Queen, heavily disguised and calling themselves 'Mr and Mrs Smith', fled to England, arriving in Newhaven on March 3, where the King immediately wrote two letters – one to Queen Victoria and the other to Coutts & Co., asking for £300. Angela, who knew the Orléans family well, at once offered financial help.

As the news from the continent grew worse, the Duke told Angela of a new duty that had been thrust upon him: 'I am to hold myself in readiness, morning, noon and night to go off, dressed as for Court, to attend the Queen's *accouchement* at a Moment's Notice!'[37] Princess Louise, the Queen's sixth child, was born on March 18. Why the Commander-in-Chief's presence should have been required on this occasion we do not know – unless it had something to do with the threat of violence from England's own revolutionaries, the Chartists.

Not that the Chartists in any way intended violence against the Queen's person. Disgusted with the reformed Parliament's failure to ease the misery of working people and incensed by the harsh administration of the new Poor Law, they wanted the vote, and an end to 'all monopoly and oppression'. They had drawn up their radical Charter in 1838; four years later, after mass arrests, over fifty of their leaders had been transported. Now, they were preparing for an all-out confrontation with the government: a mass meeting and a march to the Houses of Parliament to present a petition with five million signatures.

The date fixed for the demonstration was April 10. Already there had been riots in various parts of the country. Fears that had been haunting the upper and middle classes for the past thirty years now seemed on the point of being realised. Great London houses were reinforced with stalwarts from their owners' country estates. As for the Duke – the dangers that he had foreseen the previous summer were upon them, and he rose magnificently to the occasion.

All troops were to be kept out of sight but ready for instant action if necessary; Angela's house was one of those in which a contingent was held in readiness. The Duke, who was expecting about 200,000 demonstrators, enrolled the same number of special constables. They came from all walks of life and included Prince Louis Napoleon, who would return to France later in the year to become President of the Second Republic and, in 1852, Emperor.

With cannon placed on the bridges and the royal family evacuated to the Isle of Wight, London was ready to meet the great Chartist threat. But the whole thing turned out to be a complete anti-climax. On the morning of the 10th far fewer Chartists than expected assembled on Kennington Common, and their leader was persuaded to take the petition to Westminster in a cab. The procession petered out. At half-past six the Duke sent a note to Angela:

> I have just returned from the House of Lords. The Mobs have dispersed. There are but two or three hundred people about Palace Yard, scarcely more than usual. Not a shot has been fired or an individual injured – nor has a single soldier been seen. In short everything has passed as I wished.[38]

Later in the evening Louis Napoleon, who had been on duty in Trafalgar Square, called at Stratton Street to report that the danger was over. Whatever the reasons for the failure of the demonstration (and rainy weather probably had something to do with it), it was seen as another triumph for the Duke of Wellington.

In that year of revolutions the Duke was as busy as ever. Most of his letters to Angela are short; in many he apologises for not being able to see her. He was at last beginning to feel his age; often tired and irritable, by the end of the summer he was worn out by the constant demands made on him. This, more than anything, probably accounts for his unusually harsh reaction when Angela committed a *faux pas* by calling uninvited at Apsley House on the morning of September 4. Exactly what took place is not clear. It was quite early, and the Duke had not long been up. It seems that Angela, having been shown into his study and requested to wait, scribbled him a note which the servant took to him. Back came the answer: His Grace was dressing and could not see her. As far as Angela was concerned, nothing untoward had happened; the Duke saw it differently. In a letter delivered later that day he vented his wrath upon her:

> I must tell you that I don't admire your little Gentillesse of this morning! If we don't respect ourselves, how can we expect that our Servants will respect us?

The Queen's Servants, the Adjutant and Quarter Master General, the Military Secretary, private Secretary, my aides de Camp, acquaintances and relatives are in the Habit of calling at all Hours. Lord John Russell* is frequently here before I have done breakfast shortly after ten o'clock. Other Ministers come also at an early Hour. They would be greatly surprized to find me still dressing, and a young Lady in possession of my room!

... If you wish to see my Room and every Article it contains, I have no objection. Fix your Hour regularly. Bring your friends with you. I will attend you. But do not be found here alone, like an *Enfant de la Maison*, and this by Official Men, entire Strangers to you. In short I tell you very firmly I will not allow it ... I did not think it possible that you would be guilty of such folly![39]

Hard on the heels of this outbust came a note of humble apology:

I am very much ashamed my Dearest Miss Angela of having written any thing to annoy you; whether you merited it or not. The fact is that when my Servant brought me your Note I was naked; and I was ashamed of his seeing me in that state; and requested him to tell you that I was dressing ... I beg you to excuse me.[40]

The incident is a strange one, particularly in view of Angela's refusal to dine alone with the Duke, which he had several times pressed her to do. She evidently saw no harm in an early morning visit. That he was extremely concerned for both their reputations there can be no doubt. The previous autumn, when she was in France, he had impressed upon her the importance of arranging for her letters to be forwarded when she left Paris, so that none of his fell into any hands but her own. And in July 1849 he was to advise her against taking a house next door to Walmer Castle: 'You may rely upon it that [you] cannot do so with Impunity. Your Name will immediately be again in the Newspapers, which cannot be otherwise than disagreeable to you.' This must have produced a hurt reaction, for the next day he wrote: 'I am sorry that you should think that I did not like that you should be near me. You will see that this not a *correct* view of my feelings.'[41]

Angela may sometimes have wondered what the Duke's real feelings for her were in the last years of his life. Often his letters were full of the old affectionate tenderness, but, increasingly, a note of irritability creeps into them. 'The whole world,' he complained, 'chooses to make use of a

* The Prime Minister.

Man eighty years of age for all purposes.'[42] As he himself admitted, it was 'fatigue of body mind and spirit' that was affecting him more than anything else:

> In fact I am worn out by perpetual worry, and going full gallop from morning till night every day! Nobody can do anything unless I am present, forgetting that I am deaf; eighty years old, and neither useful nor ornamental.[43]

There were times, now, when he felt obliged to spell out to his dear Miss Angela why it was he couldn't commit himself to engagements which he might find it impossible to fulfil:

> I wish that I could prevail upon you to devote a few minutes of your excellent understanding to the consideration of my real position. Although well and hearty and equal to the performance of any Duty required from me, I am not a Young Man . . .[44]

The Duke of Wellington, from a portrait by Benjamin Haydon at Stratfield Saye

Yet he could not bear to think that he had hurt or offended her: 'God bless you! my Dearest! You did not write anything cross to me . . . It is not you that is impatient. It is I, and I beg your pardon.' But when Angela was about to leave for the continent in October 1849 and asked him for some of the rose-water and vinegar solution that he used himself and had recommended for her eyes, he exploded in exasperation. He didn't have any of the mixture with him; did she expect him to ride miles to get her something that was so easy to make? – '. . . one spoonful of Rose water and one of distilled *Table* vinegar . . . I doubt that you require a veteran soldier 81 years of Age to do that!'[45]

More and more, the desire to be left in peace becomes a recurrent theme in his letters: 'God help me! How happy I should be if people would only leave me in tranquillity!' But his sense of humour and his gallantry never quite deserted him. 'To be sure! It does amuse me mightily at times to find a veteran eighty-two years old, deaf with all! turned into a lover!' he wrote in January 1851.[46]

Clearly, this was intended as a joke. But in the Duke's last year there were those who were determined to 'turn him into a lover'. A new friend, Mrs Margaret Jones, wife of an MP and some years younger than Angela, had entered his life. Their appearance together in the London drawing-rooms did not go unremarked. 'This Love Affair he had with Mrs Jones during his last season was very unbecoming,' wrote Mrs John Ruskin to her mother after the Duke's death. 'He always was in love with someone but had never made himself ridiculous till this one, which was a source of great grief to his family and made him laughed at by every empty-headed fool in London.'[47]

What Angela felt about it we do not know. Perhaps she sensed that one of Margaret Jones's chief attractions was that she made few demands on the old Duke. Despite Angela's outward serenity, she was not the most restful companion for an old man. Nevertheless, he always showed an unfailing interest in her affairs and a constant concern for her welfare; his friendship with her was probably the most unselfish of his life.

At eighty-two, the 'costermonger's donkey' was still in harness. Now frail and rather bent, he would make his way slowly on horseback from Apsley House to his office in the Horse Guards, where his staff often found him asleep at his desk. But his interest in life was undiminished. He was as thrilled as any schoolboy with the Great Exhibition of 1851, going almost daily to the huge glass palace in Hyde Park, though initially he had had strong reservations about it on the grounds of security. The spectacular official opening by the Queen took place on May 1. It happened also to be his eighty-second birthday, and in the evening Angela gave a splendid dinner-party in his honour.

It was from the Duke's office in the Horse Guards that Angela wrote the only one of her letters to him that has survived. She had apparently gone to watch the Changing of the Guard, and before leaving had dashed off a note to him, adding a few more lines on returning to Stratton Street:

> My dear Duke, I am just seeing the sight. Thank you. Yours affect, AGBC.
> Stratton St August 8/51 – I would write one word from your office. I felt so grand! I am just Home and saw all beautifully. I send this to give you notice Mr *Green** is in London – the person who annoys you & me by writing so much. I have had a Letter from him – You had better take no notice should he write – Goodbye.[48]

We shall never know whether the Duke kept this note for sentimental reasons, or whether it was mere chance that he did not follow his invariable practice and destroy it.

Two weeks later he was writing to upbraid her for allegedly encouraging the spread of gossip. Someone had put about a rumour – a 'calumny' in the Duke's terminology – and Angela had made matters worse by telling her friends about it: 'It appears that my calumniator is very active! and that she does not require assistance! I venture to recommend to you to have no communication with anybody respecting these calumnies!'[49]

A letter to Angela from Elizabeth, Lady Herbert, seems to point to this lady as the culprit. In it she explains that she had merely asked the Duke about the origins of a report that he was going to marry Angela. He had replied that the story had not the slightest foundation and that he did not even call on Miss Coutts often. 'I thought . . . that you might have for him the regard you would have for a father,' Lady Herbert sweetly suggested; '*We* had been friends in former days . . .'[50] Angela's response was a stiff third-person note declining further communication. It is not very flattering to learn that the man you adore has dismissed you as a mere acquaintance, even though the Duke's streak of secretiveness was something Angela could understand.

The following summer, when Angela was worried by the serious and prolonged illness of Mrs Brown, the Duke was boasting to another

---

* Mr Green was presumably a writer of begging-letters.

woman friend, Lady Salisbury, that he was 'always well, never fatigued', and had 'none of the infirmities of old age! excepting *Vanity* perhaps!'[51] He was feeling particularly happy because the distinguished guests he had been entertaining at Walmer Castle had just departed, leaving him in peace to enjoy his solitary occupations of walking, reading and letter-writing. On September 12 he wrote to Angela that he would have to put boards across the gates at Walmer Castle to prevent people peering under them: 'We are an inconveniently *Curious people* in this country!'[52]

Two days later, in the afternoon of September 14, 1852, the news began to filter through to a curious and incredulous people that the Duke of Wellington was dead.

*

'The greatest man that England ever knew is no more,'[53] wrote Prince Albert's secretary, confirming the news that had been flashed to the royal family at Balmoral by electric telegraph. The Queen herself, grieving for her '*dear* & great old Duke of Wellington', wrote in her journal: 'He seems to have gone out like a lamp.'[54] How dear the great old Duke had been to Angela Burdett Coutts was perhaps known by only a few, though many knew of their close friendship. Charles Dickens, out of tact or ignorance, wrote that he feared the Duke's death would cause her 'some natural distress'. We do not know if Angela, like the Queen, had a diary to which she could confide her innermost feelings, but it is probable that she kept her grief to herself, going about her daily duties with her usual composure and sustained by what Dickens had once called 'the materials of comfort and consolation within herself'.

The Duke was not buried until November 18 – more than two months after his death – because of Prince Albert's wish to give him a magnificent heraldic State funeral. From Walmer the body was brought to London where it lay in the Great Hall of Chelsea Hospital, surrounded by acres of black drapery, a forest of candelabra, and all the elaborate trappings of heraldic pomp. The Duke's elder son, Lord Douro, told Angela that he 'never saw anything more disappointing and devoid of good taste and feeling'. When the public were allowed in, several people were killed in the crush. The whole thing, wrote Douro to Angela, was 'a disgraceful way of doing honor'.[55] Meanwhile advertisements appeared in the press offering souvenirs (including locks of the Duke's hair) and seats for the funeral procession. Dickens thought the whole public had gone mad. It was 'a relapse into semi-barbarous practices',[56] he told Angela.

Angela attended the funeral with the family, accepting Lord Douro's invitation to set off from his house: 'It will be better for your comfort that you should start from and return here,' he had written. In the story of her friendship with Wellington, nothing is more remarkable than the deference shown to her by the Duke's two sons after his death. 'My time is at your disposal to call on you when you please,' wrote Douro (who, although now the second Duke, insisted on using his old name with her). He would be giving copies of the death mask, he told her, '*to no ladies but to you: that is "notre affaire"*.'[57]

All this lends weight to the rumour – current even today – that the Duke and Angela were secretly married (his sons, presumably, being in on the secret). Not a shred of evidence has been found to support it, however; and the Duke's own letters provide the strongest possible evidence against it. Not only is there his rejection of her proposal in February 1847, but there are passages in his later letters which, had he indeed been secretly married to her at the time he wrote them, would make no sense at all. To believe the rumour, one would have to believe either that these passages were deliberate falsehoods designed to mislead any third party reading the letters, or that they were jokes in rather questionable taste. Neither seems very likely. If we take the Duke's letters at their face value – and he was the most honest of men – then we must conclude that he never really wished to marry Angela and that he did not do so.

What is more possible is that the consideration, respect and affection shown by the Duke's sons were shown not because Miss Coutts was their father's widow, or even – solely – because she had been his very dear friend, but because she was – Miss Coutts. She had evidently got to know Lord Douro and his brother well and they had a warm regard for her. But there was more to it than this. By 1852, the year of the Duke's death, Angela had become a personage in her own right – someone who commanded the respect even of Wellington's sons. As a public figure, she was esteemed as much for her character and good works as for her wealth and position. As a private individual, though still outwardly the 'quiet and unpretending person' that Disraeli had observed in 1838, she had come to accept deference as natural and had grown accustomed to exercising her will. No one had encouraged her more in this than the Duke of Wellington, even though he had thwarted her desire to marry him.

With the Duke's younger son, Lord Charles Wellesley, and his wife Sophia her friendship seems to have been particularly close. 'I often think of you and grieve for you dear', wrote Sophia after the Duke's death. The following August, when Angela was about to leave for the continent, Lord Charles ended an affectionate letter: 'Now Good bye My dear Miss Coutts come back refreshed, but not a giant, for you are tall enough already.' And in September, after the first anniversary of the Duke's death, there is another sympathetic letter from Lady Charles:

> Truly dearest I have thought much of you, the recurrence of this period brings back so vividly the thoughts and feelings of the past, and I have often felt thankful for you that your well regulated mind & naturally happy disposition have by God's blessing enabled you to bear as you have done the trials of the past year.[58]

There was a shadow hanging over the Wellesleys – the progressive blindness of Lord Charles, for which they searched desperately for a cure all over Europe. There are several cheerful but poignant letters from Charles to Angela, written in pencil in a shaky, illegible hand. In one of them he jokes about her own unreadable signature, which had 'puzzled his secretary nearly to death'. In July 1858 Lord Douro writes that his brother is much worse: 'Pray go to S. Saye and make a little stay there. It is impossible to say that you will ever have another opportunity.'[59] Charles died later that year, aged fifty.

Angela's association with the Duke's family ended only with her own death. Douro and his wife were childless, but the Charles Wellesleys had five children of whom she was very fond. After Wellington's death she commissioned a picture from James Thorburn of the Duke with his grandchildren. She had at first wanted him at breakfast, but Douro told her firmly that this wouldn't do – the breakfast table was 'a terrible stumbling block'. It would be better to have him in the library reading his letters before breakfast and giving the covers to the children: 'You saw the scene at Walmer, do you not prefer the picture to be of that which you remember?'[60] The picture, a charming miniature on ivory, is now at Stratfield Saye. Of the four children shown, the youngest, Mary Angela, then aged three, was Angela's goddaughter. The elder boy, Henry, became the third Duke, and was one of the pall-bearers at Angela's funeral.

Eight

URANIA COTTAGE

> There is a lady in this town who from the window of her house has seen such as you going past at night, and has felt her heart bleed at the sight. She is what is called a great lady, but she has looked after you with compassion as being of her own sex and nature, and the thought of such fallen women has troubled her in her bed.
> She has resolved to open at her own expense a place of refuge near London for a small number of females, . . . and to make a HOME for them.[1]

Thus Charles Dickens, in his thousand-word 'Appeal to Fallen Women'. Written in the autumn of 1847, the 'Appeal' was a fervent plea to young prostitutes to exchange the certain prospect of 'long, long years of shame, want, crime and ruin' for the chance to 'begin life afresh and . . . win a good name and character'. It was given to selected girls to read in their prison cells, and, so the prison governor assured Dickens, affected them 'very heartily indeed'.[2] No doubt they were impressed by its melodramatic representation of their plight, and tempted by the hope it held out of their becoming 'the faithful wives of honest men'. They must, too, have recognised the sincerity of the anonymous writer who assured them that he wrote 'as if you were my sister' and who signed himself 'YOUR FRIEND'.

Prostitution, the 'Great Social Evil', was a particularly large blot on the country's moral escutcheon. Although Dr William Acton's famous book* did not appear until 1857, the subject had then been a cause for public concern for some fifteen years or more. In October 1843, for instance, *The Times* had called its readers' attention to 'women – young in years, old in sin and suffering – outcasts from society – ROTTING FROM FAMINE, FILTH AND DISEASE' in 'the richest city of God's earth'. Men should learn not to theorize but to act: 'God knows there is much room for action nowadays.'[3]

For Angela, more aware than many of the need for action, the evil

---

* *Prostitution, Considered in Its Moral, Social, and Sanitary Aspects.*

was one that it was impossible to ignore. Her house fronted on to Piccadilly. Night after night there were young girls soliciting on her very doorstep. For many of them the alternatives were stark: 'starvation or sin'.[4] What could be done? In spite of the outspokenness of *The Times* article, this was not a subject to be discussed or even mentioned in polite society. Nevertheless, by the spring of 1846 Angela had found a way of mentioning it to Charles Dickens. She had had an idea: she would build an 'asylum' for some of the very youngest of these girls, a place of refuge and reform where they could be weaned away from their old habits with the ultimate aim of starting a new life in the colonies.

A number of institutions already existed for the 'rescue' of 'fallen women'. The oldest was the Magdalen Hospital, founded in 1758. Robert Dingley, its chief founder, intended it to be not 'an House of Correction, but an happy Asylum', where 'the utmost Care and Delicacy, Humanity and Tenderness'[5] were shown. Whether this policy still prevailed in the 1840s is doubtful. But in any case, one of the Magdalen's worst features was that it made no provision for its inmates after their year's stay was up. They were often forced back on to the streets, ending up in jail or in the hated workhouse (there was not much to choose between the two). More recently-founded establishments included the London Female Penitentiary and others of that ilk, whose régimes tended to be as grim as their names. From the start, Miss Coutts's 'Home', as Dickens was to christen it, set out to be different.

Dickens entered into the project with enthusiasm. His own sympathy with these 'sad aspects of humanity' (he was never at a loss for a euphemism) had been strengthened by the experience, some years before, of serving on a coroner's jury at the inquest on a new-born baby, the child of an unmarried servant called Eliza Burgess. The jury had to decide whether Eliza was to be committed for trial for the minor crime of concealing the birth, or the major one of infanticide. Through Dickens's exertions, which were supported by the coroner, they found for the lesser offence. The 'poor desolate creature', wrote Dickens many years later '. . . dropped on her knees before us, with protestations that we were right – protestations among the most affecting that I have ever heard in my life'.[6]

He had introduced the 'Great Social Evil' into his novels, hoping to do 'great things' with Nancy, the prostitute in *Oliver Twist*. In fact, like many of his female characters, 'fallen' or otherwise, Nancy is something of a caricature, uttering cliché-ridden speeches and often behaving in a most unconvincing way. By contrast, Dickens's approach to the institution that Angela was proposing was down-to-earth and practical.

His first letter to her on the subject, dated May 26, 1846, brings out his compassionate but clear-sighted approach to these 'tarnished and battered images of God'. Though they were still in the very early planning stages, he was already clear in his mind about the philosophy that should underlie the whole venture. As he told Angela, any girl admitted to the asylum should have it explained to her that

> she has come there for *useful* repentance and reform, and because her past way of life has been dreadful in its nature and consequences, and full of affliction, misery, and despair to *herself*. Never mind society while she is at that pass. Society has used her ill and turned away from her, and she cannot be expected to take much heed of its rights or wrongs.

What the girls would be taught, he continued, 'would be grounded in religion, most unquestionably'. But it would be essential to have 'a system of training established, which, while it is steady and firm, is cheerful and hopeful'. Hope was to be fostered by holding out the prospect of becoming 'Virtuous Wives' with 'happy homes of their own' in a far-distant land; for emigration, it seemed, was the only answer for those who would relapse into their old ways if permitted to return to their former haunts. He thought the government might be able to assist by informing Angela 'into what distant parts of the World, women could be sent for marriage, with the greatest hope for their future families, and with the greatest service to the existing male population'.

'I do not know whether you would be disposed to entrust me with any share in the supervision and direction of the Institution,' writes Dickens modestly towards the end of this letter. 'But I need not say that I should enter on such a task with my whole heart and soul.' Ever practical, he then suggests that, before proceeding further, Angela will need to have 'all the results of previous experience . . . as regards scheme, plan, management, and expence', both in England and elsewhere. This he offers to obtain for her. He is going to Paris later in the year and will gather all the information he can from similar institutions there. He will then prepare a digest of this accumulated experience, British and foreign, in 'the plainest and clearest form'.

This admirable letter – it is some 2,000 words in length – ends on a eulogistic note that jars with what has gone before:

I have that deep sense, dear Miss Coutts, of the value of your confidence in such a matter, and of the pure, exalted, and generous motives by which you are impelled, that I feel a most earnest anxiety that such an effort as you contemplate on behalf of your Sex, should . . . , if undertaken at all, be undertaken to the lasting honor of your name and country . . .[7]

There is no reason to doubt his sincerity; yet such passages – and similar ones appear elsewhere in his letters to Angela – verge uneasily on the obsequious and cannot be explained entirely by his enthusiasm for the project in hand. Why should he adopt this tone with Miss Coutts, with whom he was now on terms of easy friendship? The answer would seem to lie partly in his ambivalent attitude towards women – which to some extent reflected the prevailing ethos – and partly in the character (or supposed character) of Angela herself.

As we have said, the women in Dickens's novels (particularly in the earlier ones) tend to be caricatures. The 'good' women, like David Copperfield's Agnes, are altogether too perfect. He himself, it is said, fully believed in his implausible creations, though aware with another part of his mind that real women were not like that. But he had known one real woman whose early death made it possible for him to idealise her for the rest of his life. This was his sister-in-law, Mary Hogarth. She came to live with Charles and Catherine shortly after their marriage and died suddenly, aged seventeen, in 1837. Dickens was heartbroken. Mary was 'the light and life of our happy circle', he wrote. 'I solemnly believe that so perfect a creature never breathed . . . She had not a fault.'[8]

In Angela Burdett Coutts we have another real woman who was almost too good to be true. That is how she has come down to us, and the image is a reflection of how she must have appeared to her contemporaries. From most of what has been written about her she emerges, like one of Dickens's paragons, as a strangely one-dimensional figure, all goodness, sweetness and light. Dickens did not regard her as beyond criticism; he was ready to tell her if he thought her wrong or mistaken. But she was in some degree Mary Hogarth's successor. She probably came nearer than any other woman he knew to representing the stereotype of virtuous womanhood that he depicted in his novels, a stereotype that was part of the Victorian myth about women. In Miss Coutts, myth and reality almost became one – or so it seemed. So it is, perhaps, not surprising that Dickens, when writing to (or of) her, sometimes got carried away and slipped unconsciously into the rhetoric usually reserved for his novels.

*

Angela did not immediately proceed with the projected 'Home' (or Asylum, as they at first called it). For one thing, she was fully occupied with her plans for St Stephen's; for another, Dickens, who was clearly anxious to be involved in planning and running the institution, went abroad in the summer of 1846 and did not return home until the following spring. In the meantime, they corresponded regularly about the new venture.

We cannot be sure that Angela shared from the beginning the overall approach that Dickens put forward in that first long letter. But the fact that this approach was the one largely adopted in the end is as much to her credit as it is to his. Certainly she saw the wisdom of Dickens's judgment on a number of practical matters. She agreed, for instance, that it would be unnecessary to build a house specially for the purpose, since they would be bound to find one suitable for adaptation. Later, he successfully discouraged her from choosing a locality where the houses had no gardens: 'Have you thought of that? The cultivation of little gardens, if they be no bigger than graves, is a great resource and a great reward . . . I earnestly hope you will be able to make it a part of your training.'[9]

One thing that worried Angela was the question of holding out marriage as a kind of bait to entice the girls into the Home. But she withdrew her objection when Dickens assured her that he had not intended making marriage 'the immediate end and object to be gained'; it was to be kept in view 'as the possible consequence of a sincere, true, practical repentance, and an altered life'.[10]

One wonders what Hannah Brown, up till then Angela's chief adviser on nearly all matters, made of this new collaboration with the now world-famous Mr Dickens. It has been suggested that she did not approve, perhaps regarding the subject as unsuitable for a young maiden lady (Angela was in her early thirties). There is no evidence of such disapproval. William Brown, Hannah's husband, became a member of the management committee of the Home and seems to have taken a fairly constant interest in it. And Hannah herself visited the house shortly after it had opened and must have reacted favourably, for Dickens found her report of it 'extremely cheering'.

On Dickens's advice, Angela consulted while he was away two men with wide experience of the problem that she was tackling. These were George Chesterton, governor of Coldbath Fields Prison in Clerkenwell, and Augustus Tracey, governor of the Westminster Bridewell Prison. Dickens knew both men well. He particularly admired Chesterton, and declared that he knew 'nothing of him but what is good'; indeed, Chesterton was universally respected for the way in which he had reformed Coldbath Fields since becoming governor in 1829.

Coldbath Fields, a huge mixed prison where most of London's prostitutes were sent for punishment, had certainly changed since the beginning of the century, when Sir Francis Burdett had campaigned against the scandalous conditions there. What Sir Francis thought of Chesterton's régime – if he knew of it – is not recorded. A firm believer in the treadmill and other forms of hard and totally unproductive labour, Chesterton enforced a tough discipline. In this he had the unqualified support of Charles Dickens – for it comes as something of a shock to realise that the tender-hearted Dickens, while sympathetic to young offenders and fallen women, believed strongly that hardened criminals should be subjected 'relentlessly' to 'some degraded kind of hard and irksome work, belonging only to gaols'.[11]

For the 'determined thief, swindler, or vagrant', whatever his background or personal circumstances, Dickens saw little hope. But the 'poor creatures' whom Miss Coutts wished to help were a very different case. Both Chesterton and Tracey, he assured her, were 'well acquainted with the good that is in the bottom of the hearts' of these girls; and his own optimism never wavered. He even disagreed with Chesterton on the question of excluding habitual drinkers from the Home. They mustn't assume, he argued, that there was 'no hope of drunkards', for drunkenness was 'well nigh inseparable' from such a miserable and degrading mode of existence.[12]

Angela appointed both Chesterton and Tracey to the management committee of Urania Cottage, and it was from their prisons that most of the first inmates came.

In May 1847, a year after he and Angela had first discussed the project, Dickens took Chesterton to see a house in Shepherd's Bush, about three miles out of town, that he thought would be suitable. It was, he reported to Angela, 'retired, but cheerful. There is a garden, and a little Lawn ... A stable would have to be changed into a wash-house, and I would decidedly fence the garden all round. It seems to me to want only that.' This was Urania Cottage. The following month it was taken, at sixty guineas a year, and he hoped that they would be able to open before the winter weather set in, 'while the garden is green and sunny'.[13]

That Urania Cottage did not, in fact, receive its first inmates until November was in no way due to lack of application on Dickens's part. He chafed at what seemed like unnecessary legal delays – her solicitor was 'so very tardy' – though he had to admit it was 'sound sense and justice' for Angela's position to be safeguarded. (In August she asked the Duke of Wellington's advice about a legal document, which could have been connected with Urania Cottage.) Dickens's task was not made any easier by the fact that he seemed fated never to find Angela at Stratton Street when he called. She spent part of the summer in Finchley, later going to Sandgate; and it seems doubtful whether they managed to see each other at all, though Dickens was anxious for Angela to meet the matron – whom Chesterton had found – before her appointment was confirmed.

Dickens himself was preoccupied that summer with more than Miss Coutts's Home for fallen women. Apart from writing *Dombey and Son*, he was involved in amateur dramatics. In July, his company of writers and artists gave two benefit performances of Jonson's *Every Man in His Humour*. For Dickens, as producer, manager and administrator, it was another outlet for his restless energy. By late August he was back at Coldbath Fields, interviewing potential candidates for Urania Cottage. 'If you would not dislike it,' he wrote to Angela,

> I should particularly like you – you can sit in the room perfectly unnoticed and unknown – to see, at Mr Chesterton's House of Correction, the young women who are coming from there, as they are, and in their prison dresses. You will feel so much more, afterwards, the change that, with God's leave, will be worked in them.[14]

Two months later he wrote again – evidently unaware that she was in France – urging her to 'come with me to Mr Chesterton's, where there is nothing to shock you but the sight of women in captivity'.[15] In fact, according to Chesterton, who mentions the Home in his book *Revelations of Prison Life*, Angela visited the prison only once. She was in no sense a field worker, and never pretended to be.

There is no doubt that Dickens was the guiding spirit behind the whole venture. He supervised the alterations to the house, dealt with the furniture and fittings, laid in all the linen and chose the dresses – 'as cheerful in appearance as they reasonably could be – at the same time very neat and modest';[16] he installed the superintendent, worked out a routine of daily activities, picked suitable texts for the living-room and bedrooms, and ordered books of instruction. He also wrote the 'Appeal to Fallen Women', sending a copy to Angela with his letter of October 28, in which he reported progress:

> I am in a state of great anxiety to talk to you about your 'Home' (that is the name I propose to give it) with which I have been very busy for some time, and which will be ready for the reception of its inmates, please God, on Saturday fortnight. I have a perfect confidence in your approving of the details, but it would be most interesting to me to talk them over with you.

His confidence was not misplaced, for it would seem that Angela, who did not return from abroad for another month, was content to leave most of the details to him. Some weeks earlier, he had written: 'I take it for granted that I have your authority to proceed with the fittings in all respects.'[17] However, to make absolutely sure that there should be no misunderstanding between them, he now re-stated the underlying purpose of the Home:

> The design is simply, as you and I agreed, to appeal to [the inmates] by means of affectionate kindness and trustfulness, – but firmly too. To improve them by education and example – establish habits of the most rigid order, punctuality, and neatness – but to make as great a variety in their daily lives as their daily lives will admit of – and to render them an innocently cheerful Family while they live together there. On the cheerfulness and kindness all our hopes rest.[18]

She must not, he added, 'see the house until it is quite ready'. Despite his 'great anxiety' to talk to her, he was obviously enjoying himself hugely.

His letter elicited an immediate reply from Angela. She was concerned among other things about the appointment of the chaplain. He must not be appointed until her return, she wrote. Dickens hastened to assure her that he had had no intention of concluding the matter in her absence. Then, concerned lest the wrong kind of religious instruction should ruin their whole design, he continued:

> I have great faith in the soundness of your opinions in reference to the religious instruction; knowing you to be full of that enlarged consideration for the special circumstances under which it is to be administered in this case ... I trust that those enlightenments to

> which you refer, are to be found in the *New* Testament? I am confident that harm is done to this class of minds by the injudicious use of the Old . . .

He was convinced that it would be wrong for the chaplain to interview the girls individually, as Angela had suggested:

> It would decidedly involve the risk of their refusing to come to us. The extraordinary monotony of the refuges and asylums now existing, and the almost insupportable extent to which they carry the words and forms of religion, is known to no order of people so well as to these women.

The girls needed no clergyman to impress on them 'the sinfulness and degradation of their lives'. And he was equally sure that their past lives should never be referred to, and that any such reference by the superintendent would be sufficient grounds for her dismissal.

The great point to be remembered was that 'these unfortunate creatures are to be *tempted* to virtue. They cannot be dragged, driven or frightened.' For these 'doomed women' had had no 'chance or choice . . . It would have been a social marvel and miracle if some of them had been anything else than what they are'. For this reason, it would be essential to find a chaplain who was 'not only a well-intentioned man, as I believe most clergymen would be, but one of the kindest, most considerate, most judicious, and least exacting of his order.'

In the event, the chaplain's duties appear to have been divided between the several clergymen whom Angela appointed to the management committee – none of whom, one suspects, fulfilled the conditions laid down by Dickens.

'I hope there is nothing whatever, in the business arrangement, which is not in working order', he writes towards the end of this marathon letter, the longest he ever sent her. And indeed, he seemed to have thought of everything. He was writing 'a little address' for the superintendent, Mrs Holdsworth, to read to each girl as she came in, and had had printed a schedule of 'domestic duties and their allotment'. Arrangements were being made for 'washing and dressing, and putting away of clothes, and everything of that kind . . . with a view to every chance and mischance to which we are exposed'. Bedtime was to be at the realistic hour of ten o'clock, to avoid 'the danger of shutting them up, with unoccupied minds, at preposterously early hours'.[19]

The stage was set for a most interesting experiment in social work. In the middle of November, while Angela was still in France, the first girls moved into the Home.

*

For a girl coming straight from Mr Chesterton's prison, Urania Cottage must indeed have been a haven. The simple comforts provided must have seemed like unbelievable luxuries, and the general atmosphere, after the grim discipline of Coldbath Fields, almost too good to be true. Of all the many little incidents recorded by Dickens, nothing is more touching than the reaction of the very first girl to be admitted, who 'cried very much when she saw her Bed'. Indeed, it says much for the powers of persuasion of Dickens and Chesterton – not to mention the fortitude of the girls concerned – that the first two inmates had stayed on voluntarily in Coldbath Fields for *three weeks*, because the Home was not ready to take them in. No wonder they were 'wonderfully happy and grateful' and had 'altered in appearance in a most extraordinary manner' when Dickens saw them a week or so later.[20]

Despite his insistence that the running of the Home should be based on affectionate kindness and cheerfulness, it must have been extremely difficult for the girls to adjust to its order and discipline, and to a way of life so completely different from what they had been used to. For some, it proved impossible. Inevitably it is these problem cases, brought to life by Dickens's vivid pen, that provide us with some of the most fascinating reading about Urania Cottage.

There was, for instance, Isabella Gordon, a persistent trouble-maker who, after being interviewed by the committee and told to go to her room, 'danced upstairs . . . holding her skirts like a lady at a ball'. She was soon dancing to a different tune, however, for the verdict was that she should be expelled. With half a crown for a night's lodging she was seen off the premises into a dark November evening, with everyone, including the staff, crying bitterly. Isabella herself, 'now that it had really come to this, cried, and hung down her head', and when Dickens passed her on the road afterwards she was 'going slowly away, and wiping her face with her shawl'. But though depressed by the whole affair, he was convinced they had done right, for 'it was impossible to relent, with any hope of doing good'.[21]

For young Sesina he had less sympathy. She was 'the pertest, vainest, . . . and most deceitful little minx in this town'. Ordered to her room for insolence on the night of Isabella's departure, she refused to get up the following morning. Dickens instructed the matron, Mrs Morson, to give the girl her own clothes and tell her she was to leave at once. If she was still there when he arrived, he would call the police 'and give her in custody for being there without our consent and making a disturbance'. His letter to Dr Brown continues:

> On receipt of this message she parleyed a little, and, after making a slight pretence of being ill, threw her nightcap to one end of the room and her nightgown to the other, and proceeded, very leisurely, to dress herself . . . Before she went, she told Mrs Morson 'that she know'd Miss Coutts's address, and would write her a good long letter, telling her what treatment was had there.' I passed her afterwards, walking in a jaunty way up Notting Hill, and refreshing herself with an occasional contemplation of the shop windows . . . I think she would corrupt a Nunnery in a fortnight.[22]

Of Mary Ann Stonnell's misdemeanours we have no details. All we know is that she left the Home after a few months and was soon back in prison, where she received a vist from Miss Coutts. This was, perhaps, the occasion that Chesterton remembered. Her visit drew from Mary Ann the following letter:

> I take the liberty of writing a few lines to thank you for the kindness you have shown to such an unworthy creature as I have been to leave such a good home and I thank you for taking the trouble you have to come and see me who am not worthy of such a kind benefactress I hope Madam that you will forgive me for I am very sorry for what I have done.[23]

'Stonnell, *in prison*,' commented Dickens, 'will always, I think, be tolerably good. Out of it, until – perhaps – after great suffering, I have no hope of her.'[24]

As for 'that very bad and false subject, Jemima Hiscock', she may well have caused Dickens to regret his optimism about drunkards. He had always mistrusted her, because she had 'made the most pious pretences of any [girl] in the place'. When she 'forced open the door of the little beer cellar with knives, and drank until she was dead drunk', making 'a very repulsive exhibition of herself', she was instantly expelled. Dickens was convinced she had had spirits smuggled in from outside, for 'no woman of that Jemima Hiscock's habits could get so madly intoxicated with that weak beer'.[25]

The staff sometimes caused as many headaches as the girls. The first matron, Mrs Holdsworth, always seemed to Dickens 'to have a secret idea that her charges [were] her natural enemies'. She also objected, 'with a face of most portentous woe and intensity', to being asked 'to get up on every alternate washing-day'. Dickens was exasperated. 'It is intolerable to be met with such mincing nonsense from those toiling and all-enduring dowagers,' he told Angela, urging her to keep Mrs Holdsworth and her deputy 'to their tether'.[26] Then there was the 'rather thorny and irritating' Mrs Furze, who seemed determined 'to serve as a sort of human rasp, or file, or nutmeg-grater, in respect of the general establishment'.[27] It was a 'prodigious comfort' to Dickens when Angela found a diplomatic way of getting rid of her. As for Miss Cunliffe, though he liked her at first, she turned out to be 'a woman of an atrocious temper' whose 'idea of hectoring and driving' the girls was 'the most ignorant and the most fatal that could be possibly entertained'.[28]

It was over a member of staff that Angela and Dickens had their only major disagreement – as far as we know – in connection with Urania Cottage. This was in December 1847, only a few weeks after the opening. Dickens had had some difficulty in finding a young assistant to the somewhat formidable Mrs Holdsworth; 'many ladies', as he told Angela, 'were afraid of it, and evidently shrank from the association'. But he was delighted with Mrs Fisher, whom he engaged while Angela was still abroad. She was

> a widow of six and twenty – very youthful looking – vitally interested in the project – of mild sweet manners – accustomed to teaching young people – and who has known great sorrow ... I wish you could have seen them at work, on the first day of this lady's engagement – with a pet canary of hers walking about the table, and the two girls deep in my account of the lesson books, and all the knowledge that was to be got out of them, as we were putting them away on the shelves.[29]

Alas! the admirable Mrs Fisher, with all her good qualities, her eminent suitability for the job and her evident enjoyment of it, had a defect, which in Angela's eyes was sufficient to outweigh all other considerations and to debar her from the position. She was dismissed; and her dismissal drew from Dickens possibly the nearest thing to a rebuke that he ever wrote to Angela:

> I cannot but say that I greatly regret her departure, and that the cause of it, is extremely painful to me, as it involves a point, on which,

though I have no sympathy whatever with her private opinions, I have a very strong feeling indeed – which is not yours. At the same time I have no doubt whatever, that she ought to have stated the fact of her being a Dissenter, to me, before she was engaged, and I should then, before engaging her, have most certainly stated it to you. With these few words, and with the fullest sense of your very kind and considerate manner of making this change, I leave it.[30]

Mrs Fisher left within a month, and was replaced by Mrs Graves, a lady 'of a delicate gentility' whose 'sombre aspect' matched her name.

However, on all other matters connected with the Home Angela was ready to accept Dickens's suggestions and recommendations. She herself visited Urania Cottage regularly when she was in town – Saturday was her usual day – but was content to leave the day-to-day running of its affairs to Dickens, who was by far the most active member of the management committee. He was at Shepherd's Bush at least twice a week in the early days, more often if there was an emergency. He paid the bills and the staff salaries (the matron received a pound a week, paid quarterly), submitting detailed accounts to Angela. He also interviewed prospective inmates – a most time-consuming process – and wrote up the girls' past histories in a 'case-book'. His policy was never to tell the superintendent or her deputy the full circumstances of any case; he disclosed only what he considered necessary in the way of a 'particular caution or piece of advice in reference to any Individual'.[31]

It was Dickens who suggested that his friend John Hullah should give the girls singing lessons. Hullah, whose group singing classes had become the rage since he began them at Kay-Shuttleworth's training school in Battersea in 1840, had in 1836 composed the music for a one-act opera, *The Village Coquettes*, for which Dickens wrote the libretto. Dickens had 'very great hopes of the beneficial influence' of singing, which seemed 'so much the kind of ingredient we want'.[32] He it was, too, who searched 'high and low' for a cheap second-hand piano – and some time later told Angela how a Mrs Chisholm* had asked him 'if it were true that the girls at Shepherd's Bush "had *Pianos*"'. 'I shall always regret [he added] that I didn't answer yes – each girl a grand, downstairs – and a cottage in her bedroom – besides a small guitar in the wash-house.'[33]

---

* Mrs Caroline Chisholm founded the Family Colonization Loan Society in 1850, to help poor families to emigrate to Australia.

To encourage good behaviour among the inmates, a 'Marks System' was introduced based on the theories of the penal reformer Alexander Maconochie, whom Dickens knew. Under such headings as truthfulness, industry, temper, punctuality, etc., the girls were awarded good marks, which were saved up to be converted into cash when they left the Home. Dickens at first proposed that the marks should be valued at 3*d.* for twenty, or 12*s.* 6*d.* a thousand; the amount 'earned' by each girl, he estimated, would be about half a crown a week, or five guineas a year. But this must have been thought too generous – it was, after all, not far off a housemaid's wages – for the price was later fixed at 6*s.* 6*d.* a thousand, which for an average score of 8,000 marks a year came to only £2 12*s.* 0*d.* Still, the girls appear to have taken the whole business very seriously and to have valued their marks, as the cautionary tale of 'Little Willis from the Ragged School' shows. This young woman was told that, 'unless she behaved very well, she should have no marks for a month'. Dickens described the sequel to Angela:

> I wish you could have seen her come in diplomatically to make terms with the establishment. 'O! Without her marks, she found she couldn't do her work agreeable to herself' – 'If you do it agreeable to us,' said I, 'that'll do.' – 'O! But,' she said, 'I could wish not to have my marks took away.' – 'Exactly so,' said I. 'That's quite right; and the one way to get them back again, is to do as well as you can.' – 'Ho! But if she didn't have 'em giv' up at once, she could wish fur to go.' – 'Very well,' said I. 'You shall go tomorrow morning.'[34]

In spite of all the failures, there was an encouraging rate of success. At the start Dickens had forecast that about half the inmates would be 'reclaimed'. And so it proved to be, according to the statistics he gave in an anonymous article called 'Home for Homeless Women' that appeared in his periodical *Household Words* in April 1853. During the five and a half years since the Home had been opened, fifty-seven girls* had been admitted, of whom ten were expelled and fourteen left of their own accord. The remaining thirty-three emigrated, and, though three 'relapsed on the passage out', the rest were all doing well and seven had married.

Seen in the context of the whole problem – there were 8,000

---

* The Home could accommodate about a dozen girls. Angela at one time considered taking over the house next door to enlarge the establishment, but this apparently proved impracticable.

prostitutes known to the police in London alone in 1850[35] – the achievement of Urania Cottage was a drop in the ocean. But the fact that thirty young women had started a new life away from the squalor and misery of the shadow side of London is of no small importance, and we can agree with George Chesterton that Miss Coutts 'had good cause to be satisfied with her charitable labours'.

Not all the inmates were prostitutes. Chesterton, writing of those in his prison, says that many of the 'frail and suffering creatures' were unwilling 'to accept so great a boon'; and he concludes that they shrank from 'the irksomeness of quiet domesticity, and the prospect of expatriation'.[36] No doubt this was partly true. But it was not, perhaps, so much quiet domesticity that they shrank from, as the prospect of entering domestic service. A housemaid's life was often one of unremitting drudgery, particularly if she was the only servant employed by a hard-up family with pretensions to gentility. 'Many strong girls', according to an article in the Journal of the Workhouse Visiting Society, had 'utterly lost their health before they were twenty years of age from the effect of the cruel labour exacted from them . . . the time necessary for food and rest being too often denied.'[37] No wonder that, with wages for a maid of all work at between £6 10s. and £10 *per annum* (plus allowances for tea, sugar and beer), many girls chose a 'life of shame' as the lesser of two evils.

In his *Household Words* article (which did not reveal the Home's identity or that of its foundress), Dickens mentions the categories of young women who had been admitted to Urania Cottage during the first five years. His list reads like a catalogue of female misery:

> Starving needlewomen of good character, poor needlewomen who have robbed their furnished lodgings, violent girls committed to prison for disturbances in ill-conducted workhouses, poor girls from Ragged Schools, destitute girls who have applied at Police Offices for relief, young women from the streets; young women of the same class taken from the prisons after undergoing punishment there as disorderly characters, or for shoplifting, or for thefts from the person: domestic servants who have been seduced, and two young women held to bail for attempting suicide.[38]

At Urania Cottage, perhaps the nearest place to a home, indeed, that they had ever known, these girls regained their health and strength. They had daily lessons, were trained in domestic skills, tended their little gardens, sang hymns with Mr Hullah, and were read improving literature. After a year or so they were ready to leave the firm but kindly discipline of the Home and to embark on the long, uncomfortable, hazardous voyage to South Africa or Australia. They travelled steerage (at £10 to £15 a passage), in twos and threes, clinging to each other and to their new-found respectability. The conditions on most emigrant ships were such that it was surprising so few of the girls 'relapsed'.

They did not arrive completely friendless at their far-off destinations. These were the places where Angela had founded her bishoprics; she knew the governors of the Cape and South Australia, as well as the church leaders, and could call on all of these to keep an eye on her protégées.

Each girl who did well represented a small miracle, and was a living tribute to the humane and realistic principles on which Urania Cottage was run. In November 1856, nine years almost to the day after it had received its first occupants, Dickens went to Shepherd's Bush for a committee meeting and found one of the old girls home on a visit from South Africa. 'It was very pleasant,' he reported to Angela,

> to see Louisa Cooper, nicely dressed and looking very well to do . . . She brought me for a present, the most hideous Ostrich's Egg ever laid – wrought all over with frightful devices, the most tasteful of which represents Queen Victoria (with her crown on) standing on the top of a Church receiving professions of affection from a British Seaman.[39]

'Such,' as Philip Collins has remarked, 'is the reward of the successful social worker.'[40]

For Angela, the reward in this particular case had come two years earlier, when Louisa Cooper had written to her on the eve of her departure for the Cape:

> As I am about to leave England I am most anxious that one of my last acts should be to thank you my kind Benefactress for all your goodness to me . . . I often think of your kind and gentle words and the thoughts of them has many times been a comfort to me and will be when I am in a far distant land . . . may every blessing be yours Dear and Honnored Lady and may all the young people at the Home prove deserving your bounty . . . I often think of Urania Cottage and the many happy hours I have spent there . . . with your permission I will take the liberty of writing on my arrival at the Cape may every blessing be yours' Honnored Madam is the prayer of your Humble Servant.[41]

Nine

GUARDIAN OF THE POOR

By the end of the 1840s, philanthropy had become for Angela almost a way of life. 'I am always looking about and considering what *next*,' she told her cousin Frances Harrowby in a letter of September 10, 1849, in which she reflected on the 'alarming' increase in the population of London and other towns. Much of the misery among the very poor, as she realised, was due to the exodus of people from the country to the already crowded towns, where they were forced to live in squalor and degradation. It was an evil that

> spreads far & wide & extends deep into the foundations of our social state. Whole parishes exist without that which ought to constitute a Parish – Church accommodation [and] instruction, a mixture of rich to support and carry on the various good works for the amelioration of the physical & moral condition of the poor.[1]

Instinctively, when thinking of the ideal community, she had in mind the village centred on church and squire, where everyone knew his place and there was 'a mixture of rich to ameliorate the physical and moral condition of the poor'. To her, as to the majority of her contemporaries, this was the natural order of things. In devoting herself to philanthropy she was both following a long aristocratic tradition and helping to sustain a social structure which, in the towns especially, had already broken down.

To say this, however, is not to undermine her achievements. Within the limits of her social vision (which was the one prevailing at the time), she tried to seek out the causes of poverty and to provide lasting solutions. She did not subscribe to the widely-held view that poverty was due to defects in personal character. While many Victorians rigidly classified the poor into the 'deserving' and the 'undeserving', Angela believed that the 'wheat and tares' (one of her favourite biblical images) grew side-by-side in every section of society.

Of all her projects, the 'model parish' in Westminster, built in memory of her father, was always dearest to her heart. It could be called the most typically 'Victorian' of her schemes, in that the Church was seen to be playing the central rôle in improving both the spiritual and material condition of the surrounding population. Over the years Angela's dream was realised and the church of St Stephen's became the centre of a parochial organisation that included schools, guilds, clubs, friendly societies, Bible classes, district visiting and missionary activities, and a soup kitchen providing about 10,000 hot dinners a year.

Among a mass of correspondence recently discovered in a chest in the tower of St Stephen's are many letters relating to the building of the church, schools and parsonage. Things did not always go smoothly. A recurring theme is the vexed question of heating and ventilation. Church, schools and vicarage were all heated (or supposed to be heated) by the same system, and in none of them did it work efficiently. In winter the church congregation froze while the school-children fainted in overheated classrooms; and in the Reverend William Tennant's newly-built house no fires could be lit because there were no chimneys. Even after fireplaces and chimneys had been installed Tennant was reporting that the rooms were full of smoke, and as late as 1861 more alterations had to be made.

The three schools — boys', girls' and infants' — were always full and received glowing reports from HM Inspectors. As early as September 1848 an Inspector was recommending that five St Stephen's boys should be apprenticed as pupil teachers; the following year he selected three girls of fifteen for the same purpose. 'The progress of the scholars is very satisfactory and reflects great credit on the industry and skill of the Teachers,' he wrote, adding that the boys were 'quiet and obedient apparently without undue severity on the part of the Teachers.'[2]

Much later, in the seventies, the name of Matthew Arnold appears in the school log books as an Inspector. He was, generally speaking, 'greatly pleased' with what he found, and in 1880 he singled out for praise the girls' grammar, geography and arithmetic.

Angela was determined that the girls in her school should be proficient in domestic subjects, since running a home on a limited budget was what most of them were destined to do. In the past, it had always been assumed that a girl would learn such things from her mother. But a woman who worked long hours in factory, shop or mill (or on piece-work in her own home) had little time or energy left to instruct her daughters. So needlework, cookery and household management were subjects the schools had to be prepared to teach.

Some years before Lord Ashburton launched his movement for the teaching of 'Common Things' in schools, a laundry had been installed in St Stephen's girls' school, each pupil bringing her bundle of clothes to be washed. It was 'a pleasant sight to see the row of little girls standing at their tubs', wrote William Tennant to Angela. This was a branch of education 'likely to give great satisfaction to all sensible parents'.[3]

Unfortunately, not all the parents were sensible – or so one of the schoolmistresses complained to Angela in March 1852:

> The School is composed chiefly of the children of small shop-keepers, and the better class of mechanics. . . . In many cases, they are as troublesome as the children themselves, and very seldom work with the Mistress in the Education of their Children . . . When I endeavoured to carry out your wishes at the Laundry, for example, I was asked if we intended to bring up the girls as Servants of all work.[4]

There was the rub! The small shop-keeper and the superior mechanic had their feet on the lowest rungs of the middle-class ladder, and by strenuous efforts their children might climb a little higher. Cleanliness might be next to godliness, but one achieved status in that status-conscious society by employing someone else to wash and clean and by doing as little as possible oneself.

It was not Angela's fault that these parents spurned her well-intentioned efforts on behalf of their daughters. The fact was that her school, though in one of the poorest parts of London, was not attended by the very poorest inhabitants. *They* went to the Ragged Schools, if they went anywhere. The artisans who sent their children to St Stephen's were poor, but they could usually afford to pay – only a matter of pence per week, but that was all that was needed to cover the running expenses. By the end of 1849 the boys' school was almost self-supporting, with receipts of £134 against outgoings of £140 for the year. Only the infants' school, wrote Tennant to Angela in 1851, 'though full of children will never I think produce an income sufficient to cover the expenses'.[5] Even so, the gap was never very wide: in 1857, for instance, the half-year's expenditure for all three schools amounted to £254, of which £233 was covered by fees.

School treats were paid for by Angela. Among items meticulously itemized in Tennant's neat hand are 'magic lantern and slides – £20 14s. 0d.' for the first 'school feast' on New Year's Day, 1849. In 1852, no less than 400 pounds of cake was purchased at a cost of £10, together with ten pounds of butter and thirty-two quarts of milk. In the summer of 1851, Angela paid for the whole school – 445 children and nine teachers – to visit the Great Exhibition. In later years there were outings to Richmond Park, and to Holly Lodge.

To the boys', girls' and infants' schools was added, in the early 1860s, an evening school offering 'instruction in all branches of ordinary learning, together with Mechanical Drawing for Engineering and Building Purposes'. This early experiment in evening classes for the poor had by the 1890s become the Westminster Technical Institute, with classes in a wide variety of subjects from Art, Bookkeeping and Botany through Carriage-building and Millinery to Physiography and Shorthand. There were, too, courses in the three Rs for members of the Metropolitan Police Force – with 'special attention given to the writing of police reports'.

*

Despite increasing prosperity in the country as a whole during the fifties, it was a decade of public unrest. The euphoria and complacency that had been engendered by the Great Exhibition were rudely shattered by the horrors of the Crimean War. In the ill-equipped, hungry and fever-ridden British army as many men died of cholera and other diseases as were killed by the enemy. Angela arranged, through Dickens, for a large 'hot closet' for drying clothes to be sent out to the military hospital in Scutari. It arrived, in parts, in April 1855, and was greatly appreciated by Florence Nightingale and the army medical staff.

At home, meanwhile, little effort was being made to tackle the problem of the urban slums. In an angry article in *Household Words*, Dickens castigated the government for its failure to improve the living conditions of working people. When Angela told him that she was 'in a maze' about it, he replied that working men

> never will save their children from the dreadful and unnatural mortality now prevalent among them (almost too murderous to be thought of), or save themselves from untimely sickness and death, until they have cheap pure water in unlimited quantity, wholesome air, constraint upon little landlords ... to keep their property decent under the heaviest penalties, efficient drainage, and such alterations in building acts as shall preserve open spaces.

The 'worthless Government' would never pay any attention to these things 'until they are made election questions and the working-people unite to express their determination to have them'.[6]

Dickens was not exaggerating. Living conditions for the poorest inhabitants of London had if anything worsened by the middle of the century, owing to the wholesale buying-up of land for 'improvements' such as new roads and railways stations. In Westminster alone, an estimated 12,000 people had to find new accommodation in run-down areas already bursting at the seams with humanity, and it was a similar story elsewhere. Those who had two rooms let out one of them; those with one sub-let parts of it. In one room six or more people might live, sleep, eat – and die, the corpse sometimes remaining unburied for up to a fortnight until enough money had been saved for a coffin. Many a slum landlord, on the other hand, could afford to live in a comfortable suburban house and drive his own carriage.

Sanitation was non-existent. Running water was an unheard-of luxury, the street an open sewer. Epidemics of cholera and typhus carried off thousands; thousands more suffered from chest complaints and diarrhoea. A number of government reports had led to the setting up of the General Board of Health in 1848, but the new body had no means of enforcing its recommendations. In the same year cholera broke out again, and by September 1849 over 6,500 had died in London. The enormity of the problem, disagreement about remedies, and above all lack of public will, made progress painfully slow. Efficient sanitation for all – and a corresponding drop in the death rate – had to wait until much later in the century.

One reason for the lack of public will was the widespread belief that the real evil was not poverty, but pauperism. It was this belief that had swept the Poor Law Amendment Bill through Parliament in 1834. William Cobbett called it the 'poor man robbery Bill'.[7] It abolished the expensive, inefficient and much-abused system of paying allowances – out-relief – from parish funds to 'able-bodied paupers' (that is, the unemployed), and set up in its place the hated union workhouses. Unions were groups of parishes run by elected Guardians of the Poor under the supervision of a Central Board of Commissioners. Henceforth, anyone applying to the Guardians for relief would be offered the workhouse, the purpose of which was to act as a deterrent. Fear of the workhouse, it was believed (and rightly), would make 'able-bodied paupers' think twice before entering it.

The new Poor Law, wrote Edwin Chadwick, Secretary of the Poor Law Commission, was like 'a cold bath – unpleasant in contemplation but invigorating in its effects'.[8] In fact, its effects were often extremely harsh – harsher than had been intended by the reformers. Many people died rather than enter the workhouse, and some died prematurely once they were there. Inhumane, even brutal, treatment was not uncommon, particularly of children, old people and unmarried mothers. Husbands were separated from wives, children from their parents; the sick and feeble-minded were often lumped together with the so-called 'able-bodied'. Sir Francis Burdett disliked the new law because it damaged the relations between rich and poor, master and workman. Angela is said to have hated it all her life.

Economically, the new Poor Law was a success: there was a dramatic reduction in the amount spent by parishes on poor relief. But no attempt was made to deal with the new problem of urban poverty. Private philanthropy, it had been assumed, would take over where the Guardians of the Poor left off; and in fact there was an impressive increase in voluntary charity during the first half of Victoria's reign. But the philanthropists faced a formidable task. They were trying to grapple with massive social problems whose causes they did not really understand. The myriad charitable organisations did undoubtedly do much to relieve distress; but the relief was often disappointingly short-lived, and indiscriminate giving tended to encourage the kind of dependence on charity that the new Poor Law had been designed to eradicate.

Angela had always recognised the perils of 'stop-gap' charity, though she was also quick to respond in emergencies. 'My object is not to make dependents on my bounty,'[9] she once wrote, and she always sought long-term solutions to the problems she was dealing with. Her approach was clear-sighted and unsentimental. Once her Westminster buildings were under way, she turned her attention to housing and sanitation. With Dickens as her enthusiastic adviser and collaborator, she planned to build some good, cheap flats for working people in the East End. And she also intended to tackle the thorny question of sanitation by setting up a 'pilot project' in Westminster.

Part of the trouble was that many people imagined that to install running water and drainage was prohibitively expensive. In fact, as Bishop Blomfield pointed out, if small landlords co-operated to provide these services the weekly cost would be less than the price of a glass of gin — $1\frac{3}{4}d$. Angela hoped to prove to a group of landlords in Westminster just how reasonably they could improve their property and the health of their tenants. In the autumn of 1852 she paid for a survey to be carried out by the General Board of Health of a block of houses owned by eighteen landlords, and obtained estimates for the installation of a water supply and efficient drainage. The next step was to approach the landlords and try to persuade them to have the work done. As an inducement, they were told that if the final bill exceeded the original estimate (£420 to improve 150 houses), Miss Coutts would pay the difference.

Unfortunately, the landlords proved to be less reasonable than Angela and Dickens had hoped. They not only balked at the proposals; they objected to the involvement of William Tennant, vicar of St Stephen's, in the negotiations. Clearly the kindly, well-meaning Mr Tennant was not the right person to deal with these decidedly tough customers, as Dickens realised. The 'Westminster proceedings', he told Angela in May 1853,

> are so entirely out of Mr Tennant's way, and he uses such a very little hammer instead of a mallet, that he must never be left to himself in it. It is like a pigeon taking the chair at a meeting of Bulldogs.[10]

A few days later the bulldogs showed their teeth by getting one of their number to write to Dicken's friend Mark Lemon, editor of *Punch*, 'complaining', as Dickens told Angela, 'of the proposed improvements, and of "being put by Miss Coutts under the parsons"'. Could she not give Mr Tennant a hint 'to be practical and business-like above all things, *and not on any account to talk to them as if they were children*'?[11]

But the matter had been dragging on for months, and it is clear that, parsons or no parsons, the landlords were determined to resist Angela's efforts to help them improve their property. By the end of May, over six months after the survey had been carried out, Dickens was debating with Dr Brown the advisability of Angela's offering to pay one-third of the cost. He felt very doubtful about it. As he pointed out, those who objected on grounds of cost would merely hold out to get a higher proportion, while those who objected on principle would very likely be unmoved. Shortly after this, Dickens, who had been overworking, fell ill and left for a holiday in Boulogne. There is no further mention of the plan in his later letters, and it can only be assumed that it had to be abandoned.

In Bethnal Green, meanwhile, Angela had run into trouble over her plan to build 'model dwellings' for the poor. The site she had chosen was in an area described as 'one of the worst centres of sickness and fever in the East End'. Nova Scotia Gardens, as this plague spot was inappropriately called, had been the scene of a notorious murder by body-snatchers in 1831. It is possible that Angela had heard about the place from Harriot St Albans, who, as it happened, had been paying a regular pension to the wife of the leader of the gang. The victim was a 14-year-old Italian boy, who was first drugged with laudanum and then suspended, head first, in a well. The next day his body was hawked round the London hospitals.

The most distinctive feature of Nova Scotia Gardens in 1850, however, was a huge stinking mound of rotting refuse (similar to the dust heaps in *Our Mutual Friend*), some fifty or sixty feet high. Barefooted children ran up and down it and played on the top, and old women scavenged at the bottom. When Angela bought the site in 1852 for £8,700, she apparently did not realise that the dust-contractor, who was now her tenant, was as anxious to see his rubbish mountain preserved as she was to remove it. He applied to the courts for time to find 'an alternative place to carry on his business', and was granted the maximum period – seven years. As always, Angela had been careful to consult a number of people before embarking on her plan, but in this instance she seems to have been badly advised. Work on the building of Columbia Square, as it was to be called, was inevitably delayed; but, never completely defeated, Angela had a temporary school and some lodging-houses put up in the interim.

Though Dickens was not involved in the detailed planning, Columbia Square was built on the principles laid down by him in a letter to Angela of April 18, 1852. He strongly urged what was then coming to be the accepted view: that large blocks of flats were preferable to 'the absurd and expensive separate walnut shells' that the poor habitually occupied. Not only did large houses have better foundations and thicker walls than small ones; they also enabled the tenants to enjoy the benefits of 'gas, water, drainage, and a variety of other humanising things which you *can't* give them so well in little houses'.[12] Such advantages, Dickens argued, compensated for the 'overgrown shadow' cast by a large block.

Work on Columbia Square was eventually started in 1859, and it was completed three years later. Its four solid rectangular blocks probably did cast overgrown shadows; but they were well provided with the amenities Dickens had described, with some to spare. Few 'model dwellings' at that time or later could boast a library, 'club-room' or play areas for the children. Twenty-five years later, Beatrice Webb, working as a voluntary rent-collector and manager of a dock-side block, found that the only meeting-places for the children were the lavatories: 'Boys and girls crowd on these landings – they are the only lighted places in the buildings – to gamble and flirt.'[13]

On the outside, Columbia Square presented a somewhat grim and Gothic appearance. It was five storeys high, with huge gaunt arches housing the staircases, and a roof-line jagged with the vaulted tops of dormer windows. Inside, a corridor ran the whole length of the block on each floor, with the apartments leading off it on either side. These were of one, two, or three rooms, let at weekly rents of between 2s. 6d. and 5s. Each floor had two washrooms, one for men and one for women, with hand-basins, sinks, baths and w.cs. The baths were a luxury not often accorded to working-class tenants, then or later. Even the admirable Octavia Hill, an energetic champion of the poor and sometimes called the grandmother of modern social work, once told a Parliamentary Committee on Housing: 'If you have water on every floor that is quite sufficient for working people.'*[14]

Angela's architect, H. A. Darbishire, had his own ideas about what working people needed in order to live healthily. Fresh air, he considered, was the main requirement. To ensure a plentiful supply in all weathers he installed permanently open windows at both ends of the corridors, positioned doors and windows in the flats so as to produce maximum draughts, and used doors 'that do not fit too close'. It was necessary to resort to these methods, he told a meeting of the Architectural Association, because 'a ventilator, once discovered, instantly becomes useless. It is pasted over, if small; and if large, is made the receptacle of every cast-off garment, from a bonnet to an old shoe'. The pasting over of walls was in any case discouraged, for they were neither plastered nor papered, but painted with two coats of distemper 'of a warm and cheerful tint'. There was thus 'no harbour for vermin' and the colour could be 'easily renewed at a trifling expense'.[15]

Whether the tenants of Columbia Square hankered after the insanitary fug of their separate walnut shells is not recorded; but the flats were always full occupied, with a waiting-list. About 180 families could be accommodated, or some seven or eight hundred people altogether.

Columbia Square was not the first block of 'model buildings' to be erected but it was probably the most luxurious. For this reason, it was later criticised as being of little long-term importance because 'it depended too exclusively on the eagerness of a wealthy woman to give

---

* In 1945, 89 per cent of families in Bethnal Green were without bathrooms (Rose, p. 263, *see* Bibliography).

away large sums of money'.[16] Certainly the blocks built by such bodies as the Metropolitan Association for Improving the Dwellings of the Industrious Classes were more spartan. What these societies hoped to do was to attract capital by operating on a semi-commercial basis with a modest return of five per cent on the money invested. Angela, who had lavished nearly £45,000 on Columbia Square, was content with a mere two-and-a-half per cent or less.

As it turned out, the five-per-centers were only partially successful: at a time when investors could obtain 20 to 30 per cent on their capital, only the most public-spirited were prepared to put money into working-class flats for such a low return. In 1862 the American banker George Peabody gave £150,000 (later increased to £500,000) to set up a trust 'to ameliorate the condition and augment the comforts of the poor'[17] of London. The money was used to build flats, and by the end of the century the Trust was housing 20,000 people. But, says a modern commentator, 'Peabody Buildings were to become a by-word all over London for their gloom.' And Charles Booth, in his *Survey of London Labour*, wrote of 'the great blocks of modern model dwellings, sacrificing all aesthetic and many human considerations'.[18]

Had she been prepared to make similar sacrifices, Angela might have housed twice as many people as she did at Columbia Square for the same money. Who is to say that she was wrong?

*

The Duke of Cambridge once called Angela 'an English institution'; but she was never an institution in the sense of being an impersonal doler-out of alms. Not only was she personally involved in all the major schemes she undertook – schemes which made her name a household word throughout the country – but, for nearly seventy years, she dispensed charity to vast numbers of individuals in every kind of personal distress. It is impossible to estimate numbers, but she must have come to the aid of thousands, from impoverished parsons to out-of-work artisans, from children orphaned by disaster or disease to a young girl drugged and raped by a 'surgeon'. In some cases the initial appeal came from friends or relatives; but many wrote personally to the lady of Stratton Street, often as a last resort to save themselves from the workhouse or the bailiffs.

Sometimes disaster would strike a whole group of workers, like the Spitalfields hand-loom weavers, thrown out of work by a treaty of 1860 which brought a flood of French silks on to the market. Supported by Angela, the East End Weavers' Association helped in finding alternative employment; some weavers were set up in small shops, others encouraged to emigrate to Australia or Canada. At about the same time, Angela started a 'sewing school' in Brown's Lane, Spitalfields, which as well as providing regular work for destitute seamstresses and casual employment for their menfolk, became a centre for welfare services throughout the district. From here food and wine were distributed to the starving, blankets and other necessities loaned to expectant mothers, and relief given to elderly couples who had sold all their household treasures to pay the rent. Young girls starting out in service, and boys embarking on a career in the merchant navy, were provided with outfits made on the premises.

Many families were hardest hit in the winter, when expenses were heavy and work often non-existent. Particularly severe weather, like that of the 1860/61 winter when there were five weeks of continuous heavy frost, could be disastrous. The records show that during this period the number of paupers in the metropolis rose from an average of about 96,750 to well over 135,000. Facilities provided under the Poor Law were adequate, reported a Select Committee, but not everyone wanted to use them. It was the old story: so great was the reluctance to enter the workhouse that, according to the chairman of the Bethnal Green Board of Guardians, many would have died of starvation had they not been relieved by private charity. Among those who turned to Angela were the tanners of Bermondsey; she gave them money to save their homes and sent an adviser to help them sort out their relief applications.

Even for a skilled worker in regular employment, the prospect of real hardship was never far away. In 1856 Angela published a book about her prizes for the teaching of 'Common Things' (to be discussed below), which contains a fascinating Appendix giving the weekly budgets of a number of working-class families in London. These figures were intended to show how, with prudent budgeting, it was possible for the poor to live within their means. What strikes the modern reader is the paucity of those means and the precarious balance that existed between sufficiency and want.

John Taylor, a bricklayer, earned 30s. a week but was out of work for at least three months of the year. He lived with his wife and two children in one room in 20 Grange Street, off the Hampstead Road, for which he paid 3s. 6d. a week. They spent about 4s. on meat, slightly less on bread and flour; candles and soap came to $9\frac{1}{2}d.$, 'starch, blue and soda $3d.$, beer $1s.$ $8\frac{1}{2}d.$ (twice as much in summer as winter), . . . schooling $3d.$' Clothes were bought 'as we can', and in summer they tried to save for the lean winter months.

A carpenter earning 30–35$s.$ a week was slightly better off; he could afford an excursion or two by rail for himself, his wife and three children. His lodgings cost him $5s.$ $3d.$; schooling was $6d.$ The family had 9lb of brisket of beef at $5d.$ a pound each week. But John Caughlin, a labourer, could spare only $2s.$ $6d.$ or less for meat out of his weekly wage of just under £1. He couldn't afford cheese, but sometimes got cheap fish from the market – 'a very large plaice for $4d.$, or two for $6d.$, or a piece of cod at $2d.$ a pound, which saves meat and butter'.[19]

Slightly higher up the social scale, a London clerk might earn £100 a year (on which he would pay income tax of between £4 and £5). An interesting comparison is provided (unwittingly) by Angela's friend Lady St Helier, who wrote that a debutante 'coming out' in the sixties could expect to receive about £100 a year as an allowance from her father. 'Nothing could exceed the simplicity and economy practised by the young ladies of my time', she assures us, adding that the £100 did not pay for Court dresses, which were provided by the young lady's parents.[20]

One economy that the poor were obliged to practise was in the consumption of water. In some streets this essential commodity might be available from a stand-pipe turned on for half an hour a day; in others, from a communal pump. Often it was polluted and helped to spread disease. Until such time as pure water could be piped to every house, drinking fountains were a useful source of supply; Angela built a number in London and elsewhere, also supporting the Metropolitan Drinking Fountain and Cattle Trough Association. Two of her fountains are now well-known landmarks, one in Victoria Park, Bethnal Green, the other in Edinburgh. The Victoria Fountain cost over £5,000 and was inaugurated with great ceremony in June 1862. Henry Darbishire had on this occasion excelled himself to produce an extraordinarily ornate octagonal structure incorporating Gothic arches, white marble cherubs, and a roof that has been described as a 'cross between something from a French château . . . and the onion cupolas of Central Europe'.[21] The red granite drinking trough and fountain on the corner of George IV Bridge and Candlemaker Row in Edinburgh was built in 1872 in memory of 'Greyfriars Bobby', a small dog that lingered near the grave of its master in Greyfriars churchyard for fourteen years. On a column on top of the fountain sits the bronze figure of Bobby; an inscription in English and Greek tells his story.

In spite of efforts to sweeten London's water supply, cholera struck again in the summer of 1867. A list of the provisions distributed during one week in August on Angela's behalf gives an idea of her involvement in the relief operations: 500 pounds of rice, 250 pounds of arrowroot, plus smaller quantities of sago, tapioca and oatmeal; 20 gallons of beef tea, 30 pounds of blackcurrant jelly, 80 quarts of milk a day from her own farms, 25 gallons of brandy and 50 gallons of port. All this was in addition to clothing, bedding, and 1,850 meal tickets to the value of a shilling each. Angela added five nurses to the three already working in the area, and a doctor, two sanitary inspectors, and four men to distribute the vast quantities of disinfectant also supplied by her.

On several occasions Angela was asked to stand for election as a Guardian of the Poor in Bethnal Green, but she declined, saying that she lived too far away. Quite likely she had no wish to be involved in the administration of the hated Poor Law. But in any case, as *Punch* pointed out, what need was there for an election when Miss Coutts had 'long been the Guardian of the Poor of all London'?

*

Guardian of the Poor she may have been; but she was no champion of her own sex. According to Charles Osborne, she did not have a particularly high opinion of women generally. She certainly seemed to prefer the company of men, perhaps finding women dull by comparison. But what helped to make women dull was the circumscribed lives they led. Angela was not interested in the movement for higher education for women. She was in many ways very conventional, for all her forays into the masculine worlds of banking, science, public health, slum clearance and, later, wholesale food distribution. 'She showed how a capable woman could transact all the different affairs of life with as great ability as a man,' wrote Lady St Helier, but 'she was in opposition to all the later developments of the women's question.'[22]

In part, this attitude sprang from her belief in the immutability of the existing social order. 'To whatever class a person may belong,' she once wrote, 'an industrious discharge of the duties of that position in life is a social and religious obligation.'[23] Thus, in encouraging the teaching of domestic subjects in schools she had in mind something more than the practical advantages to working-class girls, as she made clear to the

Reverend Henry Baber, Chaplain of Whitelands Training College, where she instituted a system of prizes for 'Common Things' in 1854. The great end of such training, she told Mr Baber, was 'to render both pupil-teachers and children useful and happy in their respective stations'.[24]

In this she was only echoing the view of Kay-Shuttleworth and of nearly everyone else at that time who was concerned with educating 'the labouring poor'. All agreed that the purpose of such education was, in Kay-Shuttleworth's words,

> to rear the population in obedience to the laws, in submission to their superiors, and to fit them to strengthen the institutions of their country by their domestic virtues, their sobriety, their industry and forethought.[25]

Moral training, above all, was what was needed. And Angela was convinced that training in 'Common Things' produced 'more moral qualities than many other pursuits'.[26]

In 1856 she published the results of her Whitelands experiment in a little book, *A Summary Account of Prizes for Common Things . . .* , including in it her letter to Baber (which had been edited and revised by Dickens), her address to the students at the first prize-giving, and selections from the girls' prize-winning essays. The Appendix contained, besides the budgets of working-class families mentioned earlier, hints on housekeeping, cheap cookery, first-aid and care of clothes, many of which had been supplied by Hannah Brown.

The book was a modest success. An enlarged edition came out a year later, and another in 1860. *The Times*, devoting a leading article to 'Common Things', congratulated Angela on her enterprise. She would earn the country's gratitude, it said, if she succeeded in fostering a better understanding of household economy among the lower classes. But it thought the essays themselves too full of moral platitudes – a fair comment, when one considers a typical sample: 'How beautiful is the character of the devout and humble poor! What pleasure it is to help such forward in their path!'

Dickens, too, while welcoming the book, was unimpressed with the essays, particularly those that attempted to answer the question: 'How do you teach that the possession or want of self-respect is betokened by dress, and that moral habits are influenced by dress?' He found them 'not natural – disagreeably like one another – and, in short, just as affected as they claim to be unaffected'. When Angela protested, he stuck to his guns. To him, 'a love of colour and brightness' was 'a portion of a generous and fine nature'. He would not 'strike this natural common thing' out of the heart of a girl who was going to be a poor man's wife. The evil was in the abuse, not in the use, he insisted.[27]

It was not the first time they had disagreed about bright colours in dress. Some months earlier, Angela had sent him a swatch of dull cotton material called derry which she proposed using for overalls at Urania Cottage. His letter of protest has become famous, and bears repeating:

> I return Derry. I have no doubt it's a capital article, but it's a mortal dull color. Color these people always want, and color (as allied to fancy), I would always give them. In these cast-iron and mechanical days, I think even such a garnish to the dish of their monotonous and hard lives, of unspeakable importance . . . Derry might just as well break out into a stripe, or put forth a bud, or even burst into a full blown flower. Who is Derry that he is to make quakers of us all, whether we will or no![28]

Derry's great virtue, of course, was cheapness: $3\frac{3}{4}d.$ a yard, to be precise. Very likely it could not be had with a bud or a flower, or even a stripe; assuredly it was not available in the gingham-like checks so beloved by the ladies of the day from Queen Victoria downwards. The Duke of Wellington had admired these colourful checks: in an envelope marked 'Duke of Wellington's favourite Poplins' Angela kept a collection of little swatches of material in combinations of pinks, golds and mauves. As different from Derry as a soufflé from a suet pudding, they were at least twelve times as dear.

Angela herself loved beautiful clothes, but saw it as a duty to discourage a similar love in the lower classes. To her cause she enlisted the support of the two prison governors, Chesterton and Tracey. 'I beg you will not hesitate to employ my name,' wrote Chesterton, 'in confirmation of the undoubted fact, that a love of dress is the cause of the ruin of a vast number of young women, in humble circumstances especially.'[29] He had a point, of course: how could a young servant on her miserable wages afford to buy pretty clothes? Stealing from her employer, or prostitution, were strong temptations if she hankered after the finery of her 'superiors'.

The Recorder of Hull, another ally, went further. It was 'almost impossible,' he declared, '. . . to get, or retain, a respectable, modest and trust-worthy female servant' – and the reasons were not hard to find:

Young women in that class of life are monstrously over-educated for their stations and callings; ... their minds are distempered and inflated by a smattering of knowledge and accomplishments totally unfitted for them, disturbing all their notions of dutiful, respectable and happy subordination, and giving them a disgust for the plain paths of duty.[30]

A strange passage to quote, as Angela did, to an audience of young women who would soon be engaged in teaching working-class girls! No doubt it was intended as a warning of the dire consequences of filling their pupils' heads with ideas 'above their stations'. In the same year, 1859, that she quoted this letter in her Whitelands speech, Angela was asked by a charitable association in the North to donate prizes for a competition on domestic subjects that was being held among factory girls. In five pages of tortuous prose she replied that she greatly doubted whether public competitions and examinations had any beneficial effect, 'physically or morally', on the character of women 'in any condition of life'. Examinations for schoolmistresses were a necessary evil, but in other cases the publicity and excitement involved, coupled with the strain of study, were likely to be harmful to 'the bodily health and mental Constitution of the female Working Classes'. Nor did such activities make for happiness at home,

> for I cannot bring myself to think it is a comfortable thing for a Man to come home and find his Wife Daughters etc absorbed in the same anxieties and excitements as himself, especially if he be of a studious nature and unable to keep the house together himself. It may be said such pursuits would produce an active home life and strengthen family affections, but it is a question whether this is the usual result of intellectual exertion in other Classes.[31]

Much of this would have been endorsed by many intelligent, even intellectual women, though others were already working towards the revolution in women's education that would come later in the century. 'Be good, sweet maid, and let who will be clever,' wrote Kingsley; and Tennyson's Princess Ida abandoned her ideal of freedom through education, realising it is better to be 'Not learned, save in gracious household ways.'[32] These sentiments were widely subscribed to by members of both sexes. Angela, whose own 'intellectual exertion' was not inconsiderable and who counted some of the greatest minds of the day among her teachers, would not have disagreed.

Ten

DOMESTIC MATTERS

Little is known about Angela's relations with her sisters. But what evidence there is suggests that she was closer to her Stuart cousins – Frances, Countess of Harrowby, and Lord Dudley Coutts Stuart – than to her immediate family. She apparently bore Dudley no grudge for his part in the Bacon affair, recognising that in this, as in other matters, he was prompted by the highest motives. Though many regarded Dudley's preoccupation with the Polish cause as quixotic, he was universally admired for his 'gentle yet noble character, his refined intelligence and generous public life, expressed so perfectly in his chivalrous face'.[1]

Dudley died in Stockholm in November 1854 while on a mission to the King of Sweden on behalf of the Poles; his sister Frances died five years later. But Lord Harrowby, Frances's husband, survived his wife for many years and was always a true friend to Angela. It was to Harrowby that Angela unburdened herself when she heard the news of Dudley's death:

> Poor dear Frances – How keenly she must be suffering. I do not write to her yet as I am sure she will not doubt my earnest sympathy and she knows I should feel myself much grieved for Dudley was always kind and generous in his feelings towards me – from him, Fan and yourself I have always experienced kindness when I met with little from other relations who had known me or might have known me better than yourselves. I must not take up more of your time but this affliction has opened up the memory of many old sorrows . . .[2]

The relations who 'might have known me better' can only have been her sisters, whose behaviour at the time of her inheritance had so upset her. Being closest to her, they had hurt her most, and after seventeen years the wounds had still not healed.

Further proof of the strength of her feelings on this point is provided by a letter to her from Charles Douro, 2nd Duke of Wellington, written at about the same time. Dudley's death, she had told Douro, reminded her of circumstances she could not forgive. In reply, Douro confessed that he himself harboured resentment (against whom, and for what reason, he did not say), much as he would like to extinguish it: 'It is uncomfortable; it is inconvenient; it is unsatisfactory for rarely gratified.' Humble people, he had noticed, 'in their quiet way are the most resentful though they would not for the world be revenged'.³ He was writing against himself, he added; but he could well have been

Dudley, 2nd Earl of Harrowby, whom Angela referred to as 'ever my best and truest friend', by George Richmond

writing of Angela, whose own sense of injury clashed with her notions of Christian humility and forgiveness.

Angela had been generous to her sisters. But when the youngest in the family has unlimited wealth, sets herself up in an independent establishment, and is regarded by the world as a 'distinct and distinguished personage', she is bound to incur the hostility of the others. As Lord Harrowby himself had written with insight when he had first met 'the heiress' at Lady Burdett's house in December 1837,

'What a strange position, & how much it must disturb . . . the natural relation of the sisters.'

Dickens's letters to Angela contain no mention of her sisters, beyond an expression of sympathy on the death of Sophia, the eldest, in December 1849. But there are a few scattered references in the Duke of Wellington's letters which give the impression that Angela was the person the others automatically turned to when they wanted anything done. 'Your sisters,' sighed the Duke on one occasion, 'are awkward persons to deal with!'[4]

Strangely enough it was Susan, who had complained bitterly of Angela's 'unkindness' in refusing to get her husband, John Trevanion, out of debt, who was to become closest to Angela in later years. Trevanion died in 1840, but Susan lived on until 1886. Joanna, the third sister, died unmarried in 1862. Clara, the fourth sister, remained single until 1850, when she surprised the family by marrying an elderly clergyman, James Money, who had numerous offspring by his first wife. Two and a half years later, on September 18, 1852, Clara Money gave birth to a son, Francis.

Francis Burdett Thomas Money, known as Frank, was a special baby for a number of reasons, not the least of which was the age of his mother: Clara was forty-six. He was the only descendant in that generation of his illustrious grandfather, Sir Francis. And he was Angela's heir. Provided she did not marry and herself produce a son, her half-interest in the bank and all the other property would one day pass to Frank Money.

In later years Frank would become a source of anxiety and distress to his Aunt Angela. Bitter quarrels would once more raise the spectre of the 'painful experiences of early life', and eventually Angela and her sister Clara would become completely estranged. But for the time being Angela was delighted with her nephew, whose birth took place four days after the death of the Duke of Wellington. Her friends wrote to congratulate her, happy that she had a new interest to take her mind off her loss. She was a doting aunt. Dickens teased her about it: 'I think that must be all a mistake about that Suffolk baby your nephew,' he wrote, 'because (it is a remarkable fact) we have in this house the only baby worth mentioning'[5] – his ninth and last child, Edward, known as Plorn. The many subsequent references in his letters to the rivalry between the 'Suffolk baby' and the 'baby who defies competition' are an indication of the feelings of pride and pleasure that young Frank aroused in his aunt.

Domestic Matters

Unfortunately, the same could not have been said of another young relative. Amy, youngest of the ten children of William Jones Burdett, Sir Francis's brother, was Angela's cousin and god-daughter. Her father, as a younger son with a large family, may well have cast covetous glances in the direction of his niece's fortune; but of that we know nothing. He had died in 1840. His eldest son, Francis, who was about Angela's age, stood to inherit the baronetcy if, as seemed likely, Angela's brother Robert died without issue.

Angela took a well-meaning but perhaps over-zealous interest in her uncle's large family. In her privileged position, and with her strong family feeling and reverence for her father's memory, she seems to have felt a kind of general responsibility towards the Burdett clan. Amy, born in 1836, may have been a favourite with her godmother; at any rate Angela took a particular interest in her and offered to pay for her education. But by 1848, when Amy was twelve, a tussle had developed between her mother and godmother. Mrs Burdett was going abroad and wanted to take Amy with her. Angela wanted Amy to stay in England with *her*.

As usual, she turned to the Duke of Wellington for advice. 'I cannot discover . . . any ground on which you can detain Miss Burdett from her parent,' the Duke told her. She had 'no power of preventing the parent from taking her child out of the Kingdom.' Nor would it be right, he cautioned, for Angela to speak to Amy about the matter without Mrs Burdett's knowledge or consent. All she could do was put to the mother the reasons for wishing to keep the daughter, 'and in what respect you think that such detention would be an advantage to the young lady!'[6]

Perhaps Angela succeeded in persuading Mrs Burdett, for she did pay for Amy to go to school in England, either then or later. In the spring of 1852, when Amy was sixteen, she ran away from school and made her way to Belgium, where she met a young Irishman called Richard Guinness Hill; they were married that August. Amy allowed a year to go by and then wrote to her godmother to beg forgiveness: 'Though I must ever regret & lament the manner in which I left you, still I can only be too thankful that Fate brought me to Belgium where I met my dear husband.'[7] Will Angela allow her to bring her dear husband to be introduced?

Four drafts of a reply in Angela's handwriting indicate that she would allow nothing of the kind. There is no way of telling which one she finally sent, but the intent is clear. Amy had addressed her as 'My dear Angela' (they were, after all, cousins); each of the drafts begins

'Dear Mrs Hill'. Amy had pleaded her youth in mitigation; she was old enough, retorted Angela, to have known what she was doing. 'The whole affair was at the time & remains perfectly incomprehensible to me,'[8] she wrote. She was glad to hear that Amy's eldest brother approved of the marriage, but she declined to see either Amy or her husband.

A harsh reaction – but one that has to be seen in the light of Angela's situation. 'You will think me very suspicious but I am taught to be so from experience,'[9] she once wrote to Dudley Stuart about a request for money she had received. It was not only in matters of charity that she had learned to be wary. In her relationships with others she was often cautious and mistrustful. For all the confidence that she had acquired, she could never be absolutely sure that it was herself and not her money that people were interested in. 'You, like me, are supposed to be made of Gold,' the Duke of Wellington had written, 'and everybody supposes that it is only necessary to touch you to partake of the Prize.'[10] Angela shrank from the touch of people who might take advantage of her. In doing so, she may well have repulsed those who would have shown her genuine affection.

*

If Angela watched over the Burdetts like a matriarch, she was equally concerned about the reputation and fortunes of her grandfather's bank. And just as her interference was sometimes disliked by the family, so her intervention in bank affairs frequently disconcerted the partners. In 1846, as we have seen, she clashed head-on with Edward Marjoribanks, the senior partner, over the clerks' salaries and the appointment of a new partner. By January 1848 they were at loggerheads again. There had been serious disagreements among the partners, and Angela longed to sort things out. Her own exclusion from bank affairs, she was convinced, was as detrimental to the bank as it was to herself.

Once again she consulted the Duke of Wellington, sending him a letter to Marjoribanks that she had drafted. It was, he replied, 'unanswerable'. It clearly explained her position in the House, and the necessity for her to have 'more knowledge of and controul over its proceedings'. It was 'likewise very forcible', continued the Duke, lapsing into Angelic long-windedness,

> on the subject of the Necessity of keeping concealed from the Publick the differences of opinion and disputes among the partners, which on account of their remaining undecided, on account of the exclusion of

Miss Coutts from any share in the decisions, must lead to delay in Business and eventual loss and Injury.

Marjoribanks, it appeared, had been making all the decisions without consulting the other partners. Angela's letter, the Duke thought, 'admirably brought out' that this state of affairs was caused by

> the exclusion from all Influence of *the Person* who has the largest amount of Interest in the due settlement of every Question, and who has been repeatedly acknowledged by all to be perfectly capable, and sufficiently studious and diligent to acquire a knowledge of every Question brought before her, so as to be able to form a correct Judgement upon the same![11]

As before, the Duke was encouraging her in a line of action that was not really defensible under the terms of the Duchess of St Albans' will. To a woman of Angela's ability and determination it was of course extremely irksome to be denied any part in the business built up by her grandfather. Coutts & Co. was, after all, essentially a family firm, and there was no one in it to represent the family interest except herself. Two of the senior partners, Edward Marjoribanks and Sir Edmund Antrobus, had brought sons into the firm; the third, William Coulthurst, would bring in a nephew in 1857. One day, it was assumed, young Frank Money would become a partner. Meanwhile, understandable as Angela's efforts were to be given a voice in bank affairs, she herself had no real right to such a voice.

She never gave up, however, and over some things she got her way – mainly, one suspects, because she was prepared to plough back considerable sums from her share of the profits into the business. Between 1840 and 1873, for instance, she is reported to have spent over £53,000 on improvements to the premises in the Strand. It was at her suggestion – and at her expense – that a dining-room and library were provided for the clerks, together with facilities 'for their convenience and general comfort'. In August 1863 she visited the Strand to discuss these arrangements and to go over the new offices with William Coulthurst. The visit, reported Coulthurst to Edward Marjoribanks Jr, was a great success. Miss Coutts had 'minutely inspected every part [of the new offices] and declared herself *perfectly delighted*'. As for the arrangements for the clerks, these

> gave her the greatest satisfaction as it was a subject she had long had at heart. The carrying out of the arrangement she wished to leave to

us as we thought best and she would like to be informed from time to time & would assist in anything she could.[12]

'Miss C,' replied Marjoribanks,

as she says herself, has her peculiarities, but the readiness she has shown for converting old chambers to so good a purpose I am confident would never have been done by those who went before her.[13]

Not until 1865 did Angela succeed in having a descendant of Thomas Coutts accepted as a partner in the bank. This was Henry Ryder, afterwards fourth Earl of Harrowby, the son of her cousin Frances. It was a plan that she had had 'many years at heart', she told Henry in a letter of congratulation. It must indeed have been gratifying to have a representative of her family in the bank at last after nearly thirty years of dealing with the partners on her own, even though she was now on better terms with them.

Henry Ryder became her chief contact and confidant at the bank. She bombarded him with lengthy and illegible letters. Once a week, when she was in town, Henry drove from the Strand to Stratton Street to have tea with her and tell her all the news. He was quite a bit younger than his formidable cousin and always remained somewhat in awe of her. As for Angela, she never accepted that she was anything less than 'head of the House'. 'The interests and prosperity of my Grandfather's House (confided to me for many years now) have been so very dear to me as a matter of feeling,'[14] she told General Knollys, the Prince of Wales's Comptroller, when the Prince appointed Coutts to be his bankers in 1862. For her, the bank was an extension of the family. Indeed, at times it seemed almost to take the place of family.

*

It is hard to think of Angela as a maternal woman. She did not, as far as we know, long for children of her own. Concerned all her life for the welfare of the young, she was probably, like many childless women, fond of individual children in small doses. She was attached to the Duke of Wellington's grandchildren, keeping an eye on them while their parents, Lord and Lady Charles Wellesley, were abroad in the summer of 1854. 'Poor little creatures, how happy they must have been to see you,' wrote Sophia Wellesley, thanking Angela for her 'delightful account of my darlings'.[15]

Another youngster in whom she took a great interest was Charley

Dickens. She was not, as has sometimes been claimed, his godmother. But she was the good fairy who sent him each year a magnificent Twelfth Cake for his birthday, and who took him for drives to Hampstead. In September 1845 she offered to pay for his schooling. Dickens gratefully accepted. He and his wife, Kate, were worried by the 'strange kind of *fading*' that came over Charley sometimes, and were loth to send him away to boarding-school at the age of nine. He went instead to King's College School, London, but his career there was cut short by scarlet fever. When he recovered he returned to the small private school he had attended previously, and Angela paid the fees.

The public school she had originally had in mind for Charley was Marlborough, but in the end he went to Eton, which was the suggestion of his schoolmaster. Angela approved, but Dickens thought Harrow 'a better school for a boy who has to live in after years by his own exertions'.[16] Future events perhaps proved him right, though Charley's bankruptcy at the age of thirty-one could not be laid entirely at the door of the easy-going Eton system (the headmaster in his day was the humane and charming Dr Hawtrey). In fact, Charley did well at Eton, earning a 'most brilliant' report during his first term; but his abilities were not stretched there and he lacked perseverence. He was 'the best of boys', warm-hearted and affectionate; but, overshadowed by his brilliant father, he had difficulty making up his mind what he wanted to do. Eventually deciding on a business career, he left Eton just before he was sixteen to spend a year in Leipzig learning German, during which Angela paid all his expenses.

Dickens, whose high hopes for his 'quick and sensitive' eldest son were never fully realised, wrote many anxious letters to Angela about the boy's future. In his view there was 'one great want' in Charley's character: he had

> less fixed purpose and energy than I could have supposed possible in my son ... With all the tenderer and better qualities which he inherits from his mother, he inherits an indescribable lassitude of character – a very serious thing in a man – which seems to me to express the want of a strong, compelling hand always beside him.[17]

There could not have been a quality more foreign to Charles Dickens's nature than lassitude.

Angela did her best to help, trying both to stiffen Charley's resolve and to calm his father's fears. 'You letter is as wise as it is kind,' wrote Dickens. '... Your speaking to [Charley] will have great weight with him, I do not doubt.'[18] She arranged for Charley to enter the bank of Baring Brothers, where he worked successfully for several years. In 1860, with financial backing from Barings, he went to China, later starting his own business. But it was perhaps inevitable that the boy who had had the 'strong, compelling hand' of his remarkable father 'always behind him' in childhood should have found himself lacking in purpose when he reached manhood.

*

Inhibited in her relations with her own closest family, Angela continued to find solace in the affectionate companionship of Hannah Brown. Of Hannah's support and allegiance she was never in any doubt. Hannah was the one person she trusted absolutely, whom she could talk to without fear of being misunderstood, to whom she turned for comfort when there were family quarrels or disagreements with the bank partners, or when the demands of her charitable work threatened to overwhelm her.

Hannah's marriage seems in no way to have affected the bond between the two women. In this unusual three-cornered relationship it must have been Hannah who held the key. She was devoted to Angela, who had given her the kind of life few governesses would have dreamed of; she also loved her husband. It was up to her to keep them both happy. Not that she was necessarily a scheming woman. But she was a woman who had had to make her own way in the world from an early age; of necessity she had learned to be adaptable. She was also down-to-earth, shrewd and resourceful. She evidently succeeded in maintaining a balance between the demands of Angela on the one hand and of her husband on the other.

By all accounts, the Browns' marriage was a happy one. Her pet name for him was 'Darkie'; he called her 'Tiny' or his 'Little Mouse'. Quiet, steady and dependable, William Brown was the complete opposite of his lively, argumentative wife. He remains to some extent a shadowy figure. Liked and respected as he was, the impression is that for most of Angela's friends his chief *raison d'être* was as a member of her establishment. Dickens, asking Angela to dinner one day, included the Browns in the invitation thus:

> I need not go through the form (I hope) of writing separately to Mrs Brown, for of course we assume herself and Mr Brown to be included in the plural 'you'.[19]

It can certainly have been no hardship to be automatically included in an invitation to dine with Charles Dickens. But, had William been a more ambitious or self-seeking man, he might well have chafed at the loss of independence that resulted from his joining Miss Coutts's household. Presumably, however, when he married 'Tiny' Meredith he accepted that his life would change quite radically. As far as we know, he was content with his new rôle and proud to be associated with Angela's philanthropic work.

Sometimes he took himself off on bachelor trips with his friend Henry Crabb Robinson. In 1850 they went to Paris with the artist, J. J. Masquerier. Robinson described the trio in a letter to his brother: he himself, in his sixty-sixth year, was 'expected to supply *animal spirits*', while Dr Brown, 'by implication, I presume, undertakes to watch over our bodies and health, and do his best to set us right if we go wrong'.[20] The following year the three friends toured Germany. In Dresden they attended a performance of *Twelfth Night* in German. Brown, noted Robinson, knew the play so well that he could follow the translation throughout. William's love of Shakespeare was shared by his wife and by Angela, whose interest had first been kindled by her father.

It was while in France after another tour with Robinson in the autumn of 1855 that William Brown was taken seriously ill. They had joined Angela and Hannah at Bordeaux, where Robinson left the party to return to England. On October 22 he received a letter informing him that Brown was dangerously ill at Montpellier. 'Miss Coutts was desirous that I should not hear the news abruptly,' wrote Robinson in his diary. 'Whenever Brown's death takes place it will be, to me, a real loss.'[21]

William Brown died the following day, October 23. Hannah was overcome with grief. Angela, herself in a state of shock, arranged for the body to be embalmed and sent home to Stratton Street. A few days later she and Hannah arrived in Paris. By great good fortune, Charles Dickens and his family had recently settled in Paris for the winter. Dickens offered to take charge of all the funeral arrangements. 'In Miss Coutts's peculiar circumstances – so isolated in the midst of her goodness and wealth – it has been a great blow to her,'[22] he wrote to W. H. Wills, his sub-editor at *Household Words*. With characteristic sympathy and insight, he had put his finger on the irony of her situation.

Returning to London, Dickens immediately put in hand the building of a vault under St Stephen's church, where Dr Brown was to be buried. His reference, in a letter to Angela, to 'future use of the vault in a similar way' is an indication of her desire to be buried there also when the time came. 'Pray offer my affectionate love and sympathy to Mrs Brown,' he wrote, 'and believe me to be entirely devoted to you in every happiness or sorrow that can ever befall you.'[23]

No one could have been more devoted in attending to every detail of the funeral, down to the 'scarves, hatbands, etc . . . all the mourners exactly alike'. Everything was to be as simple and quiet as possible, 'such as', wrote Dickens to Mrs Brown, 'I feel sure that his honest pride and manly feeling would have approved.'[24] At that stage Hannah could not bear the thought of any unnecessary pomp or ritual, though the carved and decorated memorial to her husband that was erected in the church the following year could hardly have been more elaborate.

William and Hannah Brown had been married for just under eleven years. Marrying in their mid-forties after a very long wait, they had been a quietly devoted couple. The loss of her 'Dear Darkie' inevitably drew Hannah even closer to the woman she called her 'Darling', from whom she had hardly been separated for more than a few days at a time since becoming her governess thirty years before. From now on they were to become even more inseparable. Hannah, in her widowhood, needed Angela's love and sympathy just as much as Angela, 'so isolated in the midst of her goodness and wealth', needed Hannah's. 'God bless you!' wrote Dickens to Mrs Brown. 'Only think what a friend you have beside you, in the noblest spirit we can ever know, and what an inestimable blessing you possess in her. A hundred times, God bless you!'[25]

*

Soon after Dickens had returned to Paris after Dr Brown's funeral, Angela wrote to ask him if he could recommend anyone to be her secretary. For years he had acted as her unpaid almoner, but there was a limit even to his phenomenal energy. In June 1853 he had only just avoided a breakdown. Now, deprived of Dr Brown's practical help as well as of his wise counsel, Angela felt the time had come to appoint a confidential secretary who could take some of the load off her, and Dickens's, shoulders.

Hard-pressed as he was, Dickens hated the idea of anyone taking his place. His work with Miss Coutts meant a lot to him. He wondered

> whether a daily messenger with a Dispatch Box could not put me in possession of all such business, and whether I could not, with some small additional remuneration to one of my trustworthy people at the office, do all you want.

Meanwhile, he thought that his sub-editor, W. H. Wills, might be willing to help her on a temporary basis. It was 'impossible to find a more zealous, honorable, or reliable man'[26] than Wills.

Wills, solidly dependable, was an ideal choice from all points of view. Dickens had already delegated to him some of the work he did for Angela, so it was not completely unfamiliar to him. And, since Wills was used to working under his supervision, Dickens was able to retain some control over what happened while being relieved of the donkey-work. The following January, after careful deliberation, Angela offered Wills the post. He retained his job at *Household Words* and received £200 a year from Angela. He worked with her for twelve years, fully justifying the glowing reference that Dickens had given him. He even mastered her handwriting, which was (and is) extraordinarily difficult to decipher mainly because so many of the sloping letters look alike. The modern reader is often left, in Dickens's phrase, 'on a wide ocean of conjecture'.

Dickens was delighted with the arrangement, which ensured the continuance of his 'special relationship' with Miss Coutts. He little knew that, just over two years later, this relationship would be virtually ended by a change in his own personal circumstances – a change that was the culmination of one of the most miserable periods of his life.

In May 1855 he had begun *Little Dorrit*, in 'a state of restlessness impossible to be described – impossible to be imagined – wearing and tearing to be experienced',[27] as he told Angela. The book has been called 'the work of a man disillusioned by everything he turns to',[28] a book which depicts the world 'as a vast prison in which jailers and the jailed are equally confined'.[29] Linked with his despair over English society as he saw it was a deepening dissatisfaction with his personal life. 'The skeleton in my domestic closet,' he told his friend Forster, 'is becoming a pretty big one.'[30]

That Charles and Catherine Dickens were not a devoted couple must have been evident to many of their friends, including Angela. According to her secretary, Osborne, she never thought they were particularly suited, nor did she think very highly of Catherine, whom she referred to rather disparagingly as 'poor dear Mrs Dickens'. But, as Angela herself may have reflected, it would have been difficult to find a woman who *was* suited to such an extraordinary man as Dickens. He is said to have been exasperated by Catherine's lethargy – the 'indescribable lassitude of character' that Charley had inherited – but ten pregnancies plus several miscarriages, not to mention the strain of being married to Charles Dickens, would have made many women lethargic.

In the summer of 1857 Dickens threw himself into a new venture, a series of theatrical performances to benefit the family of an old friend who had just died. Angela had never approved of his acting; he had teased her about 'the mournful spectacle of your friend upon the boards'.[31] She may have regarded it as unsuitable for a man of his public standing, but she also knew how much it exhausted him. 'I have just come back from Manchester,' he wrote now to Hannah Brown, 'where I have been tearing myself to pieces, to the wonderful satisfaction of thousands of people.'[32] To Angela he wrote praising the performance of a young actress called Maria Ternan. But it was Maria's 18-year-old sister Ellen who had captivated him. This new emotion, coming on top of the despair he already felt, threatened to overwhelm him.

He and Catherine struggled on, keeping up appearances. By the end of 1857 the situation was becoming desperate. Dickens had moved into his dressing-room and had the communicating door to Catherine's bedroom sealed up. In December, Angela and Hannah went to dine and hear the reading of the Christmas number of *Household Words*. Old friends that they were, it would have been impossible for them not to have sensed the tension that filled the house. A month or so later, a furious note from Dickens betrayed the state of his feelings. Catherine had requested Angela's help in finding a job for her brother. Dickens, who had already approached Angela on the subject, was 'inexpressibly vexed' to find that Catherine had written

> in my absence and without my knowledge ... I had not told her of the contents of your last note to me, concerning him. That is her excuse, and I hope you will forgive her more freely and readily than I do.[33]

Angela may well have considered that there was nothing to forgive.

Within a few weeks, matters had come to a head. Ironically, in the midst of the crisis, Dickens visited Urania Cottage and learned that a girl called Sarah Hyam had been found in the parlour at four o'clock in the morning with 'the Police Constable *employed to watch the place*'. Sarah was instantly discharged. 'She behaved quietly and respectfully — told no lies and made no defence,'[34] wrote Dickens to Angela. At the time he was furiously defending himself to his wife and in-laws against allegations of adultery with Ellen Ternan. He always maintained that he had not been unfaithful to Catherine, which at this stage was probably true.

On May 9, Dickens wrote to tell Angela that his marriage was in

Angela in middle age, a wood engraving by P. P. Skeolan

ruins. He could no longer keep silent, he wrote, to one who had been so near and dear a friend for so many years, and he believed she was 'not quite unprepared' for what he had to say. His marriage had been miserable for years: 'Nature has put an unsurmountable barrier between us, which never in this world can be thrown down.'

Though insisting that he had not 'the faintest thought of influencing you on either side', he had some pretty damning things to say about Catherine. The children had never loved her, he doubted whether anyone could be found who would be prepared to live with her (Charley in fact did so for some years), and there was even a hint of mental disturbance: she had 'fallen into the most miserable weaknesses and jealousies' and 'her mind has, at times, been certainly confused besides'. As for himself, while admitting his 'many impulsive faults' he believed that he was 'very patient and considerate at heart, and would have beaten out a path to a better journey's end than we have come to, if I could'.[35]

What did Angela make of this letter? 'Don't think the worse of me; don't think the worse of her,' he had written; and he hoped she might 'pity us both'. No doubt she did; but she could not be expected to approve of the separation. Marriage was an indissoluble bond, however miserable the partners sometimes made each other. As for the 'insurmountable barrier' between them, it was a little late, after twenty-two years, to talk of incompatibility. Her instinctive response, dictated by convention, upbringing and religious conviction, was to try to bring them together again. But there was another consideration. She must have been aware that the easy intimacy of her own friendship with Charles Dickens depended on his being respectably, if unhappily, married. Separated from his wife, Mr Dickens could not be received at Stratton Street and Holly Lodge on the same terms. From all points of view, it would be better for them *not* to separate.

Angela got in touch with Catherine and, a week or so after receiving Dickens's letter, sent a note round to the *Household Words* office asking him to call. Her messenger brought back his reply:

> I think I know what you want me for. How far I value your friendship, and how I love and honour you, you know in part, though you can never fully know. But nothing on earth – no, not even you – no consideration, human or Divine, can move me from the resolution I have taken . . .[36]

On the same day, Catherine Dickens wrote to thank Angela for 'your true kindness in doing what I asked. I have now – God help me – only one course to pursue. One day though not now I may be able to tell you how hardly I have been used.'[37]

Scandalous stories were now being circulated about Dickens. Against the advice of friends he rushed into print on the front page of *Household Words* to deny 'misrepresentations, most grossly false, most monstrous and most cruel'. Meanwhile, he had embarked on a series of public readings from his books, which were a triumphant success. His reputation was as high as ever, apparently unaffected by all the scandal. Certainly Angela did not believe any of it. She told Crabb Robinson, who called in July for 'a very friendly chat about Dickens's unwise advertisement of domestic calamities', that she was satisfied there had been 'nothing criminal – nothing beyond *incompatibilité d'humeur* – to require a separation, which should have been done quietly'.[38]

In August, Angela tried to move Dickens by writing to him of a visit Catherine and the children had paid her. The bitterness of his reply must have shocked her. Catherine, he wrote, had never cared for the children and they had never cared for her. 'The little play that is acted in your Drawing-room is not the truth, and the less the children play it, the better for themselves.'[39] But he apparently did not blame Angela for her intervention: his letters to her in the last months of 1858 were cheerful and affectionate.

Convention dictated that Angela should have little to do with Dickens after the separation. She can perhaps be faulted for not rising above convention; but Dickens appeared to accept the situation, though there is a wistful, almost pathetic note in the few letters that have come down to us from the sixties. That there *are* so few letters is one of the strongest reasons for believing that the break between them was almost complete – though neither seems to have admitted it openly to the other, and Dickens did not perhaps admit it to himself.

In April 1860, when they saw each other for what may have been the last time, Angela again urged Dickens to consider a reconciliation with his wife. It was, he wrote the next day, 'simply impossible that such a thing can be'. Angela had been afraid that his unhappiness might affect his writing; he assured her that he was 'quite as hopeful, cheerful, and active, as I ever was . . . If *I* were soured, I should still try to sweeten the lives and fancies of others, but I am not – not at all.'[40]

He was not soured; but he was saddened by the ending of their 'special relationship'. His work for her ceased; Urania Cottage, to which he had devoted so much time and energy, could not survive without him and was soon closed. 'I continually live over again, the years that lie behind us,'[41] he wrote to Hannah Brown in 1862.

*

While Dickens went from triumph to triumph on his public reading tours, Angela was scoring her own modest successes as a public speaker. Charles Osborne recalled many years later her 'musical, flexible, and expressive' voice, and her manner – 'quiet, simple, and wholly free from any trace of affectation or self-consciousness'.[42] The Reverend Julian Young, one of her most enthusiastic admirers, wrote that her speech at the Whitelands prizegiving in 1866 was

> admirable for its tone, for its sterling good sense, for the practical familiarity with the subject of education it displayed, for the sympathy with the young it evinced, for the felicity of its phraseology, and for the self-possession and suavity of her deportment.[43]

Of that speech there is no record; but the one she gave the previous year was published as a separate booklet. Part of it was concerned with the serious business of choosing a husband – something that Angela herself had so far avoided doing. 'A woman rules the family after her husband's spirit,' she had declared; 'his influence is inevitably felt, and he is either her mainstay in the trials of life or the weight which crushes her.' A girl should therefore choose her companion for life with

> at least something of the same caution a prudent woman exercises in selecting her gown ... It is possible in both cases to have some approximate idea of what will wear well, and suit your ideas of what is really good. If, after due care, the selection should prove unfortunate, she must be patient, and by sedulously and affectionately fostering the good dispositions which she knew existed in her husband when she married him, she may win him from bad habits or from evil counsellors.[44]

The message was clear: marriage was for life, and though a woman might be crushed by its weight she could not think of discarding her husband as she might an ill-fitting gown. If Dickens ever read this speech, it must have brought a wry smile to his face.

It is interesting that certain traits Dickens found so exasperating in

Catherine – her untidiness and absentmindedness, for example – he was quite ready to condone in Miss Coutts. Indeed, Angela's untidiness, like her handwriting, was a source of amusement to them both. He once wrote to ask her if she had a letter he wanted to quote from: 'If you have, I write in the profound conviction that your surprising development of the organ of Order, will enable you to find it in a moment!'[45]

Angela with Mrs Brown in 1864. On the right is Henry Wagner, who, it is said, would have liked to marry Angela

Of course, Angela was an extremely busy woman with a mass of correspondence to deal with. She was also a great hoarder. So it was hardly surprising that letters and documents sometimes got mislaid. On one occasion she wrote to ask Dickens to buy the tickets for some Urania Cottage girls who were emigrating. She sent him the money – £40 – but omitted the all-important information about the ship. Since he was in Broadstairs and she was in London and the ship was due to sail within forty-eight hours, there was nothing he could do about it. Sometimes a note asking him to dine at short notice would arrive after the appointed hour; or she would forget to mention the date or time.

Small faults that rankle in an uncongenial marriage partner can have an attractive piquancy when observed in a close friend; and in any case Dickens, who felt so bitterly towards Catherine at the end, had always been unswerving in his devotion to Angela. If his admiration sometimes led him to adopt an unpleasantly cloying, almost fawning, tone with her, there can be little doubt of his sincerity. He had found in her a true friend. If ever he needed 'such help as your generosity and friendship could give me,' he once wrote, 'I would ask it of no one else in the world and would unfalteringly turn to you.'[46] It is often hard to express gratitude in a simple, unselfconscious way. When Charley was on the point of leaving for China in 1860, Dickens wrote to Angela:

> My Dear friend I cannot trust myself on the ground that lies trembling at the point of my pen. Many reasons, old and new, unnerve me. I think you know how I love you – how I could do anything in your name and honor, but thank you.[47]

Between 1860 and his death ten years later, Dickens drove himself as relentlessly as ever, with arduous reading tours, a new weekly periodical, and his three last books, *Great Expectations*, *Our Mutual Friend*, and the unfinished *Mystery of Edwin Drood*. His health was beginning to fail; in his mid-fifties he looked like an old man. But he was still full of zest for life, he still had an irresistible charm, and he was perhaps more admired and loved than ever before. In one of his last letters to Angela that have survived he wrote to acknowledge her New Year greetings for 1865: 'I send you out of my innermost heart my wishes for your happiness through many coming years, and my ever grateful and faithful remembrance of many years that are gone.'[48] He was then nearly fifty-three; in five and a half years he himself would be gone. Angela, two years younger, would live for another forty.

Eleven

WIDER STILL AND WIDER

In December 1861 another marriage of twenty-two years' duration came to an end. Prince Albert, whose constitution had never been strong, succumbed to one of the dread diseases of that insanitary age, typhoid. At forty-two, Queen Victoria was left a widow with nine children. Utterly desolate, she went to ground like a wounded animal, refusing for years to allow herself to be seen by her subjects. Inevitably, after a time, their sympathy waned, and it turned decidedly sour when the Queen's infatuation with her Highland servant, John Brown, became known. In fact, this rough-mannered but devoted attendant set the Queen on the road to recovery, a process which was to be continued by Disraeli in the seventies. But her prolonged seclusion, and the gossip about Brown, helped to make the sovereign more personally unpopular in the mid-sixties than perhaps at any other time in her reign.

As Victoria's popularity diminished, so Angela rose steadily in public esteem. The richest heiress in England had become the most charitable lady in the land. While the Queen, lonely and depressed, withdrew more and more into herself, Angela looked serenely out on the world with her calm, untroubled gaze. Though she did not court publicity, she no longer shrank from it. Her long face with its finely-chiselled mouth, deep-set eyes and broad brow framed with smooth dark hair was familiar to millions through the popular illustrated papers; her tall, spare figure was instantly recognised in public places. For her, the sixties were years of achievement. She was in the prime of life, emotionally secure, full of energy, ready for fresh challenges and eager to embrace new causes.

If there was one place that cried out for her particular brand of practical philanthropy it was Ireland. In common with many others, Angela had given money to relieve the terrible sufferings of the late forties, but she was aware that this could only be a palliative. In 1862 she began what was to be a long association with one particular district in the extreme south of the country – the little town of Baltimore and the group of islands to the south-west of it. After receiving an appeal from the parish priest, she sent W. H. Wills to Ireland to report on conditions in the area. He found 'a degree and amount of misery which I could not have believed compatible with human life'. The dislike of the Irish for the workhouse was, he wrote, 'fanatical'.[1]

Angela sent copies of the report to Sir Robert Peel (son of the former Prime Minister), who was Chief Secretary to the Lord Lieutenant of Ireland, and to William Gladstone, then Chancellor of the Exchequer. Sir Robert, she told Gladstone, blamed the people for not going to the workhouse, but she herself did not wonder at the 'intense repugnance of the Irish to . . . expose their families to so corrupt an influence'.[2] As a result of Wills's report, Peel instructed the Poor Law authorities at Skibbereen to give some out-relief. At his suggestion, Angela opened stores in the area to sell basic foodstuffs at minimum cost and to distribute clothes and blankets. Where possible, she wrote, these stores must be made to pay for themselves, to avoid the 'demoralising effects' of free hand-outs.

Meanwhile, having paid for three parties of emigrants to go to Canada, she searched for ways of helping those who remained to become self-sufficient. Could other vegetables besides the potato be cultivated? Her friend Sir Joseph Hooker, director of Kew Gardens, was consulted. Would sheep safely graze there? She had a flock sent over. She made energetic efforts to promote the sale of Irish embroidery in London and tried to encourage the local fishing industry, at that time almost non-existent.

The local gentry were sceptical about the peasants' ability to handle the large boats needed for deep-sea fishing. It was not until 1879, when Angela was approached by the new parish priest, Father Davis, that action was taken to form a proper fleet. With an interest-free loan from Angela of £10,000, administered by Father Davis, the men were able to buy the boats they needed, each having a share in a 30- to 40-ton vessel costing up to £500. The scheme was a success. Baltimore was transformed into a prosperous community and within five years the fishing plant was valued at £50,000. The Irish journalist T. P. O'Connor, a friend of Angela's, writing after her death of his own visit to Baltimore, declared: 'Never have I seen an experiment where philanthropy, conducted on sound business lines, produced results so enormous, so immediate, and so beneficent.'[3]

Angela herself, visiting the country for the first time in 1884, unconsciously borrowed Dicken's phrase about his son Charley to sum up her impressions of the Irish character: there was everywhere, she said, an 'indescribable lassitude', which

> appears to hang over all – children, peat, crops, goats, men and women, animate and inanimate nature. The country seems to be perishing from itself . . . The man who lives by himself, for himself, with no ties outside himself, on his plot of ground, even when surrounded by animal comforts, lacks that motive power for improvement which is created on the one hand by competition and comparison, and on the other by community of interest.[4]

Lack of the 'motive power for improvement' was anathema to a good Victorian like Angela. In one district of Ireland, at least, she had created the conditions in which improvement could take place, and in doing so had helped to bring about a minor miracle.

*

Probably no one who approached Angela for help in church building or restoration ever went away empty-handed. Several churches in London (apart from St Stephen's) were built with her aid, and in the 1860s she built a second St Stephen's, in Carlisle, where the congregation had been meeting in a furniture warehouse. She restored the churches at Ramsbury, where her parents were buried, and in the adjoining parish of Baydon, where she built model cottages for the villagers and gave them land for allotments.

Her interest in the colonies remained a strong one all her life. In 1858, when the mainland of British Columbia (Canada) became a Crown Colony, she promptly endowed a bishopric there, her third, at a total cost of £50,000. She also provided funds for a girls' school, Angela College. The Church in St Helena and Mauritius also received her help. She gave funds for Sir Henry James's topographical survey of Jerusalem and even offered to pay for the restoration of Solomon's aqueducts in the city, but her offer was not taken up. She introduced modern equipment into the cotton industry of southern Nigeria and helped to found societies for the protection of the Aborigines in Australia.

Africa always held a special fascination for her. From Robert Gray, 'her' bishop of Cape Town, she received long letters describing the trials and rewards of his office. Filled with a missionary zeal for converting the heathen and building churches and schools, this 'nervous, bookish, ungregarious'⁵ old Etonian travelled round his vast domain in a waggon drawn by eight horses – a form of transport he greatly enjoyed, or so he assured Miss Coutts. In a tenth anniversary letter of June 29, 1857, he reported that he now had ninety clergy, having started with thirteen. He had also become Metropolitan, with jurisdiction over the two new bishoprics of Natal and Graham's Town.

Home on a visit the following year, Gray attended a dinner given by Angela for David Livingstone, who was about to set off on his ill-fated Zambesi expedition. In December 1856 Livingstone had returned to England to a hero's welcome after three years' travelling in southern Africa during which he had covered nearly six thousand miles and made 'the first authenticated crossing of the continent from coast to coast by a European'.⁶ He now dreamed, as he wrote to a friend, of 'an English colony in the healthy highlands of central Africa',⁷ which he was convinced would be to the mutual benefit of the English and the Africans. The British government, however, was not at that time interested in acquiring new possessions; the 'scramble for Africa' would not begin until much later.

So Livingstone kept his colonial ambitions to himself, laying emphasis instead in his speeches and writings on the great commercial potential of the territory he had explored. In December 1857 Parliament voted him £5,000 for a new expedition to investigate and assess the agricultural and mining prospects of the area and to chart the Zambesi, the river Livingstone already saw as 'God's highway', the link between the fertile Batoka Plateau and the coast.

Amidst the general euphoria that surrounded the public idol, Dickens sounded a note of scepticism. Dr Livingstone's deductions, he warned Angela, 'must be received with great caution. The history of all African effort, hitherto, is a history of wasted European life, squandered European money, and blighted European hope'. It would be 'a great thing to cultivate that cotton and be independent of America', but in his opinion India would be a better place in which to seek 'that happy end'.⁸

Angela, however, was unlikely to have been moved by Dickens's arguments. She had already espoused this new cause with all her customary energy. Dr Livingstone was just the sort of man to inspire her sympathy and allegiance. It is even possible that she was one of the few friends to whom he confided his vision of a British colony in south-central Africa which would bring civilisation and Christianity to the natives and stamp out the slave trade. From what we know of her, Angela would have warmly approved such a plan and given him every encouragement. Nor would his secret have gone further than her drawing-room. According to Charles Osborne, she would have made a great diplomatist: that sphinx-like face gave nothing away – although, insisted Osborne, it could be expressive enough when she wished it to be.

As it turned out, Dickens's misgivings were justified. Livingstone had been dangerously optimistic about a number of factors: he had played down the rigours of the climate and gambled on the navigability of the Zambesi. His expedition was a failure; a number of lives were lost, including that of his wife, Mary, and hopes were certainly blighted – his own most of all. He returned home in 1864 to a very different reception from the one he had received in 1856. The following year he left England for the last time. By November 1871, when Henry Morton Stanley 'presumed' to find him in Ujiji, on Lake Tanganyika, Livingstone had been all but forgotten by his countrymen. It was Stanley's accounts, when he arrived in England the following August, of the 'brave, noble hearted and heavenly minded Dr Livingstone'[9] that made him a national hero all over again.

Angela, however, had never lost faith in him – or so it would seem from a letter she wrote in November 1869 to Sir Roderick Murchison, President of the Royal Geographical Society. She was delighted, she told Murchison, to hear news at last of her 'valued friend Livingstone' and looked forward to 'shaking him again by the hand'. She hoped Sir Roderick would promise to dine with him in Stratton Street 'if all goes well'.[10] But the last European hand that Livingstone was to shake was Stanley's, when the two men parted in March 1872. Just over a year later, after an incredible last journey during most of which he was ill and exhausted, Livingstone died. He was sixty – a year older than Angela. 'If he had but come home with Stanley: but we may not talk of *ifs*,'[11] wrote Hannah Brown to a friend when news of his death reached England. His body, which had been carried by his African followers 1,500 miles from the depths of the interior to Zanzibar, was brought home and buried in Westminster Abbey on April 18, 1874.

*

Robert Gray, Bishop of Cape Town, was not in the same class as the great Dr Livingstone. But he enjoyed a modest success, during his home leave in 1858–59, as a lecturer on his own African experiences. He little knew that, shortly after his return to South Africa, he was to become embroiled in a controversy that would cause a storm in England and shake the Anglican Church to its foundations. Concerned essentially with the delicate balance of authority between Church and State, it brought Angela, a laywoman whose money had helped to establish the Church in South Africa, into conflict with both, involving her in an enormous expenditure of time, money and mental effort.

For a bishop in Africa in the middle of the nineteenth century there must have been many agonising moral dilemmas. In 1862, for instance, Gray was writing to Angela of his concern over the confiscation by the government of land belonging to native chiefs, whose children he had been educating. The chiefs were now prisoners on Robben Island, 'within sight of their children whom the Government are now abandoning'.[12] It was surely not 'a proceeding worthy of a great Christian people'.

But this issue, grave as it was, was soon overshadowed by another of even greater importance, one which concerned fundamental questions of Christian doctrine. The Bible itself came under attack, and from within the Church itself – from no less a person, indeed, than the Bishop of Natal. What, pondered Gray anxiously, was he to do about Bishop Colenso?

John William Colenso, who was born in the same year as Angela, was consecrated Bishop of Natal in 1853 and had gone forth to work among the Zulus with a pure heart and a simple, undogmatic faith. For him, the authority of conscience was paramount, and his conscience soon began to trouble him. To begin with, there was the question of polygamy. Colenso voiced his misgivings in a pamphlet which suggested that, repugnant as this practice was to Christians, to force African communities to abandon it might do more harm than good.

To critics sitting comfortably at home in England, and to Gray in Cape Town, this was bad enough; but worse was to follow. When Colenso, having learned the Zulu language, began to translate the Old Testament, he was asked, 'Is all that true?' Did all the beasts and birds and creeping things, from the hot countries and the cold, really enter the Ark with Noah? 'And did Noah gather food for them *all*, for the beasts and birds of prey, as well as for the rest?'[13]

Faced with such questions, Colenso's conscience would not allow him to 'speak lies in the Name of the Lord'. His Evangelical upbringing had taught him that the Bible was the literal truth; he could no more interpret it for the puzzled Zulus in terms of poetry or allegory or symbolic statement than fly over the moon. He was a mathematician, who had made a name for himself with treatises on arithmetic and algebra. Now, looking at the first books of the Bible again and applying precise mathematical criteria, he realised that the Old Testament stories were not accurate. He worked out, for instance, how many people the Temple could accommodate and found that the answer did not tally with the stated number of the Children of Israel.

John William Colenso, Bishop of Natal, engraving by Biscombe Gardner

If the numbers were wrong, Colenso reasoned, everything else was suspect. The Bible could not be regarded as a literal historical record. Towards the end of 1862 he brought out his first book of biblical criticism. It was greeted with howls of protest, not least from Bishop Gray, upon whom the office of Metropolitan weighed heavily. In April 1863 he wrote to Angela:

> The clergy of my diocese have intimated to me their intention of bringing the Bishop of Natal's teaching to the test of a formal trial; and I shall have to cite him to answer to the charges brought against him. I trust God will enable me to see what my duty is, and seeing it, to discharge it.[14]

His Letters Patent from the Queen empowered him (or so he thought) to institute proceedings against the bishops of South Africa. Accordingly, Colenso was tried for heresy by his fellow bishops and, on being convicted, deposed from his bishopric.

But Colenso refused to be deposed. He appealed to the English courts, and in March 1865 the Privy Council issued an extraordinary judgment: Gray, it declared, had no power to try Colenso – had indeed no effective ecclesiastical jurisdiction in South Africa, which was a colony with its own independent legislature. In other words, the authority given to Gray in the Letters Patent was void. Colenso, as far as the law was concerned, was still Bishop of Natal. He returned to South Africa (whereupon Gray excommunicated him) and resumed his services in the cathedral, while his Dean, under instructions from Gray, held rival services at different times.

In England, the case excited enormous interest. The English bishops were thrown into confusion by the Privy Council's decision. Most supported Gray in the stand he had taken against Colenso. But Dean Stanley, an influential and authoritative figure, pointed out that there had been different interpretations of the Bible throughout the church's history. He himself had 'ventured to say that the Pentateuch is not the work of Moses', and that parts of the Scriptures were poetical and not historical; did that mean that he should take his place beside 'the despised and rejected Bishop of Natal?'[15] These arguments, however, did not stop the trustees of the Colonial Bishopric Fund (whose treasurer was William Gladstone, Chancellor of the Exchequer), from withholding Colenso's salary, or the missionary societies from withdrawing their support from him.

Angela, whose endowment had brought the bishopric of Cape Town into existence, was filled with dismay by the Privy Council's judgment. Whatever her opinion of Colenso (and she was, as he himself put it, 'no friend of mine'), her overriding concern was with the status of the colonial church. She had given her money on the understanding that she was helping to set up branches of the Church of England in the colonies which would be firmly anchored to the mother church. 'Without this security,' she wrote to the Archbishop of Canterbury in July 1865, 'I should not have guaranteed the Endowment funds.' Unless some way could be found of reversing the Privy Council's decision and giving effect 'to the arrangements which H.M.'s Letters Patent were intended to sanction',[16] she would ask for her money back.

But this was easier said than done. Gladstone, to whom she sent a copy of her letter to the Archbishop, thought that it was 'one of the expressions of opinion, among all those on the subject, which appears to me to put the Colenso question on the right ground'.[17] Gratifying as this was, it did nothing to advance Angela's case. What she wanted was action. Meanwhile, Bishop Gray had announced his intention of appointing a new bishop to replace Colenso. The Privy Council's decision had, in effect, freed the African Church from State Control; Gray and his clergy were at liberty to secede from the Church of England and form their own independent church. And this was what seemed to be happening.

Having drawn a blank with the Primate, Angela next assailed the Prime Minister, Earl Russell. Did he not realise the perils that might lie ahead? Without allegiance to the Crown and a recognition of its supremacy 'in all causes both Ecclesiastical and Civil', there was a danger that a misguided body of church people might acknowledge the Pope as supreme. Indeed, there were 'those working amongst us' towards this very end, and the Church of Rome was 'neither an inactive nor unintelligent spectator of these indications'. One of its archbishops [Manning] had recently declared that 'Protestantism has nearly run out its appointed course of Heresy' and that 'in a generation or two the Anglican religion will be a page of history'.[18]

Russell was a known anti-Catholic; but in this instance he was no more helpful than the Archbishop had been. Quite likely, having taken over as Prime Minister only two months previously on the death of Lord Palmerston, he had his hands full. In any case, there was little that anyone could do. Gladstone, though sympathetic, pointed out that as early as 1840 'it had become apparent that a system of State-Church legislation could not be made to run effectually through the Colonies'. It was clear that 'there must be more or less unmooring of the Colonial Churches from the old ground of Establishment'. He himself had 'faith enough in the enduring vigour of the Constitution of the Church, which the Almighty devised and adjusted'.[19]

Angela could not agree. In her view, the adjustment had been made by man, not the Almighty. In April 1866 she wrote to tell Gladstone that she now looked to Parliament to remedy the matter. In reply, he felt bound to tell her that, though the Privy Council's decision might be bad law, there was little chance of its being overturned. In his opinion, 'the restoration of the Supremacy of the Crown . . . in the Province of South Africa is practically impossible'.[20] Nevertheless, on June 18, a petition to the Queen was presented by the Bishop of London on Angela's behalf in the House of Lords. It asked the Queen 'to preserve unimpaired to Your Majesty and Your successors the exercise of Your Royal Supremacy in the appointment of Bishops and the Chief Government of the Church'.[21] But it did not succeed. And Angela's lawyers advised her that she would not be able to claim back her endowment of £17,500 because it had been paid to the Colonial Bishoprics Fund and was regarded as a general part of that fund.

From Cape Town came news from Bishop Gray that 'Dr Colenso having assailed the Old Testament is now, Sunday after Sunday, attacking the New'.[22] Nothing that Colenso did would surprise her, retorted Angela, but she was concerned with wider issues than the Natal–Cape Town controversy. Colenso, meanwhile, had sued Gladstone and the trustees of the Colonial Bishoprics Fund for his salary. In November 1866 Lord Romilly, Master of the Rolls, ruled that Colenso was Bishop of Natal and would remain so until he 'died, or resigned, or was legally removed'. The Fund had to pay up.

For Gray, finding a new bishop to 'replace' Colenso was proving more difficult than he had at first realised. In 1867 a conference of bishops from the whole English-speaking world was held at Lambeth to discuss the matter. Many of the bishops were uncertain and worried about defying the law; but the Americans supported Gray, and he got his bishop. Early in 1869, W. K. Macrorie was consecrated Bishop of Natal in Cape Town. For the next fourteen years, until Colenso's death in 1883, there were two bishops in Natal: Macrorie, accepted by the English Church, by the Church in South Africa and by most of the laity in Natal; and Colenso, recognised by English law and with his own small band of followers.

Angela had not quite given up. When Bishop Gray died in 1872 she wrote to the Secretary of the Society for the Propagation of the Gospel in Foreign Parts, asking him to use his influence to appoint a new bishop who would 'carry out the Trust I reposed in your Society'.[23] But she must have realised that the battle was lost. When the Secretary smoothly suggested a meeting so that she could put her point of view, she replied tartly that her views were well known and a meeting was unnecessary. The fact was that the independent Church of South Africa was a reality, Bishop Macrorie was a reality, and the clock could not be put back.

But if she had lost the fight in the colonies, she could at least try to ensure that her money would not continue to support the church in England if it broke away from the State – as it showed some signs of doing. In her will, she declared that her endowments had been made not to a 'community as a spiritual body or as an independent voluntary association, but to the Protestant Church of England as now by law established under the supremacy of the Crown, being Protestant'. If at any time the Church of England became disestablished or separated itself from the State, she wished her endowments to revert to her estate, the money to be used 'to promote the principles of the Protestant Reformation, civil liberty, and social well-being'.[24]

*

Why did Angela fight so passionately and go to such lengths to try to maintain the supremacy of the Crown over the colonial churches? That it should have been a matter of such importance to her is not difficult to understand when one remembers the intensity of feeling that surrounded matters of church doctrine and authority in the middle of the last century. The Church of England was being assailed from all quarters. The Oxford Movement and defections to Rome on the one hand, the new agnosticism on the other, as well as biblical criticism from Germany and the growth of scientific knowledge — all these worried faithful Anglicans and threatened their cherished Protestant beliefs. There were, moreover, deep differences of opinion among church leaders as to the best ways of meeting these various threats. Amid all the uncertainty, many Anglicans took comfort in the fact that their church was a national institution, that in the last resort it was the State which (through the courts) had authority to decide doctrinal matters. Not that anyone was likely to change his opinion or beliefs as a result of a court decision. But at a time of dithering and dissent among bishops and clergy, the power of the State was seen as a stabilising and unifying influence.

This, roughly speaking, was Angela's attitude. In common with many others, she had a certain mistrust of the clerical order, for all her close friendships with many of its members. The clergy, she felt, needed to be kept firmly in check or there was no knowing where they might lead their flock — into the waiting arms of Rome, if they were not careful. When young Lord Sandon, in a speech at the height of the Gray–Colenso controversy, referred to the 'autocracy of the clergy' and 'the rise of a priestly class', she wrote to congratulate him for putting into words a feeling which was 'deeply enshrined in the innermost hearts' of 'silent members of the English Church'.[25]

Many parsons, she considered, moved in a world that was narrow and restricted. 'I have always found it very difficult to act with the Clergy in *business* matters,' she once confided to Sir Edward Bulwer Lytton; the clergy were seldom 'men of social experience of a *catholic* kind'.[26] When she founded two geology scholarships at Oxford in 1859 she hoped that they would be taken up by Divinity students, who should be encouraged to master 'so much of natural science as to be fitted to turn this mighty lever to good effect in the minds of the laity'.[27] For her, apparently, reconciling her faith with the new scientific knowledge was not a problem. Perhaps, like her friend Faraday, she was able to keep science and religion in two separate compartments in her mind. But for many church people, lay and clerical, the 'mighty lever' of science was a dangerous implement which was liable to spring back and hit them in the face.

When William Howitt in 1869 called Angela 'a nursing-mother to the Church of England' he was perhaps being more apt than he knew. For her attitude to the Church seems to have resembled that of an overprotective mother towards a slightly wayward child who is in need of firm guidance from an authoritative father – the State. If left to make its own mistakes it might get into bad company and be ruined for life. Few women can have had such a passionate and *personal* concern for the Church as an institution. In Angela it was matched by a similar concern for the bank of Coutts & Co. One may smile at her attachment to these two temples of God and mammon; but there is something rather sad about the excessive devotion of a human being to an institution.

*

At the same time that she was battling to keep the colonial churches under the protective wing of the Crown, Angela was engaged in another crusade of a not altogether dissimilar nature. In this instance it was not a church, but a small country on the other side of the world, that needed protection. And, far from fighting alone, Angela had this time come to the aid of a new friend, the remarkable Rajah Sir James Brooke of Sarawak.

James Brooke, 'an unusual combination of idealist and man of action',[28] was born in Bengal in 1803. At sixteen he obtained a commission in the Bengal Army; six years later he was invalided to England. It has been suggested that the reason he never married was that he was wounded in the genitals; but according to two early biographers the injury was to his lung.

After travelling for some time in the Far East, Brooke developed a romantic attachment for the unexplored islands of the Malay

Archipelago. In 1838, when he was thirty-five, he inherited £30,000. He promptly bought a schooner and sailed again for the East, with Borneo as his objective. He finished up in Sarawak, a province on the north-west coast of Borneo under the rule of the Sultan of Brunei. After he had successfully mediated in a rebellion by the native Dayaks against their Brunei overlords, he was offered the province – its government, revenues and trade. He accepted, and became Rajah Brooke of Sarawak – the 'White Rajah'. At first he ruled the province in return for an annual payment to the Sultan of Brunei, but later the Sultan transferred to him the absolute sovereignty of Sarawak.

Brooke found himself ruler of a territory the size of Yorkshire in which the majority of the population, the Dayaks, had been for generations in a state of utter subjugation to the Malay ruling class. There were also a number of Chinese. The country was in a sorry state. The Malays appropriated most of the revenue; pirates attacked from the sea, head-hunters from the interior. It says much for Brooke's exceptional qualities and abilities that in his first five years as Rajah he established peace and order, won the respect and loyalty of the people, and began a determined campaign to rid the country of pirates. His aim was to create an independent state of free people. But he was worried that Sarawak, with its tiny population, might after his death be swallowed up by a large nation or taken over again by Brunei. Much of the rest of his life was spent in trying to obtain the protection of the British Crown for his little country. The British government, however, remained for the most part uninterested.

Angela first met Brooke in 1847, when he returned to England to find himself a public hero. He was invited to Windsor, received an honorary degree from Oxford and the freedom of the City of London, and was installed as a Knight Commander of the Bath. There is a story that Angela fell in love with him during this first visit to England – that, indeed, she proposed to him by letter and was turned down. In fact, her proposal to the Duke of Wellington took place in February 1847, some months before Brooke arrived in England. It is just possible that a rumour about this was started and at some point was transferred to Brooke. It seems unlikely that Angela, who was still very attached to the Duke, would have transferred her affections to Brooke, though in many ways he was just the sort of man to have appealed to her. They had much in common. Like her, he was serious and reserved. Filled with a sense of mission, he had devoted his life and fortune to the people whose ruler he had become quite by chance.

But it is unlikely that Angela ever seriously contemplated going to live in Sarawak. England was her home, London her base. How could she have controlled and directed her many projects from an island on the other side of the world? Besides, there was Hannah Brown: she would hardly have taken kindly to such an uprooting, and to leave her behind would have been unthinkable. The Rajah, who soon got the measure of Hannah, once wrote to Angela from Cairo: 'Mrs Brown would not like Egypt – we must not think of persuading her to visit it!'[29] Still less, one imagines, could she have been persuaded to visit Sarawak.

On his return to Sarawak, the Rajah finally succeeded in defeating the pirates in a decisive battle involving much loss of life. In England, he was attacked by people who knew little of the circumstances and maintained that a massacre of the innocents had taken place. A Commission of Inquiry completely vindicated Brooke, but the affair somewhat embittered him and made him suspicious in subsequent dealings with British statesmen.

In 1857, the Rajah's Chinese subjects rose in rebellion and attacked Kuching, the capital, by night, setting fire to the main buildings. The Rajah's house was destroyed and he lost everything, but he himself escaped by swimming across the river. With the help of the Dayaks the rebellion was quelled, and at the end of the year Brooke decided to return to England; he was now fifty-four and no doubt felt in need of a change and a rest after these exertions. Shortly after his arrival in England in 1858 he renewed his acquaintance with Miss Coutts and was soon a regular guest at Stratton Street.

*

If Angela never showed any inclination to live in Sarawak, she became deeply involved in its affairs. Once she had espoused the cause of James Brooke and Sarawak she did everything in her power to further it. The Rajah was convinced that only the support of Britain in some form would secure the future of Sarawak: Angela used all her considerable influence to try to persuade the government to offer a Protectorate. She also approached her friend Lord Elgin, son of the Elgin Marbles collector and later Governor-General of India. What the Rajah really wanted, she told Elgin in April 1860, was 'a recognition of existence and a claim to British protection: by the presence of a man-of-war, or gun-boat, which would act, if the interests of Sarawak required it'. And she concluded:

I don't think we have acted kindly to a countryman whom we permitted and encouraged to commence an arduous career and to foster a dangerous enterprise. I think he has fulfilled his part. He has succeeded. He has done us credit, and he has made (what is not always done in Europe) his small domain happy, prosperous and contented.[30]

But her efforts in this and other quarters were in vain, and in the end it was she who offered to provide a gun-boat. She had already granted Brooke an interest-free loan of £5,000 on the security of the revenue of Sarawak (which, her solicitor warned her, 'must be of a doubtful character'). Now, she offered a similar amount for the purchase of a screw steamer, which she and Hannah named the *Rainbow*. The gift of the *Rainbow* lifted a load from the Rajah's mind. In high spirits, he sent pressed flowers and a poem to 'the Ladies of Holly Lodge', at the same time indulging Mrs Brown's passion for riddles. 'I delight in the powers of Nonsense and beg you will never cease when in the mood,'[31] he told her.

His exuberance did not last for long, however. From Sarawak came news of a plot by disaffected chiefs to murder the entire white population. The Rajah's two nephews, whom he had left in charge, had attempted to deal with it as best they could; but he decided to return to Sarawak at once, sailing from Southampton in November 1860 with another loan of £500 from Angela and the promise of more should he need it. In fact, the situation was not as bad as he feared. But there were complications arising out of the interference of the governor of an adjoining British colony, Labuan. Once again Brooke felt the British government had let him down. He sent Angela long gloomy letters. Relations between Sarawak and England had gone from bad to worse, he wrote: 'the separation between the governments is now complete . . . Confidence is gone, and hope is dead . . . How I long to be at Holly Lodge – duty alone keeps me digging in this sand pit.'[32]

In common with Bishop Gray of Cape Town, Brooke had a tendency to self-dramatisation; but his letter of thanks to Angela when he arrived in Sarawak was deeply felt, if rather florid:

Here in my own country and amid my people I wish to say a few words. I was broken in heart, health and fortune. I looked for death as my relief. Sarawak was struggling and well nigh ruined – you gave me life by giving me hope and your help enabled Sarawak to struggle through difficulties which well nigh overwhelmed her. This is the simple truth . . . Words are useless for thanks, but judge in feelings as generously as you judge on most matters . . . My love to dear Mrs Brown. Kindness and sympathy attract me so strongly that I could almost leave undone what I came to do and return. – Farewell, ever and ever yours.[33]

The Rajah returned to England at the end of 1861, having formally appointed his nephew, Captain Brooke, Rajah Muda or heir presumptive. He was now negotiating with the Belgians, though still hoping for British support. At every stage he consulted Angela, who as well as being a trusted friend was, of course, the chief creditor of Sarawak. She tried to raise his spirits with a little heavy-handed humour. 'The Great Government Gun,' she told him on February 20, 1862, 'goes on slowly asking itself questions *how* it is to load and explode.' She had heard that the Radical MP Richard Cobden had spoken highly of the Rajah personally but had suggested he was born out of time. 'No doubt,' wrote Angela,

> the great Anti-Cornlaw Legislator [Cobden] would arrange these trifling errors of Providence better, but your friends observed to him that as the Rajah was actually amongst us in our generation, however inopportune and ill-arranged it might be, *something* must be done with him and the matter of his existence![34]

Throughout 1862 Angela and her friends persisted in their efforts to interest the British government in the Rajah's remote territory. Before the year was out, Brooke received startling news from Sarawak: his nephew, Captain Brooke, whom he had left in charge, had become convinced that the negotiations with British and foreign governments were against the interests of Sarawak, and declared his intention of going to 'all lengths to put an end to the present state of matters'.[35] What this meant in practice was not clear, but it amounted to a revolt against his uncle's authority. Once again, Sir James prepared to sail for Sarawak, borrowing from Angela for his passage. There was one thing he had to do before he left. His nephew's defiant conduct had debarred him from the succession: it was essential to leave Sarawak to someone who could be trusted to carry out the Rajah's intentions. He made a new will, which included the following clause:

> I leave, commit and devise unto Angela Burdett Coutts . . . the Succession to the Raj of Sarawak. And I do hereby nominate and appoint her to be my true and lawful Successor in the dignity and office of the Rajah of Sarawak now vested in me, to be held by her . . .

as a public trust for the good of the people together with the public property in which I have an interest appertaining to the State of Sarawak, in implicit confidence that she will arrange the future Government of Sarawak for the welfare of the people and for the security and permanency of the liberties they now enjoy.[36]

Before accepting this unique trust, Angela had consulted her friend John Abel Smith, MP, who informed the Foreign Secretary, Earl Russell, of the situation. 'If the trust you have left me, falls to me to perform,' she wrote to Brooke as he set sail, 'I will fulfil it as faithfully

Sir James Brooke, Rajah of Sarawak

for the interests and welfare of your people as my abilities and powers may permit.'[37] As for him, it was, he wrote, 'an inexpressible solace to have placed the future in your hands'.[38]

Arriving in Sarawak in March 1863, the Rajah was greeted enthusiastically by his subjects and was relieved to find that his nephew's revolt had been 'upon paper only'. Captain Brooke was disinherited and banished from the country. Sir James stayed on for some months to ensure that his rule was secure and to coach Captain Brooke's brother, Charles, for the succession. Meanwhile, in August 1863, the British government formally recognised Sarawak as an independent state under the rule of Rajah Brooke; the following January the first British consul was appointed. It was a step in the right direction and a triumph for Angela's persistence.

On Captain Brooke's return to England, he began openly to attack his uncle, who was still in Sarawak. Angela was incensed. 'I hold to my opinion that *he drinks*,' she wrote to the Rajah; 'so alone can I account for his unreasoning violent conduct.'[39] She was amazed when, a year or so later, Sir James became reconciled with his nephew. To her, it was a sign of weakness, and she did not hesitate to express her disapproval. But Sir James, though he called her his 'guardian angel' and valued her friendship perhaps more than that of anyone else during the last years of his life, refused to be influenced by her against his own better judgment. 'As I grow old,' he wrote to her in January 1865,

> I would fain live in charity with all men . . . I only wish to do what is right and Who can judge this for me? I do not sit in judgment upon your proceedings, but do you not attribute an infirmity of character to me?[40]

'Affectionate interest,' Angela replied, 'an uncalled for anxiety as to public estimation of your character and the habit of advising in your affairs prompted me to write with an absurd warmth of feeling.' She would not write more 'in reference to a matter upon which I have nothing more to say and with which I am *really* not concerned'.[41]

The Rajah, sensing that there was a good deal more that she would have liked to say, thought it better 'to deal plainly than permit a fester which cannot be healed, because hidden'. He owed her a debt of gratitude, he reminded her, which he could never repay,

> and this fact renders me sensitive, which you should remember in passing opinions upon my conduct. You would not wish me to do what I thought wrong and this should prevent our dwelling too long upon any question where we differ. We do not stand upon a footing of equality in considering measures relative to Sarawak, for I have a real and vital interest in her affairs, whilst you, as you write, are not really concerned excepting so far as your pleasure dictates.[42]

That Angela herself had not forgotten his indebtedness is evident from a letter she wrote to Mrs Brown at this time. 'As the public

Creditor of Sarawak I have a right to know the steps he may take about the Country,' she wrote. 'This amount of confidence is due to me not from friendship but from honour.' She was clearly piqued that the Rajah had 'completely transferred the concerns of Sarawak from me to another person'.[43] The bequest of the country to her had, in fact, been an emergency measure, and Sir James in due course made his nephew, Charles Brooke, his heir. Angela did not mistrust Charles as much as his brother, but she had no great liking for him.

With two such strong-minded people, disagreements were inevitable. The following year, they were at loggerheads over the Colenso controversy, which was then furiously raging. Angela felt that Colenso should have kept his views to himself. Brooke, while not agreeing with Colenso's opinions, defended his right to express them freely. He gave £5 to Colenso's Defence Fund, and wrote to the newspapers voicing his support. When Angela protested that his appearance in print was 'injurious to your position as the ruler of a Sovereign State', he replied that he 'could not keep silence when impelled to speak'.[44]

But their friendship survived the conflicts that from time to time divided them. In December 1866, Sir James suffered a stroke, and as soon as he could be moved was taken to Angela's house in Torquay. While he was recovering he learned that Lord Derby's Cabinet had turned down his offer of an absolute cession of Sarawak to the Crown. Angela now turned to Italy, opening negotiations through influential friends; but they led to nothing. As a last resort she appealed to Princess Alice, Queen Victoria's second daughter, and at the Princess's request submitted a long confidential memorandum summarising the situation:

> Whatever nation may annex or grant a protectorate to Sarawak will possess a country quite as fertile as Java, with ... an industrious population capable of and slowly accustomed to self-government. It would break any Englishman's heart to offer such a gift to any one but to the Sovereign. Nevertheless as hitherto any offer made by Sir James Brooke has been rejected by the English government it seems probable such a course may be forced upon him.[45]

The memorandum was dated July 29, 1867. Sir James, in failing health, made no further attempts himself to secure Sarawak's future. He died on June 11, 1868. The sovereignty of Sarawak was left to Charles Brooke and his heirs, and ultimately to 'Her Majesty the Queen of England, her heirs and assigns for ever'. Angela was one of three special executors appointed to safeguard the sovereignty; but her active interest in Sarawak appears to have virtually ended with the Rajah's death. Within a few years Charles Brooke had paid off the state's debts to her, and in 1872 she sold the Quop Estate, near Kuching, where she had started a model farm some eight years previously. She remained an executor until 1898, when she appointed her husband in her place.

In James Brooke, one feels, Angela met her match. He was not overawed by her fortune or by the glamour surrounding her name; while appreciating her good qualities and admiring her achievements he was not blind to her faults. Their friendship was a friendship between equals. His passionate integrity was matched by her fierce loyalty; they were qualities that each recognised and admired in the other, but which occasionally led to clashes between them. Angela was sure she knew what was right for her friend; Brooke, though he valued her advice and respected her opinions, insisted on following his own convictions. Had they married, his magnanimity might perhaps have softened her sometimes harsh judgments of men and events. This, however, can only be conjecture.

Twelve

THE BARONESS

Despite her involvement in overseas ventures, Angela's main interests were always at home. She never neglected her social life. In 1861 she had leased a house in Torquay, Ehrenberg Hall. In this delightful sheltered spot on the mild South Devon coast she and Hannah spent some months of every year, usually in winter. When Angela was in residence she was the leader of local society, entering into the life of the community and entertaining as always on a grand scale.

In the summer, they went as often as possible to Holly Lodge, which Angela had inherited in 1849 on the death of the Duke of St Albans. Situated only a few short miles from Piccadilly, Holly Lodge was an ideal place for entertaining out-of-doors, as Harriot St Albans had discovered. In Angela's day, as in Harriot's, the great lawns became the setting for splendid entertainments attended by the highest in the land, while in the meadows children released for a few hours from the London slums romped and gorged themselves on strawberries.

The glory of Holly Lodge was its setting – sixty secluded acres with spectacular views right across London to the Surrey hills. Everywhere were magnificent trees and flowering shrubs; Angela introduced many new varieties of plant life, some of them sent by Rajah Brooke and other friends overseas. When the heat in town became oppressive or work more than usually burdensome, the tranquil, beautiful grounds of Holly Lodge were soothing and refreshing. Occasionally the widowed Queen drove over for a visit, bringing with her one or two of her children or grandchildren. She, too, could relax in 'Miss Coutts's pretty place'.

A more frequent royal visitor was the Queen's cousin, Princess Mary Adelaide of Cambridge, who in 1866 married Prince Francis of Teck. Born in 1833, the Princess was a warm-hearted woman whose generous nature was matched by her generous size. She was much loved for her charitable works, in which her friend Miss Coutts was a guiding influence. Her daughter, Princess May (afterwards Queen Mary) became as attached to Angela as her mother was; her son, Francis, was Angela's godson. 'I shall like to feel that there is a new link between us and to claim for your godson some portion of the affection so warmly bestowed on his mother,'[1] wrote Mary Adelaide to her 'dearest Miss Coutts' in 1870, soon after the baby was born.

Holly Lodge was more than just a peaceful haven. Here, Angela had her model farm, with cows, goats, pigs, poultry and other livestock. The goat, she insisted, was the poor man's cow, and she did her best to encourage its wider use. Her own goats were champions and well-known at shows; the milk was sent to hospitals. She was the active President of both the British Goat Society and the Bee-Keepers' Association. She also tried breeding llamas at one time for their wool, but they did not survive the climate.

Holly Lodge

Angela's love of animals showed itself in a combination of sentimental attachment to her pets (especially her dogs) and compassionate realism towards those animals which, as she once wrote, had been 'given to man for use' and 'must never be abused'.[2] As President of the Ladies' Committee of the RSPCA she campaigned tirelessly against vivisection, the maltreatment of tram and cab horses, the inhumane transport of live cattle (she experimented with a new kind of cattle truck), and the trapping of wild birds. 'Life, whether in man or beast, is sacred,' she declared, and she condemned cruelty to animals whenever it came to her notice.

A portion of the grounds of Holly Lodge was always open for visiting school-children to play in; Angela also provided the site for the schools attached to St Ann's Church. At the bottom of Swain's Lane, Highgate is Holly Village, a miniature 'garden city' that she built opposite the south-east corner of her estate in 1865. The twelve houses, some detached, the rest in pairs, are in Henry Darbishire's best Gothic style. It is not clear whether they were originally intended for employees of Coutts & Co. or for members of Angela's own staff; but by 1867, when the *Christian Times* sent a reporter to visit them, they were occupied by 'a higher class in the social scale'.

The house the reporter saw over had 'a parlour, kitchen, washhouse and offices' on the ground floor, with three bedrooms above, 'the doors of which are all well contrived to prevent draughts, and screen the position of the beds'.[3] There were also rooms for a lodger, planned to give maximum privacy. Today, although the interiors of the houses have been modernised, the exteriors with their turrets and spirelets, gargoyles and ornamental ridges, hand-carved teak doors and Gothic windows, are much the same as they were over a century ago.

Holly Village was unique in being Angela's only 'middle-class' development. Her chief concern was and would always be the welfare of the very poor of London. Over the years she had built churches, schools and flats; had provided opportunities for training and employment; had sought to improve sanitation and donated large sums to hospitals. In popular esteem she stood second only to the Queen herself. Indeed, there was one period, during the winter of 1866/67, when she probably stood first. The Queen's popularity had reached its nadir. Reform was in the air: it was more than thirty years since the Reform Act of 1832, and working men were now demanding the vote. A new Reform Bill had been thrown out by Parliament and there had been riots in Hyde Park.

On December 3, 1866, a great Reform demonstration took place. Thousands of working men marched through central London. Their route took them along Piccadilly past 1 Stratton Street, where Angela and a few friends had gathered at the bay window of her drawing-room to watch them pass. The Reverend Julian Young has left a vivid description of the scene as the marchers, some 25,000 of them walking six or eight abreast with arms linked, came opposite Stratton Street and 'caught a glimpse of [Miss Coutts's] well-known face':

> In one instant a shout was raised, not only by the members of the procession, but by all the bystanders, 'Three cheers for Miss Coutts,'

which was taken up again and again as each rank filed by . . . I never witnessed anything like the popular enthusiasm. Every hat was raised, every arm unlinked, every eye was directed to her, every face gleamed and glistened with pleasure, as, with unaffected simplicity and a gentle movement of her head, she returned the universal greetings. For upwards of two hours and a half the air rang with repeated huzzahs – huzzahs unanimous and heartfelt, as if representing a national sentiment.[4]

That Burdett's daughter should be cheered by a Reform crowd was perhaps not surprising. But this was a spontaneous and remarkable tribute to Angela in her own right, an acknowledgment of her long-standing concern for the underdog.

Two months later, Queen Victoria was persuaded by her Ministers to open Parliament – only the second time she had agreed to do so since the Prince Consort's death. As she drove through the rain, her carriage windows lowered so that she could be seen, she was greeted by crowds of angry people clamouring for Reform. The Queen, in turn, was angered by the 'nasty faces' of her subjects, refusing to admit that her own long isolation from them could have any bearing on the matter.

The second Reform Bill was passed that summer, making a million more Britons eligible to vote. Angela, with characteristic thoroughness, had a pamphlet prepared and distributed among her tenants at Columbia Square, explaining their entitlement as electors in the new borough of Hackney.

Over the next decade, Queen Victoria emerged from her seclusion to become the revered matriarch of the British Empire. But Angela never lost the title that the Cockneys had given her: 'Queen of the Poor'.

*

In 1864, Angela had embarked upon her most ambitious scheme of all: Columbia Market. She was determined to do something to improve the food supply of the poor of London. There was certainly room for improvement.

The East Enders traditionally did their shopping in the street markets. Noisy, colourful, bursting with life, these markets were as much places of recreation as centres of trade. The range of goods offered for sale was enormous: it was said that from Whitechapel Market one could 'furnish a house, provision a family and plant a garden'. On cold nights hungry waifs clustered round the pie-man's stand to warm themselves at his brazier and sniff the hot pies they could not afford to taste. At the meat and fish stalls the frugal housewife could pick up for a few pence a plaice or some bloaters, a bit of offal, or bones for soup.

But though it was cheap, much of the food on sale was of inferior quality. Often, it had been bought from the big wholesale food markets at knock-down prices because it was no longer fresh. And the food at the local grocer's shop was unlikely to be much better. In this, as in so many things, the very poor were at the mercy of a system they were powerless to change.

What was needed, Angela decided, was a new market, one where the consumer would again, as in former times, be able to buy fresh food direct from the producer. More than that, it should be a place of beauty and inspiration. She commissioned Mr Darbishire to design a market that would rival the *Halles* of Paris and Brussels in architectural splendour. And so, as the first occupants were settling into Holly Village, a remarkable structure was beginning to rise on a two-acre site in the East End next to Columbia Square. This was Columbia Market. It took an army of labourers and craftsmen five years to build, cost nearly a quarter of a million pounds, and was opened by Angela with great ceremony on April 28, 1869, in the presence of the Duke and Duchess of Teck, the Archbishop of Canterbury, the Lord Mayor, and other dignitaries. Unfortunately, it rapidly proved to be a complete failure.

Nothing quite like it had ever been seen before – certainly not in the East End of London. It was variously described as 'this costly Gothic palace' and 'this almost cathedral pile'. The interior of the main hall did indeed bear a strong resemblance to a fourteenth-century Gothic church, with 'clusters of polished granite columns . . . in similar style to the Chapter House in Salisbury, only twice as lofty' supporting a cross-pointed roof 'groined throughout with pitch-pine'.[5] Elaborate carving and intricate wrought-iron work were everywhere much in evidence.

The buildings were designed to accommodate four classes of traders, ranging from first-class dealers who were provided with twelve large shops, to fourth-class dealers (the costermongers) for whom there were 400 spaces in the central quadrangle. In between were twenty-four smaller shops for second-class dealers and about 270 spaces in the arcades and galleries surrounding the quadrangle for third-class dealers. Lack of space was certainly not a problem.

But for once, it seems, Angela had not done her homework – or she had been wrongly advised. Her aims were laudable enough: 'to supply

Columbia Market, Bethnal Green, from The Illustrated London News, *May 1, 1869*

the surrounding poor with wholesome food at a fair rate; to bring the producer and consumer into closer communication with each other; and to promote habits of industry and thrift among the humblest class of traders'.[6] (A secondary aim was the provision of lodgings for City Clerks, whose needs tended to be overlooked by the builders of new apartment blocks.) What Angela had not bargained for was the opposition of established dealers in existing markets such as Billingsgate and Smithfield. They virtually controlled the supply of foodstuffs coming into the East End, and they could and did prevent it from reaching Columbia.

Six months after her market had opened, Angela was forced to close it. But, determined to make it work somehow, she re-opened it in February 1870 as a wholesale fish market. To ensure that fish came to Columbia rather than Billingsgate, Angela subsidised the fishermen; to encourage dealers to come to her market, she charged them nominal rents and even paid them salaries! But once again vested interests were too strong: the Billingsgate dealers did not hesitate to use any means in their power – and their power was considerable – to thwart Miss Coutts's 'noble scheme'. In the spring of 1871, realizing that she could not fight the entire London fish trade on her own, Angela offered Columbia Market to the City of London Corporation.

It was an extremely generous but somewhat embarrassing gift. The Corporation did what it could, setting up a special sub-committee to run the market. But during the years it managed Columbia its operations showed a consistent deficit and the volume of business was about a quarter that of Billingsgate. Eventually the Corporation, too, had to admit defeat, and in 1875 it gave the market back to Angela. She had, in the meantime, through her influence with members of parliament, pushed through an Act enabling a tramway to be built from Columbia Market to the nearest railway station; for she was convinced that transport was the main problem. The tramway was never built; but it is doubtful whether it would have made much difference. As Angela herself admitted in a letter to Henry Ryder in February 1874:

> The *Monopoly* of the Salesmen of Billingsgate prevents the food coming through. Fish is actually destroyed in the Market [Billingsgate] from want of room for distribution – rather disgusting ...[7]

Disgusting it certainly was. But one cannot help feeling that, even without the oppositon of Billingsgate and other rivals, Columbia Market, built with such good intentions and high hopes, was destined from the start to become a magnificent and slightly ridiculous white elephant. It was such an incongruity, this 'glittering edifice' set among some of the worst slums of London. To the Cockney housewife, setting out to buy her family's meagre provisions and accustomed to the cheerful hubbub of the street markets or the gossipy intimacy of the fusty little corner shop, Columbia must have seemed an intimidating place. With its churchy atmosphere and its exhortations in Gothic lettering to Be Sober, Be Vigilant, Be Pitiful, Be Courteous, it was the kind of place where you kept your voice to a whisper and tiptoed out as quickly as possible. It was surely a mistake, too, to prohibit Sunday trading (except for milk at certain hours), when Sunday was the only day most working people could do their shopping. And many costers must have been put off by the prominent notices banning 'profane cursing and swearing', for which there were graded fines ranging from a shilling for labourers and common folk to five shillings for 'every person of or above the degree of a gentleman'.

Many were the efforts made by Angela and, later, by her husband too to put her market buildings to good use; but all in vain. The City clerks' lodging-houses were always full; but as a market Columbia simply did not work. It was closed for the last time in 1885. 'The food supply of a great City should not be *throttled*,'[8] Angela had written indignantly to Disraeli in 1874, pointing out the seriousness of the social issues involved. She was right. But not even she could beat a system that had been established for centuries. As a modern economist has succinctly put it: 'It is in the nature of markets, as of all other public utilities, to enjoy a local monopoly which outsiders infringe at their peril.'[9]

*

In spite of being a failure, Columbia Market seems to have caught the popular imagination in a way that no other project of Angela's did. The concept was so bold, the buildings themselves so vast and splendid. Certainly it was her gift of the market to the City Corporation that prompted Mr Gladstone to consider what kind of public recognition could be made to her. On May 4, 1871, Gladstone, then half-way through his first term of office as Prime Minister, scribbled a note on a scrap of paper to the leader of the Liberal peers, Lord Granville:

> Miss B. Coutts has handed over in trust to the Corporation of London, Columbia Market ... Is there any way in wh the remarkable services of Miss B.C. to the public cd be acknd?

Back came the scrap of paper the next day with the laconic suggestion from Lord Granville scrawled in the margin: 'I like notion of peerage'.[10] Two days later, Queen Victoria recorded in her journal:

> Mr Gladstone then asked if I would not object to a Peerage being offered to Miss B. Coutts, who had made such generous and admirable use of her money. I quite approved.[11]

It was a unique offer. At the time, no woman had ever been raised to the peerage solely on her own merits.* For several days Angela hesitated. What passed through her mind we can only surmise. No doubt she remembered that her father had several times refused a similar honour; on the other hand, the prospect of adding to the prestige of the ancient and illustrious name of Burdett must have been tempting. As for herself, though she had always been 'quiet and unpretending' she did not suffer from false modesty. And any doubts she may have had about her eligibility for such an honour would have been warmly countered by Hannah Brown. For Hannah, this was probably the proudest moment of her life. She could not resist writing to tell the Prime Minister how she rejoiced in this 'noble act of recognition'.

On May 11, Mr Gladstone reported to the Queen that 'Miss Burdett Coutts, after taking a couple of days to consider an offer little expected, has accepted it.'[12] There remained only the choice of a name. The new peeress would be Baroness Burdett-Coutts – but of where? The Couttses, she told Gladstone, were 'one of the *Gypsy* families of the Lowlands of Scotland', and she supposed that

> the wandering instinct of my tribe has hindered my attaching myself to the soil – & I have only pitched a tent here and there. As you have caged the wild bird I will do my best to find it a respectable 'local habitation and a name.'

One place she was connected with was Bramcote, in Warwickshire, 'where the first Burdett founded a priory'. Then there was Holly Lodge, which was

> situated in *two* parishes – Highgate and Brookfield ... Could they not be combined then the whole property residence gardens houses & a site I gave for schools would be included.[13]

* In November 1868 Mrs Disraeli had been created Vicountess Beaconsfield as a tribute to her husband.

She would leave it to the Prime Minister to decide. He did so; and she became Baroness Burdett-Coutts of Highgate and Brookfield.

The country received the news with approbation: the Queen of the Poor had had due recognition from her sovereign. In June, the new Baroness was presented with an address from the people of Westminster; a week or so later she was mingling with the fashionably-dressed crowds at a garden party at Buckingham Palace. '*Lady* Burdett Coutts was presented on her creation,'[14] noted Queen Victoria afterwards in her journal. To the Queen, she would always be *Lady* Burdett-Coutts; but Angela herself preferred the title *Baroness*, and it was as 'the Baroness' that she became popularly known for the rest of her life.

One person who did not live to use her new title was Charles Dickens. His enthusiasm, one feels, would have been second only to Hannah Brown's. But he had died the previous June, aged fifty-eight, having almost literally worked himself to death. He was universally mourned and was buried in Westminster Abbey. Angela had kept in touch with Catherine Dickens and received a congratulatory note from her on her elevation to the peerage.

During the next few years the Baroness received a host of other honours. In January 1872 she learned of the decision of the Turners' Company to make her an honorary Freeman; the following year it was the turn of the Clothworkers. In July 1872, in a ceremony of dazzling splendour at the Guildhall, she became the first woman to receive the Freedom of the City of London. As she entered the Council Chamber, where the whole Court of Common Council was assembled – the Aldermen and Sheriffs in their scarlet robes and gold chains – she was given a standing ovation. There were more cheers as the Lord Mayor's address was read; it was presented to her afterwards in an elaborate and costly gold casket, engraved with tableaux of acts of mercy and with Angela's arms enamelled in the appropriate heraldic colours. On the inside of the lid was an engraving of Columbia Market.

Finally came a similar offer from Edinburgh: the city where her grandfather was born now wished to make her its first woman Freeman. Her great-grandfather, John Coutts, had twice been Lord Provost of Edinburgh in the 1740s, and it was his portrait that was displayed on the platform of the Music Hall when the ceremony took place in January 1874. The hall, Edinburgh's largest, was decked with flowers and flags and – according to one report – 'crowded to suffocation'. Hannah Brown, now old and frail, sat next to Angela on the platform. The ceremony, she wrote to a friend, was 'one of the most interesting *spectacles* I ever witnessed';[15] she was quite overwhelmed by the enthusiasm of the ordinary people. For Angela, it was gratifying to hear the Lord Provost speak of both her father and her grandfather: Thomas Coutts had received the Freedom of the City in 1813. It was to him, as she pointed out in her own speech, that she owed her present position and 'the ample means which alone have enabled me to further those public objects to which you have referred so kindly'.[16]

*

Angela was never one to rest on her laurels. While in Edinburgh she conducted a vigorous campaign against the ill-treatment of tram-horses there – 'miserable skeletons', as she described them, that 'toil and sweat up the inclines' of the hilly city, goaded by 'the stimulus of pain so useful when physical power fails'.[17] Boys of under thirteen, she wrote to her cousin Henry Ryder, were employed on the trams and were 'learning cruelty . . . and the *vilest* language and other habits'.[18] Fortunately she found the Edinburgh City Council more amenable on this issue than the City of London Corporation had been over the vexed question of Columbia Market. 'The *Radical* Town Council of Edinburgh have acted better & with more regard to public interest than the Conservative Corporation,' she told Henry Ryder. 'The Tramway grievances have been very greatly remedied – the Food Supply of London *burked*.'[19]

There were other preoccupations at this time – matters concerning her family and the bank that were causing worry and vexation. Public honours were all very fine, but no amount of public adulation could make up for snubs and insults from one's own family. On this occasion it was Angela's nephew and heir, Frank Money, who was the cause of the trouble. Frank, the 'Suffolk baby' whose birth she had welcomed with such delight, had now, at twenty-one, brought down her wrath on his head.

Angela had been pleasantly surprised when Frank suddenly decided to visit her in September 1873, shortly after she had arrived in Edinburgh. He had evidently decided, on the eve of his twenty-first birthday, that it would be a good idea to have a confidential chat with his rather formidable aunt, with whom he had not always been on the best of terms. As Angela expressed it to Henry Ryder, he had determined 'to put all straight . . . between us'. She was afraid the 'poor boy' was surrounded by 'adverse influences' – meaning, perhaps, his large family of half-brothers and sisters, though she conceded that his only good adviser was his half-brother Captain Albert Money.

But if there was one influence that Angela was certain was adverse not only to Frank but to herself and the bank as well, it was that of a certain family, the Churchills. A Churchill daughter had already become engaged to one of Frank's half-brothers, and Angela was convinced that the Churchills were trying to ensnare Frank into marrying another daughter, Edith. Quite apart from the fact that Frank was much too young to marry, the connection, in Angela's view, would be 'altogether uncongenial'.

Frank himself, or so it appeared from their conversation, was as uncertain about his feelings for Edith as he was about his future. He didn't want to live at home, was keen to leave Cambridge without taking a degree, and had ideas about joining the bank. This last posed problems. As Angela explained to Frank, the situation was complicated by uncertainties arising from the Duchess of St Albans's will: no one could tell 'who would be the surviving Trustee – who the Partners – how and when the Trust would finally end'. The partners, in fact, were none too keen for Frank to enter the bank, and Angela tended to agree with them.

Although her meeting with Frank did not settle anything definite about his future, Angela felt that it had cleared the air. 'Our relations are now as before – very affectionate and very confidential,'[20] she told Henry Ryder. But, within a month of Frank's visit to Edinburgh, this newly-forged confidence between aunt and nephew had been rudely shattered – by the announcement of Frank's engagement to Edith Churchill. Angela was 'bitterly disappointed', not only because of the engagement itself, but because, as she complained to Henry Ryder, she felt she had been 'both ignored and deceived or at least misled'. It was hard, she told Henry, 'to live over again the . . . painful experiences of early life', though it was not in Frank's power or in anyone else's, she added, 'to wound me now as then'.[21]

Her main objection to Frank's marriage was that the connection of Churchill & Sims – a perfectly respectable and well-established firm of timber merchants – with the house of Coutts & Co. was a wholly unsuitable one. She was not completely prejudiced against 'trade' connections *per se*. She had, as we know, a great admiration for self-made men, and was for instance delighted when Henry Ryder's son became engaged to the daughter of W. H. Smith, whom she regarded as 'a most steady and esteemed friend'. (It must be said, however, that W. H. Smith having built up his father's bookshop business into a highly successful and lucrative concern, had gone on to become an MP – later a cabinet minister – a prominent philanthropist, and treasurer of the Society for Promoting Christian Knowledge.)

Had Frank not been heir to the half-share in Coutts & Co., Angela would probably have viewed his marriage to Edith Churchill with less hostility. As it was, she saw it above all as 'a blow to the House'. She herself, she had once told Dickens, had promised the bank partners 'never to associate herself with anyone, in any kind of engagement or business, who was connected with any House or Enterprize'.[22] She felt strongly that Frank Money should be bound by the same principle. As she wrote to Lord Harrowby (ironically, in view of the storm her own marriage was to create):

> Naturally it [the bank] is founded perhaps too securely to be shaken by any one act or circumstance but its prestige may be impaired, and there are not wanting those not sorry to see or promote this and certainly not unwilling to lower my own position.[23]

To at least one of the bank partners, H. L. Antrobus,* there was something rather pathetic in Angela's fierce loyalty and protectiveness towards her grandfather's 'House'. Writing to Henry Ryder at about this time, Antrobus, though 'glad to hear that the Baroness has so strong a desire to consider the interests of the House in every way', added:

> It is sad however to think the House takes with her the place of family ties as when poor Mrs B. is gathered to her Father as she must be at some probably not very distant day, it will be a lonely existence to have no family to fall back upon – had she considered this earlier I think she would have made more of a son of Master Frank.[24]

Once more, Angela felt herself to be isolated: 'I feel a little desirous not to stand quite alone in the family,' she told Henry Ryder, who himself was so intimidated by her that he felt obliged to refuse Frank's request to be a trustee of the marriage settlement. Under ordinary circumstances, Henry told Frank, nothing would have given him greater pleasure:

> But you must consider my position. I am nearly related to Lady Burdett Coutts, and have always been on the most cordial terms with her. I am also under obligation to her for placing me here [at Coutts

---

* Hugh Lindsay Antrobus had become a partner in 1843. He was the son of Sir Edmund Antrobus, who had been a partner from 1816 to 1870, and whose own father and uncle had been two of Thomas Coutts's original partners.

& Co]. Moreover I regret to say that the circumstances of my accepting your recent invitation [to meet the Churchills] has much altered my relationship with her, which is most painful to my feelings. If I were now further to go against her wishes I fear that the breach would be much widened.[25]

Henry also declined an invitation to the wedding, which took place in April 1875. Three years later, the affair still rankled with Angela. In a letter to Henry of February 1878 she referred to Frank's '*very large* and needy relations on one side and (judging by the way his marriage was effected) scheming people of a rather second rate flashy mercantile kind on the other'.[26]

Frank and Edith had five children, but they separated in 1887 after twelve years of marriage. So perhaps Angela was right and they were never suited – though this hardly justifies her intervention and indeed was not the main reason for it. Their daughter Clara, who wrote (in her seventies) the first full-length biography of the Baroness, relates in it that, because of 'family differences', she never met her great-aunt until the spring of 1900, when Angela was eighty-six and Clara herself was in her twenties.

Frank, who took the additional surname of Coutts in 1880, did not enter the bank. He became a poet of some repute, and wrote the libretti for several operas to music by the Spanish composer Albeniz, whose patron Frank was for many years.

In 1913, the ancient Barony of Latymer, to which the Burdetts had a claim through marriage, was called out of abeyance in favour of Frank Money-Coutts, who became the 5th Baron Latymer. His son, Hugh, and his grandson (the present Lord Latymer) both made their careers in the bank; its present chairman, David Money-Coutts, is a great-grandson of Frank Money-Coutts.

*

'*When poor Mrs B. is gathered to her Father . . .*' When Lindsay Antrobus wrote this, Hannah's health was a continual source of worry to Angela. During the winter of 1873–74, when they were in Edinburgh, she had 'taken cold after cold', as one of Angela's advisers told Disraeli. It had seemed to those about the two ladies that Mrs Brown's health was 'a good deal broken'.[27]

She had survived that cold northern winter, however, and the following year they wintered in Torquay. In the middle of January

Hannah was well enough to travel to London to see Henry Irving's portrayal of Hamlet at the Lyceum Theatre. This production, which made Irving's reputation as a Shakespearian actor, had opened the previous October; it was a triumph, and ran for 200 nights. Hannah Brown became one of Irving's most ardent fans and saw his Hamlet thirty times. It was probably as much for Hannah's sake as for her own that Angela invited Irving to Stratton Street, thus beginning a friendship that would last until Irving's death in 1905.

Henry Irving was then in his late thirties, a tall spare man with a long face, black bushy brows, and deep-set dark eyes whose expression was at times piercing, at others dreaming. He was, wrote his grandson and biographer, Laurence Irving, 'the epitome of intensity – single-minded, self-centred and self-sufficient'.[28] In 1887 Angela presented him with David Garrick's ring, which had a miniature of Shakespeare mounted in it. But is was Hannah who had a really soft spot for her 'Brave Boy', as she called him; and Irving was not so self-sufficient as to be indifferent to the old lady's devotion. During the last years of her life he showed her many little kindnesses, not the least of which was reading and answering the many letters with which she bombarded him wherever he happened to be.

Reading Mrs Brown's letters grew increasingly difficult, for she was gradually going blind. After an operation in the spring of 1877 she partially regained her sight. Writing to Irving in May, Angela enclosed 'a little note of thanks in Mrs Brown's own hand ... but you will understand the poor darling *does not* see to write ... Your flowers are a great pleasure, she arranges them and *sees* the colours – indeed, as she told you, a bunch of your flowers on the table was the first object she saw *spontaneously*.'[29]

Within three months a second operation was found to be necessary, but it appears to have been less successful than the first. Her general health was improving, wrote a friend some weeks afterwards, but 'the sense of inactivity and imprisonment becomes more irksome'. She was 'never free from the oppressive sense of darkness', and was 'sometimes much depressed; at others cheerful and argumentative as usual'.[30]

Throughout the summer of 1877 Angela was, as she wrote, 'in constant attendance on my poor sorely afflicted friend'.[31] There were other matters demanding her attention. A crisis was brewing at the bank. Although the partners had not so far confided in her, she had a fairly shrewd idea of what was going on. In fact, the partners were on the horns of a dilemma, with the reputation of the bank at stake whichever way they moved. Edward Marjoribanks, Jr, now the senior partner, was on the verge of bankruptcy, and all attempts to get him to come to grips with his situation had so far failed.

By August 1877 things had come to a head. Action had to be taken and the Baroness informed. Marjoribanks, now owing nearly half a million pounds and with an imminent claim from the Bank of Scotland for £40,000, was still stalling. It would be impossible to keep matters quiet for much longer. He must be made to resign as a partner and the profits from his share used to liquidate his debts.

Angela agreed. Moreover, she offered to relieve Marjoribanks of his most pressing liabilities on condition he accepted the partners' terms. During the first week of September there was much to-ing and fro-ing between Stratton Street and the Strand, and between the Strand and Marjoribanks' house, where he had taken to his bed. His wife reported him too ill to sign the necessary papers. Angela and the partners stood firm. In a matter of days it was all over: Edward Marjoribanks' partnership was dissolved, and Angela signed an authority for loans totalling £83,500 made to him by Coutts & Co. to be repaid and charged to her account.

Meanwhile, Angela had once more plunged into relief operations. The objects of her concern on this occasion were not the poor of her own country, but the thousands of Turkish women and children then fleeing from the advancing Cossacks in the latest Russo-Turkish war. The previous year, the British public had been shocked to hear of the so-called Bulgarian atrocities – the murder of 12,000 Bulgarian Christians by Turkish irregular forces known as the Bashi-Bazouks. Now, Angela had heard from her friend Henry Layard, British Ambassador in Constantinople, of the plight of the Turkish refugees. Death, rape or mutilation awaited those who could not get away. Those who did escape were utterly destitute: by August, four months after the start of the war, there were nearly 30,000 families facing death from starvation or exposure in the coming harsh winter.

In a letter to the *Daily Telegraph*, Angela appealed for a Turkish Compassionate Fund to be set up to aid 'these cruelly treated Moslems'. She herself started off the Fund with £1,000, and within weeks it had grown to £30,000. By the beginning of October the yacht *Constance* was ready to sail for Constantinople, crammed to the gunnels with blankets and rugs, calico, flannel and serge; bandages, quinine and other medicines; tobacco, port wine, baby food, and a variety of other stores. On board as Special Commissioner to the Fund was a young man of twenty-six called William Ashmead Bartlett, an American by birth, who had recently joined the Baroness's secretariat. In a letter to Layard, the Ambassador, Angela commended Mr Bartlett as 'young and active and deeply interested – I hope you will like him'.[32]

Angela had known William Ashmead Bartlett since he was a boy of ten or so. She had met him and his elder brother when they were living with their mother in Torquay. Their father, Ellis Bartlett of Plymouth, Massachusetts, had died in 1852, the year after William's birth. On the outbreak of the American Civil War his widow had brought their two sons to England and they had settled in Devon. The boys attended a school at which Angela was invited to present the prizes and – so the story goes – she was so impressed with the recitation of William at the prize-giving that she offered to help with their education. It was probably through her influence that William later attended Highgate School. He subsequently followed his elder brother to Oxford, where he appears to have been a somewhat reluctant scholar and scraped through with a Third in Modern History. In 1872 he had attended the glittering ceremony in the Guildhall at which Angela had been presented with the Freedom of the City of London, and he was among the privileged few who lunched with the Lord Mayor afterwards.

Bartlett later described his work for the Turkish Compassionate Fund as the 'most startling episode' in his life. He was obviously deeply affected by the horrors he witnessed. He stayed in the Balkans throughout the winter, providing food, clothing, shelter and medical treatment for as many of the refugees as could be reached; the total amount spent by the Fund was about £43,000. From Tatar Bazardjik he wrote to Layard of people 'frozen white & black & blue' being shunted off in their thousands in open railway trucks 'to God knows what suffering'.[33]

In April, Bartlett was taken ill. Angela wrote anxiously to Layard that she knew every care would be taken of 'my dear young friend'. Nevertheless, 'If all in God's providence goes well with Mr Bartlett it is clear the time is come when he must return. I could not run the risk of a repetition of my interview with his poor Mother and his Brother yesterday.'[34]

By July, Bartlett was back in London. Both he and the Baroness had been decorated by the Sultan, Angela receiving the First Class and Diamond Star of the Order of the Medjidiyeh, which was also given to Queen Victoria, and the Grand Cross and Cordon of the Order of Mercy.

Gratifying as these exotic honours were, they could not lessen the load of care and worry that Hannah Brown's blindness imposed. On his return home, Bartlett wrote to Layard that the Baroness's health had been 'impaired by her labours, public and private – the latter having been peculiarly weighty – during the past year'. But he added that Mrs Brown, though now completely deprived of her sight, was 'in wonderful health for her age'. And four months later, on December 3, he could still write that 'Mrs Brown keeps wonderfully well, and Lady B.C. seems to go through her work with as much energy as ever'.[35]

Just under three weeks later, in the afternoon of December 21, 1878, Hannah Brown died.

'It has been an even greater blow to her than those who knew the relations between them could have expected,' wrote Bartlett to Layard. Perhaps Angela had been lulled into a state of false security by the apparent improvement in Hannah's general health. But in any case, nothing could really have prepared her for the shock of Hannah's death. The Baroness Burdett-Coutts, renowned the world over for her poise and serenity, was utterly crushed by the loss of the woman who had been 'the companion and sunshine' of her life. For over fifty years the sprightly, argumentative little lady had steered her through life – from her shy timid girlhood to the threshold of old age where, perhaps, the shy timid girl still hovered. Now she was alone, more alone than she had ever been before.

On the day of the funeral she was unable to meet even the close friends who had gathered at Stratton Street, and a message from her was read to them, copies of which were later distributed. In it she expressed her gratitude to her 'dearest kindest friends' who had 'ministered to my poor Darling in her darkness and affliction'. She asked for their support and comfort, hoping that she herself would be given something of the same 'courage, resignation and unfailing faith' that had sustained her friend.[36] 'By every means,' wrote Bartlett later to Layard, 'she has tried to do honour to [Mrs Brown's] memory, and to demonstrate as she always did in life that Mrs Brown was as closely allied to her as it was possible for any human being to be.'

Hannah was buried beside her husband in the vault beneath St Stephen's Church where Angela also hoped to be buried. The funeral, wrote Bartlett, 'was to all who had known the two together most impressive and painful'. Only the Baroness's 'great strength of character and self-control pulled her through . . . the ordeal'. As the coffin was lowered into the grave Angela knelt and placed both hands on it. 'There could have been few in the church who did not feel deeply for her,'[37] Bartlett told Layard.

Not until January 27 – more than a month after Hannah's death – could Angela bring herself to write to thank the Queen for her letter of sympathy which had come 'in the first hours of my grief for my dearest Earthly friend'. 'I have now,' she added, 'to pick up the threads of a life which seems strangely unreal to me.'[38]

Thirteen

A MOST LAMENTABLE ACT

For a woman as busy as Angela, picking up the threads was to some extent an automatic process. Her work was there, waiting to be done: correspondence piling up day by day, new projects to consider, existing ones to supervise. The claims on her time and her charity were never-ending; the need to plan, to organise, to make decisions was constant. In work, her friends felt, she would find the antidote to grief. 'I suppose she will resume her former life,' wrote Ashmead Bartlett to Layard, 'and throw herself with redoubled vigour into her manifold charitable schemes.'[1]

In 1879, the year following Hannah's death, there was plenty to be done. In South Africa, Britain was at war with the Zulus, who had risen under their king, Cetawayo. When news came in of the crushing defeat the Zulus had inflicted on the British forces at Isandhlwana on January 22, Angela's friend Sir Garnet Wolseley was ordered to the Cape to take command. Wolseley, a veteran of the Crimea, had distinguished himself in various colonial expeditions in India, China, Canada and West Africa. After his defeat of King Koffee in the Ashanti War of 1873–74, a new slang expression had entered the language: 'all Sir Garnet', synonymous with 'all correct'.*

To ensure that the sick and wounded in Zululand received proper medical care and attention, the Stafford House South African Aid Committee was set up, with a ladies' committee presided over by Angela. Much had been learned since the terrible days of the Crimean War, twenty-five years earlier. Now, thanks to the Nightingale Training School at St Thomas's Hospital, there were properly trained nurses available. On June 11 Angela wrote to tell Sir Garnet that seven nurses were on their way, accompanied by Surgeon-General Ross and Dr Stoker. The small team proved to be a valuable supplement to the army medical staff, ministering both to the British troops and to the enemy.

---

* Angela, who had the greatest admiration for Wolseley, possessed a champion goat called Sir Garnet which was king of her herd at Holly Lodge. It is not known whether she named the animal herself as a tribute to her friend!

By early December Mr Surgeon Ross and five of the nurses were back in England. The other two nurses remained in South Africa with Dr Stoker, whose work among the Zulus, Angela told Wolseley, was '*most* important – as a Christian work almost priceless and of *political* interest also at this moment'. If the money she had sent him from the fund was exhausted, she would 'willingly help by a hundred pounds more to maintain them temporarily if you saw your way to establishing amongst the Zulus any permanent Medical Mission'.[2] We do not know whether this offer was taken up or a permanent mission established; but by March 1880 the work of the Stafford House Committee had been completed.

In London, meanwhile, Angela's attention had been drawn to the particular needs of two groups of young women – flower sellers and art students. The flower girls needed protection and the students wanted somewhere to live. The Baroness provided both.

Angela had always been interested in schemes that helped young people to be self-sufficient. For years she had supported the 'shoeblack brigades', which provided regular work for boys from the Ragged Schools; and in 1874 she had given £5,000 to a scheme for maintaining poor boys on the training ships *Arethusa*, *Chichester* and *Goliath*. Her latest idea was a Flower Girls' Brigade for those waifs who, like Eliza Dolittle, made a meagre living by selling flowers to fine gentlemen and ladies. Each girl was allotted her own territory where the police could keep an eye on her, and attempts were made to build up a permanent clientele. At the same time, Angela tried to win the girls away from their precarious occupation by opening a factory where they could learn to make artificial flowers; or they were encouraged to go into service – an alternative whose benefits were questionable, to say the least. But the girls were grateful: they clubbed together with the watercress women and presented the Baroness with a silver statuette of a barefooted watercress seller.

The idea of a hostel for female art students came from Louisa Twining, the indefatigable workhouse visitor, who in 1861 had opened a home for workhouse girls. Angela had furnished the home and paid the first three years' rent. Learning of Miss Twining's new suggestion, she at once offered her assistance.

Angela, as we know, was not convinced of the value of higher education for girls. She is unlikely to have taken any interest in the first women's colleges, Girton and Newnham, established at Cambridge in the seventies, or in the Oxford women's colleges which were founded a few years later. Nor, one imagines, did she particularly rejoice when London University announced in 1878 that women would henceforth be eligible for its degrees and honours. In 1870 she had declined an invitation to become a member of the London School Board on the grounds that it was not a suitable office for a woman; and she was probably as much against the idea of women doctors as Florence Nightingale herself, who thought any woman who wanted to be a doctor instead of a nurse was merely trying 'to do things just because men do them!'[3] Nevertheless, as long as women stuck to 'suitable' professions, Angela was all in favour of their earning their living. Had not Hannah, from whom she had learned so much, started out as a working woman? So she supported the 'art students' home for ladies' in Brunswick Square with her name and her money, and it was still flourishing at the time of her death.

*

But no amount of charitable work, at home or overseas, however absorbing and gratifying in its results, could fill the aching void caused by Hannah's death. Picking up the threads might be comparatively easy; weaving them into a satisfying, harmonious texture was another matter. It was Hannah who had been largely responsible for the harmony in Angela's life.

Long ago, Dickens had written that Miss Coutts had 'the materials of comfort and consolation within herself'. He was only partly right. Angela's inner strength was essentially a strength of will-power. It showed itself in her quiet but inflexible determination, in her assurance of being right and her renowned self-control. Her religion – that unquestioning, unassailable Evangelical faith she had imbibed as a girl – served to reinforce these qualities. It was a religion that gave its adherents confidence in the face of death. But to someone facing the anguish of bereavement it was, perhaps, less of a comfort. The fact was that Angela's greatest consolation had always been Hannah. Relying on Hannah for so much, she had never built up emotional reserves of her own. Now she had nothing to draw on. At sixty-five she was as emotionally immature and vulnerable as a young girl, her loneliness intensified by the emptiness within.

Unable to face the thought of a summer alone at Holly Lodge, she decided to take a small party of friends on a Mediterranean cruise. She chartered a steam yacht, the *Walrus*, and invited some old friends, Admiral and Mrs Gordon and the geologist, James Tennant. She also asked Edwin Long, the portrait-painter, and his wife, and – partly in gratitude for his kindness to Mrs Brown – Henry Irving. The party was completed by William Ashmead Bartlett, the 'dear young friend' who had gone to Turkey as her Compassionate Fund Commissioner. It was Ashmead's sympathetic understanding that had helped her to struggle through the past few months. She was beginning to reply on his support and to find his presence indispensable.

They left England in July. Photographs of Angela taken on the cruise show a slight, almost shrunken figure – so fragile that it seems as if a puff of wind would blow it over. Her face, always melancholy in repose, is turned away from the camera with an expression of profound sadness. But it was impossible to be sad all the time. There was much to see and do, and Irving in particular was a stimulating companion. 'We've had a most delightful time in Spain, Tangiers and Tunis,' he wrote to his stage manager from Corfu, 'and now we are in Greece or in its Islands – nothing short of fairyland but – oh – it's devilish hot.'[4]

Wherever they went, Irving soaked up impressions like a sponge, storing them in his memory for possible future use in productions at the Lyceum. In Venice, the germ of an idea that had planted itself in his mind was fertilized, to bear fruit when he returned home that autumn in the shape of a new production of *The Merchant of Venice*. His thoughtful, sympathetic interpretation of Shylock, influenced by his observations of the Levantine Jew on his home ground, was one of the great triumphs of his career.

Irving left the *Walrus* at Marseilles early in September to return home and start rehearsals for his new season. His presence had enlivened the company, but his ebullience and intensity were perhaps a little overpowering in the enclosed world of a small ship. Now, as the *Walrus* sailed north, Ashmead Bartlett came into his own. Angela was struck afresh by the attractive qualities of this young man she had come to regard almost as an adopted son. How kind and considerate he was, how attentive and helpful – and how fond of her he seemed to be. Her affection for him deepened; the heavy load of grief lifted slightly. By the time they reached the Channel Islands she was writing to Irving with a new jauntiness.

For the last part of the voyage they were joined by two young sisters – 'nice girls,' wrote Angela to Irving, '. . . who would be pretty if they would leave their poor hair to grow as Nature meant. Life on board, you know, does not admit of much vanity'.[5] She did not add that for young Mr Bartlett it was a welcome change to have some female companions nearer his own age. His flirtation with the younger sister, Miss Shirley, did not go unnoticed by their fellow-passengers. But Angela, wrapped up in her own plans, saw nothing. In a lively letter to Irving, she described their rough passage from Jersey to Cherbourg after a slight accident to the *Walrus*. As they were entering Jersey harbour the pilot had driven the yacht on to a reef, holing her slightly, and the Captain had decided to make for Cherbourg:

> That evening a very severe predicted gale set in and we could not put to sea for a day and tossed or rather rolled about in our restless anchorage and next day crossed to Cherbourg, in a very big sea, rougher while it lasted than the Bay. Your bed mattress outside [the] deck saloon and the chairs were all thrown [overboard] and Mr Bartlett, a young lady and myself nearly followed. The dinner table on deck walked about and all sorts of other casualties . . . This little disaster changed all arrangements and we had all to get to S. Malo, where I had promised to inspect a Life Boat, by land.

France was a country full of memories for Angela. They came flooding back as the excitement of the crossing faded. It was strange, she told Irving, to live over 'an old French life quite past . . . Even at this moment the Horses neighing as the diligence enters the old French Courtyard carried me back such years!' And she ended her letter:

> You will feel how every sound, the most simple homely sight, a chord on some poor cracked instrument, unfold pictures of that life of mine which, until now, has never been without one dear little figure.[6]

The cruise was over. Soon she would be returning home to resume her lonely life. Ahead of her was the prospect of years of emptiness. But already she had decided that life on her own was more than she could bear. The idea of sharing it with anyone other than Hannah would at one time have been unthinkable; and of course it was impossible to replace Hannah. But the void had to be filled somehow. Since Hannah's death she had found her greatest comfort in the constant presence of Ashmead Bartlett. During the months that they had lived at close quarters on the yacht she had come to realise how important he was to her. At home in Stratton Street during the first winter without Hannah she realised it all the more. Whether the initiative came from him or from her we cannot say. But by the early summer of 1880 she had determined to make Ashmead her husband. She hoped, as she later wrote to Lord Harrowby, that 'the event would be in the heat of the

London season quickly accomplished & have become a nine days wonder'.[7] She was soon to discover how naïvely optimistic that hope was.

*

On Sunday, July 11, 1880, while Angela was entertaining guests at Stratton Street, a note arrived from the 82-year-old Earl of Harrowby:

> Dear Angela, You may suppose that I have been much startled by the receipt of the inclosed letter – What answer am I to give? Yr aff cousin, H.[8]

The enclosed letter, written the previous day at Windsor Castle, was in the formal third person generally adopted by Queen Victoria when corresponding with her subjects:

> The Queen is anxious to learn from Lord Harrowby privately whether a report that has reached her as to Lady Burdett Coutts's marriage is true.
>
> As the Queen has been told there are circumstances which make the marriage an unnatural one, she trusts that Lady Burdett Coutts had given the fullest consideration to this step before making her final decision.
>
> The Queen knows too little respecting this subject to offer an opinion upon it, but it would grieve her much if Lady Burdett Coutts were to sacrifice her high reputation and her happiness by an unsuitable marriage.[9]

Lord Harrowby's messenger was waiting, but Angela sent him back to Grosvenor Square empty-handed. She was not yet ready to reply. What her feelings were as she imperturbably attended to her guests we can only imagine: shock, undoubtedly, that the Queen not only knew of her proposed marriage but had seen fit to interfere; anger that those she had entrusted with her secret had let her down; apprehensiveness, now that the secret was out, about possible opposition from other quarters; and, above all, determination to have her own way no matter what.

Later in the day, she returned the Queen's letter with her answer:

> Dear Harrowby, I think you had better say (what is true) in reply to the enclosed rather singular letter, that you have no information on the subject alluded to. I am so sorry I could not answer at once but I had people with me and could not leave them.[10]

Angela had told only three people of her intention to marry Bartlett: her sisters, Susan Trevanion and Clara Money, and her solicitor, William Farrer. It had been important to win Clara's support because of the proviso in the Duchess of St Albans's will against Angela's marrying a foreigner. Bartlett, although he was a naturalized British subject and had been brought up and educated in England, was 'by birth an alien'. In marrying him, therefore, Angela would run the risk of forfeiting all her interest in the Duchess's estate – unless Clara, who was next in line to inherit the life-interest, agreed to waive her right. This, at first, Clara agreed to do. But meanwhile, not unnaturally, she had confided in her son Frank; and they had consulted their own solicitor, Arnold White.

It was the solicitors who had let the cat out of the bag, as Henry Ryder recorded in a memorandum. Angela's solicitor, Farrer, was in an awkward position: his firm also acted for the bank. About a week before Angela received Lord Harrowby's note, Farrer had dropped a hint to the partners: 'The Baroness had got a scheme in her head from which he had vainly tried to turn her and which was very foolish.' Ryder at once guessed what it was; but Farrer refused to say more: 'his lips were sealed'. Thoroughly alarmed, the partners tackled Arnold White, Clara Money's solicitor. He, too, had been sworn to secrecy; but in the end it was he who devulged the secret by remaining dumb but nodding in reply to the question: 'Is it matrimonial?' 'Is it Ashmead Bartlett?' And it was White who volunteered to contact Sir Henry Ponsonby, the Queen's private secretary, to see if royal pressure could be brought to bear. Such pressure, they all agreed, was the only thing likely to 'prevent the fatal step being taken'.[11]

The Queen was incredulous when she heard the news. 'Lady Burdett really must be crazy!' she wrote to Ponsonby. 'Since poor Mrs Brown's death she seems to have lost her balance.' And she added that she thought 'it would have been Irving, if it was to be anyone'.[12] Marriage with Irving, indeed, might have been more acceptable, on grounds of age if not of class: he was only twenty-four years younger than Angela. He also had the advantage of looking older than his forty-two years, whereas Bartlett seemed nearer twenty-five than thirty.

It was Henry Ryder's idea that the Queen's remonstrance should be made through his father, Lord Harrowby. No doubt Victoria was glad to follow the suggestion and avoid the embarrassment of entering into a correspondence with the Baroness herself. But, as those who knew

Angela might have realised, royal disapproval, however expressed, was unlikely to deter her from a course she had set her heart on.

A day or two after the Queen's letter, however, came another shock: Angela's sister Clara, acting under the advice of her solicitor, had changed her mind about agreeing to waive the forfeiture clause. If Angela insisted on marrying her young American, she must give up her life interest in the Duchess's estate. Clara probably regretted having given in to her determined younger sister, and was now convinced that she was acting in the best interests of both Angela and the bank. Her solicitor, Arnold White, seems to have been a very interfering man with a marked antipathy towards Angela. It was he who had taken it upon himself to inform Sir Henry Ponsonby in the first place; and he was to write several more pompous letters to the Queen's secretary containing a number of gratuitous observations on the character of the Baroness.

Once again, Angela found herself isolated. The only person who supported her unconditionally was her sister Susan, now nearly eighty. She was glad to think that Angela would have a protector, she said. But Lord Harrowby, though he could not approve, was kind and sympathetic. Could he, he asked in a touching little note to Angela, be of any use to her? He did not think her position was 'so simple or so unimportant to yourself and others, as to make the advice of a friend indifferent or superfluous'.[13]

Advice was the last thing that Angela wanted. But Harrowby's kind invitation did give her a chance to let off steam about the whole affair: how 'deeply grieved' she had been on receiving the Queen's letter; the 'unfortunate' attitude of her sister Clara and nephew Frank; the difficulty of her own delicate relations with the bank partners. She had scarcely expected that her intention would be 'warmly seconded'; but she had thought that, 'taking myself every safeguard for other interests, consideration for my own view would prevail'. By the end of the letter, however, the steam had run out:

> I shall probably settle at Holly Lodge sad as it is to return there . . . as I do not wish to be in London. I am much less strong than last year and whilst I have no wish to shirk social and other duties my interest in them is gone – & all is heavy & irksome since my poor dear loving friend died.[14]

Events had moved fast in the two weeks since the information had been winkled out of the lawyers by the bank partners – too fast, it would seem, for the prospective bridegroom. While Angela was away in the country for a few days, Bartlett called on her solicitor, Farrer. He had found so many difficulties in the way, he said, that he had given up the idea of marriage and released the Baroness from the engagement. The sigh of relief that went up in the Strand was echoed by many, including Princess Mary Adelaide in Kensington Palace. But the relief was short-lived. Angela, on her return to London, called on Farrer herself and demanded to know what was happening. Farrer explained about Bartlett's visit. 'That may be,' replied the Baroness, 'but I don't release him, and intend to carry it out.'[15]

Meanwhile, the newspapers had released the story to an enthralled public. 'A noble lady of vast wealth and benevolence,' *The World* coyly informed its readers, 'is about to be married to a gentleman considerably her junior.'[16] The *Standard* went further, announcing the intended bridegroom as Mr *Ellis* Ashmead Bartlett, William's brother, who had been returned as MP for Eye, Suffolk, in the recent General Election. He was already married and promptly issued a denial. Lord Harrowby wrote again to Angela. He had heard 'with regret' that her marriage was to take place after all. 'I cannot bear to think of you in such a position without a friend, to whom you can communicate your wishes and your difficulties.'[17]

In reply, Angela asked him to give her credit 'for having given the subject thought before I decided it offered me the only chance of comfort I can look to – and . . . for not selecting any for my companion but a gentleman of character'. Now that she was not and could never be 'a first object to any one (except a husband)', she had 'struggled on . . . mainly if not solely through Mr Bartlett's being constantly there'. To lose this now 'leaves me a future from which I not only recoil but which I feel I cannot face'.[18]

Her friends and relations were not at all convinced that Bartlett was 'a gentleman of character'. On July 30, Henry Ryder heard that the Archbishop of Canterbury, after an interview with the young man, had written to Angela proposing adoption. 'It is quite clear,' wrote Ryder, 'that that would satisfy him [Bartlett] and that money is *his* sole object.'[19] Far more disturbing was a letter Henry had received from an old friend of the Baroness, Mrs Gascoyne, giving details of the romance between Ashmead Bartlett and Miss Shirley on the *Walrus* the previous year. According to Mrs Gascoyne, Ashmead had told the young lady that he couldn't marry her because 'he felt obliged to marry "*a lamp-post of a woman*" (his very words, repeated again and again!) *and that her money would help on his ambition*!' Miss Shirley had written to the

Baroness with full particulars – 'even to the comparison made' – but her letter had been ignored, and the Baroness had refused to see her. 'She is like a girl of 15,' wrote the agonized Mrs Gascoyne;

> She does not *know* the storm of censure, indignation, grief, ridicule, amazement that is going on everywhere. She is quite unaware of what she is going to bring on herself! If I could see her, I would try to speak out, as Mrs Brown would have done, . . . but when I entreat her to see me for ten minutes, she makes the excuse of *business*.[20]

Another friend who knew of the shipboard romance was W. H. Smith. On September 20 he wrote to Lady Ely, one of the Queen's ladies-in-waiting and a close friend of Angela:

> I am afraid there is no doubt the marriage will take place, but it had occurred to me you might have said something as to an existing engagement between Mr Bartlett and another lady – contracted on board the yacht last year – which the Baroness might have listened to from you. I found however that proof had been produced to her – and she had disregarded it . . .[21]

Only that February, W. H. Smith (then a member of the Cabinet) had listened in astonishment as the Baroness outlined her plan to lend the government the staggering sum of £250,000 to buy seed potatoes for the starving Irish, who were suffering once again from the failure of the potato crop.* Then, Smith had been overwhelmed by the 'magnitude and goodness' of 'this most munificent proposal'. Now, he wrote sadly to Lady Ely of the 'miserable evening of a life that should have ended with the respect of all'.

*

The partners of Coutts & Co. were in an awkward position. Their collective relationship with the Baroness over the years had been, on the whole, a good one. Her name and prestige had been of immense value to the bank; so had her support during the Edward Marjoribanks affair only a few years before. As Lindsay Antrobus, now the senior partner, wrote to her, 'Several of us owe our positions in the Bank to your influence and we all readily acknowledge the liberality which we have experienced at your hands.'[22] Of course, Angela's position as 'sovereign head' of the bank was to some extent based on a myth, which it had been

---

* The dissolution of Parliament shortly afterwards presumably prevented the matter from being pursued.

in the interests of all parties to perpetuate – the myth of her enormous personal wealth. The real situation was spelled out to Sir Henry Ponsonby by the officious Arnold White:

> The idea of the great wealth of the Baroness, apart from the income she derives from the bank, is a pure hallucination. Her savings have (considering her large income) been *very moderate*. I have reason to think that, assuming she were to forfeit her interest under the Duchess's will she would not have an Income of more than £15,000 a year.[23]

Nevertheless, in the partners' view, Angela's marriage was bound to damage the bank's reputation. If she retained her close connection with Coutts & Co. there was the danger of interference from her husband – and even if he didn't interfere he would be regarded by customers and the public as taking over some of the Baroness's assumed power and influence. If, on the other hand, her connection with Coutts & Co. was severed, there would be a public scandal; and the partners would find themselves having to deal with Frank Money, for Clara had announced her intention of transferring all her interest to her son. Frank and his mother were now digging in their heels over the forfeiture clause. 'We have not arrived at our decision without much pain, anxiety, and thought,' wrote Frank to Lord Harrowby. 'But my mother is determined to adhere to that decision, for the sake of the Baroness, the Bank, and myself.'[24]

The partners could only do what everybody else was doing, from Queen Victoria downwards: wait and see what happened. 'It is positively distressing and ridiculous,' wrote the Queen in her journal on August 19, 'and will do her much harm, by lowering her in people's eyes, and taking away their respect for her.'[25] Two days earlier, large crowds had gathered outside the Savoy Chapel, in the Strand, where it was rumoured the wedding would take place at noon. The doors were opened at 11 and the chapel was soon full; but there was no sign of guests, bride or groom, and soon after 12 the chapel was closed again. The crowds hung about all day, but nothing happened, 'Perhaps,' wrote one of the bank partners hopefully, 'people will begin to think of something else.'[26]

But they did not. For the next few weeks newspapers and magazines continued to announce that the marriage would take place shortly; biographical sketches of the Baroness and Bartlett were prepared, full-page portraits published. According to the *Whitehall Review*, the delay was occasioned by 'long and tedious' financial negotiations. Nevertheless, it could report that the Baroness was 'in the best possible health and spirits'. And the following week (September 2), the journal confidently predicted that 'the financial details will be finally arranged by this afternoon'.[27]

Both these reports were untrue. When Angela visited the bank it was noticed that she looked 'very worn and far from well'. To Lord Harrowby she wrote of feeling 'greatly strained by long anxiety'. She had been 'deeply pained and . . . stunned by the conduct of those nearly connected with me'.[28] On the financial side, things were far from being 'finally arranged'. It would be another year before agreement between Angela and the Moneys was finally reached. Meanwhile, in accordance with the Duchess's will, Clara and Frank had added Coutts to their name, which prompted *Punch* to comment:

> Money takes the name of Coutts,
> Superfluous and funny,
> For everyone considers Coutts
> Synonymous with money!

If the Queen was not amused by the whole affair, neither was her Prime Minister, Mr Gladstone, who declined Angela's rather pathetic request for an interview so that she could explain her position. 'I should not embarrass you,' she had assured him. But Gladstone shrank from such a meeting. Disraeli (Lord Beaconsfield), on the other hand, whom nothing embarrassed, wrote waggishly to the Queen:

> Next to Afghanistan, I think the greatest scrape is Lady Burdett's marriage. I thought Angela would have become classical and history, and would have been an inspiring feature in your Majesty's illustrious reign. The element of the ridiculous has now so deeply entered into her career that even her best friends can only avoid a smile by a sigh![29]

Thoughout the autumn the subject was kept alive by the newspapers and society gossips. But one story the papers did not know about (or dared not print) concerned the claim by a young girl that Bartlett was the father of the child she was expecting. He had been a tutor to her brothers; she and her widowed mother had stayed in the same house in London where he had lodgings. The evidence against Bartlett certainly looked black; but once again Angela refused to believe even in the possibility of his guilt. She, who had come to the aid of many an unfortunate young woman in similar circumstances, would not see this girl who was Ashmead's accuser. If she had her suspicions she did not admit them; in any case she was too deeply committed now to think of giving Bartlett up, no matter what was said against him.

By the end of the year, Henry Ryder was writing wearily to his brother: 'From what I can learn it appears likely that the marriage really will take place before long but who can say. She is as infatuated as ever I hear.'[30] And on January 17 the Queen wrote to Sir Theodore Martin, a member of her Household, 'Lady Burdett's mad marriage, which we had *hoped* was *off* – is a most lamentable act of *self*-abasement!'[31]

The lamentable act took place at 11.30 on Saturday, February 12, 1881, at Christ Church, Down Street, Piccadilly – Angela's parish church. Although the time of the wedding had been kept secret, there was a small crowd waiting to greet the bride as she arrived. Wearing a

The marriage of Baroness Burdett-Coutts

dress of cream satin and velvet brocade with a flower-trimmed headdress and a long lace veil, she was given away by her cousin, Sir Francis Burdett, and attended by three bridesmaids. Sir Francis and his wife and daughters were the only representatives of Angela's family present; a dozen or so close friends, and Ashmead's brother Ellis, made up the wedding party.

By the time the short ceremony was over a large number of people had collected outside the church to cheer the Baroness as she drove off with her young husband. Her sister Susan had not been well enough to attend the service, but the wedding breakfast was held at her house in Chester Square. When the speeches were over, the couple returned to Stratton Street, where Angela changed into a travelling dress and bonnet of heliotrope plush. Early in the afternoon they drove to Charing Cross station, where a special train was waiting. The platform was covered with red cloth, and the chairman of the railway company was there to greet them. There were cheers from the crowd that had gathered behind the barrier as the train steamed out punctually at four o'clock. Their destination was Ashford, Kent, where they were to spend a few days at the home of Admiral and Mrs Gordon.

There was no question of Angela's taking her husband's name. He had been granted royal authority to use the name of Burdett-Coutts before his own surname, and thus became William Lehman Ashmead Burdett-Coutts-Bartlett. But it was not long before the 'Bartlett' was dropped and he became known as W. L. Burdett-Coutts. Angela always called him Ashmead. As for her, she was, and would always be, the Baroness.

There remained the question of the forfeiture clause. On the eve of her wedding, Angela had fired a parting shot (or perhaps it was more of an opening salvo) at Lindsay Antrobus, the senior partner of Coutts & Co:

> Messrs Farrer informed you I believe that in view of the legal opinion we have obtained Mr Burdett Coutts Bartlett and myself will be fully prepared to defend my continued right to hold the Duchess's property.[32]

The partners tackled Frank Money-Coutts. Since he had all along insisted that he was acting solely to prevent the marriage from taking place, would he – now that it had done so – change his mind and agree to waive the forfeiture clause? Frank replied that he himself felt inclined to do so but that he would have to consult his mother. Clara had no intention of giving in at this stage, but she was prepared to compromise.

A Most Lamentable Act

A month after the wedding, Angela's solicitor was handed an ultimatum from Arnold White on behalf of the Money-Couttses: she must acknowledge her altered position and abstain from all interference in bank affairs, in return for which she would remain in possession of Stratton Street and Holly Lodge and receive two-fifths of the income she had up till then enjoyed from the Duchess's estate.

The two sisters were now completely at loggerheads. In April Frank wrote to his half-brother that the Baroness had accepted his mother's conditions. But by July nothing had been formally agreed and Angela was still threatening to fight. Wearied by the whole affair, Antrobus wrote to Ryder:

> Could you not get Mrs M.C. to come some day when B.C. was there and lock them in together – if on re-opening the door nothing but their two tails were found it would save us all much worry and vexation.[33]

Not until November was Henry able to write to his father: 'You will I know be rejoiced to hear that the Agreement between Angela, Clara, and Frank Money Coutts is now "un fait accompli", all parties having signed it.'[34]

The agreement, in substantially the same terms as had been set out in the ultimatum eight months before, represented a defeat for the Baroness. In a memorandum written the following July, she asserted that she had consented to it only 'to avoid a law suit prejudicial to the Bank of Coutts & Co, and fatal to my sister's character'.[35] The memorandum also records that the first sum to be transferred to her account under the new arrangement was about £21,500.* Although Arnold White had probably over-estimated in putting her additional personal income at £15,000, she was still very comfortably off. But she would obviously not be able to spend the same huge amounts on philanthropy as she had in the past.

So closed that eventful year of 1881 – but not before the partners of Coutts & Co. had been treated to some high comedy by the battling Burdett sisters. On December 19 Henry Ryder was informed that the Baroness had sent a man to the Strand to remove the priceless Chinese wallpaper that had been given to Thomas Coutts by Lord Macartney, first British Ambassador to China, in 1794. The man, Banting, had been shown the door. Meanwhile, it was reported that Mrs Money Coutts's

---

* After 1892, when the bank because an unlimited liability company, Angela received a fixed annual sum of £20,000 and Clara £30,000.

solicitors had announced their intention of removing the furniture from Number 59. 'There will be some fun between them yet,' wrote Robert Pym, one of the partners, to Ryder.

Angela indignantly denied any intention of removing the Macartney paper: she had only sent Banting for a chandelier. 'I should think the gentlemen in the Strand would next expect me to send for the roof of the House,' [36] she remarked acidly. Probably nothing would have surprised the gentlemen in the Strand very much, particularly after the incident of Mr Farrer's clock. William (later Sir William) Farrer, Angela's solicitor, strongly disapproved of her marriage and did not give her a wedding present. So one day when she knew he wouldn't be there Angela drove up to his office, went to his room, and removed a clock that stood on the mantelpiece. Farrer's brother and junior partner was in the building but declined to take any action; so the Baroness got her wedding present.* Did she also, one wonders, get the chandelier from Number 59?

*

Whatever the views of those in royal and other quarters about the marriage, the Cockneys celebrated it with a song:

> She married him after all,
> With her lands and money and all;
> He's young and gay, she's old they say,
> But her heart's as sweet as flowers in May.
> Jolly good luck to Miss Coutts we say –
> She's married him after all.

For most people, of course, it was the age difference of nearly forty years that made the match not merely ridiculous, but unnatural and even disgusting. It is worth noting that, had the ages been reversed, hardly an eyebrow would have been raised. There was an obvious practical reason behind this attitude: procreation of children, the first cause for which matrimony was ordained, is possible for a man at an advanced age but not for a woman.

Practical considerations apart, however, the feeling that it is more *natural* for a husband to be older than his wife still seems to go very deep and was much stronger a hundred years ago. In 1890 Henry Ryder wrote that his only objection to his daughter's engagement was

---

* Told to the author by Sir William Farrer's grandson, Sir James Hunter Blair, Bt, who adds: 'I remember seeing a little china candlestick with a conspicuous label on the bottom "price 5/-." My mother said it was her wedding present from the Baroness.'

that she was *three years* older than her fiancé, but that since they had been fond of each other for some years it couldn't be helped! Harriot Coutts had not been bound by this convention when she married her young Duke; but even she had hesitated. That Angela should have flouted it with such apparent equanimity is remarkable. But, as she explained to Lord Harrowby, she felt that 'the very great peculiarity of my position in the world, always eccentric from youth to age, would have won for any such step as my intended marriage a kindly consideration'.[37] Though the need to conform was strong in her nature, it was certainly not the first time that she had shown a readiness to disregard convention when it suited her.

To Clara Patterson, the explanation for her great-aunt's action was simple: 'She loved him'. Others, like Henry Ryder, used the less flattering word 'infatuation'. To us, it may seem like the desperate attachment of a lonely, obstinate old woman. Yet the extraordinary thing is that many of those who knew her insisted that the marriage was a success. 'The last years of her life were happy ones,' wrote her friend Lady Helier, 'and only those who knew her intimately perhaps realised how much her husband helped her.'[38] And Mrs Patterson wrote: 'I only knew them both when she was an aged woman and he was a man between forty and fifty with greying hair, but she still adored him ... She always addressed him with the utmost affection.'[39]

Almost the only dissenting voice is that of Mrs Agatha Twining, wife of the Reverend William Twining, who was vicar of St Stephen's, Rochester Row, from 1889 to 1923. In her unpublished biographical sketch of the Baroness Mrs Twining bluntly declared: 'Both were out for their own selfish ends – he for money and position, she for personal protection. The result was a tragedy.'[40] The marriage was for the sake of appearances only, she maintained, and to prevent Bartlett from marrying anyone else. The Baroness thought that Bartlett, 'being so young ... would obey her'. But once they were married he proceeded to milk her of her remaining money and property, and she was miserable.

Mrs Twining is undoubtedly a biased and unreliable source; her sketch contains many factual errors and dubious judgments, though not all she says can be dismissed. Angela herself, in a memorandum dated March 6, 1887, referred to 'our happy though singular marriage' and paid tribute to

> my dearest Husband's ... generous efforts to carry out my wishes for Columbia and the sorely needed food supply of London. How

different this action which has involved him in expenses and anxiety to the way it was feared he would spend the means and influence his marriage with me would bring him.[41]

These are hardly the words of an unhappy woman whose money is being wrenched from her by a rapacious and unscrupulous husband.

The truth probably lies somewhere between the two extremes. We know from the statement issued by Ashmead's solicitors after Angela's death that between 1881 and 1895 she transferred nearly all her property to him, including Holly Lodge and her life interest in the Piccadilly houses (the freehold of which he bought in 1883). Whether it was wrested from her or given freely it is impossible to say. But her charitable work did not cease altogether, and in the first years of their marriage Ashmead took an active part in it; his interest probably began to flag after he entered Parliament in 1885.

Nevertheless, when one considers that philanthrophy had been Angela's life-work, the work that she had felt 'called' to do and which was the source of her immense prestige, one cannot help wondering how content she was to see it so drastically curtailed. There was much that she could have done in the last two decades of the century; though she was getting old, her mind was clear and she was still capable of planning – and she had never lacked willing helpers to carry out her schemes. 'The welfare of mankind,' her secretary Charles Osborne was to write, 'was the absorbing interest of her life.'[42] But it is hard to escape the conclusion that, in the desolate months following Hannah's death, the dread of being alone and the need to be again 'a first object' to someone had eclipsed this absorbing interest. By the time it regained ascendancy, the means to give practical effect to it were no longer there.

Whether Angela really believed herself to be 'a first object' to Ashmead we cannot say. A man of thirty who marries a woman of nearly sixty-seven is bound to look for sexual satisfaction outside his marriage. At one level of her mind, Angela must have known this, even if she avoided thinking about it consciously. There may have been an unspoken rule between them that so long as Ashmead was discreet about his affairs she would ask no questions and the subject would never be discussed between them. If, after six years, she could still call her marriage 'happy though singular', it was perhaps because the unspoken rule had been adhered to and because Ashmead had treated her with respect and consideration and, at least in some degree, returned her affection.

All the same, there must have been times when Ashmead was bitter and resentful, and Angela jealous and reproachful. Charles Osborne told his son that he had often heard Burdett-Coutts make cutting remarks to his wife; he also said that Ashmead brought his mistresses to Stratton Street. And according to Mrs Twining, when Ashmead went on a trip to America in 1890 he was accompanied by an actress. Mrs Twining's account of what happened when the Baroness found out about this is substantiated by the facts.

The incident took place in November 1890, before the Twinings were married. Angela was then seventy-six and Ashmead not yet forty. The Baroness came to see Mr Twining at the vicarage in a state of great agitation — 'so unlike her' — bringing with her three large oak cases. These contained her 'valuable archives', she told the vicar, which she was entrusting to him because she did not wish her husband to have them. Mr Twining was to keep them until her death, and was on no account to let Mr Burdett-Coutts or any of his family know that they were there.

William Twining never told his wife what was in the boxes, and was furious when one day she opened one of them and discovered that it contained letters from famous people. She was not told the full story until 1923, the year they left the vicarage. Twining, who was by then very elderly, did not know what to do with the boxes and eventually, on the advice of the Archbishop of Canterbury, sent them to Lambeth Palace.

Four days before Angela brought her boxes to the vicarage, she had accompanied her husband to Liverpool, from where he was sailing to New York to judge a horse show. It was, wrote Mrs Twining, 'most unusual for Mr Burdett-Coutts to be seen off by the Baroness'. But, so the story goes, Angela had discovered that Ashmead would not be travelling alone on his voyage to America, and had gone to Liverpool intent on preventing his companion from going with him. If this is true, it would have been a very human reaction for the old lady on returning to London to relieve her feelings by packing up her papers and taking them round to the vicar.

The large collection of Burdett-Coutts papers at Lambeth Palace Library was indeed given by the Reverend W. H. G. Twining in 1923. But they represent only a fraction of the papers Angela left at her death, and are nearly all concerned with charities and church matters. Most of her other papers, including the letters from Wellington, Dickens and Rajah Brooke, appear to have been left to Ashmead. Dickens's letters (some of which were copied by Osborne between 1887 and 1898) were sold in 1922, the year after Ashmead's death, to an American collector; those from Wellington were returned to the Duke's family. The Brooke correspondence remained in the possession of Ashmead's nephew and heir, who – after making it available to Owen Rutter* in the 1930s – deposited it in the British Museum.

That Angela did not include these valuable and important letters among the papers she gave to the vicar for safe-keeping should not surprise us. These were letters from some of the greatest men of their day, men who had been her intimate friends. They represented more than twenty years of her life, and it was one of her great delights to read and re-read them. It is highly unlikely that she could ever have brought herself to part with these treasures.

'I never saw a husband's manner to a wife more tender, more considerate, more perfect,' declared Angela's friend T. P. O'Connor after her death; 'And her affection for him remained undimmed to the last hour.'[43] While we may be sceptical about such a statement, we need not necessarily accept Mrs Twining's assertion that 'When in the public eye, they both behaved courteously and with dignity, but to those who knew the real truth, it was clever acting.' No doubt it was, at times. But could any couple have kept up such a pretence for nearly twenty-six years? It is easier to believe that both partners in this unusual marriage came to terms with their situation, and in doing so achieved some measure of happiness for themselves and each other.

For all her devotion to Ashmead, Angela must have realised that she could never be to him what she had been to Hannah. Loneliness was something she had to face and overcome; it could not be banished by taking to herself a reluctant young husband. As for Ashmead, marriage with the Baroness brought him wealth, influence and a political career. It also tied him to an elderly wife and prevented him from having a family of his own. No doubt he sometimes bitterly regretted this; but perhaps he did not allow the regret to overcome the genuine regard he felt for the Baroness. After her death, he wrote to the Archbishop of Canterbury:

> I have been more deeply touched than I can say . . . to find . . . how widespread is the understanding amongst high and low alike of the real relationship that has existed between the Baroness and myself.

See Bibliography.

What that real relationship was, we shall probably never know. If there was a large element of self-interest on both sides, so was there also, perhaps, a bond of real affection – in Ashmead's own words to the Archbishop, a 'sympathy of heart and intellect and disposition'.[44]

Fourteen

THE END OF THE STORY

As the scandal of 1880-81 faded from memory and people began to think of other things, Angela's life returned to normal. Her friends discovered, perhaps with some surprise, that the Baroness was the same person that she had been before her marriage. After a drawing-room at Buckingham Palace three months after the marriage, Queen Victoria wrote pityingly in her journal:

> That poor foolish old woman Lady Burdett Coutts was presented on her marriage with Mr Bartlett, 40 years younger than herself. She looked like his grandmother, & was all decked out with jewels – not edifying![1]

But in time the Queen, like everyone else, came to accept the situation. These two formidable ladies had much in common; but perhaps what helped to soften Victoria was Angela's work for animals. Cruelty to animals, the Queen thought, was 'one of the worst traits in human nature', and she had once written to Angela: 'It is a great satisfaction to me to know what a friend you are to poor dumb animals – who are in many cases man's best and kindest friends.'[2]

In popular esteem the Baroness stood as high as ever. Her presence still lent weight to any public occasion; her support was still canvassed, her name invoked, her voice heeded. In 1882 she laid the foundation stone of the new Westminster Town Hall; in her drawing-room in 1884 was held the first committee meeting of the Society for the Prevention of Cruelty to Children. And when Lord Shaftesbury died in 1885 she was his natural successor to head several of his favourite charities – just as she was the obvious choice to unveil his statue in Westminster Abbey three years later. Meetings and bazaars in aid of hospitals and other causes; children's flower shows; carthorse parades; prizegivings – especially for the RSPCA children's annual essay competition which was started by her – for all these and many other functions the Baroness was in demand. And the shoals of letters she received – sometimes several hundred in a day – from people in every kind of distress, were proof that she still held a unique place in the hearts and minds of the poor.

Life had never been all work for Angela, of course; she had always found time for entertaining, travelling, theatre-going and other pursuits, and she continued to enjoy all these to an advanced age. There were luncheon parties at Stratton Street, garden parties at Holly Lodge, and a succession of house guests. In 1886 she held a luncheon for Liszt, who was then seventy-five and seldom played except for his own amusement. After lunch, however, Liszt remarked on the fact that there was no piano in the drawing-room. Angela explained that she had had it removed so that he should not feel he was expected to play. 'But I would like some music!' he replied; and, when the piano was brought in, proceeded to delight the assembled company with an impromptu performance.[3]

If Ashmead sometimes neglected her, there were other men to whom she could turn for companionship and who remained her faithful friends until her death. One such 'old young friend' was Henry Wagner, who had acted as her unpaid secretary for a time in the mid-sixties. Henry had been greatly upset by Angela's marriage. His family always believed that he would have liked to propose to her himself; at forty-one, he may well have thought that he was a more eligible candidate for her hand than Ashmead Bartlett. By 1884, however, Henry had been won back to the fold and in that year was asked to dine at Stratton Street on Christmas Day, 'as you so often have in the dear past'.[4]

Angela's letters to Henry, written over a period of twenty years, are chatty and affectionate and give an impression of cheerfulness and activity. There is news of mutual friends, of moving about from place to place in England, of trips to Ireland and the continent. 'London par excellence is my home,' Angela told Henry; but she had always enjoyed travelling. In 1885 she rented Heydon Hall, Norfolk, 'a charming antique old place' which belonged 'to the elder branch of the Bulwer family, all of whom in my young days I knew so well, so it is full of interest to me and Partridges, Pheasants & Rabbits to Mr Burdett Coutts — at least so I hope!'.[5]

When Heydon Hall was given up in 1890, Angela spent more time on the continent. 'She was the last of the great travellers,' wrote her great-niece, Clara Patterson, who met her for the first time in Genoa in the spring of 1900. The Baroness had with her then 'her butler, footman and coachman, as well as her maid, and she travelled everywhere in her own carriage drawn by her own horses'.[6] She loved Paris and went there regularly. In December 1893 she set off on an extended tour of France and Italy, returning home in time for her eightieth birthday on April 21.

In 1896 she visited Corsica, and early in the following year returned to spend several months there. Apart from its links with the Bonaparte family, the island had a special interest for Angela: it was she who had been responsible for returning the remains of the great Corsican patriot, Pasquale Paoli, to his native land. Paoli, who had fought for his country's independence in the second half of the eighteenth century, had died in exile in London in 1807 and was buried in St Pancras churchyard. When the churchyard was turned into a public garden in the 1870s Angela had a memorial sun-dial erected bearing the names of some of the famous dead buried there. Later, Paoli's body was exhumed and sent to Corsica. It arrived, to great public rejoicing, on September 4, 1889.

Many of the eminent men whom Angela had known in her younger days – Dickens, Faraday, Babbage, Livingstone, Brooke, Napoleon III (Louis Napoleon) – had died well before her marriage. So had other, less exalted, friends, like the warm-hearted Julian Young, who died while staying at Stratton Street on July 3, 1873. In 1880, W. H. Wills, a true friend as well as a highly competent assistant, died. The same year saw the death of Sir Robert Burdett, and Angela found herself, with her two surviving sisters, administering the estate of the brother she had never known. In 1882 came the death of Lord Harrowby, 'ever my best and truest friend', as she would later describe him. He, more than any other man, had been like an affectionate elder brother to her.

But if the great names of former years had passed into history, a new generation of heroes had grown up who were as welcome at Stratton Street and Holly Lodge as their predecessors had been. There was, for instance, Henry Morton Stanley, whom Angela had first met in 1872 at the famous meeting in Brighton of the British Association at which Stanley recounted how he had found Livingstone the previous year. Some people were inclined to doubt the claims of this brash young American. It was even suggested that Livingstone had found *him*, not the other way round. And there were plenty of armchair geographers who were prepared to challenge the theories Stanley put forward on Livingstone's behalf about the source of the Nile. Angela, however, was one of those who championed Stanley from the first, and she became one of his firmest friends.

Stanley's life and character must have been particularly appealing to Angela. His story was an incredible and romantic one. Born John

Rowlands in Denbigh in 1841, the illegitimate son of a Welsh girl, he was dumped in the workhouse at the age of six and for nine years endured the tyranny of a sadistic schoolmaster who was responsible for the death of at least one boy and who ended his days in a lunatic asylum. One day, when he was fifteen, John seized the sadist's stick and soundly thrashed him with it, after which he escaped over the workhouse wall. At eighteen, he signed on as cabin boy in a ship bound for New Orleans. Here he was adopted by a cotton broker, Henry Stanley, and so acquired a new father and a new name.

After numerous adventures in America, Stanley joined the *New York Herald*, and it was from the *Herald* that he received the commission to 'find Livingstone'. His subsequent explorations in Africa opened up large areas of the continent to European influence, including the Congo which he secured for Belgium. Angela was one of those who actively encouraged him to undertake his last journey through Central and East Africa in 1887, which took three years and involved him in more controversy. On his return to London in April 1890 he was met at Victoria Station by the Baroness and her husband in their carriage and carried off to lodgings that had been prepared for him. He married that same year, was re-naturalised as a British citizen, and had a short and undistinguished career as an MP. He was knighted in 1899 and died in 1904.

But the hero of heroes was Charles George Gordon, immortalised as Gordon of Khartoum. This 'strange pious military man', a brilliant soldier, a visionary and a fatalist, intensely religious and with a fanatical belief in his own destiny, touched a chord of sympathy in Angela and became deeply attached to her. He hated Society. Lady St Helier, meeting him at 1 Stratton Street, found him

> a curiously listless-looking, nervous little man, with a sort of furtive look and expression as if he always anticipated something unpleasant. He was not agreeable or encouraging, and he gave very little outward evidence of the power and influence he possessed. He spoke little, and seemed bored when he was addressed or asked any question.[7]

In January 1884, Gordon, then fifty-one, was asked by Gladstone's government to go to the Sudan with a view to evacuating the British garrisons there. Sixteen months earlier a British force under Sir Garnet Wolseley had defeated the Egyptian rebel, Arabi Pasha. But the revolt against the Khedive of Egypt had not stopped there. A new leader, the

Mahdi, or 'Expected One', had risen in the Sudan and was sweeping victoriously through the country. In England, opinion was divided between those who demanded a new expedition to crush the Mahdi and those who, like Gladstone, wanted no further British involvement. Eventually the Cabinet announced its decision to pull out of the Sudan. But to appoint Gordon for the task was tantamount to guaranteeing that no such thing would happen.

The story of Gordon's stand at Khartoum is too well-known to need repeating. In attempting to 'smash the Mahdi' he was disobeying orders from the government; but as Sir Evelyn Baring, the British representative in Egypt, remarked: 'A man who habitually consults the prophet Isaiah when he is in a difficulty is not apt to obey the orders of anyone.'[8] On February 18, 1884, Gordon arrived in Khartoum; a month later, he was surrounded by the Mahdi's forces. To the disgust of Queen Victoria and the majority of her subjects, Gladstone took no action, refusing to believe that Gordon could be in danger.

A large number of people, many of them poor, wrote to the Baroness offering their small contributions if she could start a public subscription to rescue Gordon. In a spirited letter to *The Times*, she identified herself with all those who were raising their voices 'against a base surrender of the nation's good faith and honour, as well as of a gallant and Christian life'. It is said that she was one of a group of friends who, through the medium of an English merchant in disguise, smuggled a packet of letters and newspapers into Khartoum, which were 'the last words Gordon ever had from England, and which told him how deeply the national heart was stirred on his behalf'.[9] There is no mention of this in Gordon's Khartoum diary, but if such a messenger did get through it is highly likely that the initiative came from Angela. Among her papers are letters from a solicitor whose client (unnamed) had offered to accompany an expedition to rescue Gordon from the west, via Timbuctoo. This information, wrote the lawyer, had been communicated to Gladstone, who had ignored it.

By the time the relief force, under Wolseley, set off in September, it was too late. On January 26, 1885, two days before his rescuers arrived, Gordon was speared to death by the Mahdi's followers. He is said to have carried with him 'to the end' a small letter-case given to him by Angela as a keepsake on the day he left England.

*

The End of the Story

For the first few years after they were married, Ashmead took an active interest in his wife's charities. It was he who largely developed her scheme to benefit Irish fishermen. In September 1884 they visited Ireland together. Angela, whose first visit to the country this was, was given a rapturous welcome and hailed as the 'Queen of Baltimore'. On their return home they revived a plan for a fishery school to train boys from all over Ireland in deep sea fishing, seamanship, boat-building and allied subjects. The Baltimore Industrial Fishery School, built with public and private subscriptions, was opened by the Baroness in 1887. On this occasion W. H. Smith lent her his yacht *Pandora*. As they sailed down the coast from Queenstown (now Cobh) to Baltimore,

> flags and strips of coloured cloth, and even tattered handkerchiefs, fluttered from every house and cottage, and people gathered in crowds on every headland. As the vessel glided at night into the . . . harbour a hundred small fires twinkling far and near on the wild hill sides, signalled a welcome.[10]

Meanwhile, in 1885, Ashmead had followed his brother Ellis into the House of Commons. Under the Redistribution Act of that year the constituency of Westminster, which W. H. Smith had represented since 1868, was divided into three. Burdett-Coutts was returned for the Abbey Division and Smith for the Strand. Nothing could have given Angela greater pleasure than to see her husband become MP for the place her father had for so long represented. No doubt it was partly her name and influence that ensured his success; though she herself is said to have taken no part in the campaign. She did, however, enlist the help of some powerful supporters, among them Lady Randolph Churchill, fresh from the triumph of her husband's victory at Woodstock. There is a story that the dazzling Lady Randolph, formerly the American heiress Jennie Jerome, was told by a Westminster constituent that he would promise his vote if he got the same price that was once paid for a vote by the Duchess of Devonshire: a kiss. 'Thank you very much,' Jennie replied. 'I'll let the Baroness know at once.'[11]

Ashmead was a conscientious Member of Parliament who attended the House regularly and introduced several useful Bills, among them one which added an extra 300 acres to the open spaces of Hampstead Heath. If he did not cut as spectacular a figure as his brother, who was much in demand as a speaker – one might almost say as a rabble-rouser – at public meetings, he made his mark in 1900 when he reported on the conditions of the sick and wounded in the Boer War. His report led to a

Royal Commission on army medical services, and important reforms followed. He became a Privy Councillor in 1921, the year of his death.

Apart from politics, Ashmead's main interest was horsebreeding. He founded the Brookfield Stud, for which Angela provided a site adjoining the Holly Lodge grounds, and bred hackneys, Cleveland bays and Yorkshire coach horses. Brookfield became one of the largest and finest studs in the country for carriage-horses; but, wrote Agatha Twining bitterly, it swallowed up money that might have been put to better use.

With a reduced income, a husband to support, several large establishments to maintain and a life-style that was luxurious if not wildly extravagant, it was inevitable that Angela should have had little left over for philanthropy. Whether, as Agatha Twining suggests, Ashmead actually forced her to give up her remaining charities is doubtful. Certainly in one case, that of the Society for the Prevention of Cruelty to Children, it would seem that Angela's withdrawal of her support was due to reasons of her own rather than pressure from her husband.

Angela had worked for years to relieve the lot of neglected and maltreated children, both generally and in individual cases. In February 1871 she had suggested to Disraeli that a provision should be incorporated into the Preservation of Infant Life Bill – 'one of the most vital measures before Parliament' – whereby every child who was 'transferred wholly or partially from the care of its natural guardians to that of a stranger should receive the protection of the Law'.[12] Some years earlier, she had been moved to action by a particularly horrific incident at the St Pancras Workhouse. A child deserted by its parents had been taken, half-dead, to the workhouse. No doctor was called, and a voluntary worker gave evidence at the inquest that the child had been laid out for burial while still breathing and moving. The child had later died in the workhouse infirmary. The St Pancras Guardians, quite unabashed, reinstated the workhouse superintendent, who had been severely censured by the Coroner, and refused admittance to the voluntary worker.

'Such a hideous instance of callousness,' wrote Angela to the St Pancras Guardians, 'makes those shudder who feel they are forced by law to pay a rate which places the sick in similar hands.' The recipient of parochial relief, far from receiving benefit, ran the risk of being laid out before death 'whenever the nurses, matron or lady-superintendent . . . may choose to think the victim of their neglect cannot "last long," or is "nearly gone".'[13]

The End of the Story

Not only neglect but the most appalling cruelty awaited all too many of the unfortunate 'juvenile paupers' consigned to the workhouse. But there were also many children who were ill-treated and neglected by their own parents; and, as Angela pointed out in a letter to the Home Secretary in 1883, the law gave no protection to children whose parents had been convicted and punished: they remained 'in the custody and absolute power of those who have already injured them'.[14]

The London Society for the Prevention of Cruelty to Children officially came into being at a meeting at the Mansion House in July 1884. Lord Shaftesbury was elected President and Angela was one of the trustees. The secretary was the Yorkshire philanthropist Benjamin Waugh, who from the start was keen for the Society to become a national organisation. In 1889, as a result of pressure from the Society, the first of a series of Children's Acts was passed. This 'Children's Charter' acknowledged for the first time the right of a child to be fed, clothed and properly treated, and made it an offence to abandon, neglect or ill-treated a child. In the same year the Society was reconstituted as the National Society for the Prevention of Cruelty to Children; it thus came into being sixty-five years after the founding of the Royal Society for the Prevention of Cruelty to Animals. Angela, however, was not happy with this development, and in 1894 she resigned and withdrew her support. In her opinion the change to a National Society had been made 'too early', and she also objected to certain clauses in the royal charter for which the Society was applying.

It is sad that the old lady – she was then eighty – should have found it necessary to sever her connections with an organisation with whose aims she was so much in sympathy. Despite Agatha Twining's dark hints, one cannot help feeling that the objections were of a peculiarly 'Angelic' nature. Used to having her own way, the Baroness was unable to accept the majority decision and had no alternative but to resign.

The situation with regard to St Stephen's, Rochester Row, was, perhaps, rather different. When William Twining became vicar in December 1889 Angela was providing an extra £3,000 a year to meet expenditure not covered by her original endowments. Twining, an energetic and enthusiastic priest who had won great popularity during his ten years as curate, must have counted himself a lucky man. His parish was poor but thriving, with a benefactress whom everyone regarded as the most charitable lady in the land.

But he had not been vicar for long before the situation changed. The Baroness told him that she could no longer afford to pay £3,000 a year;

large reductions would have to be made. After her death, Twining wrote to the Archbishop of Canterbury to explain the problems he had had, and found that His Grace had been well aware of the situation:

> I realise very fully the contrast between the difficulties with which you have had to contend and the comparatively smooth waters in which your predecessor floated in the days of the Baroness's munificence.[15]

Here, without doubt, is the key to Agatha Twining's implacable hostility to William Burdett-Coutts. When Agatha married Twining in 1894 he was already having to contend with the difficulties referred to by the Archbishop. In Agatha's view, the money that should have been going to St Stephen's to support her husband's good works was going instead to the Baroness's husband to pay off his debts and finance his expensive tastes. Though Mrs Twining could concede the folly of 'our beloved foundress' in marrying Ashmead in the first place, she clearly saw *him* as an arch-villain.

Nevertheless, in the early 1890s, Angela undertook what was to be her last major expenditure in Westminster – the provision of a new building for the St Stephen's Technical Institute at a cost of about £7,000. Boasting fully-equipped workshops for practical instruction in technical trades and skills, the re-named Westminster Technical Institute offered courses in a wide range of vocational subjects, from carpentry, bricklaying and other trades, to domestic and commercial subjects, Civil Service examinations, technical drawing and applied art. The Institute was a source of immense pride to Angela, who gave scholarships to 'deserving children of poor parents' from her own and other schools. Students from the Institute carried off many of the prizes given by the City and Guilds and other bodies.

Meanwhile, changes had taken place in the organisation of the St Stephen's schools. In 1876 the Townshend elementary schools had been opened next door, built with a large trust fund left by the Reverend Chauncey Hare Townshend, of which Angela was a trustee. The Townshend Schools were free, and were attended by children of the very poorest parents, many of them living outside Westminster. Under the Education Act of 1890, however, all parishes were obliged to provide free elementary education for their children. The Townshend schools were therefore moved to smaller premises, the St Stephen's (fee-paying) schools were expanded, and some of the funds from the

Townshend Trust were used to help meet the deficit on the running of the St Stephen's schools that Angela had hitherto always paid.

In 1901, the schools were amalgamated, becoming the Burdett-Coutts and Townshend Foundation Schools. But, to the great distress of the Twinings and many of their parishioners, the schools and Institute were now to be administered, not by the parish of St Stephen's, but by the new 'agnostic' London County Council. Once again, Mrs Twining was convinced that a 'sinister influence' had been at work on the Baroness: she even claims, in her biographical sketch, that the 'handing over' of schools and Institute to the LCC was illegal because it went against the terms of the Townshend Trust. In fact, the records show that the schools' Board of Governors in 1903 consisted of five nominees of the Baroness, two of the Bishop of London, and one each from the LCC and the Westminster City Council; so church influence

One of the last photographs of the Baroness, taken in the late 1880s

was not entirely lacking. But William Twining's name does not appear as a governor, and for many years afterwards there was no direct link between the schools and St Stephen's church.

For the Twinings, who were devoted to the Baroness, 'losing' the schools was a bitter blow, and undoubtedly feeling ran high in the parish. But it has to be remembered that by then (in the words of a modern commentator), 'the world of secondary education had become a chaotic wilderness, full of vague jurisdictions and overlapping functions'. The one certain thing that had emerged by the end of the century was that the State would have to involve itself in secondary education – 'supplementing, guiding, and organising the work of private philanthropists'[16] – just as it had done since 1870 in the primary, or elementary, sector. In fact the Education Act of 1902 acknowledged for the first time that *all* educaton from kindergarten to university was a public responsibility. Under the Act, voluntary schools became eligible for grants from the rates, and in return had to submit to a measure of control from the local education authorities.

So in 'handing over' her schools and Institute to the LCC, Angela was in effect anticipating an inevitable development, though she herself may not have recognised it as such at the time. One has to remember that in 1901 she was eighty-seven. It would have been surprising if her husband, who as an MP was presumably *au fait* with what was happening in the field of education, had *not* been her guiding influence.

*

That poverty and distress were as great in the last two decades of the century as they had ever been was proved by Charles Booth's massive and authoritative survey *Life and Labour of the People of London*, the first volume of which appeared in 1889. People were beginning to realise that philanthropy, even administered on the so-called 'scientific' lines advocated by the Charity Organisation Society (founded in the 1860s), was inadequate to cope with the problems that Booth's study revealed. Education was not the only area in which the State would have to play a larger rôle. Already there was talk of old-age pensions, of unemployment pay, and of free meals for school-children.

Whether Angela welcomed this development it is hard to say. In 1884 – some years before the apppearance of Booth's survey – she had written to Herbert Spencer to congratulate him on an article called 'The Coming Slavery' in which he inveighed against State 'interference'. Spencer, an ardent individualist whose philosophy at that time still carried great weight, directed part of his attack against the growing power of the Civil Service – 'the despotism of a graduated and centralised officialism'. But his main point was that increased public expenditure on such things as education, housing, and so on encouraged people to think that 'everything is to be done for them and nothing by them . . . Every additional State interference strengthens the tacit assumption that it is the duty of the State to deal with all evils and secure all benefits'. The end result, he warned, would be enslavement to the State.[17]

Angela told Spencer that he had put into words what 'many of the best amongst us feel'. She felt that 'the shadow of the Coming Slavery' had been hanging over many recent social and political changes. 'To anyone, like myself,' she wrote,

> not in harmony with the events of life in which I am placed, and yet who is of necessity compelled to act in that life, the problem of what to do is extremely difficult . . . Instinctive piety and love to man and God gives the truest guide to good.[18]

What she did not, perhaps, realise was that the same instinct which had prompted her and others to help their fellow-men was now motivating those who urged that the community should play a larger part. No doubt the prospect of charity administered by a faceless bureaucracy worried many people. But it was gradually being seen that the scale of the problem was so large that only the State had the financial and administrative resources to cope with it. It was not enough to rely entirely on the charitable impulses of the better-off.

In 1893, nine years after her letter to Spencer, Angela produced a report for the Chicago International Exhibition of Women's Work entitled '*Women's Mission, a Series of Congress Papers on the Philanthropic Work of Women, by eminent writers, arranged and edited . . . by the Baroness Burdett-Coutts*. In her preface, she referred to the enormous social changes that had been brought about by the Industrial Revolution. The growth of trade, she thought, though it had destroyed the old order, had brought great blessings, including one that was often overlooked: the rise of 'an immense middle-class, vast in number and extremely well-to-do, . . . out of the ranks of the artisan and manufacturing class'. But it had also brought the evils of

> overcrowding, feverishness of factory work in close rooms; . . . temptation to spirit-drinking as a goad to exhausted energy; . . . dissociation of labour from nature, and from common human

sympathies ... and the destruction of homely life and of the stamina of the race by the absorption of whole families into the mill.

'Individual influence,' she concluded, 'was quite incompetent to remedy such evils as these.'[19] And she went on to mention Shaftesbury's work in pressing for legislation to limit hours of work and restrict the employment of women and children.

To the Charity Organisation Society, obsessed with the idea of self-sufficiency, State support meant pauperisation. In opposition to the growing feeling of the age, the COS continued to proclaim that 'public action demoralized but private charity, properly administered, offered redemption'.[20] Angela, of course, had acknowledged the importance of self-sufficiency long before the COS came into being. But a life-time's experience must have taught her that there were some people – the aged, the sick, the unemployed, not to mention young children – for whom self-sufficiency was impossible.

Every year, practically until her death, *The Times* published her appeals for funds for the Destitute Children's Dinner Society, of which she had become President on Shaftesbury's death. By 1890 it was estimated that about 300,000 hot meals were being provided each winter at sixty centres. The children paid a halfpenny when they could afford it; many paid nothing. There is a directness and simplicity about Angela's letters which is in refreshing contrast to the laboured style of her earlier years: 'This I know is not Christmas time, nor the proper pleading season,' she writes in February 1893, '. . . and men's minds are not turned to hungry children, but there they are, and they want comfort and food.'[21] In 1906, the year of her death, an Act was passed empowering local authorities to provide free meals for school-children. It was condemned by many in the Charity Organisation Society as an open invitation to parents to evade their responsibility and spend their money on drink.

The workhouse cast its grim shadow particularly over the old. In 1887 Angela wrote to *The Times* about the case of Thomas Ansdells, aged eighty-eight, who had literally starved to death rather than go to the workhouse where he would have been separated from his wife. One of the many appeals she received was from 65-year-old Henry Davids, an unemployed clerk whose last two employers had gone into liquidation and who hadn't even the money to advertise for a situation. Such cases were compelling proof of the need for unemployment relief and old-age pensions.

The first half of the twentieth century was to see a gradual drawing together of voluntary and State philanthropy into a partnership in which each came to recognise the importance of the other. That the State would emerge as the senior partner was inevitable; but its debt to the private philanthropists was considerable. Although Angela died before this development really got under way, the signs of change were already apparent in the 1890s. It is to be hoped that she, who had looked upon her great means as a trust to be used for the benefit of others, would have welcomed this acceptance by the community at large of its responsibility to care for its weakest members.

*

Like her old friend the Duke of Wellington, Angela remained in harness to the last, chairing committees, making speeches, writing appeals to move the hearts and open the purses of her fellow-countrymen, and dealing with her vast pile of correspondence. 'I left early,' one of her friends wrote in his diary after a visit to Stratton Street in June 1897, 'as a meeting was about to take place, and the room filled up with bishops and dowagers.'[22]

Though as a young woman she had often been prone to colds, chills, earache and other ailments, in old age the Baroness was noted for her excellent constitution. When she was over eighty her doctor told her she had the firmest and most regular pulse he had ever felt. She greatly enjoyed a good meal and was partial to strong tea – so strong that others found it undrinkable. Lord Ronald Sutherland Gower, meeting her in Corsica in 1897, thought she looked 'wonderfully young for her eighty-two years ... [not] a day older than she did a quarter of a century ago'.[23] On the other hand, it is recorded that the Shah of Persia, to whom the Baroness was presented by the Prince of Wales in 1889, looked into her face and exclaimed '*Quelle horreur!*' But the Shah was a law unto himself: on the same visit to England he also 'expressed his wonder that Lord Salisbury did not take a new wife'.[24]

To her great-niece Clara Patterson, the Baroness did not give the impression of great age: 'Her hair was dark, not white, and she gave no suggestion of fragility. She was more like some old rock jutting out of the sea, storm-worn but untroubled still.'[25] Others remarked on her stateliness, her dignified bearing and old-world manners. T. P. O'Connor, a great admirer, felt 'a sense of reserve, of stern self-control, almost of frigidity' in her presence. 'You were not long in the company of the Baroness without realising that you had to deal with no slushy philanthropist; no weak, good-hearted, soft-headed lover of humanity.' Nevertheless, beneath the 'icy manner' was 'a heart burning with affection' for mankind.[26]

As the century drew to a close, Angela felt the isolation of one who has outlived most of her friends. But there was always the younger generation. The last of her heroes, Cecil Rhodes, was a year or two younger than her husband. At seventeen, he had left his father's rectory in Herefordshire for his brother's cotton farm in Natal. He soon turned to diamond mining, and at thirty-six was head of De Beers Consolidated Mines, the largest corporation in the world. He shared his friend Gordon's instinctive sympathy with the native races. But even more did he share Livingstone's belief that the hopes of the world for liberty and progress rested with the British, who had a special duty and mission as colonisers. He dreamed of 'an Empire so vastly enlarged that it could impose its Peace on all the nations of the world'.[27] He himself acquired, through negotiation sometimes backed by force, the vast stretches of land in south-central Africa that came to be called Rhodesia.

Like Gordon, Rhodes had a charismatic personality but could be shy and awkward in company. Ill-health made him drive himself on to try to complete what he wanted to do before he died. Like so many others before him, he found the antidote to these disturbing qualities in Angela's serenity. From Lady St Helier we get a glimpse of him at a dinner party at Stratton Street, absorbed in conversation with his hostess for almost the entire evening. He was at that time Prime Minister of the Cape, an office he held from 1890 to 1895. He died in South Africa in 1902, aged forty-nine. He left six million pounds, the bulk of it to be used for the scholarships that bear his name.

On December 22, 1899, Angela's last surviving sister, Clara, died at the age of ninety-four. Susan had died in 1886. We do not know if Angela and Clara, who had quarrelled so bitterly, were reconciled at the end. A year later, on December 11, 1900, Henry Ryder died. He was sixty-four, and had succeeded his brother Dudley as Earl of Harrowby only nine months before. The death of both brothers in the same year was a sad loss to Angela. Not only had she been greatly attached to them, especially Henry, but she was reminded of the death of their father, old Lord Harrowby, whose friendship had meant so much to her.

On April 21, 1904, she was ninety, and Ashmead arranged a luncheon party for thirty at Stratton Street. The house was filled with flowers – roses, lilies, orchids, and her favourite white lilac. Among the

The End of the Story

guests were several with famous names from her past – Gladstone, Wilberforce, Peel – as well as her cousin Sir Francis Burdett, her old friends the Wolseleys, and her godson Prince Francis of Teck (his mother, Princess Mary Adelaide, had died in 1897).

One person who was unable to attend the birthday party was Henry Irving. He had been knighted in 1895 and was now, at sixty-six, the grand old man of the theatre. In September 1904 he began a farewell tour of the provinces, opening with *The Merchant of Venice* in Cardiff; a year later, on October 13, 1905, he collapsed immediately after a performance of Tennyson's *Becket* at the Theatre Royal, Bradford, and died the same evening. His body was brought to London and, because his flat at 17 Stratton Street was too small for the purpose, Angela offered her house for the lying-in-state. His funeral took place in Westminster Abbey on October 20.

The Baroness survived her old friend by more than a year. Though she was now extremely deaf, her mind was as clear as ever. Her travelling days were over; she now divided her time between Stratton Street and Holly Lodge. But on fine days she still went out for a drive, always with a dog on her lap. She visited the schools in Rochester Row, staying to watch 'the little ones at work', as the log book recorded. On February 18, 1906, she entertained to tea a small boy called Charles Howard and his father. Charles, aged eleven, had rescued a little girl of five from drowning the previous year. Angela had read about the incident in the newspapers and had written to the Royal Humane Society, who awarded Charles a certificate. The Baroness had it framed, and the overawed young hero received it from her hands in the drawing-room of 1 Stratton Street.

Letters still came pouring in from all over the world. Not all of them were requests for help. George Anderson of West Ham wrote on April 28, 1906:

> I thank you Dear Baroness for helping us over a terrible time and now that I am earning good wages and in no need of help say with as much thankfulness as ever I did in the old days, 'God bless our Baroness.'[28]

Another letter, from America, was addressed to 'The Queen of the Costers, England'. 'Try 1 Stratton Street,' a Post Office official had written on the envelope. The letter was from a former costermonger whom Angela had helped to emigrate to Canada and who had later moved to California. Perhaps this latest in her collection of titles pleased the Baroness more than all the rest. The coster was, after all, the archetypal Londoner; and London, as she had once told Henry Wagner, was her home *par excellence*.

In October 1906, Angela left Holly Lodge to spend the winter at 1 Stratton Street. Here she was among her most treasured possessions – a remarkable mixture of the priceless and the paltry that filled the house from top to bottom. Only she knew the true value of the individual items in this huge and motley collection. Her money, she had once written, 'brought little I cared for personally'. Her Shakespeare First Folios, her pictures and other rare manuscripts were worth thousands; but not as much as the old Christmas cards she had kept for her own special reasons. There were cabinets full of exquisite china; but a cracked jug with her father's portrait on it meant more to her. And then there were the letters . . . boxes and boxes of them, many still with their envelopes, all bundled together and carefully labelled.

Surrounded by these memories of nearly seventy years, Angela was nevertheless not one to live in the past. Right up to her last illness she took a keen interest in what was going on in the world. Despite her deafness, she still enjoyed conversation; and she loved to sit at the bay windows watching the traffic in Piccadilly. As she liked to point out, the traffic was much noisier in former days when the streets were paved with cobbles and horse-drawn vehicles rattled over them.

It was at Christmas-time that a troublesome cold she had had for some weeks developed into acute bronchitis. On Christmas Day she dined downstairs for the last time. On December 28, so Mrs Twining tells us, she sent for the Bishop of London and asked him to convey a message to the Twinings: 'I am so grievously sorry for what I did over the schools and to the Church, and that I behaved so badly to the Vicar, who did all in his power to help me.'[29] Two days later, she died. The 'strange story' had come to an end.

EPILOGUE

So overwhelming is the sheer volume of Angela's charitable work, not to mention its extraordinary diversity, that any attempt at a critical assessment can seem almost churlish. But to accept unquestioningly the traditional view of her – the great and noble lady, wise, kind and munificent, inspired by the highest motives and herself inspiring those about her by her serenity and goodness – is to reduce her to a cardboard character straight out of a bad Victorian novel. Even Clara Patterson, though down-to-earth and unsentimental about her great-aunt, felt obliged to apologise for mentioning some of her failings; Angela's name, she wrote, had been 'surrounded with so much glamour that one is apt to forget that as well as a great lady and a great philanthropist, she was a human being'.[1] Yet it is surely the human being who interests us most.

In recent years there have been dissenting voices. David Owen, in his study of three centuries of English philanthropy, claimed that Angela's influence had been exaggerated: her large-scale undertakings like Columbia Square, he considered, were too idiosyncratic to be valuable as 'pilot projects'. And K. J. Fielding, writing of her work with Dickens, bluntly asserted that her judgment and ability had been 'overpraised'. In his view, 'she owed her eminence to her long life, a sense of duty, and her great inherited wealth'.[2]

This, clearly, is an oversimplification. But it does remind us that Angela's charitable work needs to be seen in context. At a time when philanthropy was practised on a larger scale than ever before, she was not the only very rich person with a social conscience. If she gave away more than anyone else – an estimate in the 1880s put the figure at between three and four million pounds – it was partly because she had more to give. And certainly her long life contributed to her reputation.

If Angela has a claim to be unique among Victorian philanthropists, it may rest on the fact that she made a *career* of philanthropy. She regarded it almost as a profession, and she cultivated a professional approach to it – a shrewd, businesslike approach that her grandfather

Coutts would have applauded. To administer her fortune was no easy task. On the whole she tackled it with good sense, method and imagination, generally allowing herself to be guided by those with greater experience than herself. She operated, like Oxfam and other modern agencies, on two levels, giving emergency relief where necessary but always seeking long-term remedies.

The major blunder of Columbia Market was largely due to lack of understanding of the people and processes involved. She relied on her advisers, who were not necessarily the best-informed on the subject. Dickens might have warned her of the pitfalls; but Dickens had faded from the scene by the time she started to plan her market. So she went ahead, determined to make it work and seemingly unaware that people whose livelihood is threatened will fight to the bitter end to protect themselves and their interests.

If true charity consists in helping people to help themselves, Angela's most truly charitable achievements were in the fields of education, training and employment. She did not, as far as we know, ever question the abysmally low level of wages, still less the system that brought them about. But nor did she accept the prevailing view that those without work were lazy, incompetent, or lacking in moral fibre. She assumed that the unemployed wanted to work and she tried to create work for them, encouraging them to acquire new skills or to start a new life in the colonies. Her aid to the East End weavers and Bermondsey tanners, her 'sewing school' in Spitalfields, the Westminster Technical Institute, and perhaps above all her Irish fishery scheme, are all examples of practical philanthropy at its best.

Today, the relics of her benevolence are remarkably few. Ironically, perhaps, the best-preserved of all her projects is the 'middle-class' Holly Village, in Highgate. The houses originally built for retired servants and bank clerks are now regarded as some of the most desirable properties in the area. Columbia Market, used at various times as a warehouse, an air-raid shelter and a refuge for homeless families, was demolished in 1960. Had it survived a few years longer it would surely have been caught up in the conservation boom and preserved as a building of historic interest.

As for Mr Darbishire's draughty flats in Columbia Square, they were condemned as unfit for human habitation in the late 1950s: one child in three, it was alleged, left them with pneumonia. They were pulled down and a council estate built in their place. A cluster of small streets leading off Columbia Road – Baroness Road, Angela Gardens and Georgina

Gardens – are reminders of the area's former associations. Further East, in Victoria Park, Hackney, can still be seen Angela's Gothic drinking fountain. Running north to south from Mile End to Limehouse is Burdett Road, opened in 1862 a few weeks before the fountain; Coutts Road leads off it on the west side.

On the other side of London, in Westminster, the parish of St Stephen's Rochester Row is thriving, though the church has lost the top of its spire. The present school in Rochester Street (off Rochester Row) is known as the Burdett Coutts and Townshend Foundation Church of England Primary School; there is now no secondary school. The Westminster Technical Institute has become the Hotel School of Westminster College.

To understand the special place that Angela held among her contemporaries it is necessary to understand the rôle that philanthropy played in Victorian society. It has been said that 'the ideal national narcissistic images of the nineteenth century were of progress, expansion and wealth'.[3] And the ideal virtues, it could be argued, were the Evangelical virtues of moral earnestness, social responsibility and concern for the oppressed – a concern in which, no doubt, fear and guilt played a part. In philanthropy both these sets of ideals were embodied. Philanthropy served to display wealth and it gave expression to religious and humanitarian impulses. Though some people deplored charitable giving because it interfered with the 'natural economic order', to the majority it was (in David Owen's words) 'one of the glories of British civilisation and one of the forces that made for social stability'.[4]

That the richest woman in England, the head of a sucessful banking business, had devoted herself to philanthropy – while by no means denying herself the fruits of her wealth – must have been a source of immense satisfaction to many of her countrymen. It would probably be too much to say that she represented the conscience of the rich. But to read of her latest benefaction, or to pass by her model buildings and magnificent market in the East End, must have produced a warm glow in the heart of many a prosperous Englishman. As for the poor, they cheered her because of what she had done for them; but they revered her, too, because she symbolised the 'noble ideal' of benevolence on the part of the rich and privileged towards the poor and downtrodden.

*

Although it is probably true that Angela has been overpraised, her achievements were obviously considerable. Her sense of social responsibility, her clear-sighted generosity and practical sympathy were all admirable. While many gave to charity for dubious reasons of publicity, power, or self-perpetuation, she was not concerned with personal glory, though she enjoyed the public honours that came her way.

But her character, like most people's, was the result of a complex inter-weaving of many diverse strands. She was no ideal being without fault or foible. The image that she presented to the world, and which has been preserved almost intact to this day, was incomplete and at times almost deliberately misleading. She was a woman in whose life and character there were many contradictions. It could be said of her, as Mrs Gaskell wrote of Florence Nightingale, that she was 'so excessively gentle in voice, manner, and movement, that one never feels the unbendableness of her character when one is near her'.[5]

To all outward appearances a shining example of conventional Victorian womanhood, Angela in fact enjoyed a degree of independence undreamed of by most women at the time. Living in her own house, free from parental control, she never experienced the kind of 'petty grinding tyranny' that Miss Nightingale had to endure from her family until well into her thirties. She could form her own friendships, follow her own interests, travel when and where she pleased; she had an absorbing and satisfying 'career' and could call on the services of influential men to help carry out her charitable schemes.

Yet it is difficult to believe that she was a really happy, fulfilled woman. There is an aura of pathos about her, a bleakness which belies the richness and variety of her life. Dickens was surely right when he said that she was isolated by her wealth and position. She was essentially a lonely person, wary of close contacts with others. Outwardly posed and serene, she was in some ways a vulnerable child.

Her apparent maturity must have been one of the qualities that impressed Harriot St Albans and led her to choose Angela to be the custodian of Tom Coutts's fortune. Morally and intellectually, perhaps, Angela was ideally suited for the task. But emotionally she was completely unprepared for some of the less pleasant consequences of being the richest heiress in England. Even to leave her father's house, a necessary first step if she was to establish her new status, was a difficult and painful move – one which would probably not have been possible without the support of Hannah Meredith.

Angela was no rebel, as her father had once been. Nor, at twenty-three, did she have anything like Harriot's experience of life. It is hardly surprising that, thrust into the limelight and remembering the sneers and jibes that had been directed at Harriot, she should have taken refuge in an ultra-conventionalism that would give no scope to the gossips and scandalmongers. This need to be socially beyond reproach, to attain a position that was secure and impregnable, may have been a factor in her intense desire to marry the Duke of Wellington.

Her proposal to the Duke was, of course, a highly unconventional act; indeed, it is one of the most astonishing acts of her life. Scarcely less surprising is the way in which she continued to pursue the Duke with a naïve persistence which irritated and embarrassed him in his last years. Thirty years later, she showed the same naïve persistence in her determination to marry Ashmead Bartlett. 'It appeared,' as Clara Patterson says, 'an act of folly on the part of one who had seemed ever to be the acme of wisdom, self-possession and dignity.'[6] But it is doubtful if, in matters concerning her own feelings, she had any more wisdom in her sixties than she had had in her thirties.

As for her self-possession, this was not based on a mature knowledge and acceptance of her own strengths and weaknesses. It was partly the result of her Evangelical faith – that faith which, it has been said, gave its followers 'an inaccessible and irrefutable self-assurance'.[7] But it came also from the knowledge of being always first in Hannah Brown's affections. For, whatever Angela's feelings may have been for the Duke and for Ashmead, Hannah was the great love of her life. Whether or not there was a Lesbian element in their relationship is a question that can probably never be answered and which need not be discussed here. What matters is that it was for Angela a relationship of dependence, which had the effect of stunting her emotional development. Throughout her life she seemed incapable of understanding her feelings and how they affected her behaviour.

There is evidence for this emotional immaturity in her blind devotion to her father's memory; in her harsh treatment of her young cousin Amy and her estrangement from other members of her family; in her rather pathetic loyalty to the bank and the church; in her inability to forget the hurts of the past. But its most poignant manifestation was, of course, her marriage.

Yet it may be that during the twenty-six years of her marriage Angela attained at last the true serenity that comes with a measure of self-knowledge and self-acceptance. Clara Patterson wrote that marriage 'softened the Baroness', giving her 'a more understanding outlook with regard to individual relationships, . . . which so far had been reserved for humanity as a whole'.[8] This new understanding extended perhaps also to herself, enabling her to come to terms with the essential loneliness of her position.

Those who met her in old age were struck by her unaffected simplicity and her kindness, especially to the young. There was still a lot of the child in her. A few years before her death she gave a young niece for her seventeenth birthday a picture book of animals; attached to the pages were strings which, when pulled, caused the appropriate animal noises to be emitted. It had amused the Baroness and she thought it would amuse her nearly grown-up niece.

'It is a melancholy reflection, but there has seldom been a niche in history for a good woman,'[9] wrote the anonymous author of a magazine article shortly after Angela's death. But it seems to me that she was forgotten so quickly partly because she left behind an image of a woman who was as near perfection as any woman could be. As Lytton Strachey wrote of the widowed Queen Victoria's efforts to deify Prince Albert, 'the picture of an embodied perfection is distasteful to the majority of mankind'.[10] It is distasteful because a 'perfect' person is not a real person, someone we can believe in.

What Angela tried to conceal (though it is there in her face) was the unhappy, vulnerable, fallible, less admirable side of herself. It would be a mistake if, in reviving her memory, we were to perpetuate the pretence. For if she was not, in any sense but the most obvious one, 'made of Gold', she was surely all the more human for it.

SELECT BIBLIOGRAPHY

MANUSCRIPT SOURCES

Royal Archives(*RA*), Windsor Castle

Bodleian Library, Oxford, Department of Western MSS.
   Burdett and Burdett-Coutts Papers

British Library, British Museum, London:
   Osborne Papers (Add. MSS. 46402–08)
   Babbage Papers
   Gladstone Papers
   Layard Papers
   Murchison Papers

Harrowby MSS, Sandon Hall, Stafford

Wellington MSS, Stratfield Saye

Disraeli Archives, Hughenden Manor

Lambeth Palace Library, London: Burdett-Coutts Papers (1374–88); Davidson Papers

Pierpont Morgan Library, New York: Dickens correspondence; miscellaneous letters from Angela Burdett Coutts

Westminster Public Library, Buckingham Palace Road, London: Papers from St Stephen's Church, Rochester Row

Hove Area Library: Wolseley Papers

University of London Library: Two letters from ABC to Herbert Spencer

Hertford Record Office: Six letters from ABC to Sir Edward Bulwer Lytton

Correspondence and papers of Henry Wagner, in the possession of Sir Anthony Wagner

Mrs Agatha Twining's unpublished memoir of ABC: *A Great Foundress*, in the possession of The Hon. John Twining

PUBLISHED SOURCES

Books written or edited by Angela Burdett Coutts:

   A Summary Account of Prizes for *Common Things* offered and awarded by Miss Burdett Coutts at the Whitelands Training Institution (1856, 1857, 1860 (enlarged edn))

   Address of Miss Burdett Coutts to the Pupils of the Whitelands Training Institution. (1866)

   The Ambulatory Schoolmaster (London, 1865)

   Woman's Mission: A series of congress papers on the philanthropic work of women by eminent writers, arranged and edited with a preface and notes by the Baroness Burdett-Coutts (London, 1893)

Other works

Anderson, W. E. K. (Ed.): *Journal of Sir Walter Scott* (Oxford, 1972)

Barron-Wilson, Mrs Cornwell: *Memoirs of Miss Mellon, afterwards Duchess of St Albans* (2 vols. New edition, London, 1886)

Blackwood's Magazine, February 1907, pp. 297–304: 'Lady Burdett-Coutts, by one who knew her well'.

Broughton, Lord (John Cam Hobhouse): *Recollections of a Long Life* (ed. Lady Dorchester, 6 vols, London, 1910)

Cockshut, A. O. J.: *Anglican Attitudes* (Collins, 1959)

Coleridge, E. H.: *The Life of Thomas Coutts, Banker* (London, 1920)

Collins, Philip: *Dickens and Crime* (Macmillan, 1962)

Collins, Philip: *Dickens and Education* (Macmillan, 2nd impression, 1965)

Colvin, Christina (Ed.): *Maria Edgeworth: Letters from England* (Oxford, 1971)

Cooke, C. Kinloch: *A Memoir of HRH Princess Mary Adelaide, Duchess of Teck* (2 vols. London, 1900)

Dickens, Charles: *The Pilgrim Edition of the Letters of Charles Dickens* (vols I–IV, Oxford, 1965–77)

Dickens, Charles: *Dickens' London, selected essays* (ed. Rosalind Vallance, Folio Society, 1966)

(*See also under Forster, Johnson, Lehmann and Osborne*)

Dictionary of National Biography

Fielding, K. J.: *Charles Dickens, A Critical Introduction* (Longman, 2nd edn 1965)

Fielding, K. J.: 'Dickens to Miss Burdett Coutts', *Times Literary Supplement*, 2 and 9 March 1951

Fielding, K. J.: Articles in the *Dickensian*:

'Women in the Home' – Vol. XLVII, No. 299, pp. 140–142 (1951)
'Dickens's Novels and Miss Burdett Coutts' – Vol. LI, No. 313, pp. 30–34 (1954)
'Nova Scotia Gardens and what grew there' – Vol. LXI, No. 346, pp. 112–118 (1965)
'Casby and the Westminster Landlords' – Vol. LXI, No. 347, pp. 155–160 (1965)

Fielding, K. J.: 'Miss Burdett Coutts – Some Misconceptions', *Nineteenth Century Fiction*, March 1954, pp. 314–318

Forster, John: *The Life of Charles Dickens* (new edn. ed. A. J. Hoppé, 2 vols, J. M. Dent, 1966)

Galbraith, Georgina (Ed.): *The Journal of The Reverend William Bagshaw Stevens* (Oxford, 1965)

Gordon, D. G. H: *Fifty Years of Failure* (London, 1905)

Gower, Lord Ronald Sutherland: *Old Diaries* (London, 1902)

Hare, Augustus J. C.: *The Story of My Life* (6 vols, London, 1896–1900)

Heasman, Kathleen: *Evangelicals in Action* (Geoffrey Bles, 1962)

Houghton, Walter E.: *The Victorian Frame of Mind, 1830–1870* (Yale University Press, 1957)

Hudson, Derek (Ed.): *The Diary of Henry Crabb Robinson, an abridgement* (Oxford, 1967). *See also under Robinson*

Hurt, John: *Education in Evolution* (Hart-Davis, 1971)

Select Bibliography

Irving, Laurence: *Henry Irving* (Faber & Faber, 1951)
Jeal, Tim: *Livingstone* (Heinemann, 1973)
Jeune, Mary (Lady St Helier): *Memories of Fifty Years* (London, 1909)
Johnson, Edgar (Ed.): *Letters from Charles Dickens to Angela Burdett-Coutts* (Jonathan Cape, 1953)
Johnson, Edgar: *Charles Dickens, His Tragedy and Triumph* (2 vols, Gollancz, 1953)
Lehmann, R. C.: *Charles Dickens as Editor* (London, 1912)
Longford, Elizabeth: *Victoria R.I.* (Pan Books, 1966)
Longford, Elizabeth: *Wellington, Pillar of State* (Panther, 1975)
Longmate, Norman: *The Workhouse* (Temple Smith, 1974)
Mackenzie, Compton: *My Life and Times, Octave One* and *Octave Two* (Chatto & Windus, 1963)
Martin, Ralph G.: *Lady Randolph Churchill* (Cassell, 1969)
Martineau, Harriet: *Autobiography* (3 vols, London, 1877)
Monypenny, W. F. and Buckle, G. E.: *The Life of Benjamin Disraeli, Earl of Beaconsfield* (2 vols, London, 1929)
Moore, Thomas: *Memoirs* (ed. Lord John Russell, 8 vols, London, 1853–56)
Moorman, J. R. H.: *A History of the Church in England* (A. & C. Black, 3rd edn, 1973)
O'Connor, T. P.: 'The Baroness', *P. T. O.*, 12 January 1907
Osborne, Charles C. (Ed.): *Letters of Charles Dickens to The Baroness Burdett-Coutts* (John Murray, 1931)
Osborne, Charles C.: 'The Genesis of Mrs Gamp', *Dickensian*, Vol. XXIII, No. 201.
Owen, David: *English Philanthropy, 1660–1960* (Harvard University Press, 1964)
Patterson, Clara Burdett: *Angela Burdett-Coutts and the Victorians* (Murray, 1953)
Patterson, M. W.: *Sir Francis Burdett and His Times* (2 vols, Macmillan, 1931)
Pollock, Sir John: *Time's Chariot* (Murray, 1950)
Reid, T. Wemyss: *Life, Letters and Friendships of Richard Monckton Milnes, 1st Lord Houghton* (2 vols, London, 1890)
Robinson, Henry Crabb: *Diary* (ed. Thomas Sadler, 3 vols, London, 1869). See also under Hudson
Robinson, Ralph M.: *Coutts' – The History of a Banking House* (London, 1929)
Rose, Millicent: *The East End of London* (Cedric Chivers, 1973)
Russell, Bertrand: *Portraits from Memory and other essays* (Allen & Unwin, 1956)
Rutter, Owen (Ed.): *Rajah Brooke and Baroness Burdett Coutts* (Hutchinson, 1935)
Sala, G. A.: *Life and Adventures* (2 vols, 2nd edn, London, 1895)
Seed, Philip: *The Expansion of Social Work in Britain* (Routledge & Kegan Paul, 1973)
Stern, Walter M.: 'The Baroness's Market: The History of a Noble Failure', *The Guildhall Miscellany*, Vol. II, No. 8, September 1966, pp. 353–366.
Strachey, Lytton: *Queen Victoria* (London, 1929)
Symondson, A. (Ed.): *The Victorian Crisis of Faith* (SPCK, 1970)
Teck, Duchess of (by command of): *Baroness Burdett-Coutts, A Sketch of her public life and work, prepared for the lady managers of the World's Columbian Exposition* (1893)
Wellington, 7th Duke (Ed.): *Wellington and His Friends: Letters of the First Duke* (Macmillan, 1965)
Woodham-Smith, Cecil: *Florence Nightingale, 1820–1910* (Reprint Society, 1952)

Young, G. M.: *Victorian England, Portrait of an Age* (Oxford Paperback, 1973)
Young, G. M. and Handcock, W. D.: *English Historical Documents*, Vol. XII(1), 1833–74 (Eyre & Spottiswoode, 1956)
Young, J. C.: *A Memoir of Charles Mayne Young, Tragedian, with Extracts from his Son's Journal* (2 vols, London, 1871)
Young, J. C.: *Last Leaves* (ed. by his wife, London, 1875)

Newspapers
The Times
The Daily Telegraph
The Scotsman
The Standard
The World
The Christian Times
The Glasgow News
The Illustrated London News
The Penny Illustrated Paper
Vanity Fair
The Whitehall Review

REFERENCES

See Select Bibliography for full references

Prologue

1 Archdeacon Wilberforce to Randall Davidson, Archbishop of Canterbury, December 28, 1906. Lambeth Palace Library, Davidson Papers, vol. 124, fos 151–2.
2 Davidson to Wilberforce, December 29, 1906. *Ibid*. fos 153–4.
3 Compton Mackenzie, *Octave One*, p. 125.
4 Gordon, *Fifty Years of Failure*, pp. 212–13.
5 Young, *A Memoir of Charles Mayne Young*, vol. II, p. 246 (entry May 29, 1856).
6 Wilberforce to Davidson, January 2, 1907. Lambeth, Davidson Papers, vol. 124, fo. 155.
7 C. B. Patterson, *Angela Burdett-Coutts and the Victorians*, pp. 225–6.
8 W. Burdett-Coutts to Davidson, January 6, 1907. Lambeth, Davidson Papers, vol. 124, fos 156–9.
9 Duke of Wellington to ABC, August 14, 1847. *Wellington and His Friends*, p. 245.
10 Quoted in *The Standard*, January 10, 1907.
11 Martin, *Lady Randolph Churchill*, p. 312.
12 *Daily Telegraph*, December 31, 1906.

Chapter 1

1 Thomas Coutts to the Rev. W. B. Stevens, June 1794. Galbraith, *The Journal of the Reverend William Bagshaw Stevens*, p. 162.
2 Letter in the *Morning Post*, March 25, 1822 (quoted in Robinson, *Coutts': The History of a Banking House*, p. 18).
3 Quoted in Robinson, p. 58.
4 Thomas Coutts to the Earl of Stair, December 25, 1783 (quoted by Robinson, p. 53).
5 Robinson, p. 55.
6 T. Coutts to Georgiana, Duchess of Devonshire, June 15, 1792 (quoted in Robinson, pp. 42–3).
7 M. W. Patterson, *Sir Francis Burdett and His Times*, vol. I, p. 24.
8 *Ibid.*, p. 25.
9 Galbraith, *The Journal of the Reverend William Bagshaw Stevens*, p. 130 (entry January 24, 1794).
10 *Ibid.*, p. 84 (entry May 24, 1793).
11 *Ibid.*, p. 20 (entry May 13, 1792).
12 Francis Burdett to Mrs Jones, April 19, 1789 (quoted in M. W. Patterson, *Sir Francis Burdett and His Times*, vol. I, p. 11).

13 M. W. Patterson, vol. I, p. 15.
14 Galbraith, p. 130 (January 26, 1794).
15 *Ibid.*, pp. 168–9 (August 5, 1794).
16 *Ibid.*, p. 170 (August 12, 1794).
17 F. Burdett to T. Coutts, January 2, 1795 (quoted by M. W. Patterson, vol. I, p. 31).
18 F. Burdett to T. Coutts, January 5, 1795 (*ibid.*, pp. 31–2).
19 Russell, 'Lord John Russell', *Portraits from Memory and other essays*, p. 111.
20 M. W. Patterson, vol. I, p. 59.
21 Sir F. Burdett to T. Coutts, January 28, 1798 (M. W. Patterson, vol. I, p. 33).
22 *Ibid.*
23 MS. Bodleian (quoted by M. W. Patterson, vol. I, pp. 275–6).
24 Crabb Robinson, *Diary*, vol. II, p. 10.
25 Quoted by Robinson, *Coutts': The History of a Banking House*, p. 46.
26 T. Coutts to Lady Burdett, July 12, 1815. MS. Bodleian, Eng. Letters c. 62.
27 T. Coutts to Lady Guilford, June 1817. *Ibid.*
28 MS. Bodleian (quoted by M. W. Patterson, vol. II, p. 357).
29 Quoted by Robinson, p. 48.
30 'Declaration' of T. Coutts. MS. Bodleian, Eng. Letters c. 62.

Chapter 2

1 ABC to Miss Nora Money-Coutts, December 24, 1902. C. B. Patterson, *Angela Burdett-Coutts and the Victorians*, p. 8.
2 Sir J. Brooke to ABC, November 9, 1859. Rutter, *Rajah Brooke and Baroness Burdett Coutts*, p. 68.
3 Young, *A Memoir of Charles Mayne Young*, vol. I, p. 365.
4 Moore, *Memoirs*, vol. II, pp. 157–9 (September 7–8, 1818).
5 J. C. Hobhouse to Sir F. Burdett, January 9, 1821. M. W. Patterson, *Sir Francis Burdett and His Times*, vol. II, pp. 530–2.
6 The Rev. J. Tate to W. Friend, August 19, 1810. MS. Bodleian, Eng. Letters d. 98.
7 Sir F. Burdett to Robert Burdett, May 19, 1815. *Ibid.*
8 Sir F. Burdett to Robert Burdett, March 12, 1819. *Ibid.*
9 Moore, vol. II, p. 158 (September 7, 1818).
10 Samuel Bamford: *Passages in the Life of a Radical* (1844) (quoted by M. W. Patterson, vol. II, pp. 418–19).
11 Moore (as 9).
12 Anderson, *Journal of Sir Walter Scott*, p. 13 (entry November 25, 1825).
13 Lady Bute to T. Coutts, September 19, 1815. MS. Bodleian, Eng. Letters c. 62.
14 Lady Bute to T. Coutts, 1817 (quoted by Robinson, *Coutts': The History of a Banking House*, p. 147).
15 Lady Frances Sandon to Frances, Dowager Marchioness of Bute, June 14, 1827. MS. Harrowby, LXI, fo. 391.
16 Anderson, pp. 13–14 (November 25, 1825).
17 Quoted in Anderson, p. 14.
18 King George IV to Harriot Coutts, June 14, 1827 (quoted in Robinson, p. 145).
19 Harriot, Duchess of St Albans to Sir W. Scott, July 16, 1827 (quoted in Robinson, p. 146).
20 Quoted in M. W. Patterson, vol. II, p. 551.
21 Quoted in Heasman, *Evangelicals in Action*, p. 16.

References

22 Quoted in Houghton, *The Victorian Frame of Mind*, pp. 241–2.
23 G. M. Young, *Victorian England*, p. 4.
24 ABC to Joanna Burdett, August 1834. MS. Bodleian, Eng. Letters c. 64.
25 ABC, *Common Things*, p. 134 (1857 edn).
26 Lady F. Sandon to Dowager Marchioness of Bute, June 17, 1829. MS. Harrowby, LXII, fo. 119.
27 Sala, *Life and Adventures*, vol. I, p. 28.
28 Sir F. Burdett to Duchess of St Albans, July 29, 1829 (quoted in M. W. Patterson, vol. II, p. 538).
29 Sir F. Burdett to Duchess of St Albans, July 12, 1831. *Ibid.*, pp. 538–40.
30 Duchess of St Albans to Sir F. Burdett, July 19, 1831. *Ibid.*, pp. 540–1.
31 Sir F. Burdett to Lady Burdett, August 1, 1834. *Ibid.*, p. 624.
32 Sir F. Burdett to ABC, March 11, 1836. MS. Bodleian, Eng. Letters d. 98.
33 Sir F. Burdett to Joanna Burdett, November 25, 1836. MS Bodleian, Eng. Letters c. 64.
34 Sir F. Burdett to Lady Guilford, August 7, 1837 (quoted by M. W. Patterson, vol. II, p. 651).
35 Barron-Wilson, *Memoirs of Miss Mellon*, vol. II, p. 285.
36 Sir F. Burdett to ABC, August 7, 1837. MS. Bodleian, Eng. Letters d. 98.
37 Sir F. Burdett to Lady Guilford, August 7, 1837. M. W. Patterson, vol II, pp. 651–2.
38 The will is set out in full at the end of Mrs Barron-Wilson's biography.
39 Viscount Sandon to 1st Earl of Harrowby, August 10, 1837. MS. Harrowby, LXIII, fo. 385.

Chapter 3

1 Sir F. Burdett to ABC, September 17, 1837. MS. Bodleian, Eng. Letters d. 98.
2 Thomas Raikes, *Journal*, iv, p. 345 (quoted in *Dictionary of National Biography*).
3 Sir G. Sinclair to ABC, September 2, 1837. MS. Bodleian, Eng. Letters d. 98.
4 Lady Frances Sandon to 2nd Earl of Clare, August 24, 1837. MS. Harrowby, LXIII, fo. 389
5 Viscount Sandon to Lady Frances Sandon, December 10, 1837. MS. Harrowby, LXIII, fo. 446.
6 Monypenny, *The Life of Benjamin Disraeli*, vol. II, p. 21 (undated letter (1838) from Disraeli to his sister Sarah).
7 Hare, *The Story of My Life*, vol. IV, p. 71.
8 RA, Queen Victoria's Journal, December 5, 1838.
9 *Ibid.*, March 15, 1838.
10 Martineau, *Autobiography*, vol. II, pp. 121–6.
11 Broughton: *Recollections of a Long Life*, vol. VI, pp. 149–50.
12 Lady Burdett to ABC, August 22, 1838. MS. Bodleian, Eng. Letters d. 98.
13 C. B. Patterson, *Angela Burdett-Coutts and the Victorians*, p. 68.
14 Jane Austen: *Emma*, vol. I, chapter 1.
15 Lady Frances Sandon to 2nd Earl of Clare, August 24, 1837. MS. Harrowby, LXIII, fo. 389.
16 Lord James Stuart to Lady Frances Sandon, December 1, 1837. *Ibid.*, XLII, fos 411–12.
17 Sir F. Burdett to ABC, July 27, 1838. MS. Bodleian, Eng. Letters d. 98.

18 Lady Burdett to ABC, August 11, 1838. *Ibid.*
19 *The Times*, June 29, 1840.
20 E. Marjoribanks to Sir F. Burdett, October 1, 1838. MS. Bodleian, Eng. Letters d. 98.
21 Sir F. Burdett to ABC, October 4, 1838. *Ibid.*
22 Sir F. Burdett to ABC, September, 1842. *Ibid.*
23 Lady St Helier: *Memories of a Vanished Generation* (quoted by C. B. Patterson, p. 50).
24 Sir F. Burdett to ABC, June 1839. MS. Bodleian, Eng. Letters d. 98.
25 Charles Dickens to ABC, September 5, 1857. Johnson, *Letters from Charles Dickens to ABC*, p. 347.
26 Leigh Hunt to John Forster, quoted in Forster, *The Life of Charles Dickens*, vol. I, p. 66.
27 Forster, vol. I, p. 65.
28 Charles Dickens to E. Marjoribanks, July 6, 1840. *The Pilgrim Edition of the Letters of Charles Dickens*, vol. II, p. 95.
29 Sir F. Burdett to ABC, November 27, 1838. MS. Bodleian, Eng. Letters d. 98.

Chapter 4

1 This account of Dunn's activities has been compiled mainly from the Law Reports in *The Times* of the following dates:

    June 20, 1840   March 1, 1847
    June 30, 1840   August 1, 4, 1853
    November 5, 6, 10, 1840   July 11, 1856
    February 8, 1841

2 Sir F. Burdett to ABC, October 25, 1838. MS. Bodleian, Eng. Letters d. 98.
3 Queen Victoria's Journal, June 10, 1840. Quoted in Longford, *Victoria*, p. 188.
4 Charles Dickens to ABC, April 27, 1853. MS. Pierpont Morgan.
5 Charles Dickens to Mrs Brown, August 7, 1853. Johnson, *Letters from Charles Dickens to ABC*, p. 229.
6 Charles Dickens to ABC, July 15, 1856. MS. Pierpont Morgan.
7 Longford, *Victoria*, p. 189.
8 Compton Mackenzie, *Octave Two*, p. 230.

Chapter 5

1 Broughton, *Recollections of a Long Life*, vol. VI, pp. 149–50.
2 Dickens to C. Sumner, July 31, 1842. Quoted in Johnson, *Charles Dickens, His Tragedy and Triumph*, vol. I, p. 228.
3 Osborne, *Letters of Charles Dickens to Baroness Burdett-Coutts*, p.13.
4 Dickens to J. Forster, September 24, 1843. *Charles Dickens, The Pilgrim Edition*, vol. III, p. 572.
5 Dickens to ABC, January 22, 1841. Johnson, *Letters from Charles Dickens to ABC*, p. 28.
6 ABC to Dickens, January 23, 1841. *Pilgrim*, vol. II, p. 192, fn.
7 Dickens to ABC, April 20, 1841. Johnson, *Letters*, p. 30.
8 *Ibid.*, p. 29.
9 Dickens to ABC, August 16, 1841. Johnson, *Letters*, p. 31.
10 ABC to Dickens, August 19, 1841. *Pilgrim*, vol. II, p. 359, fn.

References

11 Young, *Last Leaves* (from Preface by his wife).
12 Young, *A Memoir of Charles Mayne Young*, vol. II, p. 108 (entry May 28, 1846).
13 *Ibid.*, vol. I, p. 373.
14 Moore, *Memoirs*, vol. VIII, pp. 9–10.
15 Colvin, *Maria Edgeworth*, p. 579 (the remark is Maria Edgeworth's).
16 ABC to Babbage, January 7, 1855. BM, Babbage Papers, 37,196.
17 Dickens to ABC, February 3, 1857. Johnson, *Letters*, p. 335.
18 Colvin, pp. 581–2.
19 Johnson, p. 32.
20 *Pilgrim*, vol. II, p. 359, fn.
21 Dickens to ABC, November 24, 1841. Johnson, p. 33.
22 Dickens to ABC, July 2, 1842. *Ibid.*, p. 38.
23 Dickens to ABC, April 24, 1843. *Ibid.*, p. 42.
24 Dickens to ABC, October 5, 1846. *Ibid.*, p. 88.
25 Forster, *The Life of Charles Dickens*, vol. II, p. 108.
26 Dickens to ABC, March 23, 1851. Johnson, p. 183.
27 Dickens to ABC, September 20, 1852. *Ibid.*, p. 207.
28 Dickens to ABC, November 27, 1853. *Ibid.*, p. 244.
29 Quoted in Johnson, *Charles Dickens, His Tragedy and Triumph*, vol. II, p. 863 (Dickens to Georgina Hogarth, May 5, 1856).
30 Dickens to ABC, July 28, 1843. Johnson, p. 46.
31 Dickens to ABC, September 17, 1845. *Ibid.*, p. 72.
32 G. M. Young, *Victorian England*, p. 61.
33 Dickens to ABC, September 5, 1857. Johnson, p. 347.
34 Colvin, p. 585.
35 Dickens to ABC, September 16, 1843. Johnson, pp. 50–4.
36 Dickens to Forster, September 24, 1843. *Pilgrim*, vol. III, p. 572.
37 *Ibid.*

Chapter 6

1 Dickens to ABC, January 13, 1844, Johnson, *Letters from Charles Dickens to ABC*, p. 60.
2 Quoted by M. W. Patterson, *Sir Francis Burdett and His Times*, vol. II, p. 661.
3 Disraeli Archives, Hughenden. A/X/A22.
4 Sir F. Burdett to Robert Burdett, May 9, 1831; Lady Burdett to R. Burdett, April 26, 1836. MS Bodleian, Eng. Letters d. 98.
5 Lady C. Bacon to Sir R. Burdett, March 31, 1844. MS. Harrowby, LXIV, fo. 186.
6 MS. Bodleian (quoted by M. W. Patterson, vol. I, p. 309).
7 Sir R. Burdett to Lady C. Bacon, April 7, 1844. MS. Harrowby, LXIV, fo. 188.
8 Count D'Orsay to Lord D. C. Stuart, March 25, 1844. *Ibid.*, LXIV, fo. 184.
9 Lady C. Bacon to Lord Brougham, May 1, 1844. *Ibid.*, LXIV, fo. 197.
10 Lord Brougham to Lord D. C. Stuart, undated (May 1844). *Ibid.*, LXIV, fo. 200.
11 ABC to Lord D. C. Stuart, May 14, 1844. *Ibid.*, LXIV, fo. 197.
12 Lord D. C. Stuart to ABC, July 31, 1844. *Ibid.*, LXIV, fo. 205.
13 Dickens to ABC, March 18, 1844. Johnson, p. 64.
14 Dickens to ABC, October 13, 1843. *Ibid.*, p. 56.
15 Dickens to ABC, August 7, 1843. *Ibid.*, p. 48.

16 Dickens to Forster, March 30, 1844. Quoted in Johnson, *Charles Dickens, His Tragedy and Triumph*, vol. I, p. 536.
17 Lord Brougham to Lord D. C. Stuart (undated, but referred to by Stuart in his letter to ABC, below). MS. Harrowby, 1059, fo. 219.
18 Lord D. C. Stuart to ABC, March 1, 1845. *Ibid.*, LXIV, fo. 217.
19 ABC to Lord D. C. Stuart, March 3, 1845. *Ibid.*, LXIV, fo. 219.
20 The Rev. E. Coleridge to ABC, May 6, 1846. Lambeth Palace Library, Burdett-Coutts Papers, 1384, fos 33–4.
21 G. M. Young, *Victorian England*, p. 44 (fn.).
22 Miss C. Sinclair to ABC, July 22, 1847. Westminster Collection, E1.
23 Lord Brougham to ABC, undated (July 1847). *Ibid.*
24 Miss Sinclair to ABC, July 22, 1847.
25 Mrs M. Howley to ABC, June 30, 1847. Lambeth, B-C Papers, 1384, fo. 107.
26 Young, *A Memoir of Charles Mayne Young*, vol. II, p. 119.
27 Lieven–Palmerston Correspondence, ed. Lord Sudley (Murray, 1943), p. 297.

Chapter 7

Note: Letters from the Duke of Wellington are quoted from the originals at Stratfield Saye unless otherwise stated. WHF = *Wellington and His Friends* (*see* Bibliography).
1 Wellington to ABC, August 14, 1846.
2 Quoted by Longford, *Wellington*, p. 190.
3 Wellington to ABC, July 28, 1840.
4 Longford, *op. cit.*, p. 501.
5 Charles Arbuthnot to Wellington, August 5, 1834. Quoted in Longford, *op. cit.*, p. 366.
6 Longford, *op. cit.*, 372 (Diary of Anna Maria Jenkins).
7 Quoted by Longford, *op. cit.*, 252.
8 *Correspondence of Sarah Spencer, Lady Lyttelton, 1787–1870*. Edited by Mrs Hugh Wyndham, 1912, p. 334.
9 Sir F. Burdett to Baroness North, August 31, 1839, MS. Bodleian, Eng. Letters c. 64.
10 Wellington to ABC, October 24, 1846.
11 Wellington to ABC, August 31, 1846.
12 Draft letter written by Wellington with his letter to ABC of November 19, 1846.
13 Wellington to ABC, November 24, 1846.
14 Wellington to ABC, October 30, 1846; November 25, 1846.
15 Wellington to ABC, January 1, 1847.
16 Wellington to ABC, January 5, 1847.
17 Wellington to ABC, January 9, 1847.
18 Wellington to ABC, January 12, 1847.
19 Wellington to ABC, February 4, 1847.
20 Wellington to ABC, February 6, 1847.
21 Wellington to Miss Jenkins, January 13, 1835. Quoted in Longford, *op. cit.*, p. 373.
22 Wellington to ABC, February 8, 1847. WHF, pp. 242–3.
23 Wellington to ABC, February 11, 1847.
24 Wellington to ABC, April 27 or 29, 1847.
25 Wellington to ABC, June 5, June 14, 1847.
26 Greville, *Memoirs*, July 13, 1847 (quoted by Longford, *op. cit.*, p. 470).

References 277

27 Longford, *Victoria*, p. 500 (quoting Lord John Manners).
28 Wellington to ABC, August 26, August 29, 1847.
29 Wellington to ABC, October 2, 1847.
30 Wellington to ABC, October 15, October 20, October 17, 1847.
31 'Declaration' of T. Coutts. MS. Bodleian, Eng. Letters c. 62.
32 Wellington to ABC, November 9, 1847.
33 Wellington to ABC, October 30, 1847.
34 Philip Collins, 'The Rich Full Life' (*TLS*, January 13, 1978).
35 Wellington to ABC, December 30, 1847.
36 Wellington to W. F. Spicer, March 22, 1848. Longford, *Wellington*, p. 463.
37 Wellington to ABC, March 9, 1848.
38 Wellington to ABC, April 10, 1848.
39 Wellington to ABC, September 4, 1848. WHF, pp. 264–5.
40 Wellington to ABC (2nd letter, same date).
41 Wellington to ABC, July 19, 20, 1849.
42 Wellington to ABC, December 31, 1848.
43 Wellington to ABC, July 10, 1849.
44 Wellington to ABC, June 19, 1849. WHF, p. 275.
45 Wellington to ABC, June 21, October 3, 1849.
46 Wellington to ABC, November 10, 1850; January 31, 1851.
47 Quoted in Longford, *Wellington*, p. 471.
48 ABC to Wellington, August 8, 1851. Wellington MSS.
49 Wellington to ABC, August 23, 1851.
50 Lady Herbert to ABC, August 1851. Wellington MSS.
51 Wellington to Lady Salisbury, August 29, 1852. Longford, *Wellington*, p. 486.
52 Wellington to ABC, September 12, 1852. WHF, p. 290.
53 Col. Phipps to Prince Albert, September 15, 1852. Quoted by Longford, *Wellington*, p. 489.
54 Queen Victoria to King Leopold of the Belgians, September 17, 1852. Longford, *Wellington*, p. 490. Queen Victoria's Journal quoted in Longford, *Victoria*, p. 287.
55 Second Duke of Wellington to ABC, November 11, 13, 1852. Wellington MSS.
56 Dickens to ABC, September 23, 1852. Johnson, *Letters*, p. 208.
57 Second Duke of Wellington to ABC, November 5, October 25, November 4, 1852. Wellington MSS.
58 Lady Charles Wellesley to ABC, November 1, 1852; Lord Charles Wellesley to ABC, August 12, 1853; Lady Charles Wellesley to ABC, September 20, 1853. Wellington MSS.
59 Second Duke of Wellington to ABC, July 8, 1858. *Ibid.*
60 Second Duke of Wellington to ABC, May 9, 1853. *Ibid.*

Chapter 8

1 'An Appeal to Fallen Women,' Johnson, *Letters from Charles Dickens to ABC*, pp. 98–100.
2 Dickens to ABC, October 28, 1847. *Ibid.*, p. 98.
3 *The Times*, October 12, 1843.
4 Letter to *The Times*, 1857, quoted in Longmate, *The Workhouse*, p. 158.
5 Quoted in Owen, *English Philanthropy*, p. 58.
6 'Some Recollections of Mortality' (*All the Year Round*, May 16, 1863).

7 Dickens to ABC, May 26, 1846. Johnson, pp. 77–83.
8 Dickens to unknown correspondent, June 9, 1837; to Thomas Beard, May 17, 1837. Quoted in Johnson, *Charles Dickens, His Tragedy and Triumph*, vol. I, pp. 196, 198.
9 Dickens to ABC, October 5, 1846. Johnson, *Letters*, p. 87.
10 Dickens to ABC, July 25, 1846. *Ibid.*, p. 85.
11 'In and Out of Jail' (*Household Words*, May 14, 1853). Quoted by Collins, *Dickens and Crime*, p. 55.
12 Dickens to ABC, May 26, 1846; January 12, 1847. Johnson, pp. 80, 89.
13 Dickens to ABC, May 23, 1847, June 27, 1847. *Ibid.*, pp. 92, 94.
14 Dickens to ABC, August 26, 1847. *Ibid.*, p. 95.
15 Dickens to ABC, October 28, 1847. *Ibid.*, p. 97.
16 Dickens to ABC, November 3, 1847. *Ibid.*, p. 106.
17 Dickens to ABC, September 26, 1847. MS. Pierpont Morgan.
18 Dickens to ABC, October 28, 1847. Johnson, pp. 96–8.
19 Dickens to ABC, November 3, 1847. *Ibid.*, pp. 101–8.
20 Dickens to ABC, November 20, 1847. *Ibid.*, p. 109.
21 Dickens to Dr Brown, November 6, 1849. *Ibid.*, pp. 152–4.
22 Dickens to Dr Brown, November 7, 1849. *Ibid.*, pp. 154–5.
23 M. A. Stonnell to ABC, August 31, 1848. *Ibid.*, p. 128.
24 Dickens to ABC, September 8, 1848. *Ibid.*, p. 128.
25 Dickens to ABC, April 17, 1850. *Ibid.*, pp. 169–70.
26 Dickens to ABC, November 1848, August 10, 13, 1848. *Ibid.*, pp. 134, 121, 122.
27 Dickens to ABC, October 26, 1848. MS. Pierpont Morgan.
28 Dickens to ABC, January 27, 1849. Johnson, p. 140.
29 Dickens to ABC, November 20, 1847. *Ibid.*, p. 110.
30 Dickens to ABC, December 29, 1847. *Ibid.*, p. 110.
31 Dickens to ABC, December 9, 1847. MS. Pierpont Morgan.
32 Dickens to ABC, February 8, 1848. *Ibid.*
33 Dickens to ABC, March 4, 1850. Johnson, p. 166.
34 Dickens to ABC, November 19, 1852. *Ibid.*, p. 214.
35 'Prostitution' (*Westminster Review*, 1850). Quoted in Houghton, *The Victorian Frame of Mind*, p. 366.
36 G. L. Chesterton: *Recollections of Prison Life*. Quoted in Collins, *Dickens and Crime*, pp. 98–9.
37 Quoted by Longmate, p. 159.
38 'Home for Homeless Women' (*Household Words*, April 23, 1853). Quoted by Johnson, pp. 100–1.
39 Dickens to ABC, November 15, 1856. *Ibid.*, p. 329.
40 Collins, *Dickens and Crime*, p. 110
41 Louisa Cooper to ABC, October 20, 1854. Johnson, p. 272.

Chapter 9

1 ABC to 2nd Countess of Harrowby, September 10, 1849. MS. Harrowby, LXIV, fo. 362.
2 Quoted in letter of The Rev. W. Tennant to ABC, September 27, 1849. Westminster Collection, G1.
3 The Rev. W. Tennant to ABC, November 18, 1850. *Ibid.*, J8.

References

4 St Stephen's schoolmistress (no name) to ABC, March 23, 1852. *Ibid.*, J5.
5 W. Tennant to ABC, August 10, 1851. *Ibid.*, F4.
6 Dickens to ABC, October 26, 1854. Johnson, *Letters from Charles Dickens to ABC*, p. 273.
7 Longmate, *The Workhouse*, p. 59 (Cobbett's speech in House of Commons, August 13, 1834).
8 *Ibid.*, p. 62 (Edwin Chadwick to Lord John Russell, 1838).
9 Quoted in Teck, *Baroness Burdett-Coutts, A Sketch*, p. 136.
10 Dickens to ABC, May 3, 1853. MS. Pierpont Morgan.
11 Dickens to ABC, May 10, 1853. Johnson, p. 224.
12 Dickens to ABC, April 18, 1852. *Ibid.*, p. 199.
13 Beatrice Webb, *My Apprenticeship*. Quoted by Rose, *The East End of London*, p. 265.
14 Quoted by Rose, p. 264.
15 *Ibid.*, pp. 257–8.
16 Owen, *English Philanthropy*, p. 378.
17 *Ibid.*, p. 380.
18 Quoted in Rose, p. 268. The previous comment is hers (p. 261).
19 ABC, *Common Things* (Appendix to 1856 edn).
20 Jeune, *Memories of Fifty Years*, p. 66.
21 Rose, p. 242.
22 Jeune, p. 224.
23 Quoted in Teck, *Baroness Burdett-Coutts, A Sketch*, p. 43.
24 ABC to The Rev. H. Baber, December 16, 1854. ABC, *Common Things*, 1857 edn, p. 107.
25 F. Smith, *The Life and Work of Sir James Kay-Shuttleworth*, 1923, p. 87 (quoted in Hurt, *Education in Evolution*).
26 ABC to the The Rev. H. Baber, *op. cit.*
27 Dickens to ABC, March 5, April 9, 1857. Johnson, pp. 338–9.
28 Dickens to ABC, November 15, 1856. *Ibid.*, pp. 328–9.
29 G. L. Chesterton to ABC. Quoted in *Common Things*, 1857 edn, p. 101.
30 *Common Things*, 1860 edn (Address of ABC, 1859).
31 ABC to the Secretary (?) of the Central Committee of the Institutional Association of Lancashire and Cheshire, May 1859. MS. Pierpont Morgan.
32 Charles Kingsley, *A Farewell*; Tennyson, *The Princess*.

Chapter 10

1 Forster, *The Life of Charles Dickens*, vol. II, p. 83.
2 ABC to Second Earl of Harrowby, November 21, 1854. MS. Harrowby, XLII, fo. 37.
3 2nd Duke of Wellington to ABC, November 28, 1854. Wellington MSS.
4 1st Duke of Wellington to ABC, October 29, 1850. *Ibid.*
5 Dickens to ABC, May 19, 1853. Johnson, *Letters from Charles Dickens to ABC*, p. 225.
6 1st Duke of Wellington to ABC, September 22, 1848. Wellington MSS.
7 Amy Hill to ABC, undated (Autumn 1853). *Ibid.*
8 Draft letters, ABC to Amy Hill. *Ibid.*

9 ABC to Lord Dudley Coutts Stuart, September 22, 1846. MS. Harrowby, XXV, fo. 156.
10 1st Duke of Wellington to ABC, August 14, 1847. *Wellington and His Friends*, p. 245.
11 1st Duke of Wellington to ABC, January 28, 1848. *Ibid.*, p. 259.
12 W. M. Coulthurst to Edward Marjoribanks, August 21, 1863. MS. Harrowby, LXVI, fo. 23.
13 Edward Marjoribanks to W. M. Coulthurst, August 22, 1863. *Ibid.*, LXVI, fo. 25.
14 ABC to General W. Knollys, December 28, 1862. RA, T3/113.
15 Lady Charles Wellesley to ABC, June 14, 1854. Wellington MSS.
16 Dickens to ABC, December 22, 1848. MS. Pierpont Morgan.
17 Dickens to ABC, January 14, 1854. Johnson, p. 254.
18 Dickens to ABC, January 18, 1854. *Ibid.*, p. 256.
19 Dickens to ABC, June 10, 1854. MS. Pierpont Morgan.
20 Crabb Robinson, *Diary*, vol. III, p. 363 (letter to his brother).
21 *Ibid.*, pp. 440–1 (entry October 22, 1855).
22 Dickens to W. H. Wills, October 28, 1855. Lehmann, *Charles Dickens as Editor*, pp. 182–3.
23 Dickens to ABC, October 31, 1855. MS. Pierpont Morgan.
24 Dickens to Mrs Brown, November 3, 1855. Johnson, p. 309.
25 *Ibid.*, p. 310.
26 Dickens to ABC, November 16, 1855. Johnson, pp. 310–11.
27 Dickens to ABC, May 8, 1855. *Ibid.*, p. 296.
28 Fielding, *Critical Introduction*, p. 177.
29 Johnson, p. 202, fn.
30 Dickens to J. Forster, April 1856. Forster, vol. II, p. 198.
31 Dickens to ABC, March 23, 1851. Johnson, p. 183.
32 Dickens to Mrs Brown, August 28, 1857. *Ibid.*, pp. 345–6.
33 Dickens to ABC, February 2, 1858. *Ibid.*, pp. 352–3.
34 Dickens to ABC, April 14, 1858. MS. Pierpont Morgan.
35 Dickens to ABC, May 9, 1858. Johnson, pp. 354–6.
36 Dickens to ABC, May 19, 1858. *Ibid.*, pp. 356–7.
37 Mrs Dickens to ABC, May 19, 1858. *Ibid.*, p. 357.
38 Hudson, *The Diary of Henry Crabb Robinson*, p. 297 (entry July 13, 1858).
39 Dickens to ABC, August 23, 1858. Johnson, p. 361.
40 Dickens to ABC, April 5, 8, 1860. *Ibid.*, pp. 369–70.
41 Dickens to Mrs Brown, October 24, 1862. *Ibid.*, p. 374.
42 Osborne, *Letters of Charles Dickens to the Baroness Burdett-Coutts*, pp. 16–17.
43 Young, *A Memoir of Charles Mayne Young*, vol. II, p. 309 (entry November 30, 1866).
44 ABC, *Whitelands Address*.
45 Dickens to ABC, March 28, 1853. MS. Pierpont Morgan.
46 Dickens to ABC, July 11, 1856. Johnson, p. 322.
47 Dickens to ABC, March 13, 1860. *Ibid.*, p. 369.
48 Dickens to ABC, January 4, 1865. *Ibid.*, p. 377.

Chapter 11

1 Teck, *Baroness Burdett-Coutts, A Sketch*, p. 129.

References

2 ABC to W. Gladstone, November 18, 1862. BM, Gladstone Papers, 44,399
3 O'Connor, 'The Baroness', *P.T.O.*, January 12, 1907.
4 Teck, pp. 152–3.
5 Cockshut, *Anglican Attitudes*, p. 95.
6 Jeal, *Livingstone*, p. 119.
7 *Ibid.*, p. 186.
8 Dickens to ABC, February 3, 1857. Johnson, *Letters from Charles Dickens to ABC*, p. 336.
9 Jeal, p. 351 (quoting from the *Standard*, August 6, 1872).
10 ABC to Sir R. I. Murchison, November 29, 1869. BM Add. MSS. 46,125 (wrongly catalogued as November 29, 1864).
11 Mrs Brown to H. Wagner, February 6, 1874. Wagner Papers.
12 Bishop Gray to ABC, undated (1862), Lambeth Palace Library, Burdett-Coutts Papers, 1386, fos 171–2.
13 Cockshut, p. 93 (quoting Colenso).
14 Gray to ABC, April 17, 1863. Lambeth, B-C Papers, 1383, fo. 187.
15 Cockshut, p. 110.
16 ABC to Archbishop of Canterbury, July 12, 1865. Lambeth, B-C Papers, 1383, fos 24–5.
17 W. Gladstone to ABC, October 17, 1865. BM, Gladstone Papers, 44,408.
18 ABC to Earl Russell, December 28, 1865. Lambeth, B-C Papers, 1383, fos 38–9.
19 W. Gladstone to ABC, February 19, 1866. BM, Gladstone Papers, 44,409.
20 W. Gladstone to ABC, April 22, 1866. *Ibid.*, 44,410.
21 Petition of ABC to Queen Victoria, May 2, 1866. Lambeth, B-C Papers, 1383, fo. 96.
22 Gray to ABC, April 20, 1866. Lambeth, B-C Papers, 1386, fos 195–9.
23 ABC to the Rev. W. T. Bullock, November 21, 1872. Lambeth, B-C Papers, 1386, fo. 206.
24 Will of ABC. Quoted by Osborne, *Letters of Charles Dickens to the Baroness Burdett-Coutts*, p. 195.
25 ABC to Viscount Sandon, October 8, 1867. MS. Harrowby, XLIV, fo. 1.
26 ABC to Sir Edward Bulwer Lytton, March 4, 1868. Hertford Record Office, Bulwer Lytton Correspondence.
27 Professor John Phillips to ABC, November 2, 1859. Westminster Collection, H5.
28 Rutter, *Rajah Brooke and Baroness Burdett-Coutts*, p. 31.
29 Sir J. Brooke to ABC, December 4, 1860. Rutter, p. 98.
30 ABC to Lord Elgin, April 5, 1860. *Ibid.*, pp. 71–2.
31 Sir J. Brooke to Mrs Brown, August 26, 1860. *Ibid.*, p. 85.
32 Brooke to ABC, February 4, 6, 1861. *Ibid.*, pp. 104–6.
33 Brooke to ABC, February 25, 1861. *Ibid.*, p. 109.
34 ABC to Brooke, February 20, 1862. *Ibid.*, p. 136.
35 Captain Brooke to Sir J. Brooke, November 14, 1862. *Ibid.*, pp. 148–9.
36 Will of Sir J. Brooke, January 1863. *Ibid.*, pp. 156–7.
37 ABC to Brooke, January 16, 1863. *Ibid.*, p. 158.
38 Brooke to ABC, January 19, 1863. *Ibid.*, p. 158.
39 ABC to Brooke, May 25, 1863. *Ibid.*, p. 195.
40 Brooke to ABC, January 16, 1865. *Ibid.*, p. 238.
41 ABC to Brooke, January 17, 1865. *Ibid.*, p. 239.

282 *Made of Gold*

42 Brooke to ABC, January 18, 1865. *Ibid.*, pp. 240–1.
43 ABC to Mrs Brown, January 22, 1865. *Ibid.*, p. 242.
44 ABC to Brooke, February 9, 1866; Brooke to ABC, February 10, 1866. *Ibid.*, pp. 260–1.
45 Confidential memorandum written by ABC at the request of HRH Princess Alice, July 29, 1867. RA, P23/59.

Chapter 12

1 Duchess of Teck to ABC, March 4, 1870. RA, Geo V CC52/1.
2 Letter of ABC to *The Times*, 1872, quoted in Teck, *Baroness Burdett-Coutts, A Sketch*, pp. 75–7.
3 *Christian Times*, November 22, 1867.
4 Young, *A Memoir of Charles Mayne Young*, vol. II, p. 310 (entry December 3, 1866).
5 *The Times*, April 29, 1869; *The Builder*, quoted by Rose, *The East End of London*, p. 260.
6 Quoted by Rose, p. 259 (*The Times*).
7 ABC to the Hon. Henry Ryder, February 15, 1874. MS. Harrowby, LXVI, fo. 138.
8 ABC to Disraeli, February 28, 1874. Disraeli Archives, Hughenden, B/XX/C/529.
9 Stern, 'The Baroness's Market', *The Guildhall Miscellany*, September 1966, p. 366.
10 BM, Gladstone Papers, 44,430.
11 RA, Queen Victoria's Journal, May 7, 1871.
12 RA, Add. A41/94 (May 11, 1871)
13 ABC to Gladstone, May 10, 12, 1871. BM, Gladstone Papers, 44,430
14 RA, Queen Victoria's Journal, June 23, 1871.
15 Mrs Brown to H. Wagner, January 15, 1874. Wagner Papers.
16 *Scotsman*, January 16, 1874.
17 ABC to Scottish Society for Prevention of Cruelty to Animals, December 1873. Quoted in Teck, pp. 81–2.
18 ABC to The Hon. Henry Ryder, December 10, 1873. MS. Harrowby, LXVI, fo. 130.
19 ABC to The Hon. Henry Ryder, February 15, 1874. *Ibid.*, LXVI, fo. 138.
20 ABC to The Hon. Henry Ryder, September 18, 1873. *Ibid.*, LXVI, fo. 104.
21 ABC to The Hon. Henry Ryder, October 3, 1873. *Ibid.*, LXVI, fo. 114.
22 Dickens to W. H. Wills, January 10, 1856. Lehmann, *Charles Dickens as Editor*, pp. 201–2.
23 ABC to 2nd Earl of Harrowby, February 4, 1875. MS. Harrowby, LXVI, fo. 159.
24 H. L. Antrobus to the The Hon. Henry Ryder, October 25, 1873. MS. Harrowby, LXVI, fo. 120.
25 The Hon. Henry Ryder to Frank Money, February 8, 1875. MS. Harrowby, LXVI, fo. 163.
26 ABC to The Hon. Henry Ryder, February 5, 1878. MS. Harrowby, LXVI, fo. 402.
27 John Hassard to B. Disraeli, January 2, 1874. Disraeli Archives, Hughenden, B/XXI/C/528.
28 Irving, *Henry Irving*, p. 316.
29 ABC to Henry Irving, May 9, 1877. Quoted in C. B. Patterson, *Angela Burdett-Coutts and the Victorians*, p. 193.
30 W. M. Sinclair to H. Wagner, September 4, 1877. Wagner Papers.

References

31 ABC to A. H. Layard, August 30, 1877. BM, Layard Papers, 39,012.
32 ABC to A. H. Layard, September 28, 1877. *Ibid.*, 39,015.
33 W. A. Bartlett to A. H. Layard, January 7, 1878. *Ibid.*, 39,017.
34 ABC to A. H. Layard, April 9, 1878. *Ibid.*, 39,019.
35 W. A. Bartlett to A. H. Layard, August 7, December 3, 1878, *Ibid.* 39,021, 39,023.
36 'My Message' – printed letter from ABC of December 27, 1878 read to her friends on the morning of Mrs Brown's funeral. Wagner Papers.
37 W. A. Bartlett to A. H. Layard, February 21, 1879, BM, Layard Papers, 39,025.
38 ABC to Queen Victoria, January 27, 1879. RA, S12/1.

Chapter 13

1 W. A. Bartlett to A. H. Layard, February 21, 1879, BM, Layard Papers, 39,025.
2 ABC to Sir Garnet Wolseley, December 4, 1879. Hove Library, Wolseley Papers.
3 Quoted in Woodham-Smith, *Florence Nightingale*, p. 365.
4 Henry Irving to H. J. Loveday, August 26, 1879. Irving, *Henry Irving*, p. 331.
5 ABC to Henry Irving, September 18, 1879. C. B. Patterson, *Angela Burdett-Coutts and the Victorians*, p. 196.
6 ABC to Henry Irving, October 2, 1879. *Ibid.*, p. 199.
7 ABC to 2nd Earl of Harrowby, July 18, 1880. MS. Harrowby, LXVII, fo. 109.
8 2nd Earl of Harrowby to ABC, July 11, 1880. *Ibid.*, LXVII, fo. 89.
9 Queen Victoria to 2nd Earl of Harrowby, July 10, 1880. *Ibid.*, LXVII, fo. 88. (draft in RA differs slightly).
10 ABC to 2nd Earl of Harrowby, July 11, 1880. *Ibid.*, LXVII, fo. 92.
11 Memorandum of The Hon. Henry Ryder, July 1880. *Ibid.*, LXVII, fo. 84.
12 Queen Victoria to Sir H. Ponsonby, July 10, 1880. RA, Add. L14/56.
13 2nd Earl of Harrowby to ABC, July 16, 1880. MS. Harrowby, LXVII, fo. 107.
14 ABC to 2nd Earl of Harrowby, July 18, 1880. *Ibid.*, LXVII, fo. 109.
15 Memorandum of The Hon. Henry Ryder, July 1880. *Ibid.*
16 *The World*, July 21, 1880.
17 2nd Earl of Harrowby to ABC, July 24, 1880. MS. Harrowby, LXVII, fo.141.
18 ABC to 2nd Earl of Harrowby, July 25, 1880. *Ibid.*, LXVII, fo. 143.
19 The Hon. Henry Ryder to Viscount Sandon, July 30, 1880. *Ibid.*, LXVII, fo. 157.
20 Mrs C. Gascoyne to The Hon. H. Ryder, undated (July 1880). *Ibid.*, LXVII, fo. 82.
21 W. H. Smith to Lady Ely, September 20, 1880. RA, H26/72.
22 H. L. Antrobus to ABC, August 4, 1880. MS. Harrowby, LXVII, fo. 166.
23 A. White to Sir H. Ponsonby, August 19, 1880. RA, Add. A12/560.
24 Frank Money to 2nd Earl of Harrowby, July 31, 1880. MS. Harrowby, LXVII, fo. 159.
25 Queen Victoria's Journal, 19 August 1880. *Letters from Queen Victoria*, 2nd series, vol. III (ed. G. E. Buckle), Murray, 1928, p. 134.
26 G. Robinson to The Hon. H. Ryder, August 17, 1880. MS. Harrowby, LXVII, fo. 181.
27 *Whitehall Review*, August 26, September 2, 1880.
28 ABC to 2nd Earl of Harrowby, September 11, 1880. MS. Harrowby, LXVII, fo. 230.
29 Lord Beaconsfield to Queen Victoria, September 23, 1880. *Letters from Queen Victoria, op. cit.*, p. 146.

30 The Hon. H. Ryder to Viscount Sandon, December 31, 1880. MS. Harrowby, XLIV (Pt. I), fo. 265.
31 Queen Victoria to Sir Theodore Martin, January 17, 1881. RA, Y172/36.
32 ABC to H. L. Antrobus, February 10, 1881. MS. Harrowby, LXVII, fo. 297.
33 H. L. Antrobus to The Hon. H. Ryder, July 11, 1881. *Ibid.*, LXVII, fo. 353.
34 Hon. H. Ryder to 2nd Earl of Harrowby, November 22, 1881. *Ibid.*, XLII, fo. 107.
35 Memo by ABC, July 26, 1882. BM, Osborne Papers, 46,404.
36 R. R. Pym to The Hon. Henry Ryder, December 19, 1881. MS. Harrowby, LXVII, fo. 387.
37 ABC to 2nd Earl of Harrowby, July 25, 1880. *Ibid.*, LXVII, fo. 143.
38 Jeune, *Memories of Fifty Years*, p. 226.
39 C. B. Patterson, *Angela Burdett-Coutts and the Victorians*, p. 201.
40 Twining, *A Great Foundress* (*see* Manuscript Sources, Select Bibliography).
41 ABC, Memo of March 6, 1877. BM, Osborne Papers, 46, 404.
42 Osborne, *Letters of Charles Dickens to The Baroness Burdett-Coutts*, p. 15.
43 O'Connor, 'The Baroness', *P.T.O.*, January 12, 1907.
44 W. Burdett-Coutts to the Archbishop of Canterbury, January 6, 1907. Lambeth, Davidson Papers, vol. 124, fo. 156.

Chapter 14

1 RA, Queen Victoria's Journal, May 3, 1881.
2 Queen Victoria to ABC, August 22, 1875. RA, F41/78.
3 Bram Stoker: *Personal Reminiscences of Henry Irving*. Quoted by C. B. Patterson, *Angela Burdett-Coutts and the Victorians*, p. 62.
4 ABC to Henry Wagner, December 19, 1884. Wagner Papers.
5 ABC to Henry Wagner, August 22, 1885. *Ibid.*
6 C. B. Patterson, p. 2.
7 Jeune, *Memories of Fifty Years*, p. 226.
8 Geoffrey Best: 'Evangelicalism and the Victorians' in Symondson, *The Victorian Crisis of Faith*, p. 55.
9 Teck, *Baroness Burdett-Coutts, A Sketch*, p. 189.
10 *Ibid.*, p. 156.
11 Martin, *Lady Randolph Churchill*, p. 312.
12 ABC to Disraeli, February 20, 1871. Disraeli Archives, Hughenden, B/XXI/C/522.
13 Teck, p. 64.
14 *Ibid.*, p. 65.
15 Archbishop of Canterbury to the Rev. W. Twining, January 17, 1907. Lambeth, Davidson Papers, vol. 24.
16 Owen, *English Philanthropy*, pp. 270, 273.
17 Herbert Spencer: 'The Coming Slavery' (first published in *The Contemporary Review*, April 1884). *The Man versus the State*, Watts, 1940, pp. 36, 40.
18 ABC to Herbert Spencer, April 17, 1884. University of London Library, MS. 791/175 (on permanent loan from the Athenaeum).
19 ABC, *Woman's Mission*, p. xix.
20 Owen, p. 240.
21 *The Times*, February 27, 1893.
22 Gower, *Old Diaries*, p. 304.

References

23 *Ibid.*, p. 281.
24 Hare, *The Story of My Life*, vol. VI, p. 172.
25 C. B. Patterson, p. 1.
26 O'Connor, 'The Baroness', *P.T.O.*, January 12, 1907.
27 G. M. Young, *Victorian England*, p. 183.
28 G. Anderson to ABC, April 28, 1906. BM, Osborne Papers, 46, 404.
29 Twining, *A Great Foundress* (*see* Manuscript Sources, Select Bibliography).

Epilogue

1 C. B. Patterson, *Angela Burdett-Coutts and the Victorians*, p. 228.
2 Fielding, *Critical Introduction*, p. 100.
3 Seed, *The Expansion of Social Work in Britain*, p. 7.
4 Owen, *English Philanthropy*, p. 470.
5 Mrs Gaskell to Catherine Winkworth, October 20, 1854. Woodham-Smith, *Florence Nightingale*, p. 93.
6 C. B. Patterson, p. 201.
7 G. Best, 'Evangelicalism and the Victorians' in Symondson, *The Victorian Crisis of Faith*, p. 55.
8 C. B. Patterson, p. 202.
9 *Blackwood's Magazine*, February 1907, pp. 297–304.
10 Strachey, *Queen Victoria*, p. 203.

The family tree of Angela Burdett Coutts

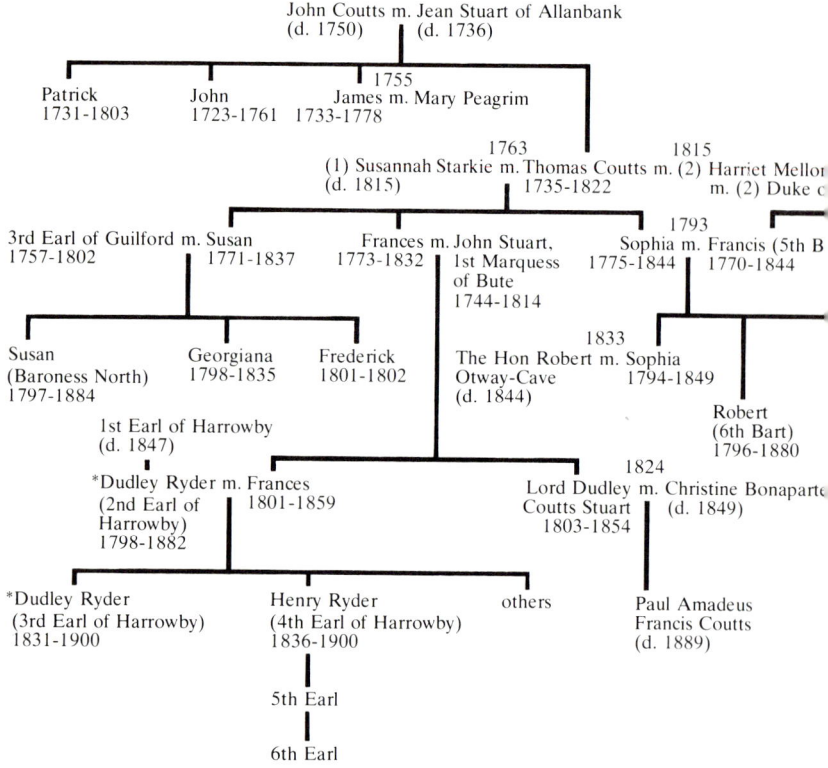

*Known as Viscount Sandon until after his father's death

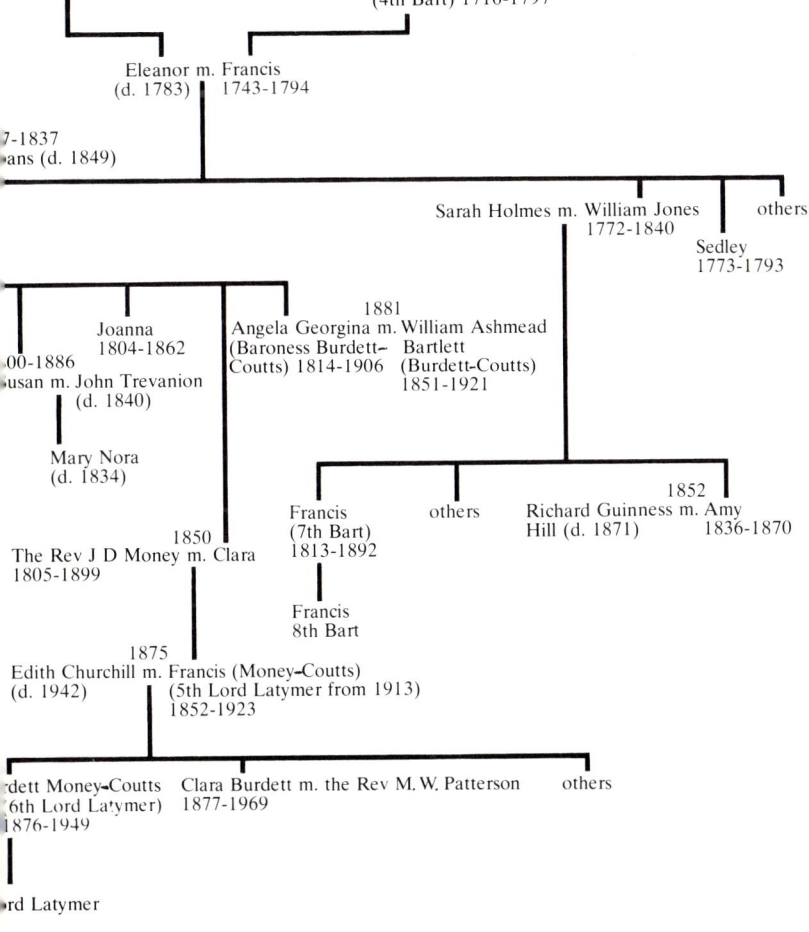

INDEX

ABC = Angela Burdett Coutts; *p.* = *passim* (scattered references). Relationship to ABC is shown in parentheses; page numbers in *italics* refer to illustrations.

Albert, Prince Consort, 61, 129, 183
Alexander, Boyd, 64, 67, 68
Alexandra, Queen, 3
Alice, Princess, 201
animals, ABC and, 204, 214, 244
Antrobus, Sir Edmund, 45, 57, 103, 169
Antrobus, Hugh Lindsay, 216, 217, 232, 236, 237
'Appeal to Fallen Women' (Dickens), 132, 139
Archbishop of Canterbury (*see also* Davidson), 108, 190–1, 207, 231, 241, 252
Arnold, Matthew, 90, 149

Babbage, Charles, 83
Bacon, Anthony, 95–6, 97–104 *p.*
Bacon, Lady Charlotte (formerly Lady Charlotte Harley), 95–6, 97–104 *p.*
Bamford, Samuel, 31
Bartlett, Ellis Ashmead, 231, 236, 249
Bartlett, William Ashmead, later W. A. Burdett-Coutts, 3, 4, 5–6, 235, 258; in Turkey, 219–20; and Hannah's death, 221–2, 223; on cruise, 226–7; engagement to ABC, 227, 229–35; marriage, 7, 235–6, 238–43, 245; and ABC's charities, 240, 249, 250, 252–4; as MP, 249–50; death, 250; character, 7, 231–2, 234–5, 239–43 *p.*
Blessington, Countess of, 77, 97
Blomfield, Charles James, Bishop of London, 57, 60, 84, 104, 106–7, 153
Bonaparte, Christine (Lady Dudley Stuart), 33 & n, 54
Booth, Charles, 157, 254
Brooke, Sir James, Rajah of Sarawak, 28–9, *199*, 203; early career, 194–6; ABC's help to, 196–201; bequeaths Sarawak to ABC, 198–9; disagreements with ABC, 200–2; death, 201
Brougham and Vaux, 1st Baron, 29, 89, 108; and Bacons, 98, 102–3
Brown, Mrs, *see* Meredith, Hannah
Brown, Dr William, 85, 119, 136; marriage, 101–2, 172; in ABC's household, 172–3; death, 173; funeral, 174
Burdett, Amy, later Mrs Hill, 167–8, 265

Burdett, Clara, later Mrs Money (sister), 19, 29, 31, 166; and ABC's marriage, 229–30, 233–4, 236–7; death, 258
Burdett, Francis (grandfather), 13–14, 16
Burdett, Francis, later 5th Bart (father), 3, *15*, 32, 35, 51, 89, *92*, 111, 113, 153, 265; birth to marriage, 13–14; marital difficulties, 14–17; Radicalism, 14, 17–18, 19; enters Parliament, 17; MP for Westminster, 18; popularity, 18, 21, 37; imprisonment, 20–1; and Lady Oxford, 19, 21, 96–7, 98–104 *p.*; and son, 29–30, 43, 95; and the young ABC, 22, 28, 29, 31, 37, 42, 44; and Harriot, 24–5, 39, 42–3, 44; as Tory, 43–5; and Harriot's will, 45, 47, 54, 57; and Dunn affair, 55–6, 62, 65, 68; last illness and death, 94–5; ABC's devotion to, 31, 37, 77, 93, 98–9, 103–4, 106, 167, 265
Burdett, Lady, *see* Coutts, Sophia
Burdett, Francis, later 7th Bart, 167, 236, 259
Burdett, Joanna (sister), 19, 29, 31, 166
Burdett, Sir Robert, 4th Bart (great-grandfather), 13, 14, 16
Burdett, Robert, later 6th Bart (brother), 34; birth, 19; early family relations, 29–30; inherits, 95; and Bacon affair, 95–7; death, 246
Burdett, Sedley, 14–16
Burdett, Sophia, later Mrs Otway-Cave (sister), 19, 21, 29, 30–1, 70, 166
Burdett, Susan, later Mrs Trevanion (sister), 19, 29, 31, 54–5, 166; and ABC's marriage, 229, 230, 236; death, 258
Burdett, William Jones (uncle), 29, 167
Burdett-Coutts, Baroness, *see* Coutts, Angela Georgina Burdett
Burdett-Coutts and Townshend Foundation Schools, 2, 252–3; *see also* St Stephen's schools
Byron, Lord, 17, 19, 22, 29, 96

charity, *see* philanthropy
Charity Organisation Society, 254, 256
Chartism, 123–4
Chesterton, George, 137–8, 141, 146, 162

Index

church, colonial, 104–5; bishoprics founded by ABC, 105, 108, 117, 147, 185–6; and Colenso affair, 188–93
Church of England (*see also* church, colonial, Evangelicalism, St Stephen's), 38, 57; ABC's devotion to, 37, 185, 194, 265; and Colenso affair, 188–93; threats to, 193–4
Churchill, Edith, later Mrs Money, 215–17 *p.*
Churchill, Lady Randolph, 249
Cobbett, William, 14, 20, 152
Colenso, John William, Bishop of Natal, 189; controversy over, 188–92, 201
Columbia Market, 206–11, *208–9*, 213, 214; end of, 262
Columbia Square (formerly Nova Scotia Gardens), flats in, 154–7, 206, 262–3
costermongers, 6, 207, 211; ABC 'Queen of', 259
Coulthurst, William, 57, 169
Coutts, Angela Georgina Burdett, later Baroness Burdett-Coutts:
 Life: I (*1814–1847*): birth, 22; childhood, 26, 28–32; affinity with older people, 29, 57, 77; in Europe, 35; Hannah as governess to, 35–7; friendship with Harriot, 40–2, 44; inherits, 45, 47; family reactions, 48, 49, 54–5; moves to Stratton St., 48–9; suitors, 49–51; at Coronation, 51–2; harassment by Dunn, 55–6, 61, 62–75; social life, 56–7, 77–8, 81–3; early charity, 57–8; meets Dickens, 58–9; begins work with Dickens, 79, 87–8, 90–2; interest in science, 83–4; reliance on Hannah, 85; parents' deaths, 94; refuses aid to Bacons, 97–101, 102–4; first large-scale charities, 104–8; lays foundation-stone of St Stephen's, 107–8 (*107*)
 II (*1847–1858*): friendship with Duke of Wellington, 109–10, 112–29; proposes to Duke, 118–19; death of Duke, 129; public respect for, 130; and Urania Cottage, 132–47; dismisses 'dissenting' Mrs Fisher, 143–4; other work with Dickens, 151–5; aid to individuals, 157–8, 160; *Common Things* published, 161; relations with sisters, 164–6; birth of Frank Money, 166; estrangement from cousin Amy, 167–8; improves bank premises, 169–70; appoints Wills as secretary, 175; tries to reconcile Dickens and wife, 178–9; break with Dickens, 179–80
 III (*1858–1878*): public esteem for, 183, 205–6, 244; overseas ventures, 183–7, 194–202; Colenso affair, 190–3; Sarawak bequeathed to, 198–9; at Holly Lodge, 203–4; work for animals, 204, 214; builds Columbia Market, 207–11; peerage, 211–13; other honours, 213–14, 220; opposes Frank's marriage, 214–17; sends Bartlett to Turkey, 219–20; death of Hannah, 221–2
 IV(*1879–1906*): resumes charitable work, 223–5; cruise on *Walrus*, 225–7; marriage plans and opposition to, 227–34; wedding, 235–6 (*235*); income reduced, 237; married life, 238–43, 245–6; charities after marriage, 240, 250, 254–7; travels on continent, 245–6; last years, 257–60; last illness and death, 1–3, 260; funeral, 6–7; will, 7, 193

 Appearance, 3, 35, 40, *41*, 49, 52–3, 64, 77–8, *177*, *181*, 183, 187, 244, *253*, 257; determination, 48–9, 100, 103, 110, 115, 130, 169, 201, 225, 251; devotion to Church of England, 37, 185, 194, 265; devotion to father, 31, 37, 77, 93, 98–9, 103–4, 106, 167, 265; Hannah's influence on, 36–7, 39, 87, 172, 174, 225, 264–5; isolation of, 168, 173–4, 216, 221, 264; 'lice on', 75–6; as public speaker, 180; relations with bank, *see* Coutts & Co.; religious beliefs, 3, 37–9, 84, 91–2, 193–4, 225, 265

 Friendships: see Babbage, Blomfield, Brooke, Brougham, Dickens, Douro, Faraday, Gordon, Hobhouse, Irving, Kay, Layard, Livingstone, Louis Napoleon, Mary Adelaide, Moore, O'Connor, Rhodes, Robinson (Henry Crabb), Rogers, Ryder (2nd Earl of Harrowby), St Helier, Shaftesbury, Sinclair, Smith, Stanley (H. M.), Wagner, Wellesley, Wellington, Wilberforce, Wolseley, Young

 Philanthropy, her approach to, 116, 148, 153, 183, 261–2; and State 'intervention' in, 254–7; church charities (*see also* St Stephen's), 57–8, 84, 185; colonial bishoprics founded by, 105, 108, 117, 147, 185–6; other charity (*see also* Columbia Market, Columbia Square, Holly Village, Ireland, Ragged Schools, Urania Cottage), 4, 57–8, 79, 87–8, 102, 116, 151–61 *p.*, 185, 204–5, 219–20, 223–5, 244–5, 250–1, 252, 256–7, 259; assessment of charitable work, 261–3

Coutts, Frances, later Marchioness of Bute (aunt), 12, 16, 20, 24, 33, 34, 45
Coutts, James, 9–11
Coutts, John (great-grandfather), 9, 213
Coutts, Sophia, later Lady Burdett (mother), *15*, 21, 28, 37, 39, 42, 45, 49, 93, 102; early life, 12–13; marriage, 14, 16–17, 18–19; and ABC's birth, 22; and father's re-marriage, 24–5; in Europe with ABC, 33; letters to ABC, 53, 54–5; last illness and death, 93–4
Coutts, Susan, later Countess of Guilford (aunt), 12, 20, 24, 25, 26, 33, 44, 45

Coutts, Susannah (née Starkie) (grandmother): marriage, 10, 11; in Europe, 12; visits Foremarke, 16; illness, 22–3; death, 24

Coutts, Thomas (grandfather), 3, 8, *25*, 54, 121, 214; early life and marriage, 9–10; controls bank, 11; daughters' education, 12–13; Sophia's marriage, 14; and sons-in-law, 16–17, 19, 20; wife's illness and death, 22–4; second marriage, 23–5; last years and death, 26–7; fortune, 11, 33, 43, 48, 264; Harriot and, 33, 35, 44

Coutts & Co., bank, 7, 13, 20, 27, 33, 34, 43, 45, 47, 51, 59; history of, 9–11; and Dunn, 69; ABC's relations with partners, 57, 114–15, 168–70; and Frank's marriage, 215–16; and Marjoribanks' bankruptcy, 218–19; and ABC's marriage, 229, 232–3, 236–8; ABC's feelings for, 170, 216, 265

Crimean War, 2; ABC's help in, 151

Darbishire, H. A., 156, 159, 207, 262
Davidson, Randall, Archbishop of Canterbury, 1–2, 5, 11, 242
Denman, Lord: and Dunn, 66–7, 70–3
Devonshire, Georgiana, Duchess of, 10, 12, 249
Dickens, Catherine (née Hogarth), 59, 78, 79, 81, 135, 171, 181–2, 213; end of marriage, 175–9; ABC on, 175
Dickens, Charles, *58*, 81–2, 97, 102, 105, 117, 119, 241–2, 262; meets ABC, 58–9; appearance, 59; early friendship with ABC, 59–60, 78–80; and Hannah, 85–7; ABC's 'almoner', 87–8; and Ragged Schools, 90–2; and Urania Cottage, 116, 132–47 *p*.; and urban housing, 153–5; and Dr Brown's death, 172–4; suggests secretary for ABC, 174–5; marriage ends, 175–9; break with ABC, 179–80; later years, 182; death, 213; feelings for ABC, 78, 135–6, 173–4, 178, 181–2; *views on*: churchmen, 84; criminals, 137; dress, 161–2; the law, 73–4; Livingstone, 186–7; social conditions, 151; Wellington's funeral, 129–30
Dickens, Charley, 59, 178, 182; ABC's interest in, 102, 117, 170–2
Disraeli, Benjamin, later Earl of Beaconsfield, 49, 88, 211, 219, 250; on Sir F. Burdett, 94–5; on ABC's marriage, 234
domestic service – *see* service, domestic
D'Orsay, Count, 97–8, 104
Douro, Arthur Wellesley, Lord, later 2nd Duke of Wellington, 129–30, 164–5; relations with ABC, 130–1
Dunn, Richard, 61, 117, 119; first harassment of ABC, 55–6; further activities of, 62–74; declared insane, 74; effect on ABC, 75, 106

Edgeworth, Maria, 85, 90
education (*see also* Ragged Schools, St Stephen's): of girls – ABC's views on, 149–50, 160–1, 163, 224–5; sectarianism in, 89–90; State and, 89–90, 252, 254; in Urania Cottage, 134, 139–40, 144
Education Acts: (1871), 4; (1890), 252; (1902), 254
emigration, 116, 133, 134, 147, 158, 184, 259
employment and wages, 47, 157–8, 158–9, 256, 262
Evangelicalism, 37–9, 42, 225, 263, 265

Faraday, Michael, 2, 83–4, 194
Farrer, William, 229–31, 236, 238
Ferrey, Benjamin, 106–7
food supply (markets), 206–7, 211
Forster, John, 59, 78, 87, 91, 102, 175
Fox, Charles James, 12

George III, King, 10–11, 12, 20
George IV, King (formerly Prince Regent), 11, 22, 25, 34
Gladstone, W. E., 184; and Colenso affair, 190–2; and ABC's peerage, 211–13; and ABC's marriage, 234; and Gordon, 247–8
Gordon, General Charles George, 247–8, 258
Gray, Robert, Bishop of Cape Town, 108, 185–6, 187–8, 197; and Colenso affair, 188–90, 192–3
Great Exhibition (1851), 127–8, 151
Greville, Charles, 98, 109, 120

Harrowby, Earls of, *see* Ryder
Harrowby, 2nd Countess of (formerly Lady Frances Sandon) (cousin), 30, 34, 39–40, 45, 48, 49, 54, 148, 164, 170
Hazlitt, William, 18, 22, 37
health, public, 152, 153, 159–60
Hill, Octavia, 156
Hobhouse, John Cam, later Lord Broughton, 29, 43, 52, 53, 64, 77, 83, 94
Holly Lodge, 4, 7, 24–6, 44, 45, 151, 197, 203–4, *204*, 212, 225, 230, 237, 240, 246, 260
Holly Village, 205, 262
Household Words (Dickens), 73, 145–6, 151, 173, 175, 176, 178–9
housing, urban, 151–2, 153–5
Hullah, John, 144

Ireland, ABC's charities in, 183–5, 232, 249, 262
Irving, Henry, 229; and Hannah, 218; on cruise, 226–7; death, 259

Kay, Dr James, later Sir James Kay-Shuttleworth, 89–90, 144, 161

Latymer, 5th Baron, *see* Money, Francis
Law, Chief Commissioner, 73, 75
Layard, Sir A. H., 219–20, 221–3
'lice' legend, 75–6

Index

Lieven, Princess de, 109–10
Liszt, Franz, 245
Livingstone, David, 84–5, 186–7, 246–7, 258
Louis Napoleon, Prince, later Napoleon III, 108–9, 124

Macrorie, W. K., Bishop of Natal, 192
Marjoribanks, Edward, senior, 45, 57, 59, 80; and Dunn, 55–6, 69, 72; ABC's difficulties with, 114–15, 168–9
Marjoribanks, Edward, junior, 169–70, 218–19, 232
Martin Chuzzlewit (Dickens), Sairey Gamp in, 87
Martineau, Harriet, 51–2
Mary Adelaide, Princess, later Duchess of Teck, 74, 203–4, 207, 231, 259
Masquerier, J. J., 32, 173
Mary Adelaide, Princess, later Duchess of Teck, 74, 203–4, 207, 231, 259
50, 51
Mellon, Harriot, later (1) Mrs Coutts, (2) Duchess of St Albans, 3, *23*, 118, 121, 203, 239, 264; early life, 23; marriage, 24, 25–6; family rows over, 24–6; inherits, 27; as widow, 32–4; re-marriage, 34–5; and the young ABC, 26, 40–2; life-style, 39–40; family relations, 40–3; death, 44; reading of will, 45–6; will, 47, 54, 114, 169, 215, 229–30, 236–7
Meredith, Hannah, later Mrs Brown, 6, 7, *36*, 52, 54, 60, 61, 176, *181*, 187, 212, 213; engaged as governess, 35; character, 36, 85–7, 172; in ABC's girlhood, 36–7; during early inheritance, 47–50, 53, 77, 85; and ABC's suitors, 49–50, 53; and Dunn affair, 55, 63–6; marriage, 85, 101–2, 112, 172–4; and Wellington friendship, 113–20 *p.*; illnesses, 86, 117, 128, 217–18; widowed, 173; death, 221; Brooke and, 196–200 *p.*; Dickens and, 79, 85–7; influence on ABC, 36–7, 39, 58, 87, 172, 225, 264–5; Irving and, 218; and Urania Cottage, 136
Milnes, Richard Monckton, later Lord Houghton, 49–50
Moffat, Robert, 84–5
Money, Francis Burdett Thomas (Frank), later 5th Baron Latymer, 169; birth, 166; marriage, 214–17; and ABC's marriage, 229–30, 233–4, 236–7
Moore, Thomas, 28–9, 31, 32, 82–3
More, Hannah, 38

Napoleon Bonaparte, 22, 34
Napoleon III, *see* Louis Napoleon
National Society for the Prevention of Cruelty to Children (as London SPCC), 244, 250–1
Nightingale, Florence, 50, 151, 223, 225, 264

O'Connor, T. P., 184; on ABC's marriage, 242; on ABC in old age, 257–8

Osborne, Charles: on ABC, 80, 160, 175, 180, 187, 240; on ABC's marriage, 241
Owen, David, 261, 263
Oxford, Jane Harley, Countess of, 19, 21, 95–7

Paoli, Pasquale, 246
Patterson, Clara Burdett, 6, 53, 217, 261; on ABC's marriage, 239, 265–6; on ABC in old age, 245, 257
Peabody Buildings, 157
Peel, Sir Robert, 105, 111
philanthropy: ABC's approach to, 116, 148, 153, 183, 261–3; individual, 38–9, 88, 105, 133, 153, 157, 158, 163, 224; State and, 254–7 (*see also* education); Victorians and, 263
Ponsonby, Sir Henry: and ABC's marriage, 229, 230, 233
Poor Law Amendment Act (1834), 43, 123, 152–3, 158
poverty, urban, 22, 57, 60, 79, 88, 106, 151, 158; ABC's attitude to, 148
prisons, conditions in, 18, 137, 138, 141, 146
prostitution (*see also* Urania Cottage), 116–17, 132–3, 162
public health – *see* health, public
Punch, 154, 160, 234

Ragged Schools, 90–2, 150
Reform, Parliamentary (*see also* Sir F. Burdett, Chartism), 18, 43, 123, 205–6; Acts (1832), 43, (1867), 206
Rhodes, Cecil, 258
Robinson, Henry Crabb, 21, 173, 179
Robinson, Joseph Armitage, 1–2, 6
Rogers, Samuel, 32, 81, 83, 120
Royal Institution, 83
Royal Society for the Prevention of Cruelty to Animals, 204, 244, 251
Russell, Lord John, later Earl Russell, 17, 125, 199; and Colenso affair, 191
Ryder, Dudley (Viscount Sandon), later 2nd Earl of Harrowby, 45, 49, 70, 105, 164–5, *165*, 216, 258; and ABC's marriage, 228, 229–39 *p.*; death, 246; ABC's 'best and truest friend', 246
Ryder, Dudley (Viscount Sandon), later 3rd Earl of Harrowby, 193, 235, 258
Ryder, Henry, later 4th Earl of Harrowby, 170, 210, 214; and Frank's marriage, 215–17; and ABC's marriage, 229, 231, 235, 238, 239; death, 258

St Albans, Duchess of, *see* Mellon, Harriot
St Albans, William Aubrey de Vere, 9th Duke of, 34–5, 45, 46; death, 203
St Helier, Lady (Mary Jeune), 159, 160, 239, 247, 258

St Stephen's 'model parish': plans for, 106, 117; work on, 148–9; after ABC's marriage, 251–2, 260; today, 265; *church* (Rochester Row): foundation stone laid, 107–8; vault in, 6, 173–4, 221; *schools*, 2; running of, 149–51; re-organisation of, 252–4; *technical institute:* begun, 151; re-built and re-named (Westminster Technical Institute), 252
Sala, George Augustus, 42
Sandon, Lady Frances – *see* Harrowby, 2nd Countess of
Sandon, Viscount – *see* Ryder, Dudley
Sarawak – *see* Brooke
Scott, Sir Walter, 22, 29; and Harriot, 32–3, 34–5
service, domestic, 133, 145, 146, 150, 162–3
Shaftesbury, Antony Ashley Cooper, 7th Earl of, 7, 38–9, 105, 244, 251, 256
Sinclair family, 48, 57, 84, 89, 107–8
Smith, W. H., 215–16, 249, 232
social conditions – *see* employment, emigration, food distribution, health, housing, Poor Law, poverty, prisons, prostitution, service (domestic), workhouse
Spencer, Herbert, 254–6
Stafford House South African Aid Committee, 223–4
Stanley, Dean, 190
Stanley, Henry Morton, 187, 246–7
Starkie, Susannah – *see* Coutts, Susannah
Stevens, Rev William Bagshaw, 13, 14, 16
Stuart, Lord Dudley Coutts (cousin): and Harriot's will, 33–4, 45–6, 54; and Bacons, 97–101, 102–4; death, 164; *99*
Summary Account of Prizes for Common Things, A (ABC), 158, 161

Teck, Duchess of – *see* Mary Adelaide
Teck, Prince Francis of, 203–4, 259
Tennant, Rev William, 149–50, 154
Ternan, Ellen, and Dickens, 176
Times, The, 4–7 *p.*, 21, 26, 65, 70, 94, 132, 161, 248, 256
Townshend elementary schools, 252–3, 263
Tracey, Augustus, 137, 162
Trevanion, John, 31, 54, 166
Turkish Compassionate Fund, 219–20
Twining, Agatha: on ABC's marriage, 239, 241–2; opposition to Ashmead, 250–4 *p.*; on ABC's last illness, 260
Twining, Louisa, 224–5
Twining, Rev William, 241, 251–4 *p.*, 260

Urania Cottage, 162, 176; first idea for, 116–17; Dickens's proposald and preparations for, 134–5, 136–41; opening of, 141; difficult girls in, 141–2; staff for, 142–4; 'Marks System' in, 145; success of, 145–7; closing of, 180

Victoria, Queen, 3, 4, 50, 57, 74–5, 81, 162, 220, 248, 266; accession, 44; mother's debts, 50–1; coronation, 51–2; marriage, 61, 63–4; attempt on life, 64; and Chartists, 123–4; widowhood, 183, 206; guest of ABC, 203; and ABC's marriage, 50, 228–9, 233–5, 244; and ABC's peerage, 212–13; ABC's petition to, 191–2; and Wellington, 111, 121, 123, 129

Wagner, Henry, 245, 260
Wales, Prince of, later Edward VII, 4, 170, 257
Webb, Beatrice, 155
Wellesley, Lord Charles, 130–1, 170
Wellesley, Lady Charles, 130–1, 170
Wellington, Arthur Wellesley, 1st Duke of, 7, 28, 30, 110, *126*, 242, 257; career after Waterloo, 111; growing friendship with ABC, 111–14, 116–18; advice about bank, 114–16, 168–9; ABC's proposal to and result, 118–19, 265; later relationship, 119–23; and Chartists, 123–4; last years and death, 124–30; and ABC's family, 166–7
Wesley, John, 37–8
Westminster Technical Institute – *see* St Stephen's
White, Arnold, 229–30, 233, 237
Whitelands Training College, 161, 163, 180
Wilberforce, Basil, Archdeacon of Westminster, 1–2, 3, 5, 7
Wilberforce, Samuel, Bishop of Oxford, 1, 109
Wilberforce, William, 38–9
William IV, King, 44
Wills, W. H., 173, 175, 184, 246
Wolseley, Sir Garnet, later 1st Viscount, 223–4, 247–8
women (*see also* education, prostitution, service (domestic), Urania Cottage): ABC's opinion of, 160; Victorian attitudes to, 135–6, 163, 264
Women's Mission: a series of congress papers . . . (edited by ABC), 255
workhouse, the, 89, 133, 146, 152–3, 157, 158, 184, 224, 250, 256

York, Frederick, Duke of, 11, 30, 32
Young, Rev Julian, 81, 82, 84, 109, 180, 205–6, 246

Zulu War, 223–4